ReFocus: The Films of William Castle

ReFocus: The American Directors Series

Series Editors: Robert Singer and Gary D. Rhodes

Editorial Board: Kelly Basilio, Donna Campbell, Claire Perkins, Christopher Sharrett, and Yannis Tzioumakis

ReFocus is a series of contemporary methodological and theoretical approaches to the interdisciplinary analyses and interpretations of neglected American directors, from the once-famous to the ignored, in direct relationship to American culture—its myths, values, and historical precepts. The series ignores no director who created a historical space—either in or out of the studio system—beginning from the origins of American cinema and up to the present. These directors produced film titles that appear in university film history and genre courses across international boundaries, and their work is often seen on television or available to download or purchase, but each suffers from a form of "canon envy"; directors such as these, among other important figures in the general history of American cinema, are underrepresented in the critical dialogue, yet each has created American narratives, works of film art, that warrant attention. *ReFocus* brings these American film directors to a new audience of scholars and general readers of both American and Film Studies.

Available or forthcoming titles

ReFocus: The Films of Preston Sturges
Edited by Jeff Jaeckle and Sarah Kozloff

ReFocus: The Films of Delmer Daves
Edited by Matthew Carter and Andrew Patrick Nelson

ReFocus: The Films of Amy Heckerling
Edited by Frances Smith and Timothy Shary

ReFocus: The Films of Budd Boetticher
Edited by Gary D. Rhodes and Robert Singer

ReFocus: The Films of Kelly Reichardt
E. Dawn Hall

ReFocus: The Films of William Castle
Edited by Murray Leeder

ReFocus: The Films of Susanne Bier
Edited by Missy Molloy, Mimi Nielsen, and Meryl Shriver-Rice

edinburghuniversitypress.com/series/refoc

ReFocus:
The Films of William Castle

Edited by Murray Leeder

Edinburgh University Press is one of the leading university presses in the U.K. We publish academic books and journals in our selected subject areas across the humanities and social sciences, combining cutting-edge scholarship with high editorial and production values to produce academic works of lasting importance. For more information visit our website: edinburghuniversitypress.com

© editorial matter and organization Murray Leeder, 2018
© the chapters their several authors, 2018

Edinburgh University Press Ltd
The Tun—Holyrood Road
12 (2f) Jackson's Entry
Edinburgh EH8 8PJ

Typeset in 11/13 Monotype Ehrhardt by
Servis Filmsetting Ltd, Stockport, Cheshire

A CIP record for this book is available from the British Library

ISBN 978 1 4744 2426 4 (hardback)
ISBN 978 1 4744 2427 1 (webready PDF)
ISBN 978 1 4744 2428 8 (epub)

The right of the contributors to be identified as authors of this work has been asserted in accordance with the Copyright, Designs and Patents Act 1988 and the Copyright and Related Rights Regulations 2003 (SI No. 2498).

Contents

List of Figures vii
Notes on Contributors ix
Acknowledgments xii

    Introduction: The Many Castles 1
    Murray Leeder

Part 1 The Early Castle

1 *When Strangers Marry*: Film Noir as Mediated Gothic 21
   Hugh S. Manon

2 Gender in William Castle's Westerns 41
   Zack Rearick

Part 2 The Gimmick Cycle

3 He Earned Our Forgiveness: William Castle and American Movie Showmanship 57
   A. T. McKenna

4 Collective Screams: William Castle and the Gimmick Film 76
   Murray Leeder

5 Ghost Show Ballyhoo: Castle's *Macabre* Will Scare You to Death 99
   Beth Kattelman

6 How to View *13 Ghosts* 115
   Eliot Bessette

7 Chaos Made Flesh: *Mr. Sardonicus* (1961) and the Mask as Transformative Device   137
   Alexandra Heller-Nicholas

Part 3 Castle, Authorship, and Genre

8 A Sick Mind in Search of a Monstrous Body: William Castle and the Emergence of Psychological Horror in the 1960s   153
   Steffen Hantke

9 "What a Wicked Game to Play?" Playfulness, Generic Hybridity, and Cult Appeal in Castle's 1960s Films   171
   Michael Brodski and Caroline Langhorst

10 "Where Did Our Love Go?" The Case of William Castle's *The Night Walker*   189
    Michael Petitti

Part 4 Castle's Legacy

11 Homo/cidal: William Castle's 1960s Killer Queers   219
    Peter Marra

12 The Cinematic Pandemonium of William Castle and John Waters   237
    Kate J. Russell

Index   255

Figures

I.1	William Castle makes a cameo on a 1973 episode of *Circle of Fear*	2
I.2	Castle's cameo in *Rosemary's Baby*	4
I.3	Castle's tombstone in Glendale, CA	14
1.1	Mildred Baxter, the Gothic/noir heroine of *When Strangers Marry*	27
1.2	Mildred and Paul Baxter pay their fares at a New York ride-share depot in *When Strangers Marry*	32
1.3	Lieutenant Blake confronts Fred Graham in front of a mail chute in *When Strangers Marry*	38
4.1	William Castle introduces *The Tingler*	77
4.2	Direct address in the opening of *House on Haunted Hill*	83
4.3	The skeleton walks in *House on Haunted Hill*	85
4.4	Frederick Loren is revealed as the puppet-master in *House on Haunted Hill*	86
4.5	Castle's introduction to *13 Ghosts*	87
4.6	Martha's fake death certificate in *The Tingler*	89
4.7	Dr. Chapin extracts the tingler	90
4.8	The tingler is projected onto the screen	91
6.1	The lion ghost appears spatially incongruous in the black-and-white version of *13 Ghosts*	121
6.2	Buck and the goggles: Buck, avid ghost viewer	128
8.1	Jean Arless contemplating the fluidity of gender roles in *Homicidal*	161
8.2	The power and terror of the disembodied voice on the phone in *I Saw What You Did*	163

10.1 Howard Trent, the patriarchal figurehead, assumes his position of power in *The Night Walker*   206
10.2 Irene Trent physically upsets the capitalist ideology underwriting her marriage   206
10.3 Castle depicts the Trent house torn asunder by Irene's disturbance of the ideological order   207
10.4 Barbara Stanwyck, unlikely scream queen   209

Notes on Contributors

Eliot Bessette is a doctoral candidate in Film and Media at the University of California, Berkeley, where he is writing a dissertation, "Thinking Through Fear in Film and Haunts," on the cognitive content of fear elicited by horror films and haunted house attractions.

Michael Brodski is currently working on his Ph.D. thesis on cinematic representations of childhood and child figures at the University of Mainz, where he also works as an associate lecturer. His main research interests include children's film and intermedial representations of childhood and children's culture, cognitive film theory, Soviet and Russian cinema and culture as well as cinematic portrayals of remembrance.

Steffen Hantke has edited *Horror: Creating and Marketing Fear* (2004), *Caligari's Heirs: The German Cinema of Fear after 1945* (2007), and *American Horror Film: The Genre at the Turn of the Millennium* (2010). He is author of *Monsters in the Machine: Science Fiction Film and the Militarization of America after World War II* (2016).

Alexandra Heller-Nicholas is an Australian film critic, broadcaster and academic and an editor at the film journal *Senses of Cinema*. She has written four books on cult, horror, and exploitation film, the most recent of which is *Ms. 45* for Wallflower/Columbia University Press's Cultographies series.

Beth Kattelman is an Associate Professor and Curator of Theatre at The Ohio State University. She holds a Ph.D. in theatre from Ohio State. She is co-editor, with Magdalena Hodalska, of *Frightful Witnessing: The Rhetoric and (Re)Presentation of Fear, Horror and Terror* (2014). Her work has been published in numerous academic journals.

Caroline Langhorst holds a B.A. in Film Studies and British Studies and a M.A. in Film Studies. She is currently working on her Ph.D. thesis on representations of sub- and countercultural tendencies in British culture (mainly 1960s to 1980s cinema and music) at the University of Mainz, Germany. Her main research interests include British and American cinema, literature and culture, Gender and Gothic Studies, popular music, and countercultural narratives, as well as youth and subcultures.

Murray Leeder is an Adjunct Assistant Professor at the University of Calgary and holds a Ph.D. from Carleton University. He is the author of *Horror Film: A Critical Introduction* (2018), *The Modern Supernatural and the Beginnings of Cinema* (2017), and *Halloween* (Auteur Press, 2014), as well as the editor of *Cinematic Ghosts: Haunting and Spectrality from Silent Cinema to the Digital Era* (2015).

Hugh S. Manon is Associate Professor and Director of the Screen Studies Program at Clark University, where he specializes in Lacanian theory, *film noir*, and digital aesthetics. He has published in *Cinema Journal*, *Film Criticism*, *Framework*, *Psychoanalysis, Culture & Society*, and numerous anthologies, including articles on Tod Browning, Edgar G. Ulmer, George Romero, and Michael Haneke.

Peter Marra is a Ph.D. candidate in Film and Media Studies at Wayne State University. His dissertation argues the queer history and function of the U.S. slasher film and its forebears. He is the author of "Strange Pleasure: 1940s Proto-Slasher Cinema," in Mario Degiglio-Bellemare et al., *Recovering 1940s Horror Cinema: Traces of a Lost Decade* (2015).

A. T. McKenna is a Senior Lecturer in Film and Television Studies at the University of Derby. He is the author of *Showman of the Screen: Joseph E. Levine and his Revolutions in Film Promotion* (2016), co-author of *The Man Who Got Carter: Michael Klinger, Independent Production and the British Film Industry 1960–1980* (2013), and co-editor of *Beyond the Bottom Line: The Role of the Producer in Film and Television Studies* (2014).

Michael Petitti is faculty in the Thematic Option honours program at the University of Southern California.

Zack Rearick is a Ph.D. candidate in Literary Studies at Georgia State University and a First-Year Writing lecturer at the University of North Carolina at Charlotte, as well as a lecturer of Literature and Composition at Catawba College. He received his Bachelors of Arts in English and Philosophy from the University of North Carolina at Charlotte and his Masters of Arts in Literature from the University of North Carolina at Wilmington. He is also the author of a chapbook entitled *Poems in Which I Am Chopped Up, Stepped On, and Sleep Deprived* (2012).

Kate J. Russell is a Ph.D. student in Cinema Studies at the University of Toronto, where she also completed her Masters. Her work focuses on intersections of laughter, disgust, horror, and eroticism. She also holds a Masters in History of Art from the University of Glasgow.

Acknowledgments

I would like to thank line editors Gary D. Rhodes and Robert Singer for their enthusiastic support and assistance, as well as Gillian Leslie from Edinburgh University Press and all of my contributors. Thanks go, too, to my family and coworkers.

Murray Leeder's "Collective Screams: William Castle and the Gimmick Film" was originally printed in *Journal of Popular Culture* 44.4 (2011): 774–96.

Introduction: The Many Castles

Murray Leeder

"I'M WILLIAM CASTLE..."

"The Graveyard Shift" was the 19th episode of NBC's *Ghost Story/Circle of Fear* (1972–3), an anthology series that only lasted one season but somehow managed to have two titles. In this episode, John Astin[1] plays Fred Colby, a night watchman at the fictional Fillmore Studios in Hollywood. Colby was once an actor for the studio, appearing in its horror films. But now the studio is closing down and Colby, whose wife (Patty Duke, Astin's real-life wife at the time) is late in her pregnancy, looks forward to changing professions. At first it seems that the biggest problems of his last shifts relate to a gang of teenagers sneaking onto the lot; however, it transpires that the monsters of the studio's heyday have a spectral existence on the grounds and are scheming to reincarnate themselves through Colby's unborn son. Colby foils them by breaking into the vault and setting the master prints of the horror films on fire, putting a stop to the cinematic monsters once and for all.

Except for making film preservationists weep, "The Graveyard Shift" is not an exceptional example of a largely forgotten show. It has a special interest, however, as the only episode of what was then called *Circle of Fear* to feature a cameo by the show's executive producer—the legendary showman, producer, and director William Castle (Figure I.1). Castle's plays the company's founder, J. B. Fillmore. Fillmore briefly appears at his old studio, full of wistful nostalgia about what he has built on the edge of its destruction: "Forty years, and soon it will all be dust."[2] Speaking to Colby, Fillmore reflects about their successful horror films: "Nobody did any better than we did, and do you know why? 'Cause I knew what the public wanted: to be scared out of their wits. That's why I gave them the most terrifying characters ever created: the

Figure I.1 William Castle makes a cameo on a 1973 episode of *Circle of Fear*.

Claw, the Wolf Man, Scarface, the Mummy, and Dr. Death." There is a particular twinkle in Fillmore's eye at the last name, which Colby has forgotten. "He never caught on like the others," says Fillmore. "An emissary of the Devil who specialized in the taking over of human bodies. Once he got bored with one, he'd move onto someone else. Men, women, even unborn children . . ." Fillmore laughs. "He probably was way, way ahead of his time."

It is at this moment that Colby realizes the nature of the threat against his unborn son. But the moment provides a pleasure of another sort through the presence of Castle, reprising a version of the perverse carnival barker/film impresario persona from his first-person introductions to most of the films of his gimmick cycle of the late 1950s and early 1960s. Like Fillmore, Castle was unapologetic about delivering "what the public wanted," no matter how direct, tasteless, and lowbrow. His cameo in "The Graveyard Shift" has the same kind of surplus quality associated with movie stardom; he makes no attempt to vanish into the character, but rather his appearance functions as an attraction unto itself. When relatively few directors were household names, Castle, like his sometime model Alfred Hitchcock, built himself into a presence, an icon, a brand.

Castle presents a potential a challenge for the auteur theory, both the strains promoted in France by the critics at *Cahiers du cinéma* and in the United States by Andrew Sarris,[3] insofar as his authorial signatures are overt, at least where his most famous films are concerned. It does not fall to a critic to "discover" an auteur in his case: he makes it abundantly clear, addressing his audience directly in advertising and the films themselves with the directness of a pitchman or a mountebank. It may be more useful to think of Castle as an early case of what Timothy Corrigan has called the "commerce of auteurism": "the author as a *commercial* strategy . . . as a critical concept bound to distribution and marketing aims that identify and address the potential cult status of an auteur."[4] While Corrigan describes this strategy as emerging with the New Hollywood generation of directors like Francis Ford Coppola, Martin Scorsese, Stephen Spielberg, and George Lucas, packaged and marketed as *auteurs*, Castle seems like an ur-example, building himself into a larger-than-life attraction with whose name a film can be marketed, much like that of a movie star.[5]

In the last years of his life, with directing largely behind him, Castle maintained a sideline as an actor, playing, as in "The Graveyard Shift," old Hollywood types: a producer in *Shampoo* (1975), a director in *Day of the Locust* (1975). Such roles fit him like a glove, and well they ought to have: he was a Hollywood insider with decades of history. And yet his most memorable screen appearance might be a brief and silent one: standing outside a phone booth in *Rosemary's Baby* (1968) near the end of a four-minute long take, stoking Rosemary Wodehouse's (Mia Farrow) growing paranoia even as he looks benign and grandfatherly. To the audience, if not to Rosemary, he is highly recognizable: he even sports his signature cigar (Figure I.2). The words "A William Castle Production" appear in the opening seconds of *Rosemary's Baby*, so the cameo is an entirely appropriate gesture toward his authorial persona.

If Castle's sole contribution to film history were as a producer (of Orson Welles' *The Lady from Shanghai* (1947) and *Rosemary's Baby*, among less remembered films), that alone would make for a remarkable career. Yet his reputation truly rests on his status as "the Master" or "King of the Gimmicks," "the Abominable Showman," or "the Living Trailer," alluded to in "The Graveyard Shift": a larger-than-life figure whose authorial persona blurs with his films in fascinating ways. And yet that identification obscures much of the full sweep of his career.

". . . THE DIRECTOR OF THE MOTION PICTURE YOU'RE ABOUT TO SEE . . ."

So who was William Castle? He was born William Schloss Jr. in New York City in 1914; his father was a German Jew. Schloss was orphaned by the age of twelve and would later adopt the literally translated surname "Castle." He soon became a man of the theatre, operating as an assistant to Béla Lugosi during a stage revival of *Dracula* and later staging a successful series of summer stock plays at the Stony Creek Theatre in Connecticut in 1939. There he

Figure I.2 Castle's cameo in *Rosemary's Baby* (1968).

drew the attention of Columbia Pictures' Samuel Marks, who recruited him to Hollywood. Certain details of Castle's biography are clouded by his own penchant for self-aggrandizing confabulation. His memoir, *Step Right Up! I'm Gonna Scare the Pants Off America* (1976), is full of entertaining but somewhat suspect episodes. Early on, he describes bluffing his way into Orson Welles' good graces to get access to the Stony Creek Theatre, where the Mercury Theatre Company had held summer tryouts. With Welles and his company relocating to Hollywood to take up an invitation from R.K.O., Stony Creek was available, and Castle smelled an opportunity. Around the same time, Castle met German actress Ellen Schwanneke, "the star of *Mädchen in Uniform* (1931), a very successful film."[6] Schwanneke was in fact a supporting player in *Mädchen in Uniform*, and had since relocated to the United States. When she flouted a request to return to Nazi Germany, she was publicized as "The Girl Who Turned Down Hitler": an advertising ploy from which Castle surely benefited (though he did not instigate it, as his memoirs imply). Castle describes conceiving of *Das ist Nicht für Kinder* as the title of a non-existent German play (to justify the casting of Schwanneke against Equity regulations)—translated to English as *Not for Children*. He describes writing the play in two days and bribing the son of his German-Jewish tailor to translate it into German. He attributed the German version to "Ludwig von Herschfeld"—"the name sounded as good as any. A new German playwright was born."[7]

However, contemporary press for *Not for Children* lists it as adapted from a script by "Ludwig Herschfield," a real Austrian playwright who died in 1945 (his play *Geschäft mit Amerika* was adapted in Britain as *Yes, Mr. Brown* (1933), a popular musical comedy). Further, consistently listed as the writer of

Not for Children was playwright Wesley Towner, a name that does not appear in *Step Right Up!*[8] In fact, *Not for Children* was adapted in Hollywood as *The Mad Martindales* (1942) a few years later, crediting Towner, Herschfeld, and Edmund Wolf as authors of the source play. If Castle were in fact, as he indicates, the author of this play, that would be notable information, yet *Step Right Up!* makes no reference to it. Are these inconsistencies attributable to Castle's faulty memory as he wrote decades later? Perhaps.

However, the baldest claim follows. Castle claims that the controversy around casting Schwanneke inspired death threats from the pro-Nazi German American Bundists. At four a.m. the night before *Not for Children* opened, he went to the theatre and, "With some lumber from backstage, I smashed windows in the theatre and overturned the box office. Then, with red paint, I drew swastikas on the walls."[9] Castle goes on to describe insisting that the play will open as scheduled, and even calling the governor of Connecticut (while posing as Orson Welles!) to demand protection from the national guard: "On the opening night soldiers with helmets and guns surrounded the theatre. Klieg lights flashed everywhere. Members of the audience arriving in formal attire were carefully inspected. It was one hell of an opening."[10] But if this were the case, the press seems to have overlooked it.

I raise these points not in the spirit of damning Castle's tendency toward self-serving deception (or even the understandable "print the legend" tendency of so much writing on Castle), but rather to explore the authorial persona Castle established for himself. Despite Castle's profile as "a sort of minor-league Alfred Hitchcock,"[11] in certain respects he also parallels Welles; the careers of the two men of theatre-turned-film entwined on a number of occasions, and both carefully constructed and managed larger-than-life public personas. Jonathan Rosenbaum writes that, "For a figure with the theatricality and imagination of Welles, exaggeration, hyperbole and flights of invention often took the place of solid facts . . . Welles often told lies as a raconteur in order to entertain."[12] Something similar can be said of Castle, who continually frames himself in *Step Right Up!* as a benign trickster, again and again getting ahead through his wits and his willingness to stretch the truth, while retaining a core of decency. From the beginning of his "gimmick" period in 1958, his films were not just pictures that happened to be directed by William Castle: they were *Castle films*, replete with his directorial persona.

Castle's reputation is so dominated by his gimmick films that we might think of his career as roughly divided into three phases: pregimmick, gimmick, and postgimmick. Of the three, the first is by far the most productive: between *The Chance of a Lifetime* (1943) and *Uranium Boom* (1956), Castle made more than three dozen B-movies, predominantly for Columbia. They included Westerns, war films, and crime films, as well as a few historical adventure movies and the like. He found work in the innumerable low-budget film series of the 1940s, directing not only *The Chance of a Lifetime* (in the Boston Blackie series) but also *The Whistler* (1944), the first feature based on the popular mystery radio serial (1942–55), and three others of that series; plus four of the *Crime Doctor* series, and *The Return of Rusty* (1946), the second of the children's series starring Ace the Wonder Dog. He would also work as a television director, including on ten episodes of *Men of Annapolis* (1957), where he became acquainted with screenwriter Robb White. The best remembered of Castle's pregimmick features is the crime thriller *When Strangers Marry* (1944), also released as *Betrayed*. Welles himself praised it in his column in the *New York Post*, "Orson Welles's Almanac": "Making allowances for its bargain-price budget, I think you'll agree with me that it's one of the most gripping and effective pictures of the year."[13]

So Castle was already an experienced director, a Hollywood insider who even received a smattering of critical acclaim, when he reconceived himself as the "King of the Gimmicks." It is also when he fostered the identification as a horror auteur. The gimmick cycle consists of six horror films, each of which has a unique and highly marketable feature that altered the cinematic experience either directly or indirectly.[14] The first was *Macabre* (1958), in which Castle claimed to have insured the audience against death by fright. He followed it in 1959 with two films starring Vincent Price: *House on Haunted Hill*[15] and *The Tingler*. In both cases, Price's finely honed "male diva"[16] persona, balancing camp humor and credible menace, perfectly matched Castle's productions and gimmicks. *House on Haunted Hill* featured "Emergo," a pop-out skeleton that flew over the audience during the climax, while the latter had maybe the most famous Castle gimmick, "Percepto," where theatre seats were rigged to vibrate at key moments. Next came *13 Ghosts* (1960), with the color process "Illusion-O" and its "ghost viewer"; the "fright break" in *Homicidal* (1961), which allowed audience members the option of leaving if they were too scared to see the ending and its shocking twist; and the "Punishment Poll" in *Mr. Sardonicus* (1961), where the audience putatively decides the fate of the villain. All but the last film had screenplays by Robb White, a prolific novelist as well as a screenwriter, who did not recall their association fondly.[17] White was also Castle's producing collaborator in Susina Associates, their independent production company, which would ultimately be purchased by Columbia.

Part of Castle's strategy was to elide the need for name-brand actors by remaking himself into a name brand: "My name was now above the title in every marquee."[18] Castle made himself into a "Living Trailer," a larger-than-life public persona who took charge of the marketing of his own films with an unusual directness. His first-person trailers were lower-rent analogs of Hitchcock's celebrated trailers. Replacing Hitchcock's dry British archness with an American carnival barker's naked perversity, they promised the unprecedented scares his pictures would deliver and warned off the faint of heart. From *The Tingler* onwards, Castle did first-person introductions to his films from "inside" them, both building his authorial cult of personality and blurring the line between diegetic and audience space in a way that paralleled many of his gimmicks. The on-screen "William Castle" is uncontained by diegetic coherence, casually breaks the fourth wall, and appears in various locations: in front of a white cinema screen in *The Tingler*, in an office setting that blends corporate banality and mad-scientist kitsch in *13 Ghosts*, in a family living room in *Homicidal*, on a foggy Victorian London street in *Mr. Sardonicus*. The appearances become more reflexive over time—he shares the screen with an animated skeleton in *13 Ghosts*, and the opening to *Homicidal* is a litany of self-referentiality: "The more adventurous among you remember our previous excursions into the macabre, our visits to haunted hills and through tinglers and to ghosts." Likewise, in the opening of *Mr. Sardonicus* Castle greets the audience as "My homicidal friends." This "William Castle" is the same figure who appeared outside theatres interviewing shocked patrons in the trailer for *Strait-Jacket* (1964); and it was his distinctive silhouette, sitting a director's chair with a cigar between his teeth, that circulated in advertisements.

Rather like the skeleton in *House on Haunted Hill*, the "William Castle" persona was by no means confined to the screen. At his frequent public promotions, where he often arrived in a hearse or coffin, he made statements like, "Ladies and gentlemen, please do not reveal the ending of *Homicidal* to your friends, because if you do they will kill you, and if they don't, I will."[19] His films are laughed at now, as they were when first released, by design, much in the manner of a carnival funhouse that combines giggles and screams. On the commentary track for the documentary *Spine Tingler! The William Castle Story* (2007), Castle's daughter Terry Castle indicates that her father "didn't take these things seriously . . . The whole thing was done in a campy way and he knew it was campy and he was having fun with it."[20] Castle recalls touring Europe to promote *Homicidal* and spontaneously crying, "Jesus, I speak German!" upon seeing his appearance in a dubbed version, to great laughter. "My surprise was so spontaneous that we kept it in every performance throughout Europe. I hadn't realized my voice had been dubbed in many languages—French, Italian, Spanish, Dutch."[21] As usual, Castle positions himself as both an authentic man having genuine reactions and as an entertainer who dissembles and exaggerates for effect.[22]

But as much as Castle clearly enjoyed his own celebrity, uneasy lay the head that wore the crown of King of the Gimmicks. He lamented that "[h]aving to create a new, fresh gimmick for each picture was becoming tiresome. Critics were now starting to attack, claiming the only reason my films were successful was the gimmicks, and I was unable to make an important thriller without one."[23] All the same, there is not a clear dividing line between his gimmick and postgimmick films. His next two features were children's films of a more straightforward kind:[24] *Zotz!* (1962) and then *13 Frightened*

Girls (1963). Both had a gimmick of sorts: in the case of *Zotz!* moviegoers received replicas of the magical amulet from the film, and *13 Frightened Girls*, also released as *The Candy Web*, featured actresses from different countries so that each could be the focus of a local advertising campaign. Yet these gimmicks are relatively extrinsic to the films themselves, and *Zotz!* and *13 Frightened Girls* tend to be excluded from the "official" bounds of Castle's gimmick cycle, perhaps unjustly, for reasons of genre.[25]

Neither of the children's films was particularly successful, and the key film for transitioning away from gimmicks was *Strait-Jacket*. In fact, *Step Right Up!* implies that it preceded the two children's films.[26] It was certainly advertised with familiar exploitation film techniques, with "WARNING! 'STRAIT-JACKET' VIVIDLY DEPICTS AX MURDERS!" as its tagline, but more than anything it was a star vehicle for Joan Crawford, newly aligned with horror in the wake of *Whatever Happened to Baby Jane?* (1962). Despite the lack of gimmicks (give or take some cardboard axes distributed to patrons, a nostalgic lark on Castle's part), it feels like a Castle film through and through, with Crawford's over-the-top histrionics standing in for the sensational attractions of the earlier films. In a sense, however, the partial position of *Strait-Jacket* within the Castle gimmick cycle speaks to the commensurability of Castle's style of gimmickry with Hollywood's general production logic, with a more traditional form of "stunt casting" substituting for the earlier gimmicks.

The late Castle is rather an odd beast. *Strait-Jacket* led to other, more serious thrillers like *I Saw What You Did* (1965), also with Crawford in a small part, and *The Night Walker* (1964). Castle later made broad comedies like *Let's Kill Uncle* (1966), *The Spirit Is Willing* (1967), and *The Busy Body* (1967), the minor but interesting science fiction film *Project X* (1968), and what may be the least classifiable film in his filmography, *Shanks* (1974). Some months after the release of *Macabre*, it had been reported that Castle was planning a theatrical adaptation of Franz Kafka's *Metamorphosis*;[27] this production was obviously (and unfortunately) not to be, but *Shanks* may give us the clearest indication of what an "artistic" Castle project would look like. This collaboration with Marcel Marceau, a silent film pastiche with aspects of a pre-*Night of the Living Dead* (1968) zombie film that also seems to be a children's film, received a DVD release in 2013 by Olive Films, but remains extremely obscure. Castle was open about his disappointment with the project in *Step Right Up!* As conceptually fascinating as it might be, *Shanks* plays more as a clumsy proto-Guy Maddinesque curio than a forgotten classic, with Castle and Marceau's sensibilities stubbornly refusing to gel.[28]

Some years earlier Castle had purchased the rights to Ira Levin's 1967 novel of New York maternity and witchcraft, *Rosemary's Baby*, with the intention of directing it himself. Robert Evans at Paramount overruled him and insisted on recruiting Roman Polanski to Hollywood to direct. Here again there exists another *Rashomon* (1950) of different tellings: Castle claims that he met with Polanski and became convinced that Evans's judgment was correct,[29] while Evans describes silencing Castle by refusing to go forward with him as a director and doubling his fee to act as producer, well before Castle ever met Polanski personally.[30] Where Castle depicts himself as a principled artist willing to sacrifice his desires when he understood that the project was in good creative hands, Evans frames him as a blusterer who was easily bought off. But no matter; it is a fascinating irony that Castle's greatest success as a producer helped usher in the new golden age of American horror related to the New Hollywood, a trend that more or less wiped away the kind of films he was making scant years earlier (as alluded to in "The Graveyard Shift"). His declining health and dwindling enthusiasm for directing led him to focus more on producing in his last years. His last film as a producer, the killer cockroach movie *Bug* (1975), had the misfortune to be released the same week as a much more successful "revenge of nature" picture called *Jaws* (1975)—so often spoken of as representing the moment when the exploitation marketing and distribution techniques associated with independents like Castle and Roger Corman were embraced by Hollywood as the "blockbuster mentality." Castle died of a heart attack in 1977 at the age of sixty-three.

CASTLE AFTER CASTLE

It is perhaps appropriate that Castle's authorial persona, always somewhat unpinned from his personal identity, should have gone through a set of permutations after his death. It should be noted that his were not the only gimmick films; rather, his efforts revealed a new marketing strategy that would be eagerly exploited by others. A notable example was *The Hypnotic Eye* (1960), which purported to hypnotize its audience using "HypnoMagic." Certain of Castle's gimmicks were appropriated early on: *Macabre*'s gimmick was egregiously borrowed by *The Screaming Skull* (1958), which promised a free casket and burial for anyone who died of fright. Later, the UK werewolf film *The Beast Must Die* (1974) blatantly borrowed *Homicidal*'s Fright Break with a "Werewolf Break," where the film pauses for the viewers to contemplate which character is the lycanthrope. Probably the second most famous "gimmick filmmaker" was Ray Dennis Steckler, best known for *The Incredibly Strange Creatures Who Stopped Living and Became Mixed-Up Zombies!!?* (1964). If Castle had been described as a poor man's Hitchcock, Steckler was a poor man's Castle, a "zero budget" auteur who acted in his films as "Cash Flagg" and reputedly lived out of his car to cut down on production costs. The gimmick for *The Incredibly Strange Creatures* was the bizarre "Hallucinogenic Hypnovision," in which people in masks would occasionally run through the theatre.

Yet Castle's larger legacy was less immediate. For within those crowds of kids experiencing the bacchanal of the gimmick films were a host of future directors who would later credit Castle as an important influence, like Robert Zemeckis, John Landis, Sam Raimi, Joe Dante and John Waters.[31] Waters has spoken about the influence of Castle numerous times (see Kate J. Russell's essay in this volume) and more recently cameoed as Castle on the television show *Feud* (2017–). Dante, a lifelong horror buff who in his youth served as the reviews editor for the fan magazine *Castle of Dracula*, paid tribute to Castle in *Matinee* (1993), in which Lawrence Woolsey (John Goodman) is an amalgam of Castle and other independent horror/science fiction directors of the 1950s and 60s. A cuddly emblem of American capitalism's most benign aspects, Woolsey is a sort of huckster saint whose monsters and gimmicks provide a paradoxical stability during the chaos of the Cuban Missile Crisis.

Another, more official Castle legacy is managed by his daughter Terry. Terry Castle had co-producer credits on remakes of *House on Haunted Hill* (1999) and *Thirteen Ghosts* (2001; the title was stylized as *Thir13en Ghosts*), produced through Dark Castle Pictures. Though these films are fairly generic horror films of their era with only a smattering of Castle's style, they serve as evidence of a millennial Castle revival. Other remakes, as yet unrealized, were announced (including *Macabre*, slated to be directed by Robert Zemeckis,[32] and *The Tingler*[33]). Terry Castle has also arranged a reprint of her father's long-unavailable autobiography and a published screenplay of *House on Haunted Hill* with his notes intact;[34] and she has established a website intended to preserve his legacy (williamcastle.com), offering new fiction inspired by her father's works, including her loosely autobiographical novel *Fearmaker: Family Matters* (2011).[35] For a time, the williamcastle.com site even hosted a blog written as if by Castle himself. Terry Castle participated in Jeffrey Schwarz's celebratory documentary *Spine Tingler! The William Castle Story*, later to be included with Columbia's five-disc *The William Castle Film Collection* in 2010.

The Castle revival has penetrated the spaces of film art. La Cinémathèque Française in Paris ran a Castle retrospective from June 19 to August 2, 2009, as did New York's Film Forum between August 27 and September 6 of that year. A broader cultural appreciation for Castle developed at roughly the same time. In 2013, the humor website Cracked.com declared him "the World's Craziest Filmmaker" in an article written by Chris Sims:

> When you think about the filmmakers who have given us the greatest spectacles of all time, you probably think of people like Steven Spielberg or James Cameron. Hell, if you've recently been clocked upside the head with a two-by-four, you might even think about Michael Bay. When it

comes to pure, unadulterated, attention-grabbing stunts, though, there's one man who stands above all others: William Castle.[36]

Castle's rising posthumous star is evidenced in the way his name is casually cited in discussions of vibrating theatre chairs,[37] and bloggers endorse him as "a fucking visionary."[38] The aforementioned *Cracked* article opines, with reference to *The Tingler*, "I don't think anybody actually thought a crazy fear monster was crushing their spine, but you can't tell me that's not a thousand times more fun than, say, anything that happened in *Avatar*."[39] This new adulation often positions Castle as a visionary auteur from a purer time, before a jaded audience faced an endless slate of new cinematic advances that fail to shake up the format as ostentatiously as something like *The Tingler*, leaving it yearning for good old-fashioned low-tech gimmickry with a hint of danger and transgression. As "kettlechips," a commenter on the *Cracked* article, states: "the 'Tingler' shtick sounds WAYY too fun for something that could exist today . . . one complaint [about the physical buzzing] would ruin it for everyone else."[40] The recent veneration of Castle stands in stark contrast to the bemused dismissal his gimmicks received, for instance, in Michael and Harry Medved's *The Golden Turkey Awards* (1980).[41]

Recognition of Castle in academia has grown steadily as well. While he was not paid much attention during the formative phase of horror studies, he is now a canonical figure. Scholarship on individual Castle films like *The Tingler*,[42] *Strait-Jacket*,[43] and *I Know What You Did*[44] coexist with broader examinations of aspects of his career;[45] outside of the academic publishing establishment, two career-spanning books on Castle have appeared as well.[46] Catherine Clepper notes that Castle's relevance to the phenomenological turn in film theory resides in the way his gimmick films are "indicative of what cinematic embodiment can mean in a material, proximate, and shocking sense, rather than as a mode of affective sympathy or reflexive mirroring."[47] Indeed, scholarship on film phenomenology and affect has referenced Castle and his gimmicks with some regularity.[48] Industrial and cultural treatments of the horror film centering on the 1950s and 60s have examined Castle's career as well.[49] On another register, the inclusion of a first-person trailer for Castle's *Homicidal* in the DVD collection *Experiments in Terror* (2005) reflects an interesting attempt to draw him into the constellation of experimental cinema. It sits alongside the trailers for *The Nanny* (1965), *Cannibal Girls* (1973), *Dr. Jekyll and Sister Hyde* (1971), and *Blacula* (1972), unpinned from their commercial function so that their unbridled strangeness is reconfigured as avant-garde.

Castle has received references and homages in other places. Joe R. Lansdale, the accomplished horror novelist best known to moviegoers for *Bubba Ho-Tep* (2002), wrote a story called "Belly Laugh, or, The Joker's Trick or Treat" for the 1990 print anthology *The Further Adventures of the Joker*, featuring the Joker rigging a movie theatre with deadly traps for Batman inspired by *House on Haunted Hill*, *The Tingler*, and *Mr. Sardonicus*.[50] Appropriately enough, the Joker says that he was among those few voting against Sardonicus's dark fate as a boy. Another homage to Castle appeared in a 1978 episode of the great Canadian sketch comedy show *SCTV* (1976–1984), imagining a Castle-directed adaptation of Agatha Christie's *Murder on the Orient Express* called *Death Takes No Holiday*. Portrayed by Dave Thomas, Castle interrupts the film to stage a *Sardonicus*-style poll on the film's ending, only to be overruled by Hercule Poirot (John Candy) and Agatha Christie (Andrea Martin) herself, the latter writing the story from within it, who accost him in the non-diegetic space of Castle's first-person audience address and strangle him. What other director could you simultaneously raise and refute the authorship of, while depicting him on screen and "killing" him a mere year after his actual death, and have this play as a gesture in relatively good taste?

"... I FEEL OBLIGATED TO WARN YOU ..."

The word "unique" is often abused, and yet it seems rather unavoidable where William Castle is concerned. Indeed, his Britannica entry declares, "A master showman, he made a unique, if minor, contribution to American motion pictures."[51] This collection hopes to show that, in the aggregate at least, his contribution has been something more than minor. It is perhaps inevitable that the essays collected here spend the most time on the gimmick films, but they also excavate Castle's earlier and later work, and contextualize the gimmick films within his long career.

The first part of *ReFocus: The Films of William Castle* is entitled "The Early Castle" and deals with his pregimmick days. Hugh S. Manon's "*When Strangers Marry*: Film Noir as Mediated Gothic" is a sustained analysis of Castle's early classic and how it uses generic noir tropes to transform the Gothic tradition. Zack Rearick's "Gender in William Castle's Westerns" focuses on an especially neglected facet of Castle's career, his Westerns.

The following part, "The Gimmick Cycle," deals with Castle's most famous films, most broadly and narratively. The first entry is Anthony Thomas McKenna's "He Earned Our Forgiveness: William Castle and American Movie Showmanship," which explores the industrial conditions of the 1950s and 60s American film industry that allowed Castle's brand of showmanship to flourish. It is followed by a reprint of Murray Leeder's "Collective Screams: William Castle and the Gimmick Film," which particularly examines *House on Haunted Hill* and *The Tingler* as profoundly reflexive texts that not only reflect but are about Castle's own authority and showmanship. It describes the gimmick films as revivals of sorts of the mode of authorship associated with early cinema's trick films.

The next three chapters provide case studies of gimmick films. Beth Kattelman offers a probing treatment of *Macabre* and its relationship to the theatrical tradition of ballyhoo, also offering an exploration of the potential for real-life "death by fright." Eliot Bessette follows with an examination of *13 Ghosts* and its themes of belief and disbelief, its links with *Psycho* (1960) and elements of its reception. Alexandra Heller-Nicholas discusses *Mr. Sardonicus* through the film's central image of the mask.

Moving partly beyond the gimmick film, the part entitled "Castle, Authorship, and Genre" assembles a series of chapters beginning with Steffen Hantke's "A Sick Mind in Search of a Monstrous Body: William Castle and the Emergence of Psychological Horror in the 1960s." Hantke examines both gimmick and postgimmick to locate Castle within the emerging paradigm of the psychological horror film, while also noting that Castle's insistence on gruesome imagery and embodied reactions somewhat distinguishes himself from other figures such as Hitchcock. Michael Brodski and Caroline Langhorst's "'What a Wicked Game to Play?': Playfulness, Generic Hybridity, and Cult Appeal in Castle's 1960s Films" also sees continuities between Castle's gimmick and postgimmick films, finding engagement with postwar social issues precisely through his playful approach to genre. Michael Petitti's "'Where Did Our Love Go?': The Case of William Castle's Disintegration of the American Marriage in *The Night Walker*," takes one of Castle's most satisfying and fascinating films as a case study while connecting it with his gimmick and postgimmick canons.

The final part chronicles dimensions of Castle's influences. First, Peter Marra traces the influence of Castle on the slasher film cycle of the late 1970s and early 1980s. His "Homo/cidal: William Castle's 1960s Killer Queers" finds an intriguing presence of queerness in some of Castle's films through their very incoherence. The last chapter, Kate J. Russell's "The Cinematic Pandemonium of William Castle and John Waters," explores Castle's relationship to perhaps his most vocal disciple, the iconic American independent director John Waters. It chronicles the influence of Castle on Waters and the relationship of shock, disgust, and gimmickry.

"... BUT DON'T BE ALARMED ..."

Michael Petitti has kindly provided us with a photograph of Castle's tombstone in Glendale, California (Figure I.3).

When I first saw it, it was a clear disappointment: I had imagined it festooned with skeletons or axes or tinglers or severed heads, or maybe a Zotz

Figure I.3 Castle's tombstone in Glendale, CA.

amulet or two. Yet it is a reminder that there was so much more to him than just the showman, both personally and professionally. And there is surely something resonant in the simple inscription: "Forever." This collection does not and cannot cover all of Castle's many facets, but it hopes to increase our understanding of such a dynamic, provocative and, yes, unique filmmaker.

NOTES

1. Astin previously acted in Castle's film *The Spirit is Willing* (1967).
2. "The Graveyard Shift" echoes the collapse of the Hollywood studio system's production model in the 1960s, which led to much traditional studio space falling into disuse.
3. For useful overviews on critical and academic approaches to film authorship, see Stephen Crofts, "Authorship and Hollywood," in John Hill and Pamela Church Gibson (eds), *The Oxford Guide to Film Studies* (Oxford: Oxford University Press, 2000), pp. 310–24; Paul Sellors, "Film Directors and Auteurs," in *Film Authorship: Auteurs and Other Myths* (London: Wallflower, 2010), pp. 6–32.
4. Timothy Corrigan, *Cinema Without Walls: Movies and Culture After Vietnam* (New Brunswick, NJ: Rutgers University Press, 1991), p. 103 (original emphasis).
5. For a discussion of Castle and the auteur theory, see Ethan de Seife, "The Branding of an Author: William Castle and the *Auteur* Theory," *16:9* 42 (2011): n.p.
6. William Castle, *Step Right Up! I'm Gonna Scare the Pants Off America: Memoirs of a B-Movie Mogul* (New York: Pharos, 1992), p. 17.
7. Ibid. p. 21.
8. My thanks to Jane Bouley for sharing with me her history of the Stony Creek Theatre.
9. Castle, *Step Right Up!*, p. 27.
10. Ibid.
11. Robert Bloch, *Once Around the Bloch: An Unauthorized Autobiography* (New York: Tor, 1993), p. 294.
12. Jonathan Rosenbaum, *Discovering Orson Welles* (Berkeley: University of California Press, 2007), p. 94.
13. Quoted in Castle, *Step Right Up!*, p. 95.
14. The costs of the gimmicks belonged to the theatres, so the more elaborate, like Emergo, Percepto and Illusion-O, would frequently go unrealized.
15. While the film was advertised as *The House on Haunted Hill* and is referred to as such in many other sources, including *Step Right Up!*, the title sequence within the film lacks a definite article.
16. See Harry M. Benshoff, "Vincent Price and Me: Imagining the Queer Male Diva," *Camera Obscura* 23.1 (2008): 146–50.
17. Robb White interviewed by Tom Weaver, "An Outspoken Conversation with Robb White," *Film Fax* 18 (1990): 60–5, 94–5.
18. Castle, *Step Right Up!*, p. 159.
19. Quoted in *Spine Tingler! The William Castle Story*, dir. Jeffrey Schwarz (U.S.A.: Automat Pictures, 2007).
20. Quoted in ibid.
21. Castle, *Step Right Up!*, p. 160.
22. For a discussion of the interplay of comedy and horror in Castle's films, see Murray Leeder, "The Humor of William Castle's Gimmick Films," in Cynthia J. Miller and A. Bowdoin Van Riper (eds), *The Laughing Dead: The Horror-Comedy Film from* Bride of Frankenstein *to* Zombieland (Lanham, MD: Rowman & Littlefield, 2016), pp. 87–101.
23. Castle, *Step Right Up!*, p. 165.
24. The gimmick cycle was clearly targeted at young audiences, making the recurring themes of adultery, disintegrating marriages, and spouse-murder all the more baffling.
25. More fully a postgimmick Castle film was *The Old Dark House* (1963), a reworking of the 1932 James Whale classic that anticipates Castle's weak comedies of the later 1960s.

26. In his own autobiography, Robert Bloch, screenwriter for *Strait-Jacket*, politely says of Castle's account of their first meeting with Crawford, "Actually, that's not quite how it really happened" (*Once Around the Bloch*, p. 298) and goes on to give a notably different version.
27. Philip K. Scheuer, "Roland, Costars Have Cuban Date," *Los Angeles Times*, August 29, 1958, p. 7.
28. *Shanks* is ironically the only film directed by Castle to have been nominated for an Academy Award—for Alex North's original score.
29. Castle, *Step Right Up!*, pp. 192–4.
30. Robert Evans, *The Kid Stays in the Picture* (Beverly Hills, CA: Phoenix, 2002), p. 142. For another account, see Jason Zinoman, *Shock Value: How a Few Eccentric Outsiders Gave Us Nightmares, Conquered Hollywood, and Invented Modern Horror* (New York: Penguin, 2011), pp. 11–17.
31. Stephen King recollects watching *The Tingler* in his non-fiction book *Danse Macabre* (New York: Gallery, 1981), pp. 196–7. It was clearly a unifying event for a generation of future horror specialists.
32. Dana Harris, "Silver, Zemeckis go Dark in Castle 'Macabre' Redo," *Variety*, May 10, 2000, <http://variety.com/2000/film/news/silver-zemeckis-go-dark-in-castle-macabre-redo-1117781468/> (accessed June 1, 2017).
33. Brad Beveret, "'Tingler' to Scare Again," *Comingsoon.net*, November 15, 2004, <http://www.comingsoon.net/movies/news/502891-tingler_to_scare_again> (accessed June 1, 2017).
34. William Castle and Robb White, *House on Haunted Hill: A William Castle Annotated Screamplay* (William Castle Productions, 2011).
35. Terry Castle, *Fearmaker: Family Matters* (William Castle Productions, 2011).
36. Chris Sims, "5 Great Moments from the World's Craziest Filmmaker," *Cracked*, January 27, 2013, <http://www.cracked.com/blog/5-great-moments-from-worlds-craziest-filmmaker_p2/> (accessed November 26, 2013).
37. Mike Bracken, "Will These Home-Theater Chairs Change the Way You Watch Movies in Your Living Room?" www.movies.com, October 2, 2013, <http://www.movies.com/movie-news/tremor-fx-home-theater-chairs-vibrate-to-onscreen-action/13701> (accessed November 8, 2013).
38. Will Millar, "William Castle, Part One," *In Advent of the Zombie Holocaust*, June 24, 2012, <http://www.movies.com/movie-news/tremor-fx-home-theater-chairs-vibrate-to-onscreen-action/13701> (accessed February 26, 2013).
39. Sims, "5 Great Moments."
40. Ibid.
41. The Medveds grant Percepto the prize of "Most Inane and Unwelcome 'Technical Advance' in Hollywood History," with Emergo one of the runners up. Strikingly, the Medveds find little to say about these gimmicks and what makes them so "inane" beyond simply describing them. Harry Medved and Michael Medved, *The Golden Turkey Awards: Nominees and Winners—The Worst Achievements in Hollywood History* (New York: Perigee, 1980), pp. 161–6.
42. Mikita Brottman, "Ritual, Tension and Relief: The Terror of 'The Tingler'," *Film Quarterly* 50.4 (Summer 1997): 2–10; Kjetil Rødje, *Images of Blood in American Cinema: The Tingler to The Wild Bunch* (New York: Routledge, 2016), esp. pp. 52–5.
43. David Sanjek, "The Doll and the Whip: Pathos and Ballyhoo in William Castle's *Homicidal*," *Quarterly Review of Film and Video* 20:4 (2003): 247–63.
44. Marc Olivier, "Gidget Goes Noir: William Castle and the Teenage Phone Fatale," *The Journal of Popular Film and Television* 41.2 (2013): 41–52.

45. Including my essay "Collective Screams: William Castle and the Gimmick Film" (*Journal of Popular Culture* 44.4 (2011): 774–96), reprinted here, and Catherine Clepper's "'Death by Fright': Risk, Consent, and Evidentiary Objects in William Castle's Rigged Houses," *Film History* 28.3 (2016): 54–84.
46. John W. Law, *Scare Tactic: The Life and Films of William Castle* (Lincoln, NE: Writer's Club, 2000), Joe Jordan, *Showmanship: The Cinema of William Castle* (Albany, GA: BearManor Media, 2014).
47. Clepper, "Death by Fright," p. 55.
48. For example, Angela Ndalianis, *The Horror Sensorium: Media and the Senses* (Jefferson, NC: McFarland, 2012), pp. 166–7; Xavier Aldana Reyes, *Horror Fiim and Affect: Towards a Corporeal Model of Viewership* (New York: Routledge, 2016), p. 104.
49. Kevin J. Heffernan, *Ghouls, Gimmicks, and Gold: Horror Films and the American Movie Business, 1953–1968* (Durham, NC: Duke University Press, 2004), esp. pp. 96–104; Blair Davis, *Battle for the Bs: 1950s Hollywood and the Rebirth of Low-Budget Cinema* (New Brunswick, NJ: Rutgers University Press, 2012), esp. pp. 63–5, 77–82.
50. Joe R. Lansdale, "Belly Laugh, or, The Joker's Trick or Treat," in Martin H. Greenberg (ed.), *The Further Adventures of the Joker* (Bantam Books: New York, 1990), pp. 1–30.
51. *Encyclopaedia Britannica*, s.v., "William Castle," by Michael Barson, <https://www.britannica.com/biography/William-Castle> (accessed May 25, 2017).

PART I
The Early Castle

CHAPTER 1

When Strangers Marry: Film Noir as Mediated Gothic

Hugh S. Manon

Of William Castle's 1944 film *When Strangers Marry*, Orson Welles wrote the following: "Making allowances for its bargain-price budget ... it's one of the most gripping and effective pictures of the year. It isn't as slick as *Double Indemnity* or as glossy as *Laura*, but it's better acted and better directed by William Castle than either."[1] In retrospect, Welles is of course correct to compare Castle's "'B' minus" crime thriller to two contemporaneous films that critics would later identify as keystone films noirs. However, a great deal can be gained by resituating the female-centered narrative of *When Strangers Marry* as part of the upsurge, in 1940s Hollywood, of the Gothic romance, best exemplified by films such as *Rebecca* (1940) and *Gaslight* (1944). *When Strangers Marry* appears at a critical point in film noir's development, while at the same time illuminating the Gothic as a crucial generic precursor to noir's bleak, newsprint-obsessed crime narratives, of which it is a pointed example. More acutely than *Double Indemnity* (1944) or *Laura* (1944), Castle's film develops a set of generic film noir tropes by mediating the Gothic. The word "mediate" is being used here in two ways: both as an indicator that the classical Gothic is being transformed and reframed by Castle's film, and as a way of denoting the ostensible catalyst for this transformation: the proliferation of modern telecommunications media in mid-century American life.

As I argue below, the traditional Gothic is a genre at great pains to highlight, and derive chills from, a phenomenon that psychoanalyst Jacques Lacan terms "the gaze" (*le regard*), an individual's sudden realization that they occupy a field of vision at odds with their own perspective. The gaze is most commonly experienced as a sense that one is being watched, especially when the existence or position of the watcher is not confirmable. In Gothic narratives, the characteristic isolation of the (usually) female protagonist is punctuated by a series of signifiers that lack signifieds: she sees distant figures whose presence lacks any rational explanation, hears voices that lack any clear source. Shadows emerge at the periphery of her vision, and then vanish. Messages are received, but the sender's motives remain strange. Objects impossibly appear, disappear, or change places. The hired help is either oversolicitous or rudely uncooperative, but always suspicious. An uncanny aura of death and decay pervades even the most banal of activities. In all of these encounters, what the Gothic heroine discerns is precisely *the sense of a beyond*, which is precisely the feeling the gaze evokes in the human subject. Although William Castle and other auteurs of the cinematic Gothic surely did not read Lacanian theory, we can nonetheless begin to appreciate how Lacan's conception of the gaze as an impossible blot in the field of vision has a strong bearing on the narrative and aesthetic qualities of the Gothic. Indeed, it would not be wrong to state that the Gothic is the *genre of the gaze*, provided we come to terms with the various plot elements and filmmaking techniques that make the Gothic narrative a distinct form of horror story, as a well as a distinct form of crime story.

Castle's brilliant intervention in *When Strangers Marry* is to perpetuate the gothic gaze via the fragmentary signification of mid-century media: telegrams, phone calls, radio broadcasts, and especially newsprint. His Gothic heroine is repeatedly hemmed in, demoralized, and confounded by the persistent interruptions of analog media transmissions—communications that are supposed to provide signifying clarity and closure, but instead only convey strangeness and lack. Beginning with a discussion of the film's trenchant incorporation of references to cinema and radio, I go on to explain that the film's near-constant references to newsprint provide a special case of the mediated Gothic, insofar as headline news is film noir's particular fetish, a narrative and stylistic obsession that is just beginning to develop in 1944, but which will increase exponentially in noir as the genre crystallizes later in the decade.

MURDER AMIDST MEDIA

When Strangers Marry announces its engagement with media *per se* in its very first shot sequence. Produced by the King Brothers for Monogram Pictures, a Poverty Row studio known for quickly created, low-budget B action films, the film begins with an abrupt camera push to a close-up of a man wearing a papier-mâché lion's head. The image is accompanied by a non-diegetic lion's roar. We are at the Hotel Philadelphia, whose rooftop sign flashes the message "WELCOME LIONS," but the cheaply cartoonish mask and the roar on the soundtrack makes a different announcement: *this will not be an ostentatious MGM production*. By jokingly referencing a studio that is out of Monogram's league, Castle sets the tone of his own production aesthetic, which makes up for its lack of financial wherewithal through inventiveness and an embrace of its own limitations. The result, at least according to Welles, is a film that punches above its weight—not quite MGM, but far better than expected from Monogram.

The lion's head is worn by a conventioneer named Sam Prescott (Dick Elliott), whose drunkenness becomes the source of the narrative's inciting incident. Prescott enters the nearly empty hotel bar flashing around a large wad of money ($10,000 cash, he says), part of which he drops on the floor while paying for drinks. An ominous man in a fedora, whose face we never see and who never speaks, helps Prescott to pick up the cash. When the bartender (Lou Lubin) notes that the convention has made it impossible to find a room anywhere in the city, Prescott invites the stranger to share his own room. "Any friend of Sam Prescott's," Prescott says, nearly toppling over, "is a friend of mine." The two leave together, with Prescott drunkenly cackling and the identity of the man in the fedora still obscured.

In the scene that follows, the young William Castle's directorial talents become amply evident. In both narrative and stylistic terms, shot-by-shot, it is difficult to think of more complex or nuanced interplay of word and image in a Hollywood B-picture. The overall scene exists to establish that Prescott is dead, presumably killed for his money by the faceless stranger. Such a scene could have been handled straightforwardly, in the manner of a classical detective whodunit, through a perfunctory discovery of the corpse and a couple of memorable clues, while nonetheless producing the kind of visceral shock 1940s audiences expected from a quickly paced crime film. What Castle delivers instead, however, is a kind of leap-frogging, dialectical meditation on the unidirectional connectivity of electronic media and the oblivious anonymity of modern urban life—two themes that pervade the noir-tinged Gothic melodrama that follows. By incorporating media as part of the crime scene, and by aggressively manipulating cinema's capacity to obfuscate and then deliver, tease and then satisfy, Castle intuits and thus exploits the structure of the gaze, which for Lacan "is always a play of light and opacity."[2]

As the hotel bar closes for the night and Prescott exits with his new "friend," the camera dissolves to a daylight shot of a window veiled by a diaphanous curtain that billows in the breeze. Through the window, the camera reveals numerous other windows belonging to the building across the street—perhaps another hotel or an office building. The camera holds on this image while a friendly male voice emerges on the soundtrack: "That's right. Now take a deep breath. Ready? Now, no fair cheating—a deep breath, I said! That's right. Inhale . . . Exhale . . ." At this moment, before the camera moves, it is unclear—one is tempted to say conspicuously opaque—who is speaking these words and why.

In psychoanalytic theorist Michel Chion's terms, the disembodied voice we hear is an example of an "acousmatic voice," a voice whose ominous, captivating power derives from the fact that it cannot be attached to any speaker. If the Lacanian gaze can be understood as a seen presence whose meaning is unknown and undiscoverable, the acousmatic voice is a heard sound whose source cannot be known, because it is conceptually (and in this case literally) out of frame.[3] This disjunction of sound and image is soon remedied when the camera pulls back to reveal a console radio standing between two large windows. The voice comes neither from within the room, nor from a window across the way, but instead from a radio studio in some other part of the city, broadcasting a calisthenics program in the style of Bernarr Macfadden or (later, on television) Jack LaLanne. At the point that Castle's camera visually connects the acousmatic voice to its source, the source is revealed to be yet another form of acousmatic voice.[4] Chion makes the case that "radio is acousmatic by nature" and that "[i]n radio, one cannot play with showing, partially showing and not showing." However, Castle's approach wryly undermines the acousmatic ontology of radio by *disembodying the radio itself*, initially withholding and then revealing the very technology that is the cause of the *acousmêtre*.

This initial dialectical movement, using the camera-pull to provide an objective source for the voice, but not a physically present body who speaks, represents a nascent version of the kind of carnivalesque gimmickry Castle will more aggressively deploy in later films such as *The Tingler* (1959) and *13 Ghosts* (1960). For Castle, technology is not something to be blindly accepted or taken for granted, but something to be toyed with, exploited, and even perversely made to undermine itself. In a strong sense, the camera-pull that unveils the radio forecasts the famous "Club Silencio" sequence in David Lynch's postmodern film noir *Mulholland Dr.* (2001), in which a lilting Spanish rendition of Roy Orbison's "Crying" on the soundtrack is abruptly decoupled from the singer's (Rebekah Del Rio) moving lips when she falls unconscious to the floor and is carried off stage. Similar to Lynch's emcee (Geno Silva), who tells the audience, "No hay banda; there is no band," Castle's quirky reveal tells us that there is no human speaker for the words we hear, only a radio speaker. He is saying "Gotcha!" but also "see what I just did there?" Modern electronic media can be deceptive, even discombobulating, and Castle uses media to deceive his own audience, while at least partly admitting the trickery in which he is engaged.

But the dialectical machinations of the scene do not stop there. As the voice on the radio continues to coach his audience through a series of exercises, the camera pans right to reveal a chambermaid (Virginia Sale) who has entered the room carrying a vacuum cleaner and some clean sheets. We listen along with her: "Bend, stretch, bend, stretch. Touch your toes! . . . Ah, you can do it. That's better."[5] The maid pauses to shake her head at the radio in a mildly scornful way, although it is unclear whether she is disappointed with the room's former guests, who apparently left without turning off the radio, or with all the non-working middle-class housewives in the city who, unlike her, have the luxury of staying at home to consume such programming. Regardless, we have arrived at the scene's second meaning: that modern urban existence depends on workers whose labor goes unseen, but who, in our absence, gain unfettered access to the spaces we inhabit. Castle's sequence does not excise the activities of a mere chambermaid; it goes out of its way to include her—and not only her physical body, but something of her agency, as evinced in her disapproving little shake of the head. With the maid established not as an object, but as a full-fledged subject, we can now proceed to the third dialectical collision this complex scene wants to stage.

As the maid leaves the sitting room and enters the bedroom, her voice displaces the radio voice, but in a manner that is similarly decoupled from any moving lips on screen. We see the maid plug in her vacuum and the camera tilts down so that it fills the frame, as its loud motor fills the soundtrack. The voice of the maid, whose face no longer appears, seems to come from nowhere: "Look now, I've got twenty-six rooms to clean and I can't upset my schedule . . ." Just as the context for the radio voice was unclear, the exclusive close-up on the vacuum disallows any sense of who the maid is addressing. Again the camera resituates, pulling back to provide the answer: Prescott is sitting in a chair in the middle of the room with the lion's-head mask still on. Is he asleep, hung over as usual? Switching off the vacuum, the maid approaches him wearily: "Please, Mr. Prescott, don't be difficult. Mr. Prescott?" She lifts the mask and screams in horror, signaling that Prescott has been murdered—an ironically immobile endpoint for the sequence, given all the liveliness of the radio exercise show, the harried maid, and the nimble movements of Castle's camera.

To sum up, the Hotel Philadelphia scene in *When Strangers Marry* represents a complex interplay in which the partialness of the viewer's knowledge—specifically shots in which one hears but does not see—alternatingly impedes and facilitates the maid's plot-initiating discovery of Prescott's corpse. The room initially appears lively and upbeat by virtue of the calisthenics instructor's pleasant encouragements, but in reality it is a drunken man's death chamber. Here, as in all films noirs, things are not what they appear at the surface. However, the more crucial point concerns Castle's meaning-deprivation technique, in which both radio and cinema are self-reflexively put on display. To do so establishes noir deception less as a matter of wartime paranoia, and more as a question of media-technological anxiety. In effect, Castle's version of noir transports the viewer, like a radio wave, beyond the vision-obstructing walls and curtains of an urban hotel suite to show us what it looks like to see too much. Such epistemological translucence is of course not what average citizens experience moment-by-moment in their everyday lives. Rather, films noirs like *When Strangers Marry* permit their viewers an experience that is all but impossible in the real world: an exceptional boundary-crossing gaze that allows them to see precisely *just how much they fail to see* in their everyday interactions.

The dialectical merge-points in the hotel sequence ultimately come full circle when we realize that we have witnessed a murder and its discovery only so as to recognize ourselves, metaphorically, in one of the many oblivious windows across the way—windows through which scores of occupants could have seen a lurid murder-by-strangulation, but didn't. The scene's opening shot, recalling paintings by American realist painter Edward Hopper such as *Apartment Houses* (1923), *Room in Brooklyn* (1932), *Night Windows* (1928), and *House at Dusk* (1935), serves as a metaphor for all the blind, oblivious eyes out there in the world, and in this way pointedly exemplifies the fundamental paradox of the Lacanian gaze: "I see only from one point, but in my existence I am looked at from all sides."[6] Such reflexive framing (a window-frame which "looks out," only to frame a series of other frames which seem to "look in" at this banal scene of a woman cleaning a hotel room, a scene that will come to mean so much more) succinctly conveys the enjoinder to *look and see what you're missing* that is noir's prime directive.

WHEN GENRES MARRY

In a strong sense, the female protagonist of *When Strangers Marry* is our surrogate, our avatar in the story-world, owing to the fact that her lack of knowledge mostly coincides with our own. Young bride Mildred Baxter (Kim Hunter) is often affectionately referred to as "Millie," both by her husband Paul (Dean Jagger) and her ex-boyfriend Fred (Robert Mitchum); however, to hypocoristically excise the "-dred" from her name does nothing to abate the dread of her moment-by-moment experience. Mildred's plot-line combines two anxiety-driven genres, updating the classical Gothic "Bluebeard" scenario, in which a young bride is deceived at every turn by her (apparently) murderous new husband, to incorporate the traversal of a paranoid film noir cityscape, in which every mundane encounter is a potential threat. As such, Castle's film knots together his earlier focus on crime genres with his later horror output. Mildred's inquisitive pursuit also represents a quantitatively scarce, but qualitatively striking 1940s character type identified by Samantha Lindop as a combination of the Gothic heroine and female investigator, seen elsewhere in *Shadow of a Doubt* (1943), *Born to Kill* (1947), and *A Kiss Before Dying* (Gerd Oswald, 1956).[7] However, unlike the male investigators who appear in Castle's other 1940s films, Mildred Baxter is a true naïf, unaccustomed to marriage or big city life, and more than ready to be "gaslighted" when her narrative

Figure 1.1 Mildred Baxter, the Gothic/noir heroine of *When Strangers Marry* (1944).

commences (Figure 1.1). In the early sequence on the train, Mildred reveals that she came from a small Ohio town, and that she married her husband, whom she is *en route* to meet, after having met him only three times. This eponymous premise, that Mildred "married a stranger," represents the most conventional launchpad for the narrative type known as the modern Gothic romance.[8]

According to Diane Waldman, the modern Gothic romance subgenre involves a tightly defined narrative premise:

> [A] young inexperienced woman meets a handsome older man to whom she is alternately attracted and repelled. After a whirlwind courtship . . . she marries him. After returning to the ancestral mansion of one of the pair, the heroine experiences a series of bizarre and uncanny incidents, open to ambiguous interpretation, revolving around the question of whether or not the Gothic male really loves her. She begins to suspect that he may be a murderer.[9]

Within this hallmark subgenre of 1940s Hollywood, Waldman situates such films as *Suspicion* (1941) and *Secret Beyond the Door* (1947), as well as lesser-known films such as *Undercurrent* (1946) and *Sleep, My Love* (1948). Waldman does not mention *When Strangers Marry*, perhaps because it is not set in a remote mansion, but it seems clear that Castle has made a deliberate effort to substitute the urban milieu of New York City for the Gothic manse, trading the looming parapets, strange portraits, forbidden rooms, and mysterious tunnels of the traditional female Gothic for the hotel rooms, diners, jazz clubs, theatre lobbies, etc., that will become hallmarks of film noir. Castle's modern city is labyrinthine, mostly dark, populated by uncooperative locals, and above all prone to abrupt turnabouts and audiovisual shocks. It is also, however, a milieu positively obsessed with the medium of newsprint and its ontology.

Castle's substantial innovation in *When Strangers Marry*, and what perhaps more than anything justifies discussing the B-picture film in the same breath as A-list films noirs such as *Double Indemnity* and *Laura*, is his effort to develop noir's obsession with media, and especially its fetishization of headline news. Typical of this media-centric approach is a scene in which Mildred goes to the movies with husband Paul, exits the theatre to make a phone call to ex-boyfriend Fred, learns that Paul has mysteriously resigned all his sales accounts in Philadelphia, aborts the call, exits the phone booth to find a newspaper, checks a telegram to recall a specific date, purchases the Philadelphia newspaper for that date from a newsstand, cannot read the newspaper because of the dim street lights, goes to a well-lit diner, and when she finally reads the story of the so-called "Silk Stocking Murder," comes away with more questions than answers about her husband's possible involvement. This sequence, I argue, is a perfect example of the way film noir both adapts and reframes the Gothic romance by mediating it.

The sequence culminates in Fred meeting Mildred at the diner. She expresses her deep concerns that Paul may be involved in the murder, a conclusion the audience has been strongly encouraged to share. Fred retorts, "You mean to tell me you made up your mind just from reading this paper?" In this incredulous line of dialogue, Fred gives voice to an underappreciated major theme in film noir, and one that Castle helps to cement. *When Strangers Marry* could have remained a modern Gothic romance, but for the repeated complication of the plot via headline news. Unlike in *Rebecca* or *Gaslight*, the suspicion that the husband is a murderer is facilitated by the daily circulation of newspapers, which swings the film's overall trajectory sharply into noir territory. As film noir coalesces around a set of archetypes and narrative gambits in the late 1940s, it becomes positively obsessed with the bombastic and often lurid epistemology of headline news, as well as the ways in which the press both represents and exploits mysterious true crime stories.

In order to assert that noir, among its other distinguishing generic qualifications, is the genre of headline fetishism, that noir is somehow fixated on the very idea of newsprint as a cultural paradigm, what exactly would one need to prove? Since numerous films throughout the history of cinema have resorted to newsprint for reasons of narrative economy (i.e., as a relatively cheap and effective way to advance the plot) there can be no tenable argument that noir is unique in resorting to the on-screen appearance of news headlines. Nor does it seem likely that noir utilizes a greater or lesser quantity of on-screen headlines than, say, the screwball comedy or the musical. Setting aside these debates about quantity, any argument about newsprint as a gravitational center for noir must take a two-pronged approach. First, we must demonstrate that the ontology of daily news, both in its garish representation of above-the-fold crime stories and in its structure of daily and semi-daily circulation, inflects noir both thematically and formally. And second, we must establish that the narrating function of on-screen headlines is substantially different from the function of headlines in other genres of the period. The quality of noir's headlines, then, is the real issue—not their quantity. Headlines appear everywhere in Hollywood film, but film noir treats them in a peculiar way, and it is only by specifying this peculiarity that any illumination of film noir's remarkable "nose for news" can be explained.

I will thus propose the following axiom: *When news appears on screen in film noir, it appears as recognizably false information; information that has already been, or will soon be, undercut by the behind-the-scenes activities we witness.* Indeed, in the vast majority of cases, noir headlines could very plausibly be followed by a voice-of-God narration stating, ". . . but you, the viewer, know better . . ." Though the viewer of course never hears this point of clarification so literally enunciated, noir's point is no less clear. From breakfast-time perusers to serious armchair detectives and conspiracy theorists, everyone knows that the attractiveness of the headline news story derives not from its production of an answer, but from its raising of a question—the arrival on the reader's doorstep of a problem which can't be solved, but which one can fantasize about by reading between the lines.

The news-craving public (fans of the tabloids, the scandal sheets, and yellow journalism) entertain the fantasy that something dreadful and horrific is possible in everyday life; they are in love with the idea that danger is not so much really imminent, but is present without being seen. Given these presumptions, one way to conceive of noir's on-screen headlines is not as a source from which the viewer can glean basic plot information, but as signifying a lack of signification, connoting a sense of "who knows what the truth is?" In a word, news in noir is a gaze—an obfuscating, impassable point of juncture between here and the beyond. Crucial to this effect is the fact that noir reveals criminality from the inside. While screening a film noir, the viewer is witness to a complete, totalized, behind-the-scenes truth, and in turn, noir's on-screen headlines deliver either a misrepresentation of or a gateway to the "inside scoop" that the narrative displays. These two realms of truth, the between-the-lines and the behind-the-scenes, are for all purposes utterly equivalent. Noir simply brings this connection to the forefront. Epicentral to film noir even when it is not shown, the news headline does not represent a solution, but instead functions as a veil between the oblivious eyes of the public and the private gaze of the various criminal agents who stoke the conflicts of film noir's narratives.

THE GAZE AND THE VEIL

In his book *The Real Gaze: Film Theory After Lacan*, theorist Todd McGowan explains that the look, which is on the side of the subject, is not the same as the gaze, which is on the side of the object. In this way, the gaze is not determined by or associated with the viewer's perspective, but instead is a necessarily distorted, nonsensical point around which the visual field is organized. The gaze is "the point at which the visual field takes the subject's desire into account":

> If a particular visual field attracts a subject's desire, the gaze must be present there as a point of an absence of sense. The gaze compels our look because it appears to offer access to the unseen, to the reverse side of the visible. It promises the subject the secret of the Other, but this secret exists only insofar as it remains hidden.[10]

In phenomenological terms, the gaze involves the emergence of a blot, stain, or veil within the subject's field of vision: an apparition whose inert refusal to signify, or deliver meaning, turns the entire scenario on its head. In the presence of a gaze, things are no longer what they seemed. Everything is suspect and all bets are off as to what the future holds.

When Strangers Marry is a film chock full of gazes, and gaze-structures: the unseen face of the man at the bar, the delayed letter from Fred to Mildred, the unfriendly and abrupt phone call from Paul to his new bride, the disappearance of the man from the cafeteria window, etc. Well-established in the Gothic genre, such blot-like devices actively confront both the protagonist and the viewer with a question they must work to answer, a problem that the narrative will ultimately resolve. However, a second, less obvious form of gaze appears in Castle's film, pervading its *mise-en-scène* and defining the narrative's status as film noir. The curtained window in Prescott's hotel room is an example of this type of gaze, which takes the form of an actual veil, but more importantly for noir, a *veil seen from the inside out*.

When Strangers Marry presents the viewer with two distinct modes of narrative, effectively halving the film along the lines of genre. Despite some stylistic blending and shared tropes, the first two acts of the film are largely a Gothic melodrama, whereas the third act is unremittingly noir. The splice occurs when Mildred comes to sympathize with Paul, despite the fact that he may have committed the Philadelphia murder she has read about. Whereas we initially viewed the gaze/veil from the outside, alongside the confused Mildred, in later scenes we see it exclusively from the inside, as Mildred becomes Paul's accomplice in evading the law. From the moment the two go on the lam to evade the New York homicide detectives who, at the behest of Lieutenant Blake (Neil Hamilton), have staked out Paul's apartment, the viewer's perspective shifts from the locked-out curiosity of the Gothic heroine to the portrayal of an "inside scoop" regarding a notorious noir murder case.

This generic pivot point in the narrative is marked by Castle in a striking way: a kind of directorial autograph. When Paul leaves the apartment, he is neither arrested nor questioned by the two plainclothes homicide detectives standing by the door. Why? Because the photo Mildred has given to the police, in lieu of a photo of Paul, is a photo *of William Castle himself*. Lee Server calls this "an impudent Hitchcockian cameo," but the crucial factor is that the cameo is a mediated one; Castle appears not as a pedestrian on the street, as Hitchcock does in many films, but instead in the form of a photograph, ostensibly a forgotten possession of the previous occupant of Paul's apartment, spotted on the mantelpiece by Mildred in an earlier scene. To properly read this strange meta-textual moment requires us to put it in line with two others: the film-opening shot of the lion's-head mask, which parodically references MGM, and the early scene when a hotel page walks through the lobby saying "Call for Mister King . . . Call for Mister King," referencing the film's producers, the King Brothers. Having established the film as referential, but in a semi-invisible way that only scholars and serious cinephiles will apprehend, Castle reserves the point of generic juncture, when Gothic becomes noir, for the appearance of his own face. In doing so, he certifies this moment of hybridity as authorial, as his own signature approach, but in a manner that accords with the surreptitiousness of a noir mastermind.

Although other directors of the period were engaged in various forms of Gothic-noir hybridization, and I am thinking here especially of *Gaslight*, *Bluebeard* (1944), *Experiment Perilous* (1944), and *Dark Waters* (1944), Castle's film, which debuted amidst this pack in August of 1944, is clearly the most noir in tone and aesthetics, as well as being the most aggressively hybridized. It would thus not be incorrect to claim that Castle either invented the form, or had a very strong role in establishing it, opening the door to later Gothic noirs such as *The Two Mrs. Carrolls* (1947), *Secret Beyond the Door*, *Les Diaboliques* (1955), *Mulholland Dr.*, and the television series *Dexter* (2006).

Beginning at the precise point when Castle's photo deceives the police, Mildred (and the viewer as well) is no longer confounded by the uncanny gaze of the Gothic, in which various punctiform objects, both visual and sonic, create a sense of incompleteness and alienation. Instead, the alliance of Mildred and Paul in their effort to flee New York conducts them through a broad series of encounters with the public eye—some overly suspicious, and others entirely oblivious to their presence. It is in these encounters that we become aware of a second type of gaze, a persecutory noir gaze that renders the entire urban landscape one of paranoia and threat, even and especially when things seem mundane and pedestrian. Two scenes are crucial in this regard: the couple's encounter with a long-haul cab driver, and their brief respite in a Harlem jazz club. In each sequence, the noir-era slang term "spot" is an unspoken keyword; the stakes concern whether Paul and Mildred will be spotted (in other words "outed" for being the criminals they do not appear to be) either by police or the news reading public.

Having decided to flee the city, Mildred and Paul go to a ride-share depot. The last car of the night is leaving for Louisville, and Mildred buys two tickets (Figure 1.2). When the driver (Billy Nelson) arrives, he is reading the daily newspaper as he walks through the door. He glances at Paul, then at the paper, then back at Paul. The driver and passengers depart. As they drive though the city, Mildred tries to appease the crying toddler of the visibly tired woman

Figure 1.2 Mildred and Paul Baxter pay their fares at a New York ride-share depot in *When Strangers Marry*.

seated next to her. All the while, the driver is staring suspiciously at Paul in the rear-view mirror. In an eye-line match shot, we see the newspaper item that concerns the driver: "KILLER ESCAPES: Description of Silk-Stocking Murderer Revealed By Police." The prominently listed height, weight, eye color, etc., match Paul exactly. Paul fidgets in his seat, pulling down the brim of his hat. Suddenly, the tension of the child crying and the driver's glare become too much. Paul demands that they stop; police sirens are heard.

The scene underscores noir's fascination with the epistemology of headline news through exaggeration. By virtue of just a few scant descriptions, the driver becomes unreasonably suspicious that the random man in his car is Paul Baxter, the murder suspect. However, in an epistemological reversal, the fact that we know the driver's suspicions to be correct only underscores the tangential nature of the encounter, and the too-paranoid gaze of the driver. The message is not that everyone is a criminal in hiding, but that anyone we encounter could be. Here, writ large, is noir's fantasy of unsuspicion—an invitation to the viewer to look and see what they are missing in everyday life.

WITNESSING WHITENESS

The sense of noir as a realm of adjacent, unsuspected conspiracy is reemphasized by Castle in the remarkable scene that follows, one which, I argue, is largely misinterpreted in existing scholarship. The couple exit the car in an unknown part of the city and get their bearings. Mildred and Paul, who are both white, encounter a series of people on the street: a woman in a black dress exits an alley; a soldier in his dress uniform entertains his date; a tall man smokes a cigarette while leaning in the doorway of a pool hall. All of these people are black, and it becomes clear that we are in post-renaissance Harlem, an African American cultural mecca well known to audiences of the 1940s.

Distant sirens are heard, but only Mildred and Paul respond, quickening their pace and searching for a place to hide out. Boogie-woogie music wafts up to street level from a basement bar, Big Jim's. They enter and the patrons of the bar glance up for a moment: *who are these white people in the club?* The attention of the patrons quickly dissipates as the couple sit down for a beer. Soon the music stops, with the police sirens now blaring at street level, evidently just outside. Everyone looks up as if there is going to be trouble. A newsboy comes down the steps and gleefully announces: "He's won! He's won! The champ's here! Hooray for the champ!" Dressed in natty suits, a locally known boxer and his manager enter the club to the delight of the adoring club-goers. Mildred and Paul take this opportunity to exit, unseen by the crowd that has amassed around the champ.

The scene at Big Jim's is truly remarkable, a pathbreaking scene in terms of depicting black culture for a largely white mainstream audience, and in a manner that the developing conventions of the noir genre render non-tokenistic. Existing analyses of this sequence tend to interpret it as an unusually progressive depiction of black culture's resiliency in a copacetic, ebullient community apart from its white oppressors. This perspective is perhaps best articulated by Frank Krutnik in his article "Something More than Night: Tales of the *Noir* City":

> The scene overturns the containment of blacks as a servile minority in U.S. society—a situation personified in the porter who assists Millie on the train to New York—and it also casts Paul and Millie momentarily adrift from their own narrative, so they can bear witness to a self-contained social world that possesses a vitality and cohesion lacking in the America they know. Without offering the Harlem subculture as a template for the disordered society that Paul and Mille are in flight from, the film does use it as a significant barometer of that society's disjunctions—as well as allowing a tantalizing glimpse of the city as a regime that accommodates multiple cultures.[11]

The problem with Krutnik's analysis here is not that it is wrong, but that it is incomplete, especially vis-à-vis genre. Krutnik understands the scene strictly from the perspective of the two white interlopers, who "bear witness," which is not at all what Castle's *mise-en-scène* intends. To the contrary, it is the club-goers who are witnesses, albeit to a reality that they cannot (yet) see.

Remarkably, the scene begins with a full thirty seconds of action in the club before Mildred and Paul enter. Smiling customers drink and dance; the camera sinuously tracks one dancing couple as they work their way over to chat with the piano player. No words are heard in the scene until the end, when the newsboy arrives. All meaning is conveyed via facial and bodily expression, as the enthusiasm of the dancers and onlookers contrasts with the alienated, furtive exchange of looks between Mildred and Paul. In a set of long shots, the two appear almost invisible in the back left corner of the room, the loud music having taken away their voices. From this use of camera and sound, we get the sense that Mildred and Paul are at once overwhelmed and entirely marginal; they do not fit in the picture they have entered. The space of the bar, like the street above, belongs to the black patrons, is "owned" by them, and the appearance of two white folks is at most a fleeting curiosity to the denizens of Lenox Avenue. Mildred and Paul are entirely surrounded by black culture, subsumed by it. Their diminutive presence itself is what strikes the viewer most. A series of long shots make the couple seem small and unimportant, a blot to the viewer, if not to the patrons, who go on with their revelry. In its binary of seeing and missing, with Mildred and Paul hiding in plain sight, the scene does not exist to exoticize black culture, or to put it on display, so much as it requires the viewer to "bear witness" to whiteness as such.

However, there is more to this arrangement than its effort to nominate whiteness as race, and this secondary meaning, as with all things noir, bears on the epistemology of headline news, a factor that the scene's conclusion makes explicit. Mildred and Paul's out-of-place-ness is subtly underscored by the fact that the bar is full of music, improvised by the piano player in a live performance, but until the newsboy arrives, Big Jim's is utterly devoid of any trace of media: no radio, no jukebox, and no telephone can be seen. Perhaps this is the real reason why Mildred and Paul are so ill at ease; the abundantly evident cultural differences between blackness and whiteness are not their primary problem, but instead the fact that the scene is too im-mediate, too non-electronic and real, and the couple thus find themselves out of their (mediated) element.

In a provocative thought-experiment, it may be useful to consider Castle's scene at Big Jim's as a race-inverted parallel to the two famous scenes at Jerry's supermarket in Wilder's *Double Indemnity*. In these scenes, Phyllis Dietrichson (Barbara Stanwyck) and Walter Neff (Fred MacMurray) meet "sort of accidentally on purpose," and in plain view of the public eye, to plot and then cover up the murder of Phyllis's husband. In the scenes at Jerry's, numerous shoppers pass by the conspiratorial couple, but the shoppers are so focused on their day-to-day activities that they do not so much as glance at Phyllis and Walter. However, it should also be noted that literally every patron of Jerry's supermarket is white, a fact which, given the period, does not strike the viewer as remarkable. The scene cannot, then, be a true racial inversion of the scene at Big Jim's, because this would entail Phyllis and Walter being the lone black shoppers in the store. Were this the case, their whispered communiqués surely would arouse suspicion. As the scene stands, and in light of what we see in Castle's film, it becomes clear that *Double Indemnity*'s two white co-conspirators are exnominated (i.e. not "named out" as such), both in their status as white, and in their status as murderer and accomplice.

This thought experiment highlights the racial/political departure of Castle's scene at Big Jim's. By situating his white protagonists as "other," whiteness itself becomes a kind of stain: what are these white folks doing in Harlem? The black patrons initially notice Mildred and Paul for their whiteness as such, but in a crucial second step, after a few moments the couple is left alone with their beers. Despite the weirdly antisocial, downbeat behavior of Mildred and Paul at the club, in effect *nothing comes of their whiteness*. The point of comparing Castle's scene to analogous ones in *Double Indemnity* is not to say that, in terms of their depictions of race, Castle is more progressive than Wilder because Castle dares to include a scene in a Harlem club. Rather, to the extent that Castle's scene depicts a progressive leveling of race, or sense of humanistic equality, the scene effectuates this racial leveling in tandem with noir's obsession with the pre-retrospective epistemology of front page news. By "pre-retrospective," I simply mean that the entire scene forecasts a future conversation amongst the patrons of Big Jim's, one that will take place immediately after the following day's newspaper hits the stands. We can imagine one of the patrons, or maybe the bartender, paper in hand, accosting the waiter: "Hey, remember those white folks who came in here last night? You served them beers. I think that guy was the Silk Stocking murderer!"

The fact that the scene at Big Jim's is resolved by the appearance of a newsboy lends credence to this interpretation. The point of the scene is that *two* news stories are co-present, both available to the eye, but only one of them, the arrival of the champ, is properly apprehended by the club's patrons. The second story, that is to say the noir story, will only come into focus with the arrival of the morning edition. In the moment of its happening, Paul and Mildred's flight from the police is gazed at by the club patrons, but not seen. In this respect, as newsreaders and unknowing witnesses, black people and white people are depicted as just the same: oblivious to a mediated truth that comes too late for anyone to take action, but never too late for the public's entertainment.

THE PURLOINED LETTERHEAD

If Lacanian theory is correct to place great emphasis on the gaze as "the point at which the visual field takes the subject's desire into account," then the Gothic needs to be reconsidered as a gaze-focused, or gaze-driven genre. The Gothic always entails the emergence of a strange, perhaps impossible, non-signifying blot into the realm of otherwise normal places and activities, and this blot serves as a kind of tip-off to the fact that the protagonist has drifted into the field of vision of a malignant other. This structure is the basis for the *unheimlich* quality of the Gothic. In light of this understanding, film noir can be viewed as a kind of geometral inversion of the Gothic, as if a glove or envelope has been turned inside out. Most notably, whereas the Gothic conventionally entails a protagonist witnessing a series of vexingly strange apparitions, film noir conveys a very different sense that *nothing* will emerge to tip us off to the presence of evil behind the scenes. Noir is, in effect, a reconceptualization of the Gothic gaze as both pedestrian and universal, which is to say that, in noir, the world of everyday appearances seems to "stare back" without anything to indicate that there is anything beyond it. Whereas the Gothic gaze is localized to a certain castle, room, or cemetery, the gaze in noir is at once mundane and pandemic.

Gothic narratives center on a protagonist who knows she (or less often, he) really is in physical danger, and every last little creak, rustle, or shadow comes to mean something. Film noir pointedly differs in its evocation of a realm of criminal conspiracy from the inside. In stressing the difference between these two positions, and sometimes, as in *When Strangers Marry*, by shifting the protagonist from one position to the other, noir infuses our cultural idea of the modern world with fright and horror. What then does it mean to say that *When Strangers Marry* is a hybrid of Gothic and noir, and what is to be gained in saying so? Among other things, such a claim entails that the long-established tropes of the Gothic, including especially the (frequently architectural) veils beyond which reside the source of Gothic conspiracy, are being mediated in noir by newsprint. Whereas the truth of the Gothic resides in a locked-up basement, attic, or hidden passageway, the conceptual core of noir involves an omniscient criminal eye imagined beyond the headlines, which are never entirely true. As such, noir compulsorily depicts the perspective of an oblivious public eye that sees nothing, or at least nothing of the conspiracies playing out in plain sight, which will only become transparent in light of the next morning's papers. If the Gothic generates horror based on the obscure, distant, partialized emergence of horrible threats, such grotesquery is at odds with noir's depiction of an underworld that is fully in view, right there at the surface of things, and quite banal-seeming.

As I have argued, William Castle's *When Strangers Marry* involves a masterful imbrication of established Gothic tropes and nascent noir ones. Nowhere is this more evident than in the film's conclusion. As Mildred and Paul strive to escape the public eye as they traverse New York, Mildred remains unaware that it is in fact Fred who is the real murderer: a gaslighting Gothic antagonist *par excellence*. Interestingly, it is the least technological form of mediated communication (the mailed letter, an ancient form more appropriate to Ann Radcliffe's literary Gothics than to 1940s New York) that trips up the media-dependent murderer at the center of the film's narrative.

The identity of the murderer finally becomes clear when Mildred receives a delayed letter that Fred wrote to her, proposing marriage. Yet, the crucial element of the note is not what Fred has written, but the mechanically printed stationery on which his message appears: from the Hotel Philadelphia. Viewing this letterhead, all the discoveries made by Mildred, the police, and the press are knotted together to reveal a new meaning: Fred is the Silk Stocking murderer. The stationery, combined with Fred's cursive postscript that "I just got hold of that present I promised you," certifies that Mildred is finally seeing things clearly. She escapes the rooftop garden where they have met, missing what the viewer clearly sees: Fred was on the verge of pushing her off the roof to her death.

However, it is a second purloined letter that trips up Fred, leading to his arrest. Late in the film, Lieutenant Blake of NYPD Homicide talks with

Figure 1.3 Lieutenant Blake confronts Fred Graham in front of a mail chute in *When Strangers Marry*.

Fred in the hallway of his hotel, while two detectives search his room for the stolen $10,000. Known only to the viewer, Fred has the money in an envelope, addressed to himself at a different location, which he drops into the mail chute when Blake isn't looking. As other letters clatter down the chute from above, Fred becomes visibly nervous, sweaty, and begins to prattle (Figure 1.3). Blake takes notice, commands his detectives to hold Fred where he is, and proceeds down to the lobby to meet a postman at the mail drop. Fred's letter is not there. But when a man on an upper floor drops his own last-minute letter into the chute, Fred's envelope full of money becomes unstuck, falling to the lobby and exploding open in front of Blake and the postman. It is as if the circulatory mechanisms of the big city themselves have intervened. Finally an "on time" connection is made, as the ironclad evidence of Fred's guilt drops into the hands of the police.

Just prior to this climactic discovery, a statement by Lieutenant Blake to Fred sums up the film's major theme, and in a strong sense the very foundation of noir: the concept of public unsuspicion:

> You know, you'd be surprised how much it takes to convict a murderer. You have a jury of twelve ordinary people. They've never even seen a murderer. They expect some wild-eyed maniac with blood on his hands.

When you show them someone who looks the same as they . . . they just don't believe you.

In the estimation of Lieutenant Blake, whose snappy professionalism and world-weary skepticism position him as a truth-teller, modern crime entails not just misrepresentation, but a kind of widespread simulacrum, in which criminal deception is immediately adjacent to our own daily activities and interactions. Modern criminals look just the same as everyone else. This insight likewise speaks to noir's revision of the traditional Gothic, wherein crime really is maniacal and bloody, bound up with dark hidden secrets, ulterior motives for marriage, and generations-old familial wealth.

By locating a Gothic residue within the noir canon, and by connecting this structure to Lacan's conception of the gaze as a signifier without a signified, we can begin to understand Castle's approach as the milestone noir Orson Welles proclaimed it to be. In modernity, the ultimate locus of uncanny isolation is not a remote Gothic estate or a creepy castle, but the cellular partitioning of the modern city, in which one's immediate neighbors are often complete strangers. In this way, *When Strangers Marry* is a critical signpost for film noir, marking a shift from a spatially situated Gothic gaze, in which things are not what they seem, to an omnipresent yet temporally contingent noir gaze, in which there is always more than meets the eye.

NOTES

1. William Castle, *Step Right Up! I'm Gonna Scare the Pants Off America* (Los Angeles: William Castle Productions, 2010), p. 92.
2. Jacques Lacan, *The Seminar of Jacques Lacan, Book XI: The Four Fundamental Concepts of Psycho-Analysis*, trans. Alan Sheridan (New York: Norton, 1978), p. 96.
3. Michael Chion, *The Voice in Cinema*, trans. Claudia Gorbman (New York: Columbia University Press, 1999), p. 18.
4. This turnabout recalls the drawing back of the curtain in Fritz Lang's proto-*noir* masterpiece *The Testament of Dr. Mabuse* (1933), a film Chion brilliantly theorizes; in Lang's film, the pseudo-source of Mabuse's voice is not a radio, but a horn-style loudspeaker connected by wire.
5. To my ear, the voice on the radio sounds like that of Richard Gaines, the actor who played Mr. Norton, the stuffy insurance company boss who is famously dressed down by Barton Keyes (Edward G. Robinson) in *Double Indemnity*. I mention this trivia only because I draw parallels between the two films elsewhere in this chapter.
6. Lacan, *Seminar*, p. 72.
7. Samantha Lindop, *Postfeminism and the Fatale Figure in Neo-Noir Cinema* (London: Palgrave Macmillan, 2015), 132–3.
8. The film was originally supposed to be titled *Love From a Stranger*, and was shot in seven days for a budget of fifty thousand dollars. Lee Server, *Robert Mitchum: "Baby I Don't Care"* (New York: St. Martin's Griffin), p. 76.
9. Diane Waldman, "'At Last I Can Tell It to Someone!': Feminine Point of View and

Subjectivity in the Gothic Romance Film of the 1940s," *Cinema Journal* 23.2 (Winter 1984): 29–40.
10. Todd McGowan, *The Real Gaze: Film Theory After Lacan* (Albany: State University of New York Press), p. 6.
11. Frank Krutnik, "Something More than Night: Tales of the *Noir* City," in David Clark (ed.), *The Cinematic City* (New York: Routledge, 1997), p. 98.

CHAPTER 2

Gender in William Castle's Westerns

Zack Rearick

"Iconic horror director William Castle created a simple, but winning formula for his films: a little comedy, a lot of scares, a preposterous gimmick, and a clear sense that fright films should be fun." Such begins the description on the back of Columbia Pictures' box set *The William Castle Film Collection*. As promised, the five-disc set consists almost entirely of horror films. This set represents the general understanding of who Castle was as a filmmaker. It would be a dramatic understatement to say that Castle is remembered primarily for his gimmick-driven horror films; it would be more accurate to say that he is remembered *only* for them.

We see this borne out not only in the popular conception of Castle but also in scholarship about him. Mikita Brottman refers to Castle's work as "a wide series of feisty, carnival-style gimmicks and hokum gimcracks."[1] Catherine Clepper notes that Castle was "belittled by his contemporaries as a purveyor of meaningless thrills and carnival tricks" but quickly reminds us that he "specialized in promotional stunts, takeaway ephemera, and standardized gimmickry."[2] The small range of extant scholarship on Castle focuses almost exclusively on his gimmick horror films.

Current scholarship presents Castle exclusively as a director of horror films. This is problematic, since Castle was one of the most prolific and versatile directors of the 1950s and 60s, working with a wide variety of genres. I find this scholarly gap troublesome because it reduces Castle not just to a horror director but to a director of gimmick horror. Since Castle directed many films that do not fall into either the horror film or gimmick film categories, moving away from seeing him as exclusively a horror director is not enough. In order to appreciate the full range (and it is large) of Castle's oeuvre, we must initiate discussion of his non-gimmick/non-horror films. If this seems excessively restrictive, it isn't. In reality, over half of Castle's films fit within this category. It is rather the scholarship that has heretofore restricted our discussion.

Beginning a discussion of Castle's non-horror/non-gimmick films presents a few problems, most obviously that such a discussion must be started almost entirely from scratch. The existing materials that discuss these films in any capacity are small and mostly factual. The only productive scholarly work on Castle's non-gimmick/non-horror films appears in Joe Jordan's book *Showmanship: The Cinema of William Castle*, which takes on the monumental task of describing and analyzing all of Castle's films. Because of Castle's prolificity, these descriptions must necessarily be short and Jordan's analyses of them even shorter. Some films receive no real analysis at all and are simply summarized.

Jordan's work sets a good foundation, but it must be taken further. New scholarship must continue this conversation, advancing it down the paths that Jordan has marked off. The present volume attempts to do much of that traveling. For my part, I have decided to focus on one specific genre of Castle's non-gimmick/non-horror work: his westerns.

Before a sustained treatment of Castle's westerns can begin, however, it is important to demonstrate how they differ from his other films. Obviously, the western as a genre has different conventions than a horror film. These distinctions can be made easily. But how do we determine whether these westerns constitute gimmick films? What is the definition of a "gimmick film"? This is important because I am claiming that we must begin seeing Castle as a filmmaker who created non-gimmick films, and so we need a clear line to separate the two categories.

The definition that gets most closely at this use of "gimmick" here is the following, which comes from the Oxford English Dictionary: "a trick or device used to attract business or attention." But how do we know which features of a film count as gimmicks and which do not? Certainly, many films exist with features that make them uncommonly unique that we do not typically consider gimmick films, although these features are, like the Coward's Corner for *Homicidal* (1961), often used as selling points for the films themselves. For example, the trailer and poster for *Ben-Hur* (1959) markets the film in part on the basis of its large cast. This feature of the film dominated adverting materials leading up to the film's release. This certainly makes that feature a "device used to attract business or attention." But few would call *Ben-Hur* a gimmick film.

In part, we can attribute this to the fact that this selling point of *Ben-Hur* brings attention to a feature germane to the film itself, not something that has been added to it. Coward's Corner was a real life physical location that existed outside of the boundaries of the film *Homicidal*, and many of Castle's other famous gimmicks (e.g. the vibrating seats in 1959's *The Tingler*) were as well.

This, I think, creates the primary difference between how we talk about a film like *Ben-Hur* and how we talk about a film like *Homicidal*. For the former, advertisers have chosen to emphasize a part of the film as a selling point. We as an audience understand that the filmmaker and the advertisers are often different groups, and so we know that, while William Wyler was certainly conscious of his use of a large cast, it is unlikely that he used a large cast solely to sell *Ben-Hur* to audiences. In contrast, *Homicidal* seems to exist solely to have a film around which the ingenious Coward's Corner idea can be set (although we must note the complicated relationship between Coward's Corner's and the film's Fright Break). We as an audience do not see a clear difference between the person who made the film and the person trying to sell it to us. Indeed, Castle made it quite clear to audiences that he considered himself both. This collapse of roles gives the filmmaker the appearance of a salesman, a role that Castle embraced with gusto.

The difference between "gimmicks" and features unique to films primarily revolves around the relationship between that feature and the film itself. If the feature is something already in the film (i.e. something that would be replicated if you were to watch the film anywhere aside from a theatre), then we should not term it a gimmick. If it is something that has been added to the film, something that can only be experienced if one goes to see the film in theatres, then we can term it a gimmick.[3] Much of the confusion results from the idea that non-gimmick films can have gimmicks. Instead, I suggest that we use words like "selling points" or "unique features" when speaking of these aspects of non-gimmick films.

This all has much to do with our discussion of Castle's westerns because, under my definition, one would not regard them as gimmick films, and so they fall, as do nearly all of Castle's non-gimmick films, outside of the existing Castle scholarship.[4] Like much of his genre work, Castle's westerns are unified by their difference. No two are alike. Set in a variety of historical and geographical settings, the westerns explore a range of theoretical and social issues. The films approach gender in characteristically different ways, ranging from conventional (such as 1954's *Masterson of Kansas*) to radically subversive (such as 1955's *The Americano*). Though all the films fall into the same genre, they are as different as they could be otherwise. Some of them star clean-cut heroes, some of them notorious anti-heroes; some of them feature extended gunfights or warfare, some of them are less action-based and more character-driven; some of them are about love, some of them are about war, some of them are about money. Because of the great variety in these films and because of the dearth of scholarship on Castle's non-gimmick films in general, investigation of Castle's westerns makes for a difficult endeavor. Finding a starting point for this discussion was the first and most critical task for this paper. I decided to use the westerns' treatment of gender as an entry point. Many other such entry points remain, but a paper in this present volume only has space for one. I have chosen gender as my focus because the films treat gender in radically different ways from one another, highlighting the inconsistency from film to film that characterizes Castle's westerns as a larger whole. Exploring these different approaches will begin a conversation worth having and will give us better insight into Castle's underappreciated talents as a director in the western genre.

The western as a genre lends itself to difference. Because it is "ostensibly grounded in the facts of history, genuine locations, and the biographies of actual individuals, the western seems a distinctly American form."[5] Jordan notes Castle's adherence to this rule: "most of [Castle's] Westerns . . . evolved around real life events and locations."[6] Of course, the western's treatment of gender does not replicate such variety. The "established conventions" of the genre reflect the "implicit gender . . . politics which now appear explicitly offensive."[7] Westerns are mainly films about men, and women in these films often serve merely as plot points with no more (and, indeed, sometimes less) depth than the inanimate objects (money, guns, land) which preoccupy the western.

Castle's westerns cannot be said to deviate from these conventions entirely. Even the most subversive among them regards women as meaningful characters primarily in their relations to the men with whom they associate. Castle uses them mostly as romantic objects, and, even when they act outside of the boundaries of traditional gender norms, they usually do so out of devotion to the men whom they love. Rarely do Castle's films pass Alison Bechdel's famous "Bechdel test," meant to gauge whether a film truly gives a voice to its female characters, and his westerns in particular do not fare well under this set of criteria. The majority of Castle's westerns feature women in roles meant to supplement the films' male heroes. Using Pam Cook's notion that women in Westerns are both "peripheral" and "central," most of the women in Castle's westerns are more the former than the latter.[8] Only two of the films include female characters who occupy roles prominent enough that one may consider them to exist alongside rather than in service of their male counterparts: Nita in *The Law vs. Billy the Kid* (1954) and Marianna in *The Americano*.

Much scholarly work functions under the assumption that a work's subversiveness itself constitutes grounds for scholarship. Blake Lucas is in line with most of the scholarship on gender and the western when he claims that "it's time to see the Western in a different light" and champions seeing the western "not as a masculine genre but one supremely balanced in its male/female aspect and one of the finest places for women characters in all of cinema." His fear that failing to do so "presents the deepening possibility that the classical Western, a genre without equal in its 1946–1964 golden age, may come to be undervalued and rejected" is common among scholars who talk about westerns and gender.[9] Implicit in this claim and in the strong focus on the most gender-subversive westerns in these works of scholarship is the notion that subversiveness should determine which films to focus on when discussing gender. Lucas, Cook, and other scholars like them highly value subversive portrayals of gender and spend most of their time discussing them.

Under this model, it is easy to see why Castle's westerns, with their mostly "peripheral" women, have not attracted much attention. But subversive portrayals of gender are not the only portrayals of gender worth talking about. Castle's westerns are worth discussing chiefly because he is a director worth writing about, and because they are an under-discussed segment of his larger corpus. Their varying levels of subversiveness do not compromise their importance to Castle's canon or to film studies as a whole. Still, although Castle's westerns mostly do not violate the major gender(ed) conventions built into the genre, many of them deviate meaningfully from the implied gender politics of those conventions. Because a larger conversation about these films does not exist, I will discuss all of Castle's westerns, examining their individual approaches to gender.

The subversiveness of female characters in Castle's westerns can be broken down into two traits, which the individual characters possess to varying degrees: autonomy and sexual uninhibitedness. Female characters in conventional westerns have little individual autonomy; they exist mostly to serve the men to whom they are connected, and they rarely have motivations aside from romantic devotion. Such conventional characters also stay within the kind of boundaries set for how female characters could and could not express sexual interest in westerns. Such characters' attraction was also typically directed toward one male character. Few westerns contain female characters who display interest in more than one male character, and even fewer who act on their sexual urges with more than one male.

Autonomy for female characters in westerns can be measured in two principle ways, both of which connect more broadly to the chief concerns of the western as a genre: motivation and the ability of the female character to protect herself. Male characters in westerns are typically motivated by a few general things: money, land, and self-protection (with romance occupying a lesser but still important role). Because these things comprise the chief concerns of the western as a genre, the ability for a character to be motivated by these concerns reflects directly on the degree to which he/she enjoys autonomy. When a female character has her desire for a male companion as her only motivation, she experiences a restriction of possible motivations that her male counterparts do not. The possession of money or land would indicate that a female character has motivations outside of her relationship with a male character. Jordan speaks of this kind of motivation when he says of the main female character in *The Americano*, who owns her own ranch, that her "independent stature is what enables her to succeed in a male-dominated society."[10] Additionally, the ability of a female character to defend herself would show the character's capability of getting by in the violence-driven world of the western without needing a male character to save her. Kidnapping, the ultimate violation of self-protection, is a common subplot in westerns. In these films, the kidnapping and rescue of the female character proves both her (male) rescuer's strength and also his devotion to her. In being kidnapped, female characters become explicitly stripped of their autonomy. In contrast, a female character capable of protecting herself by means of violence displays the kind of autonomy broadly afforded to her male peers.

The westerns that use gender in the most conventional ways in Castle's corpus are *The Law vs. Billy the Kid*, *The Battle of Rogue River* (1954), and *Masterson of Kansas*. I do not say that women are not important to these films. In fact, *The Law vs. Billy the Kid* features one of the most prominent female roles in all of Castle's westerns, Betta St. John as Billy the Kid's lover, Nita Maxwell. The plot of the film revolves around the relationship of Nita to the titular anti-hero, so much so that so Jordan remarks, "in essence, *The Law vs. Billy the Kid* is a love story."[11] This move by the film comes as a surprise to those already familiar with the typical representation of Billy the Kid as "an impassionate killer." This love story, however, conforms to the gender norms of the genre and the period in its depiction of the devoted female lover who we as the audience do not know apart from her relationship to the male main character. We see Nita only as one half of a romantic relationship, whereas Billy the Kid has concerns outside of his relationship with her, particularly a feud with a local man. Billy the Kid's tragic death at the end of the film represents the end of the story for us; we cannot envision Nita's life beyond this relationship because the film never situates us in her world apart from their romance. Although Nita has a vital role in the film, it never strays outside of the boundaries of the stock western romance.

One can certainly say the same for the primary female characters in *The Battle of Rogue River* and *Masterson of Kansas*. The latter has its most important female character, Amy Merrick (Nancy Gates), in the most minor of roles and does not warrant discussion here. *The Battle of Rogue River*, like *The Law vs. Billy the Kid*, has its most prominent female character as a romantic sidekick to the male lead. The poster aptly characterizes the role that Brett McClain (Martha Hyer) occupies in the film: "Fight to death ... While a woman waits." Appropriately, Brett spends most of her screen time in the film waiting. Her most significant contribution to the film's plot is her kidnapping, and the kidnapping itself never even takes place; instead, the lie about its occurrence suffices to break the peace treaty that is the film's principal focus.

Unlike Nita, however, Brett does not remain completely devoted to one man for the duration of the film. An example of sexual uninhibitedness, she flirts with both the film's protagonist (Major Frank Archer, played by George Montgomery) and its antagonist (Stacy Wyatt, played by Richard Denning). Brett's polyamory amounts to a combination of the two characteristics I have identified as being the markers of the subversiveness of female characters in westerns. The ability to be motivated by attraction to two men displays a kind of autonomy, although this still inhibits these characters from motivations not centered on men. Still, the ability to pick between two men (or at least to indicate their attraction to two men) gives these characters a semblance of power not afforded to most female characters in westerns. Additionally, such polyamory shows these characters as sexual beings. Sexual desire prompts the state of indecision that women like Brett face when they are torn between two potential lovers, a decision that often involves the potential violation of marriage vows. However, like nearly all the women in Castle's westerns, Brett eventually ends up with the protagonist, fulfilling the marriage (sub)plot.

Jesse James vs. the Daltons (1954) also includes a woman whose primary function is to be a romantic object, but the character in question (Kate Manning as played by Barbara Lawrence) also possesses the two characteristics I have identified as subversive. She displays an overt sexuality, bordering on the wanton, atypical of her counterparts in Castle's other westerns. After Joe Branch (Brett King) saves Kate from being hanged, she makes clear sexual advances toward him. Her request to change into his clothes necessitates her stripping naked for him, and, although she does so behind a tree and thus out of sight, she implies that she would prefer to do so in front of him. For a moment, the audience feels unsure whether she will appear nude in front of the camera. This is a moment of rare sexual tension in the otherwise conservative sexual world presented in Castle's westerns. Women in these films do not become nude frequently, and Kate's flirtatious nudity, although never revealed to the audience, represents a singular instance of bare sexual invitation. We have difficulty deciding initially if these advances result from a genuine attraction to Joe, or if Kate merely offers herself as a sexual reward for his saving her life. As the film progresses, Kate's importance to the story diminishes (often the case with women in these films), but her playful and inviting nudity, echoed in Castle's westerns only by a similar scene in *The Americano*, leaves an impression on its viewers.

In addition to her explicit sexual advances, Kate displays autonomy via violence, although this autonomy is compromised as the film progresses. When Joe meets Kate initially, a group of men are about to hang her. Although she cannot save herself in this specific scenario, her violent past situates her as a person who has the ability to commit the kind of violence necessary to protect oneself in a western; in fact, her near-death experience comes as a result of previous violence. She claims, "I have killed a man, and I will kill another man for the same reason!" Although Joe has saved her, she distrusts him. She states that she does not fear him and only needs his help because, at the moment, he has a gun and she does not. Not your typical helpless western female. However, despite her ability to defend herself, Kate never does so during the film itself, and, in addition to being on the verge of execution at the beginning of the film, the film's antagonists kidnap her later, a classic stripping of the autonomy of females in westerns. As with most of Castle's westerns, even when a woman displays subversive characteristics, she ultimately finds herself still relegated to traditional roles.

Jordan also sees Kate as a progressive representation of women in film, but for different reasons. Citing the cinematographic elements of the film's final scene, in which Joe and Kate marry and ride off, Jordan argues that the two are positioned as equals and that this positioning "represents a step towards the independence of women, "[alluding] to the beginning of a new era for women."[12] Perhaps Jordan makes too much out of the scene, in particular the political implications of the placement (and displacement) of the characters' hats, but I find the overall sentiment that Kate inaugurates a somehow "new" iteration of the traditional cinematic woman a reasonable one.

The Gun That Won the West (1955) features a female character in a similar role: Maxine "Max" Gaines (Paula Raymond), the wife of the film's main character, "Dakota" Jack Gaines (Richard Denning). Jack's desire to repair his damaged marriage to Max brings him out of the stupor of alcoholism that has thus far prevented him from participating in the war that comprises the major plot of the film. She is consigned to the sidelines once he has made his decision though, and, as the title suggests, the film focuses not on Max but on a new version of weaponry and its consequences for territorial battle. Jack may be brought to the action by his love for Max, but his involvement in that action (and his previous lack of involvement) serves as the fulcrum of the film. Like Nita, Max ends up as a typical western love object, devoted entirely to serving and caring for Jack.

Max does exhibit the polyamorous tendency that we saw in Brett; having failed repeatedly in her attempts to get her husband to give up drinking, Max begins to become attracted to Jim Bridger (Dennis Morgan), a friend of Jack's from his army days who serves in place of Jack as the film's major male character until Jack gets back on his feet. Bridger rejects Max's advances, but Max's adulterous leanings, though perhaps justified by the disastrous state of her marriage and by Jack's self-destruction, represent another instance of exploratory romantic feelings experienced by Castle's western female characters.

The three most subversive of Castle's westerns in terms of gender are *Fort Ti* (1953), *The Conquest of Cochise* (1953), and *The Americano*. *Fort Ti* and *The Americano* notably have two female characters of importance, a trait unique in the canon of Castle's westerns. In the former, the film's male lead (Captain Jebediah Horn, as played by George Montgomery) meets and falls in love with Fortune Mallory (Joan Vohs). The attraction between the two becomes obvious during a nighttime scene in which Fortune and Jebediah prepare to sleep next to each other by a tree. Jordan notes that "the tension between the two is undeniable," and "the following morning, they are together, away from the camp and isolated from the other rangers."[13] Only a surprise attack from the Native American group who constitute the film's antagonists disturbs this "moment of serenity." The portrayal of Fortune Mallory is mostly conventional. In fact, Jebediah's thoughts on the subject of womankind, which he shares after he kisses Fortune for the first time, position him in direct contradiction with the notion of female autonomy. He remarks that "woman is soft" and rejects Fortune's notion that women can survive by themselves (what Fortune playfully terms his "deadly ethics"). As the film concludes, he seems to have conceded to Fortune's earlier claim that "a man needs a woman" by kissing her, but he does not indicate that he has reconsidered his feelings on their survival abilities.

But Fortune is not the woman who has the longest-standing relationship with Jebediah. Running Otter (Phyllis Fowler), the spouse of one of Jebediah's closest friends, has been attracted to him for a long time. Running Otter's relationship with her husband and Jebediah can only be described as complicated. When we meet Running Otter, she immediately begins passionately kissing Jebediah as her husband and Fortune look on. Her husband remarks, "There is Running Otter, my wife. You wouldn't think [her husband] is like her father . . . We live in a crazy world, mademoiselle. I am old enough to be her father, but I am not. He is old enough to be her husband, but she thinks of him as a father. But it is fine this way. Between the three of us, we are pretty good family." The idea of Running Otter considering Jebediah as a father comes, her husband believes, from the fact that Jebediah found her alone and starving in the woods and brought her to her husband to be raised by him. After Running Otter sees Fortune, she runs off in a jealous rage, and her husband remarks resignedly, "We are married, but I still don't understand her sometimes." We learn that Running Otter only married her husband because he saved her life by taking her in as an orphan and raising her, and that she considers her marriage an unhappy one, later calling it "paying a debt."[14] Running Otter accuses Fortune of being a spy for the French to get her out of the way so that she can have Jebediah to herself. But Jebediah decides to trust Fortune, leaving Running Otter with a husband who, although he loves her enough to keep the fact of her deceitful accusation to himself, she decides she can no longer remain with. Faced with the prospect of staying with him (and knowing that, once Jebediah finds out that she has lied to him, he will no longer be attracted to her), she stabs herself in the stomach with her husband's knife—the only instance of suicide in Castle's westerns. Because violence is a sign of autonomy in westerns, in some ways the decision to kill oneself is an act of the most extreme autonomy. The ability to inflict violence on oneself, in particular to take one's own life, shows a power seemingly denied to these film's male characters, whose self-destructive tendencies do not extend so far and whose lives only end at the hands of others. In *Fort Ti*, that violence is rooted in sexual uninhibitedness, as Running Otter's sexual encounters with Jebediah (which we know have been going on for a long time prior to the beginning of the film) display the ability to choose more than one sexual partner. Of course, Running Otter kills herself because of her romantic and sexual rejection, so, in the end, her autonomy remains constrained by gender politics.

Still, the complex relationships between men and women in *Fort Ti* clearly fall outside of the bounds of the typical western. *The Conquest of Cochise* is equally subversive. Consuelo de Cordova (Joy Page), who Jordan terms "the heroine of the film," "does not find happiness upon the story's conclusion," skirting the marriage plot that most of the women in these films ultimately fall into.[15] Consuelo gives us another example of polyamory because she displays attraction to both Major Tom Burke (Robert Stack) and the Native American chief Cochise (John Hodiak). Tom is "presented to the audience as a compulsive womanizer," who, despite having been with another woman earlier in the film, "becomes enamored with Consuelo the second he lays eyes on her."[16] However, Consuelo does not reciprocate his affections, despite Tom's best efforts to court her. A group of Native Americans under the leadership of Cochise capture Consuelo. It soon becomes clear that Consuelo is becoming attracted to Cochise. Cochise responds favorably to this development. He allows Consuelo to touch him affectionately, although he does not attempt to court her as openly as Tom does. But such a relationship is not to be. In the final scene of the film, Tom comes to rescue Consuelo from captivity, but she hesitates to leave because she prefers Cochise. Unfortunately for Consuelo, even though Cochise has shown attraction to her, he claims, after a short speech about the difficulty of their relationship in the future, that she must go because the laws of his tribe state that he must "marry within his people." We find this odd enough at first because this law had not previously prevented Cochise from showing affection to Consuelo, but it becomes even more so when one of Cochise's men says, as Consuelo walks away with Tom, "Cochise, there is no law that a chief must marry within his people," prompting Cochise to cryptically reply, "I know."

Though Consuelo leaves with Tom, we get no indication that they will become romantically attached. Jordan contrasts *The Conquest of Cochise* to *Jesse James vs. the Daltons*, saying of the former that, "upon the story's resolution, a man and a woman do not live happily ever after."[17] Consuelo does not end up with either Tom or Cochise, although she shows interest in both of them at various times throughout the film. We see here again the subversive tendency toward polyamory that indicates an ability to make choices about one's destiny. However, Consuelo's autonomy is undermined both by the fact that she (like many other female characters in Castle's westerns) is kidnapped, and by the fact that she is spurned by Cochise despite choosing him as a mate, preventing her from being totally in control of her romantic and sexual destiny.

The best of Castle's westerns, *The Americano*, is also the most subversive. Jordan rightly notes that "the women of *The Americano*, although characterized as sex symbols, possess an empowering nature."[18] He speaks specifically of the film's female lead, Marianna (Ursula Thiess) and of the seductive Brazilian Teresa (Abbe Lane). These women exhibit the two traits that I have marked as indicators of gender subversion in fuller force than in any of Castle's other westerns.

The film's protagonist, Sam Dent (Glenn Ford), meets Marianna in hopes of finding out more information about a man who Sam sees as responsible for a recent murder. Marianna has already found her position as an autonomous character before she meets Sam. She owns her own property, meaning that, unlike any of the other women in Castle's westerns, she is self-sufficient. She does not need a man to take care of her, and she has the ability to survive in the patriarchal world of the western on her own. In fact, the two only meet because the same villain threatens them both. In this way, the film portrays Marianna as equal to Sam, perhaps even superior to him in her state in the world because he acts as an itinerant, while she owns property. Marianna embodies the characteristics that Robert Warshow associates with prostitutes in Westerns: "nobody owns her, nothing has to be explained to her, and she is not, like a virtuous woman, a 'value' that needs to be protected."[19] Sam initially bristles at these aspects of Marianna's character. He undermines Marianna's self-sufficiency, saying, "You're not as tough as I thought," and criticizes her for "dressing as a man," telling her that she would "look good dressed as a woman." We can see clear indications of his anxiety about her violation of traditional gender norms.

Although intimidated by Marianna at first, Sam quickly becomes interested in her sexually. In one of the most daring sexual scenes in Castle's westerns, Marianna takes a bath in a nearby lake and "uses her sex appeal as a means to deceive Dent." Sam "assumes the role of voyeur . . . [convinced] that she is naked underneath the water."[20] As with Kate in *Jesse James vs. the Daltons*, Marianna teases the man who looks at her with the possibility of seeing her nude. Unlike Joe, Sam shows little hesitancy in seeing Marianna's naked body. When Marianna warns Sam that she intends to come out of the water, he replies, "I'm ready if you are." Marianna gives Sam a chance to rethink his position, but he says that he is "sure" that he does not want to look away. Unfortunately for the "devastated" Sam, Marianna "emerges from the lake in a cream-colored bathing suit." Jordan sees an undermining of traditional gender roles along the lines of sexuality in this scene: "[Marianna] has had the upper hand all along."[21]

Marianna is flanked by another female with both autonomy and the ability to express her own sexuality: a local woman named Teresa. Jordan describes Teresa as "confident" and "exhibit[ing] a high degree of control."[22] Although Sam falls for Marianna fairly soon in their relationship (whether he can admit it to himself or not), Teresa fascinates him, particularly in one of the film's most pivotal scenes in which Teresa sings the film's eponymous song, which centers, albeit subtly, around an erotic relationship. Sam responds with fascination, eagerly grabbing an English-Portuguese dictionary to apprehend the song's meaning. Although Teresa and Sam engage in a sexually charged exchange about the meaning of the song thereafter, we learn soon that she is already married—another example of adulterous tendencies in Castle's female western characters. Teresa sings "The Americano" again, but this time we (and Sam) know that she directs it at her lover. Realizing that he will never gain Teresa's love, Sam kisses Marianna passionately. Both Marianna and Teresa display significant subversive qualities. The film ends on a less than subversive note, however, with Marianna and Sam getting together only after she claims that she will give up her ranch to be with him.

In the end, Castle's westerns exhibit an interesting but uneven degree of subversiveness. They are certainly worth discussing, as they comprise a significant part of the filmography of one of the twentieth century's most prolific and underrated directors. It is my hope that, now that the conversation about Castle's westerns has begun, other scholars will follow suit, adding additional thoughts and theories. This conversation need not focus exclusively on the subversiveness of Castle's films, but there must be work that further explores these westerns, one of the many under-discussed sections of the work of a man whose talents as a filmmaker are just now being truly discovered.

NOTES

1. Mikita Brottman, "Ritual, Tension and Relief: The Terror of *The Tingler*," *Film Quarterly* 50, No. 4 (Summer 1997): 4.
2. Catherine Clepper, "Death by Fright: Risk, Consent, and Evidentiary Objects in William Castle's Rigged Houses," *Film History* 28.3 (October 2016): 55.
3. The difficulty of deciding whether 3-D—which was in Castle's time both an element of the film itself, and a feature of the film that could only be experienced by seeing the film in a theatre—falls into the category of a gimmick places my definition in line with the general scholarly indecision about the gimmickness of 3-D. For this chapter, I will not consider 3-D as a gimmick on the basis of its inseparability from the film itself. Unlike the vibrating seats of *The Tingler*, the elements of a film that make it 3-D cannot be removed from the film, although they can be ignored. I must make this distinction because Castle shot two of his westerns, *Fort Ti* and *Jesse James vs. the Daltons*, in 3-D. In my cinematic taxonomy, those films do not count as gimmick films.
4. In "Collective Screams" (*Journal of Popular Culture* 44.4 (2011): 774–96), Leeder rightly

assigns Castle's westerns to "his pregimmick days" (p. 778), identifying 1958's *Macabre* as Castle's first gimmick film (p. 782).
5. Corey Creekmur, "Westerns," in Barry Keith Grant (ed.), *Schirmer Encyclopedia of Film* (Detroit: Schirmer, 2006), p. 357.
6. Joe Jordan, *Showmanship: The Cinema of William Castle* (Albany, GA: BearManor Media, 2014), p. 127.
7. Creekmur, "Westerns," p. 357.
8. Pam Cook, "Women and the Western," in Jim Kitses and Gregg Rickman (eds.), *The Western Reader* (New York: Limelight, 1998), p. 293.
9. Blake Lucas, "Saloon Girls and Ranchers' Daughters: The Woman in the Western," in Jim Kitses and Gregg Rickman (eds.), *The Western Reader* (New York: Limelight, 1998), p. 301.
10. Jordan, *Showmanship*, p. 173.
11. Ibid. p. 154.
12. Ibid. p. 191.
13. Ibid. p. 119. Jordan speculates that Castle spent less time on developing the romantic relationship between Fortune and Jebediah "simply because an action-packed, three-dimensional sequence is potentially, yet arguably, more entertaining to theatergoers," although such a focus on violence over romance is characteristic of most of Castle's westerns.
14. Running Otter attributes Jebediah's budding love for Fortune as a racial move, saying "You want a white woman!" when Jebediah rejects her advances—although he says that he does so because she is married and because her husband is his friend. This seems odd, as he has kissed her in front of her husband only a few scenes earlier, but he never engages her sexually again in the film. It is unclear why Running Otter considers her husband to have saved her life (and thus believes she owes him the debt of marriage), rather than Jebediah.
15. Jordan, *Showmanship*, p. 124.
16. Ibid. p. 125.
17. Ibid.
18. Ibid. pp. 172–3.
19. Robert Warshow, "Movie Chronicle: The Western," in Jim Kitses and Gregg Rickman (eds.) (New York: Limelight, 1998), p. 37.
20. Jordan, *Showmanship*, p. 173.
21. Ibid.
22. Ibid.

PART 2

The Gimmick Cycle

CHAPTER 3

He Earned Our Forgiveness: William Castle and American Movie Showmanship

A. T. McKenna

Some years ago I taught an undergraduate course entitled "Showmanship and the Movies." In this course I introduced students to the well-knowns and not-so-well-knowns of cinema's showman culture, from early pioneers to figures such as Terry Turner, Kroger Babb, William Castle, Joseph E. Levine, and Harvey Weinstein. As a class, we explored showmanship in search of a definition. "What is showmanship?" I asked my class. "What is a showman? What do showmen do?" After a short silence one student responded, "They earn our forgiveness."[1] It was an incisive observation. To *earn* forgiveness is indeed the hallmark of the showman. But how is it done?

In 1944, Theodor Adorno and Max Horkheimer published their famous jeremiad "The Culture Industry: Enlightenment as Mass Deception," which contains the lamentive last line, "The triumph of advertising in the culture industry is that consumers feel compelled to buy and use its products even though they see through them."[2] But the complaint underestimates both the audience and its appreciation of the *art* of the hoodwink. "Seeing through" is often the point of showmanship, conceding to be *willingly* duped. The showman invites the audience to both see (the object) and see through (objectification), and earns forgiveness through audience complicity. This means that because showmanship is dependent on audience acceptance, it is difficult to assess objectively because its success is entirely in the eye of the beholder. But this does not mean that it cannot be engaged with fruitfully as a concept. Using Castle as a vantage point, and focusing on his "gimmick period" (*Macabre* [1958] to *Mr. Sardonicus* [1961]), this chapter provides a historical and theoretical framework for understanding showmanship.

The chapter is split into three sections. The first section positions Castle and his showmanship in a historical context. Castle may have been idiosyncratic, but he was not wholly unique. He used showmanship techniques that had been developed since the beginning of cinema, but he benefited from the friendly post-Paramount Case marketplace in the 1950s and 60s, and capitalized on developments such as saturation promotion. The second section positions Castle in the tradition of the carnivalesque, which Russian scholar Mikhail Bakhtin developed in his book *Rabelais and his World*, and argues that the carnivalesque helps us to understand Castle's "showmanship-en-abyme." The third section details how Castle's brand of showmanship became less appealing in the 1960s because of changing audience tastes and sensibilities, as popular reading strategies such as camp, cultural movements such as the Hollywood renaissance, and the industrial ructions of the studio corporatizations weakened the position of the showman as audiences found they had less need for an objectifying intermediary.

This chapter does not seek to undermine Castle's uniqueness, but rather gives a historical account of the conditions that allowed his idiosyncratic style to flourish in the 1950s and 60s. I prioritize neither contextual determinism nor individual agency, but instead position Castle at a specific time in American history, one that he capitalized on and, indeed, helped to shape.

CASTLE'S FOUNDATIONS

In his essay about William Castle, John Waters bemoans the decline of hoodwinking techniques at the movies:

> What's happened to the ludicrous but innovative marketing techniques of yesteryear that used to fool audiences into thinking they were having a good time even if the film stunk? Did the audiences care? Hell No. They may have hated the picture, but they loved the gimmick, and that's all they ended up remembering anyway.[3]

It is, in some circles at least, inadvisable to suggest that William Castle's films "stunk," and most did not. It is likely that Waters is deliberately exaggerating the badness of Castle's films in order to accentuate the excitement of the accompanying gimmick for films such as *Macabre* (audience members were insured for $1,000 by Lloyd's against death by fright), *House on Haunted Hill* (1959; presented in Emergo, whereby a plastic skeleton would fly over the audience's heads at a key point in the film) or *The Tingler* (1959; some cinema seats were fitted with buzzers to frighten audience members during the film). But the notion of the showman artfully selling his wares by exaggerating their attractions to a knowing audience is the hallmark of showmanship, and key to Castle's strategies.

Castle sought to appeal to an audience that understood what he was selling from the way he was selling it, an audience that was able to decode the nods, winks, and tongue-in-cheek hyperbole. The fact that he was selling his films and gimmicks to children, who may be considered too young to have acquired the maturity to "see through" the ballyhoo, does not make this any less true; quite the reverse. Speaking to Linda May Strawn in 1973, Castle recalled his audience from the previous decade:

William Castle: The majority of my audience was the youngsters and young adults. But then, they were a little more sophisticated.
LMS: The youngsters were?
WC: The youngsters were. My films weren't.[4]

I will return to the notion of sophistication later in this chapter (partly because Castle seems to contradict himself later in the interview). But what is important here is how an audience interacts with a showman.

In his essay "An Aesthetic of Astonishment," Tom Gunning addresses the popular myth that audiences at early film shows screamed and ran for cover during screenings of *Arrival of a Train at Le Ciotat* (1895) upon seeing a train moving toward the screen, apparently fearful that it would crash through into the screening space. For Gunning, the myth of the terrorized spectator lies in film historians' underestimation of the sophistication of early cinema audiences. Far from being "transfixed [by the] illusionist power" of image and apparatus,[5] argues Gunning, the reaction from the audience was part of a consensual illusion "well prepared for by both showmen and audience."[6] The showmen provided a way of seeing, or seeing through, to enhance the audience experience, and the audience was complicit. This is the process of objectification, as understood by an audience, which takes cues from the showman.

The showman's job is to objectify. The object may not be extraordinary, but it is the showman's job to *render* the object extraordinary. Castle's objects were movies, and the objectification was the process of showmanship and ballyhoo into which the movie was integrated. Thomas Page, who knew Castle, writes: "Castle believed that promotion should be an integral part of the entire movie going experience. Film promotion should never be separated from film creation."[7] Castle was far from alone in this belief, and if one takes a scholarly wander through film history it is remarkable how *un*important the actual film can be.

Historically, exhibition has often seen a film text nestled into a bed of attractions, distractions, contraptions, and concessions. "It was the Cinématographe, the Biograph or the Vitascope that were advertised on the variety bills in which they premiered," writes Gunning of early film shows, "not *The Baby's Breakfast* or *The Black Diamond Express*;"[8] and Ross Melnick argues that, "over the first 25 years of projected moving pictures, from 1895 to 1920, the individual film was of little significance. The basic unit of exhibition was not the individual film but the programme, and the commodity that most patrons wished to buy from the exhibitor was not access to an individual film, but time in the auditorium."[9] Later, exploitation roadshowmen would attract audiences with lurid advertising and tabloid fervor to create an "overall entertainment experience,"[10] while drive-in operators of the 1950s "turned to selling an evening of fun in which the film being screened was only a part—and not necessarily the most important one."[11] At the other end of the cultural spectrum, arthouse cinemas of the 1950s and 60s "featured art galleries in the lobbies, served coffee, and offered specialized 'intelligent' films to a discriminating audience that paid higher admission prices for such distinctions."[12]

The film functioning as a non-dominant component of a show was, as Melnick states, standard practice until around the 1920s. Subsequently, shows may have been built around film texts, but films were still only a *part*. In his study of the showman Samuel 'Roxy' Rothafel, Melnick coins a useful phrase to describe the extravaganzas orchestrated by Roxy and his contemporaries, describing them as "unitary texts."[13] He also cites Richard Koszarski's assertion that movie exhibitors, up until the 1920s, "considered themselves showmen, not film programmers."[14] In stark contrast, by the late 1950s, as Castle was finding fame for his gimmick films, Berne Schneyer of the *Film Bulletin* observed that exhibitors "are *businessmen* not *showmen*."[15] Somewhere between the 1920s and the 1950s, the unitary text and personal touch promotion became sidelined in mainstream cinema, until they were resurrected by showmen such as Castle.

Arguably, it was the increasing rigidity of the studio system that compromised exhibitor showmanship. The 1930s saw the rise of double bills and block-booking, which saw the transformation of the exhibitor into a product programmer. Theatres became screening spaces, and block-booking meant that independent exhibitors were obliged to buy a whole season of films from a studio. Promotional materials were supplied by the studio, the unitary text of which the film was just a part became a thing of the past, and the showmanship skills of the exhibitors withered.

In 1948 block-booking was outlawed following the Paramount decision. Ostensibly, this was to free independent exhibitors from the burden of being obliged to purchase a whole slate of product in order to procure the handful of films that might make a profit. But the Paramount decision brought further problems for exhibitors, as Lincoln Freeman explained to *Fortune* readers in 1955:

> Delivered of the 'ruinous' obligation to buy an entire program of pictures (block-booking), the theatre man suddenly discovered that he had lost

his inventory. Then he complained that not only was he unable to forecast what picture he would be showing next April; in order to have one to show at all, he had to enter into "ruinous" competitive bidding for a commodity that, he was convinced, was produced in minimum quantities so a higher film rental could be squeezed out of him.[16]

The withering of the exhibitors' showmanship skills, the ramifications of the Paramount case, and the threat from television all coalesced to provide a fertile ground for showmen in the late 1950s. Shortly before *Macabre*'s release, *Film Bulletin* reported on the "little picture":

> The little picture is not sold as a quality offering; it is not likely to benefit from word of mouth advertising after it opens ... The trick with the little picture is first to provide the kind of promotion that arouses audience interest and secondly to book the picture on the kind of saturation basis that gets the audience while it's hot.[17]

Big-budget, prestigious roadshow presentations such as *The Ten Commandments* (1956) or *Ben-Hur* (1959) were being produced in greater number in the 1950s, but not in anything like the numbers to sustain exhibitor requirements. Moreover, roadshow presentations were only really suitable for metropolitan first-run houses; by the time they reached the second-run houses and the provinces, often in a truncated form, the initial barrage of publicity had died down. By contrast, "little pictures," with territory-by-territory saturation and blunderbuss promotion, were an ideal solution to the provincial and second-run exhibitors' problems, and an ideal platform for the new breed of entrepreneurial showman.

It would be wrong, however, to suggest that this new breed of showman simply sprang into being in the 1950s. There are connective threads between the high showmanship of the 1920s and the little-picture showmanship of the 1950s. Exploitation movies, for example, benefited from a range of hard-sell promotional techniques to emphasize the exploitable elements of the films being sold. Although Eric Schaefer disputes the link between the classical exploitation film and the weirdies of the 1950s, there were elements that crossed over and found their way into Castle's work. Schaeffer writes:

> Going to an exploitation film was often a carnival-like event because of the extrafilmic practices that accompanied the show ... external spectacle served to compound the delirium of the viewing experience. Lobby displays, lecturers, and "nurses" selling books disrupted the more routinized attendance patterns associated with mainstream movies.[18]

The "carnival" nature of the events will be discussed in greater depth in the next section. But what is interesting is that this precise assessment could be applied to Castle's gimmick films. Castle employed "nurses" at film screenings (to attend to audience members in case they were overcome by shock or fear), lobby displays were common, and even lecturers—if one considers Castle's direct addresses to the audience in films such as *The Tingler* and *13 Ghosts*.

With exploitation roadshowmen keeping showmanship practices alive on the fringes of the movie business, the lower end of the mainstream also kept showmanship alive via producers and promoters of cheap and gimmicky movies. Castle began his movie career at Columbia, where he had worked closely with one of the most notorious low-budget producers of the 1940s and 50s, the extraordinarily prolific Sam Katzman. Katzman was nicknamed "Jungle" Sam because of the jungle settings of so many of his movies and serials, and was described by Castle as "a great showman."[19] But perhaps the best connective thread between the showman exhibitors of the 1920s and the little-picture saturations of the 1950s can be found in the person of Terry Turner, particularly in terms of the development of the multi-media saturation campaigns which were so important to Castle's gimmick film successes.[20]

Turner is a hugely important but largely forgotten figure in the development of saturation promotion.[21] As head of special promotions at RKO Pictures in the 1940s, Turner began to develop the technique that would be so influential for future showmen such as Castle: multi-media saturation promotion. In 1943, RKO released *Hitler's Children*, a low-budget propaganda film about the Hitler Youth. Alongside the print and poster promotion ballyhooing exploitable elements such as evil foreigners, democratic righteousness, violence against women, and an urgent moral message, Turner opted to spend forty percent of his promotional budget on radio announcements. *Hitler's Children* was a surprise hit for RKO, and made a profit of over one million dollars.

Although promoters such as Rothafel had had success with radio, the medium had never been used so extensively or successfully in a movie advertising campaign before. But is not only Turner's pioneering use of radio and saturation promotion to sell a film that is important, but also the *type* of film. *Hitler's Children* is, essentially, an exploitation film, but Turner subsequently used the same techniques to sell *This Land is Mine* (1943), directed by Jean Renoir and starring Charles Laughton and Maureen O'Hara. It was a financial failure—not in *spite* of the prestige of the actors and stars, but *because*, according to *Billboard*, it is "a quality film of a serious nature," and thus unsuited to Turner's aggressive selling techniques.[22] An important lesson had been learned, and the gold standard for saturation promotion had been found: the sensational film with exploitable elements. "The formula won't work for just *any* picture," Turner would later contend, "You got to get the right kind . . . or at least a gimmick."²³

Histories of saturation innovations tend to position David O. Selznick as a pioneer of the process with his release of *Duel in the Sun* (1946),²⁴ but, like *This Land is Mine*, it is an exception that proves the rule. *Duel in the Sun* is a big-budget, star-studded western, with high production values. Its saturation release was widely seen as a tactic employed by Selznick to circumvent critical appraisal. Selznick later said in a memo that he regretted the decision because it undermined his organization's "former *Tiffany* standards."²⁵

Having harnessed the power of radio, Turner would pioneer the use of television in exploitation campaigns with the re-releases of *King Kong* (1931) in 1952 and 1956 before teaming up with Joseph E. Levine to create the blunderbuss promotional campaigns for *Godzilla: King of the Monsters* (1956) and *Attila* (1954; released in America in 1958). Thus, saturation tactics became synonymous with the low-rent weirdie, and Castle cashed in and chose horror as his favoured genre.

Castle claimed to have been inspired to begin making horror films by encountering queues of enthusiastic youngsters waiting to see *Les Diaboliques* (1955), which was released in the United States in 1955. Castle recorded his thoughts in his autobiography. "They have probably never seen a real horror film," he writes, "it's been ten years or more, in fact, since Lorre, Lugosi, or Karloff . . . Young audiences are starving for this type of picture, and I want to be the one to satisfy their hunger."²⁶

In the years between the release of *Les Diaboliques* and the release of *Macabre*, horror films became increasingly common in American popular culture. October 1957 saw the television syndication of many of the Universal horrors of the 1930s, such as *Dracula* (1931) and *Frankenstein* (1931), in *Shock Theater*; this was followed in 1958 by more horrors on television in *Son of Shock*. With black-and-white horror films being shown regularly on television, color horror films from Britain's Hammer studios, such as *The Curse of Frankenstein* (1957) and *Horror of Dracula* (1958), were on movie screens. With America's youngsters increasingly accustomed to spooky movies, Castle's *Macabre* was released in 1958 into a horror-friendly atmosphere.

Young audiences, as Castle observed, may well have been hungry for horror, but exhibitors were hungrier. With studios producing fewer films, television poaching audiences, and their own showmanship skills atrophied, showmen such as Castle were a godsend, and he, Levine, and Sam Arkoff of American International Pictures all deliberately targeted anxious exhibitors with their "little pictures." *Macabre*'s opening on 125 screens in New York was, reported *Film Bulletin*, prepared "with the same care as an army general planning a big offensive campaign."²⁷ Saturation innovations, with the attendant multimedia blitzes pioneered by Turner and the kind of personal touch promotion provided by Castle, along with the gimmick of insuring each member of the audience against death by fright, all helped to assuage exhibitor anxiety.

Castle had some words of tough love for exhibitors and the industry at large before rolling out his *Macabre* campaign: "The solution for a weak box office is hard hitting exploitation with well-produced films . . . There is altogether too much lethargy in the movie business today and this includes producers, distributors, exhibitors and theatre managers."[28] This kind of rhetoric, the energetic showman-hero seeking to revitalize a tired industry, was common among the showmen of the day. Like Levine, Castle placed himself at the epicenter of promotional campaigns: Castle was not just promoting movies, he was promoting William Castle.

Where Castle differed from contemporaries such as Levine (and, arguably, Arkoff), was in that Castle was a hands-on filmmaker with many years of experience *making* films, whereas Levine was, at this time, purely on the distribution and promotion side. In his essay about Castle, Waters even positions Castle as an *auteur*. He is almost certainly being facetious or iconoclastic, given that he compares respected auteurs Jean-Luc Godard and Sergei Eisenstein unfavorably to Castle, but his assessment is worth considering. "Mr. Castle got so carried away with the promotion [of *Macabre*] that he arrived in a hearse at some of the premieres and made his entrance popping from a coffin. Was this not the ultimate in auteurism?"[29]

To position Castle as an auteur, one must recognize, as Waters does, that his authorship extended beyond the film text. Castle's roles as filmmaker and showman, as author and intermediary, were, for his gimmick films, inseparable. He presented his audience with a film to see, showmanship to see through, and vice versa. Castle took the showmanship techniques of the past (unitary texts, exploitationist ballyhoo) and contemporary conditions and innovations (exhibitor anxiety, saturation promotion) and combined them with his own personal-touch showmanship to create a carnivalesque experience, as explored in the next section.

CASTLE'S CARNIVAL: *SHOWMANSHIP-EN-ABYME*

As Castle prepared to release *Macabre*, he told the *Motion Picture Daily*, "We're in a carnival age—we've got to bark to sell our product."[30] Indeed, the title of Castle's autobiography, *Step Right Up! I'm Gonna Scare the Pants Off America*, apes a carny barker's pitch. Fellow movie showmen such as Levine also invoked carnivals and circuses to describe the movie business of the time ("We're reminding everyone that this is a circus business");[31] and scholars have invoked the carnival to describe Castle's work.[32] When Castle spoke about carnivals, he was referring to the traveling cornucopia of attractions of P. T. Barnum's lineage: freaks, acrobats, coconut shies, penny arcades, fairground rides, and so on, all underpinned by American entrepreneurial capitalism and showmanship. Within academia, however, carnival is often related to Bakhtin's notion of the carnivalesque.

Within the Rabelasian marketplace of the middle ages, as interpreted by Bakhtin, we find the roots of the modern carnival and of Castle's showmanship. Bakhtin writes that during the European carnival of the middle ages, "A special carnivalesque, marketplace style of expression was formed."[33] Quoting a book-selling carnival barker character from Rabelais's *Gargantua*, Bakhtin observes, "Besides the enormous accumulation of superlatives, typical of marketplace advertising, we find the characteristic method of testifying to the speaker's honesty: comic pledges and oaths."[34] The book the barker is selling is "peerless, incomparable, nonpareil," and he offers a "pint of tripes" to anyone who can disprove his claim. Castle, in selling *Macabre*, offered his own comic oath "pint of tripes" in the form of a life insurance policy.

This is not merely about finding parallels between the Rabelasian carnival of Bakhtin's interpretation and the American showmanship of the twentieth century. Using Bakhtin's work can help us to understand Castle's showmanship specifically, and the traditions he came from. For example, both Castle and Levine were prominent media personalities, and both used their constructed personas to sell their films. But it is Castle who owes more to the carnivalesque, while Levine's persona was rooted in American populism. These are crossover constituencies, to be sure, and the latter descended from the former, but Kevin Heffernan has drawn a useful distinction between the two carnival forms:

> As Mikhail Bakhtin has noted in his study of medieval France . . . the often terrifying world of the carnival was an occasion for the temporary inversion of cultural and moral values characteristic of feudal hierarchy. The democratized, consumerist American carnivalesque is viewed with a deep ambivalence by a Puritan sensibility that seeks to both restrain individual desires and to unleash them in consumption. Nowhere is this ambivalence more clearly expressed than in the cultivation of the young as a consumer group in the postwar period.[35]

Although Heffernan cites Castle as an exemplar "snake oil salesm[a]n" to illustrate his point, Levine is a more fitting example of the ambivalence he observes, while Castle fits better into the Bakhtinian tradition.

Both Levine and Castle invited the audience to "see through" their promotional gimmicks. In Levine's case, his instinct was to oversell with hyperbole, akin to Bakhtin's "gay and fearless"[36] marketplace talk. But a significant part of Levine's brand of showmanship depended on the cultural hierarchies of the time. He was pointedly anti-elite, and railed against real and imagined enemies within the intelligentsia ("eggheads," as he called them), while styling himself as a representative of the "little guy." He deliberately provoked the "Puritan sensibility" of Heffernan's assessment.[37] Castle took a more Bakhtinian approach.

Castle's persona of the affable, spooky uncle made no reference to social and cultural hierarchies. Like Bakhtin's carnival barker, "he is one with the crowd; he does not present himself as its opponent, nor does he teach or accuse it. He *laughs* with it. There is not the slightest tone of morose seriousness in his oration, no fear, no piety, or humility."[38] For Bakhtin:

> carnival does not know footlights, in the sense that it does not acknowledge any distinction between the actors and the spectators. Footlights would destroy a carnival, as the absence of footlights would destroy a theatrical performance. Carnival is not a spectacle seen by the people; they live in it, and everyone participates because it embraces all people.[39]

Bakhtin's is a useful way of exploring Castle's showmanship. For Bakhtin, carnival is not a spectacle because it is immersive. Immersion, however, is only one facet of Castle's showmanship. Castle's gimmick film presentations are multifocal, incorporating both spectacle and immersion. Murray Leeder argues that the viewer should embrace the multifocal nature of Castle's gimmick films, and the coexistence of humor and horror in films such as *The Tingler*: "So stubbornly we seem to cling to these oppositions: laughing *or* screaming, horror *or* comedy. Why not both?"[40] Similarly, the coexistence of spectacle and immersion is key to understanding Castle's gimmicky showmanship.

In some of Castle's later gimmick pictures he directly addresses the audience. Whereas in *Macabre* and *House on Haunted Hill* the audience is greeted at the beginning of the movie by disembodied, in-character voices, in *The Tingler* we see and hear Castle as he speaks directly to us. He enters the shot from the right, wearing a suit and tie, and introduces himself to the audience: "I am William Castle, the director of the motion picture that you are about to see." The fourth wall is broken, yet it is not; broken, because Castle speaks directly to an audience whose existence he should not be acknowledging, and unbroken because it is not there. An immersive experience, such as carnival, has no fourth wall ("does not know footlights"), but a spectacle ("seen by the people") relies on a fourth wall. This is the coexistence of apparent opposites that informs Castle's showmanship, as highlighted by Leeder's analysis of the horror/humor conundrum. Castle's showmanship was not one or the other; it was both at the same time: "the motion picture that you are about to see" is also "the motion picture I am inviting you to see through."

In much of Castle's work, the intention of the gimmick (aside from promotional opportunities) was to inspire a giddy chaos in the theatre as opposed to an immersive theatrical experience. Castle proudly records in his autobiography some of the mishaps and failures associated with his two most famous gimmicks, Emergo and Percepto.[41] Waters, also, writes about how young audience members threw popcorn boxes at the Emergo skeleton, as opposed to quaking with fear,[42] and Leeder writes about the gimmicks "backfiring,"[43] making us wonder how "well" the gimmicks were actually meant to work.

In *13 Ghosts* (1960), as in *The Tingler*, Castle appears at the beginning of the movie, this time to tell the audience how to watch the film using the ghost-viewer—a viewing device that either revealed or concealed the screen ghosts, depending on which lens you looked through. In both *Homicidal* (1961) and *Mr. Sardonicus*, the film "pauses" before the climax so that the audience can be addressed directly;[44] in *Homicidal*, spectators too frightened to see the movie's climax were invited to leave the auditorium to sit in "Coward's Corner"; and in *Mr. Sardonicus*, Castle appears on screen to conduct a "punishment poll," whereby members of the audience decide whether the titular villain should receive punishment or mercy.

Castle's gimmicks were not only to enhance the movie, but also to be "seen through" (no ghost-viewer pun intended), and provide a brief distraction by drawing attention to artifice. They were also motifs of authorship that positioned the showman as auteur by reminding the audience that this was not just a movie, but a William Castle experience, in all its unruliness. This was not an immersive experience, such as the "unitary text" identified by Melnick; nor was it mere spectacle. Castle's showmanship combined new and old tricks, it was funny and scary, it was multi-layered and multi-focal; it was *showmanship-en-abyme*.

BABY BOOMERS, CAMP, AND CORPORATIONS

The showman invites the audience to both see and see through, and earns his forgiveness by crediting the audience with the sophistication to employ multi-focal reading strategies. Which brings us back to Castle's apparently contradictory views of audience sophistication, mentioned earlier in this chapter.

> LMS: Would you say that you couldn't make the films you made for your nine-to-sixteen audiences today? Do you think that kids nine to sixteen are too sophisticated?
> Castle: Oh, God yes . . . It's amazing . . . communications—television, news media—everything is instantaneous. Therefore, everybody is growing up fast . . . I think our audiences today are a lot more sophisticated.[45]

This seems like a contradiction, having earlier in the interview credited the audience for his gimmick films with being "a little more sophisticated" than the contemporary 1973 audience. But there are different types of sophistication. As Julian Stringer observes, "a fine line has always separated the public's willingness to be seduced by the values of public showmanship from its impulse to recoil in the face of vulgar exhibitionism;"[46] and it would seem that sometime in the 1960s that line had been crossed.

Robert Ray argues that television played a key role in developing youthful tastes in the mid-1960s, citing the knowing humor of *The Monkees* (1966–8) as being a particularly important, and overlooked, influence on the cinematic developments that would become the Hollywood renaissance: "In effect, the critics who proclaimed the New American movie (and who avoided TV) overestimated the impact of formal departures that the television viewer had largely digested."[47] Popular television products such as *The Avengers* (1961–9), *The Man from UNCLE* (1964–8), *The Monkees*, and *Batman* (1966–8) did not need any objectification by a showman; a showman did not need to provide the audience with "a way of seeing." Indeed, one of the "formal departures" common to all these shows is a sensibility often ascribed to Castle's gimmick films: camp.

In 1964, Susan Sontag sought to identify the camp sensibility that had emerged as a "private code, a badge of identity even, among small urban cliques."[48] The speed with which this sensibility spread through American culture was astonishing, and a nail in the coffin of showmanship. As a consumption strategy which cherishes ironic detachment to "dethrone the serious,"[49] camp ennobles the viewer by presupposing the creator's quixotically misguided intentions and glorying in presumed ineptitude. Among the camp artifacts Sontag lists are Steve Reeves movies and Japanese monster movies, which were popularized in America by showmen such as Joseph E. Levine and Sam Arkoff, neither of whom warrants a mention. Indeed, Sontag's greatest act of showmanicide comes with her judgment that "Ripley's Believe-It-Or-Not items are rarely campy,"[50] which reduces Robert Ripley's work to the objects, and ignores the showmanship context, or objectification, he provided.

Moreover, although Sontag advances camp as a "sensibility" as opposed to a production strategy, and argues that "intending to be campy is always harmful,"[51] it was a sensibility that was already gaining traction in the mainstream by the time Sontag published her analysis; and the advance of the camp sensibility became a mode of consumption that, inevitably, affected modes of production. If audiences wanted camp, then market forces would provide it, and they did so in the form of the television shows cited earlier. This exchange meant the creation of a closed loop between the audience and the text, between object and interpretation, which negated the role of the showman-objectifier.

Castle and his gimmick films have been incorporated into the camp canon with such alacrity that any suggestion that his films and showmanship are *not* camp must be justified; but to call Castle's films and showmanship camp is not quite right. Blair Davis has argued that applying camp theory to 1950s B-movies is a limited strategy because:

> The focus ... is primarily on the "badness" of these so-called bad movies, with viewers taking an ironic or satiric stance in their assessment of a given film ... Such criticisms of the 1950s B-movie that are rooted in mockery ... have served to suppress the importance of these films to the history of cinema.[52]

Although Davis is addressing the camp interpretation of the film texts, as opposed to the wider showmanship context of films such as Castle's, the point he makes is instructive. To understand Castle's showmanship as being *not* camp may seem counterintuitive, but Castle's alignment with the carnival as opposed to camp is strengthened for the reasons Davis outlines. As Bakhtin argues, "Carnival is different from the negative parody of modern times. Folk humor denies, but it revives and renews too."[53] Of course, Bakhtin's "modern times" of the pre-Second World War Soviet Union are rather different to the cultural milieu of postwar America, but the distinction remains useful. Although camp strategies are often affectionate to the objects of derision, derision is key. Camp viewing strategies seek to denigrate the text and eliminate the intermediary in order to elevate the consumer. In this sense, camp is the antithesis of Castle's carnivalesque showmanship, which is inclusive and caters to the curious, while camp is exclusive and caters to the schooled.

This is not to say that it was camp alone that forced showmanship out of American cinema in the 1960s, but with "knowing" reading strategies incorporated into the texts of the popular culture of the mid-1960s, there was certainly less need for a showman's objectification. Castle's *auteur* status incorporated his roles of author and intermediary to such an extent that they were inseparable. But as the 1960s progressed Castle's films became less gimmicky, and his role as a showman-objectifier waned.

There was an element of personal choice in this. As Castle writes in his autobiography, "Having to create a new, fresh gimmick for each picture was becoming tiresome."[54] But the shift in the tastes and sensibilities of the young American audience at this time was palpable, as one can observe from the changing approaches of Castle and his contemporaries. As the 1960s wore on, Alfred Hitchcock sought to move away from his showman persona, frustrated that his showman antics precluded him being taken seriously by critics.[55] Arkoff and Levine also moved away from the gimmicky exploitation that had been profitable for them in the early 1960s to accommodate the changing audience tastes of young adults. Arkoff and AIP responded to the generation gap by making fewer beach and bikini movies, and more biker and counterculture movies; Levine capitalized on the new sophistications of young audiences with *The Graduate* (1967). And Castle made *Rosemary's Baby* (1968).

Alongside the sophistications of camp on television, Robert Sklar argues that the baby boomer audience developed a greater intellectual and aesthetic sophistication in movie theatres:

> Oriented to visual media as no previous generation had been ... when members of this new generation began to encounter classic European and Hollywood movies through college courses many were astounded by the wonders of past movies.[56]

Movies of the nascent Hollywood renaissance, such as *Bonnie and Clyde* (1967) and *The Graduate*, were able to take old genre forms, gangster and screwball comedy respectively, and add a generation-gap twist with anti-establishment and alienated youth motifs. *Rosemary's Baby*, based on the novel by Ira Levin, also benefited from emerging sophistications, and capitalized on the maturation of the horror movie.

Rosemary's Baby is often understood to mark a change of direction in the American horror film, incorporating prestige, production values, and respectability. Gregory Waller argues that *Rosemary's Baby* "gave birth to highly professional, much publicized, mainstream ... horror films like *The Exorcist*."[57] But the birth of a new era came at the expense of a decline of the more carnivalesque horror. In his autobiography, Castle writes movingly about his desire to be taken seriously as a filmmaker,[58] and directing an adaptation of Ira Levin's novel would have helped him in his quest. Castle owned the rights to the book, and was keen to direct, but ceded the director's chair to Roman Polanski after meeting with him to discuss the project.

The horror film had, since the beginning of cinema, been synonymous with showmanship, gimmickry, and see-through cheap thrills. Polanski was of a new generation of auteurs, and understood how things had changed; prefiguring Castle's observations about the new audience sophistication, he told *Time* magazine in 1967, "TV has changed the world by changing people's attitudes ... When they are born with a TV set in their room—well—you can't fool them any more."[59] He was, as Castle attests, the ideal choice to direct *Rosemary's Baby* and, with Castle producing and Polanski directing, the film can be seen as the passing of a baton as the horror film journeyed from the disreputable world of ghoulish delights to the cultural legitimacy of auteurism and maturity.

Along with viewer-centric reading strategies that negated the need for an intermediary, the changing sophistications of young audiences, and the cultural capital acquired by genre films, came another development in American cinema that undermined showmanship still further. Concurrent with the Hollywood renaissance were the Hollywood conglomerations, which began with Gulf and Western's takeover of the troubled Paramount Studios in 1966. Subsequently, Seven Arts bought Warner Bros. and, in 1967, Transamerica acquired United Artists. In 1969, Seven Arts sold Warner Bros. to Kinney National Services and, also in 1969, MGM sold out to real-estate magnate Kirk Kerkorian.

Castle and Levine were two of America's great barnstorming showmen, and it is odd that they should be so closely linked to the corporatization of Hollywood, yet they were. The new sensibilities and sophistications of American audiences had resulted in Hollywood's two great flim-flam men scoring the biggest hits of their careers: *The Graduate* and *Rosemary's Baby*. Thanks to the success of the former, Levine was able to sell his company, Embassy, to the Avco Corporation for an astonishing $40 million. The success of the latter, meanwhile, saw a commercial lift at Paramount following the lean years of the mid-1960s which, notes Heffernan, "signal[ed] the wisdom of its new parent, Gulf and Western."[60] Over the following months and years, Hollywood's corporate future would be sealed. But the corporate world was not fertile ground for personal-touch showmanship.

Castle, like Levine and Arkoff, had come to prominence following the Paramount case, and found success against the background of a crumbling studio system. When the studio system was finally replaced by the corporate system, the tastes and sensibilities that had sustained movie showmen through the previous decade had changed, and audiences embraced new sophistications to replace the old. But the years between the Paramount case and the corporatization of Hollywood had proved to be a fruitful time to resurrect the tactics of the past, supplement them with new innovations, and allow showmen such as Castle and his idiosyncratic style to flourish, as American cinema floundered between two epochs.

CONCLUSION

Showmanship comes in many and varied forms. Joe Kember writes that in mid-nineteenth-century Britain the term "showmanship," which had most commonly been associated with performances at venues patronized by the working class, became more "widely dispersed and applied to middle class performers."[61] Similarly, in twentieth-century America, different techniques were used at different times to attract different crowds. If Samuel "Roxy" Rothafel was "the man who gave the movies a college education,"[62] then Castle was the man who gave them grade-school rough-and-tumble. Catering to different audiences in different eras, the showmen were always the objectifiers of culture, and they used technology to help them play their role.

Showmen of the nineteenth and twentieth centuries supplemented their own skills as entertaining intermediaries by embracing the mass media. The print media was enormously important to the showmen of the Victorian era,[63] and remained so as Rothafel embraced radio and Terry Turner pioneered multi-media tactics, which paved the way for Castle's own combination of mass-media saturation and intimate, personal-touch promotion. But it may well be that communications technology has superseded the showman, who thrives in intimate settings, and therefore needs at least the illusion of intimacy. Indeed, most scholars of showmanship situate showmanship in the past, as does John Waters, who titled his appreciation of Castle "Whatever Happened to Showmanship?"

As this chapter argues, the ramifications of the Paramount decision of 1948 created conditions whereby showmanship could flourish, but changing audience tastes and sensibilities, along with Hollywood's corporatizations, dampened prospects for showmanship. But the acceleration in technological developments within the communications field is also a factor. Castle entered his gimmick period at a time when mass communication technologies could still be harnessed by a charismatic individual able to put his own personal vulgar stamp on a campaign or entertainment experience.

With this in mind, during the writing of this chapter I went to see *Rogue One: A Star Wars Story* (2016) at a cinema in Shanghai in a 4-D presentation. 4-D is a Castle-esque process that seeks to immerse the audience in the film experience. Alongside 3-D visual effects, audiences are treated to extra-filmic effects in the auditorium: air is blown toward the audience to simulate wind, seats vibrate to simulate spaceship takeoff, and water droplets are sprinkled to simulate rain. The effects are wholly underwhelming. But the patheticness of the experience would have been much more enjoyable if a showman had intervened to tell me how amazing it all was—at least then I would have been in on the joke.

ACKNOWLEDGMENT

Thanks to David Pierce and Eric Hoyt for setting up the Media History Digital Library, which has been an enormously valuable resource in writing this chapter. <http://mediahistoryproject.org/index.html>

NOTES

1. I would like to thank my former student, Caleb Umlauf, for inspiring this chapter's title.
2. Theodor Adorno and Max Horkheimer, "The Culture Industry: Enlightenment as Mass

Deception," in *Dialectic of Enlightenment*, trans. John Cumming (New York: Verso, 1997), p. 167.
3. John Waters, "Whatever Happened to Showmanship?," in *Crackpot: The Obsessions of John Waters* (New York: Scribner, 2003), p. 13.
4. Linda May Strawn, "Interview with William Castle," in Todd McCarthy and Charles Flynn (eds.), *Kings of the Bs: Working Within the Hollywood System: An Anthology of Film History and Criticism* (New York: E. P. Dutton, 1975), p. 292.
5. Tom Gunning, "An Aesthetic of Astonishment: Early Film and the (In)credulous Spectator," in Leo Baudry and Marshall Cohen (eds.), *Film Theory and Criticism* (Oxford: Oxford University Press, 2004), p. 115.
6. Ibid. p. 129.
7. Thomas Page, "Introduction," in Joe Jordan, *Showmanship: The Cinema of William Castle* (Duncan, OK: BearManor Media, 2014), Kindle edition, location 77.
8. Tom Gunning, "The Cinema of Attraction: Early Film, Its Spectator and the Avant-Garde," *Wide Angle* 6.2 (1986): 66.
9. Ross Melnick, *American Showman: Samuel "Roxy" Rosenfel and the Birth of the Entertainment Industry* (New York: Columbia University Press, 2012), p. 319.
10. Eric Schaefer, *Bold! Daring! Shocking! True! A History of Exploitation Films, 1919–1959* (Durham, NC: Duke University Press, 1999), p. 111.
11. Kerry Segrave, *Drive-In Theaters: A History From Their Inception in 1933* (Jefferson, NC: McFarland, 1993), p. 78.
12. Barbara Wilinsky, *Sure Seaters: The Emergence of Art House Cinema* (Minneapolis: University of Minnesota Press, 2001), p. 2.
13. Melnick *passim*.
14. Richard Koszarski qtd. in ibid. p. 10.
15. Berne Schneyer, "Showmanship: It Still Pays Off!" *Film Bulletin*, July 20, 1959: 11.
16. Lincoln Freeman, "The Comeback of the Movies," in Tino Balio (ed.), *The American Film Industry* (Madison: University of Wisconsin Press, 1985), p. 377. Article first published in *Fortune*, February 1955.
17. Anon., "A Market for Little Pictures," *Film Bulletin*, March 31, 1958: 9, 16.
18. Schaefer, *Bold!*, p. 131.
19. William Castle, *Step Right Up! I'm Gonna Scare the Pants Off America* (Los Angeles: William Castle Productions, 2010), Kindle edition, location 2475.
20. Kevin Heffernan notes that *The Tingler* did not receive full saturation treatment because of the expense of the Percepto gimmick (*Ghouls, Gimmicks and Gold: Horror Films and the American Movie Business* [Durham, NC: Duke University Press, 2004], Kindle edition, location 1695). However, it did open fairly widely, taking $500,000 in its first week from forty-eight theatres in New York (Anon, "*Tingler* a Hit Here," *Motion Picture Daily*, March 17, 1960: 4.).
21. Turner is not completely absent from film histories. See, for example, Sheldon Hall, "Ozoners, Roadshows and Blitz Exhibitionism: Postwar Developments in Distribution and Exhibition," in Steve Neale (ed.), *The Classical Hollywood Reader* (New York: Routledge, 2012), p. 351; Sheldon Hall and Steve Neale, *Epics, Spectacles and Blockbusters: A Hollywood History* (Detroit: Wayne State University Press, 2010), pp. 171–2. For more on Turner's development of saturation techniques, see A. T. McKenna, *Showman of the Screen: Joseph E. Levine and his Revolutions in Film Promotion* (Lexington: University Press of Kentucky, 2016), pp. 38–40.
22. Anon., "Third Big Pic Plug Drive: Air Campaign on RKO 'Sun' In High Gear," *Billboard*, August 14, 1943: 6.

23. Anon., "RKO Hails *Conqueror* with spot TV, radio saturations," *Sponsor*, February 1955: 20, 35.
24. Sheldon Hall and Steve Neale also cite *The Outlaw* (1941) as being an important precursor to *Duel in the Sun*'s promotional tactics (*Epics, Spectacles*, pp. 131–2).
25. William Paul, "The K-Mart Audience at the Mall Movies," in Gregory A. Waller (ed.), *Moviegoing in America* (Malden, MA: Blackwell, 2002), p. 284.
26. Castle, *Step Right Up!*, location 2685.
27. Anon., "Allied Artists Outlines *Macabre* Drive to N.Y. Exhibs," *Film Bulletin*, July 21, 1958: 20.
28. Anon., "'Learn to be a Barnum' Says Exploitation-Wise Producer," *Film Bulletin*, April 28, 1958: 23.
29. Waters, *Crackpot*, p. 15.
30. Anon., "Carnival Techniques Pay Off, Says Castle," *Motion Picture Daily*, April 21, 1958: 2.
31. Anon., "Joe Unchained," *Time*, February 24, 1961.
32. See, for example, Murray Leeder, "The Humor of William Castle's Gimmick Films," in Cynthia J. Miller and A. Bowdoin Van Riper (eds.), *The Laughing Dead: The Horror-Comedy Film from Bride of Frankenstein to Zombieland* (Lanham, MD: Rowman & Littlefield, 2016), pp. 91–5; Alexander Swanson, "Audience Reaction Movie Trailers and the *Paranormal Activity* Franchise," *Transformative Works and Cultures*, 18 (2015): n.p.
33. Mikhail Bakhtin, *Rabelais and his World*, trans. Hélène Iswolsky (Bloomington and Indianapolis: Indiana University Press, 1984), p. 10.
34. Ibid. p. 162.
35. Heffernan, *Ghouls, Gimmicks and Gold*, location 3883.
36. Bakhtin, *Rabelais*, p. 167.
37. For more on Levine's antagonistic relationship with critics, see McKenna, *Showman of the Screen*, pp. 51–62.
38. Bakhtin, *Rabelais*, p. 167.
39. Ibid. p. 7.
40. Leeder, "The Humor," p. 97.
41. Castle, *Step Right Up!*, location 2996.
42. Waters, *Crackpot*, p. 16.
43. Leeder, "The Humor," p. 94.
44. In *Homicidal*, the "film" does not stop, as in *Mr. Sardonicus*, but the action slows while a countdown clock appears on screen to give the "cowards" a chance to leave.
45. Strawn, "Interview with William Castle," pp. 296–7.
46. Julian Stringer, "Introduction," *Movie Blockbusters* (London: Routledge, 2003), p. 7.
47. Robert B. Ray, *A Certain Tendency of the Hollywood Cinema, 1930–1980* (Princeton, NJ: Princeton University Press, 1985), p. 295.
48. Susan Sontag, "Notes on 'Camp,'" in *Against Interpretation* (New York: Picador, 2001), p. 275.
49. Ibid. p. 288.
50. Ibid. p. 284.
51. Ibid. p. 282.
52. Blair Davis, *The Battle for the Bs: 1950s Hollywood and the Rebirth of Low-Budget Cinema* (New York: Rutgers University Press, 2012), pp. 14–15.
53. Bakhtin, *Rabelais*, p. 11.
54. Castle, *Step Right Up!*, location 3340.

55. See Robert E. Kapsis, *Hitchcock: The Making of a Reputation* (Chicago: University of Chicago Press, 1992) for a thorough study of Hitchcock's reputation-building.
56. Robert Sklar, *Movie-Made America* (New York: Vintage Books, 1994), pp. 300–1.
57. Gregory A. Waller, "Introduction," in *American Horrors: Essays on the Modern American Horror Film* (Urbana: University of Illinois University Press, 1987), pp. 4–5.
58. Castle, *Step Right Up!*, location 3338.
59. Anon., "The Shock of Freedom in Films," *Time*, December 8, 1967, <http://www.time.com/time/magazine/article/0,9171,844256,00.html> (accessed January 22, 2017).
60. Heffernan, *Ghouls, Gimmicks and Gold*, 3469.
61. Joe Kember, "The Functions of Showmanship in Freak Show and Early Film," *Early Popular Visual Culture*, 5:1 (2007): 3.
62. Golda Goldman qtd. in Melnick, *American Showman*, p. 195.
63. Joe Kember, John Plunkett, and Jill A. Sullivan, "Introduction," in *Popular Exhibitions, Science and Showmanship 1840–1910* (London: Pickering and Chatto, 2012), p. 12.

CHAPTER 4

Collective Screams: William Castle and the Gimmick Film

Murray Leeder

The first section of Tom Gunning's seminal essay "An Aesthetic of Astonishment," called "Terror in the Aisles," reflects on the "myth of the Grand Café."[1] The notion that cinema's first audiences reacted with screams, or even got up to run from the theatre in terror, has been largely discredited but remains a powerful and persistent primal scene for cinema.[2] The phrase "Terror in the Aisles," however, brings to mind another time and place, not 1895 Paris but rather across North America in 1959. A horror film called *The Tingler* marked a new technological innovation called "Percepto" that forced audiences to "scream for [their] lives." At key moments of the film, certain audience members would be jolted by a vibrating motor hidden in their seats.[3] This was the latest offering from William Castle, the director and impresario also known as "the Abominable Showman" and "the Master of Gimmicks." Castle appears in the opening moments of *The Tingler* (Figure 4.1) with the following speech, delivered with a carnival barker's perversity:

> I'm William Castle, the director of the motion picture you're about to see. I feel obligated to warn you that some of the sensations, some of the physical reactions, which the actors on the screen feel, will also be experienced, for the first time in motion picture history, by some members of this audience. I say certain members because some people are more sensitive to these mysterious electronic impulses than others. These unfortunate sensitive people will at times feel a strange tingling sensation. Others will feel it less strongly. But don't be alarmed. You can protect yourself. If at any times you are conscious of a tingling sensation, you can obtain immediate relief by screaming. Don't be embarrassed about opening your mouth and letting rip with all you got. Because the

Figure 4.1 William Castle introduces *The Tingler* (1959).

person sitting in the seat right next to you will probably be screaming too. Remember this: a scream at the right time may save your life.

My reason for pairing Castle and early cinema should be apparent. Castle's gimmicks attempt to reach out to the audience and incorporate them directly into the cinematic experience, to restore the real or imagined experience of the early cinema spectator. Castle is more Méliès than Lumière (insofar as such lines can still be drawn), an inheritor of cinema's stage magic and carnival roots (Castle claimed that he modeled his career on P. T. Barnum[4]). Castle's 1976 autobiography, *Step Right Up! I'm Gonna Scare the Pants Off America*, has him deciding to make horror films after witnessing the audience reaction at a screening of Henri-Georges Clouzot's *Les Diaboliques* (1955): "I want to scare the pants off America. When that audience gave that final collective scream, I know that's where I wanted to take them—only I want louder screams, more horror, more excitement."[5]

Gunning's influential conception of the "cinema of attractions" designates early cinema's period before the dominance of narrative storytelling, the age of the popularity of the trick film. Gunning terms it "exhibitionist cinema," characterized not by the voyeuristic absorption of the audience but by a relationship between screen and audience emblematized by "the recurring look at the camera by actors."[6] However, Gunning stresses that though the dominance of the cinema of attractions ends around 1906 in the face of narrative complexity and the closing of the diegetic universe to the point where the look at the audience becomes virtually taboo, the logic of attractions remains as a buried element of cinematic practices. It is in this light that this chapter will examine two of Castle's gimmick films—*House on Haunted Hill* (1959), featuring the pop-out skeleton gimmick "Emergo," and *The Tingler*, with its vibrating seats among a gamut of gimmicky goodies—as inheritors of the cultural practices of early cinema. To make such a claim is not to argue, as Linda Williams writes in her analysis of *Psycho* (1960), that "American cinema has reverted to the *same* attractions of early cinema."[7] I do believe that there is a certain lineage, however, between Méliès and Castle, and on some level that Castle understood this too, for Castle's work shows strong affinities for silent and early cinema. His obscure last film, *Shanks* (1974), made in collaboration with Marcel Marceau, represents an attempt to recreate a silent aesthetic well before Guy Maddin's similar efforts.[8] But rather than looking at these gimmick films as spectacles where narrative is at best decorative (the way Gunning approaches the trick film), this chapter shall explore how narrative and gimmick work together, aligned to the point where it is neither proper to say that the gimmick serves the narrative of the film nor that the narrative is a clothesline supporting the gimmick; in Castle's films, the two are inseparable.

GIMMICK!

Just what the term "gimmick film" signifies is certainly debatable. One could propose a sweeping definition in which any "hook"—a movie star, adaptation of a "presold" property, an innovative plotline—constitutes a gimmick, and certainly mainstream cinema in Hollywood and beyond has always balanced an interest in novelty with its desire to provide a standardized product. But an overbroad definition relieves the novelty of the films of Castle and his ilk, which certainly were perceived as novel. For present purposes, the term designates a series of mainly horror and suspense films, beginning in the late 1950s, that introduced innovative tricks to attract audiences by addressing them more directly than Hollywood cinema is accustomed to doing. It represents "disreputable" novelty and invention following a wave of more official innovation on the part of the film industry in the early 1950s, an attempt by the industry to combat a precipitous drop in attendance conventionally attributed to the threat from television. David J. Skal rightly places the gimmick film as "part of a larger Hollywood movement in the fifties towards more expansive presentational modes";[9] John Belton's *Widescreen Cinema* is the definitive study of technological innovation in the 1950s.[10] In 1952, American movie audiences numbered forty-two million, a drop from eighty million the year before,[11] and such a plunge required a reaction from the industry: "In 1953, almost all of the major studios were aligned with at least one major manufacturer in an attempt to adopt an image or sound technology that they hoped would soon become the new industry standard."[12] These included Cinerama, variants on stereophonic sound, and, perhaps the most successful of them all, CinemaScope, which debuted in 1953 with Fox's Biblical epic *The Robe*, chosen specifically because the prestigious production lent the new format the legitimacy of "official innovation." *The Robe* was advertised as "The modern entertainment miracle you can see without the use of glasses."[13] The dig at 3-D film, which straddled the divide between upscale innovation like CinemaScope and the disreputableness that would come to characterize Castle and his ilk,[14] may allude specifically to *House of Wax* (1953), released five months earlier by a rival studio (Warner Bros.) amid similar claims of revolutionizing cinema. A throwback to the nineteenth-century stereoscope, an important piece of cinema's technical and cultural lineage, 3-D was hoped to restore the industry's value through newness (although ironically, as Ray Zone has shown,[15] the technology for 3-D cinema has existed almost since cinema's inception). In 1953, Bosley Crowther wrote that "it is on the sale of the average picture that the whole movie industry is pegged. If it cannot sell the ordinary picture, it cannot live . . . Thus it is that they are thinking first of all of the possibilities of 3-D in imparting magnetism and novelty, they hope, to the average film."[16]

But if 3-D commenced with the hopes of transforming cinema, it would become (at least until recently) a footnote in film history, only slightly more upscale than the one-off B-movie innovations that Michael and Harry Medved lambast in their smug *The Golden Turkey Awards*. They propose candidates for the "The Most Inane and Unwelcome 'Technical Advance' in Hollywood History" from a slate of one-off gimmicks.[17] These include not only Emergo and Percepto, but a split-screen process called "Duo-Vision" and Smell-O-Vision, which speaks (or smells) for itself.[18] The Medved brothers also cite the rather complex "Hallucinogenic Hypnovision." The latter, from Ray Dennis Steckler's *The Incredibly Strange Creatures Who Stopped Living and Became Mixed-Up Zombies!!?* (1965), consisted of an extra-diegetic "swirling hypnotic wheel" on the screen accompanied by masked men running up and down the aisles. The gimmicks the Medveds single out for ridicule span from innovations resident solely in the film to those that introduce a new element *into the theatre*, be it skeletons or smells or fluorescent costumes; in other words, these are a heterogeneous set of devices united by the keyword "unwanted." So one constituent for a gimmick film is surely disrespectability. Something like Hitchcock's *Rope* (1948) is too upscale to keep company with them, and we do not conventionally think of *Psycho* as a gimmick film, though Castle himself describes Hitchcock's gambit of not allowing anyone into the theatre after the film started as a gimmick, and perhaps fairly—the restriction figured strongly in the film's advertisement.[19]

The gimmick represents the collapse of advertising and exhibition to an unusual degree. In an article promoting *The Tingler* that appeared in *Motion Picture Herald* on September 19, 1959, Castle, we are told, "is firmly convinced that in today's motion picture market, if you don't have an all-star cast you've got to have a gimmick, 'a real gimmick,' backed by a sound story and a razzle-dazzle promotion campaign." The article is full of instructions on how to install and operate Percepto, as well as suggestions for "exploitation and promotion stunts, contests and merchandising tie-ins, all practicable on the local level. 'Tingler' street dances, cooperative promotions with department stores and disc jockey promotions were proved very successful in the first three engagements." It speaks of Castle as a "self-styled living trailer,"[20] with his regular publicity tours visiting openings of his films. As John Waters writes in his tribute to Castle, "Mr. Castle got so carried away with the promotion that he arrived in a hearse at some of his premieres and made his entrance popping up from a coffin. Was this not the ultimate in auteurism? Would Jean-Luc Godard . . . have arrived in a wrecked car to promote *Weekend*?"[21]

Before moving onto Castle's films themselves, it may be advantageous to briefly examine the early life of 3-D and in particular *House of Wax* as a model for approaching Castle's work. For his part, Castle shot two 3-D Westerns, *Fort Ti* and *Jesse James vs. the Daltons* (both 1953), in his pregimmick days, and claimed to have tried to sell MGM on the merits of 3-D back in 1949.[22] Billed as the first major studio film shot in 3-D, following a number of shorts and the successful independent film *Bwana Devil* (1952) the year before, *House of Wax* was an expensive, lavish Technicolor remake of 1933's *Mystery of the Wax Museum*. Objects fly toward the screen in fight scenes and showgirls' legs jut stereoscopically into the audience during a chorus line. James L. Limbacher writes that "the film's most terrifying moment occurred when smoke from a fire seemed to pour from the screen out into the audience,"[23] an apparent collapse of diegetic space and audience space that Castle's tricks like Percepto and especially Emergo would literalize. 3-D inherently challenges the diegetic closure that we associate with the classical Hollywood style.

House of Wax contains one sequence of particular interest to the formulation of the gimmick film. As the wax museum opens, we see a line beneath a marquee reading "House of Wax," an example of *mise-en-abyme* correlating the attractions within the film to the attraction *of* the film. Out steps a barker with a paddleball in each hand, shouting "Come see the House of Wax!" He bounces balls in the direction of the faces of gawkers around him before turning it onto the cinematic audience. We see from the putative perspective of an onlooker as 3-D paddleballs bounce directly into the audience. The fourth wall finally breaches altogether as he says "There's someone with a bag of popcorn. Close your mouth, it's the bag I'm aiming at!" Pretense of narrative dissolves and the film is laid bare as a showcase for 3-D. Kevin Heffernan regards this moment as that when "the interplay between the cinema of attractions and the cinema of narrative integration in *House of Wax* is most pronounced."[24] He writes:

In many horror films, the narrative's storytelling process is often enacted in a magician or trickster figure who accompanies his acts of sorcery with elaborate gestures to the audience that have their origins in the deliberately distracting sleight-of-hand of the stage magician. In the case of *House of Wax*'s use of 3-D and stereophonic sound, the violation of the proscenium space signaled elsewhere by the magician's gesture to the audience is achieved through spectacular displays of 3-D or surround-sound channel effects.[25]

Heffernan goes on to draw on André Gaudreault's distinction between the two divergent regimes of the cinema, "exhibitionist confrontation" (often with a *monstrateur*, the showman/magician within the film who acknowledges the audience) and "narrative absorption," putting forward *House of Wax* as a prime example of both modes coexisting in a single narrative. We shall find that this is equally true with Castle's films. Gunning resists an absolute separation between the exhibitionist and narrative modes of cinema: "Although different from the fascination in storytelling exploited by the cinema from the time of Griffith, it is not necessarily opposed to it. In fact the cinema of attractions does not disappear with the dominance of narrative, but rather goes underground."[26] The gimmick film represents a more manifest than regular reemergence of the cinema of attractions, and seizes upon the logic of the magician and the fairground stretching behind cinema—(unofficial) innovation, novelty, astonishment. Castle borrows from the trick film of early cinema a desire to use the resources of cinema itself to astonish the audience.

Others have found grounds to question even Gunning's porous separation of narrative cinema and the trick film. For instance, Gunning writes that "In parallel editing the 'magical' switches from one line of action to another are not the product of a Méliès-like prestidigitator, nor indications of a marvelous overturning of the laws of space and time . . . Griffith's 'trick work' is in the service of the drama, a narrativizing of the possibilities of filmic discourse."[27] Karen Beckman, however, has objected that, "in spite of this distinction both narrative and magical forms ultimately exploit the illusions that these editing techniques make possible. Continuous narrative *is* a trick."[28] It is this non-separation between narrative and trickery that underlies my consideration of William Castle.

Castle's autobiography never mentions *House of Wax*; one rather suspects that he elides any reference to *House of Wax* because it makes a lie of his claim that he singlehandedly turned Vincent Price into a horror icon.[29] Why grant Castle pride of place among those making gimmick films? An important reason is that regarding the full scope of his career tells us something about the gimmick film's place within the Hollywood system. In many ways Castle is quite unlike Ray Dennis Steckler or the more famous Edward D. Wood, Jr., desperately low-budget independent producers who never got past the extreme margins of the film industry. Rather, Castle was a Hollywood veteran who had directed more than forty films before *Macabre*—many of them films noirs, including *The Whistler* series and the well-reviewed *When Strangers Marry* (1944, also released as *Betrayed*), and who even produced Orson Welles' *The Lady from Shanghai* (1947). Castle's insider status helps demonstrate that the gimmick film is not divorced from the general production logic of Hollywood, but in fact flows directly from it.

What makes Castle especially fascinating, however, is his own public persona as a grand showman/*monstrateur*, a latter-day director/magician of Méliès's model, and how it straddles diegetic and non-diegetic space. His on-screen appearances find Castle explicitly presenting himself as the director of the film and a perverse master of ceremonies, warning off the weak-willed and promising thrilling terror. In *Mr. Sardonicus* (1961), Castle (dressed in period clothes, half occupying and half standing apart from the film's narrative) even interrupts the film for the "Punishment Poll" on whether Sardonicus should live or die. But the appearance of agency on the audience's part is a fiction: there was only one ending, for Castle knew no one would ever want him to live. Castle's first-person persona went beyond the screen and into marketing, his persona becoming a key part of selling his films. Showmanship frequently extends to the level of theme, with many of his films borrowing the premise of *Les Diaboliques*, an attempt to scare a character to death or into hysteria by staging supernatural events. This is the case even in his first gimmick film, *Macabre* (1958), about a doctor searching for his daughter, who has been buried alive by a madman. In truth, though, the doctor has staged this whole episode in order to give his father-in-law a heart attack so he can claim an inheritance. Castle hawked the film by taking out a life insurance policy against death from fright for the audience, and in so doing inaugurated the cycle of production for the gimmick film.

In both *House on Haunted Hill* and *The Tingler* there is a considerable slippage at work between Castle and his star, Vincent Price. So complete is this identification that in the 1999 remake of *House on Haunted Hill,* Price's role is filled by Geoffrey Rush with the name "Stephen Price." Outfitted with Price's pencil-thin moustache, he is an amusement-park mogul who specializes in scaring people practically to death; this harking back to the proto-cinematic attractions of terror is one of the remake's few laudable ideas. In *The Tingler* it is Castle who initially speaks to the audience (quoted earlier), but Price who closes out the film with a parallel voiceover. During the sequence in which the tingler attacks the projectionist (to be discussed in depth later) Price delivers the exhortation to "Scream for your lives!," while the alternate version prepared for drive-ins uses Castle's voice, suggesting a basic interchangeability of the two. Moreover, the narrative of *House on Haunted Hill* concerns a struggle for authorship that builds to Price's character taking on the dimensions of a puppet-master supreme, a diegetic incarnation of Castle himself.

SKELETON DANCE: *HOUSE ON HAUNTED HILL*

House on Haunted Hill opens, after a vocal collage of screams and a frantic first-person recap of the house's bloody history by the unhinged Watson Pritchard (Elisha Cook, Jr.), with Vincent Price's face and sonorous voice floating mid-frame and addressing the audience directly (Figure 4.2). As millionaire Frederick Loren, he issues an invitation to the audience: "I've rented the House on Haunted Hill tonight so that my wife can give a party. A haunted house party . . . There'll be food and drink, and ghosts, and perhaps even a few murders. You're all invited. If any of you will spent the next twelve hours in this house I'll give you each ten thousand dollars . . . or your next of kin, in case you don't survive. Ah, but here come our other guests."[30] *Other guests*: Loren's monologue is aimed directly at the audience, not any diegetic characters. Implicitly, the audience is included in the party, invited to stay for the duration of the movie. Already, too, Castle is being self-referential, reversing the conflation of death and money in *Macabre*: instead of money for dying, we're to get money for living. It also anticipates one of Castle's later gimmicks, the "Fright Break" in *Homicidal*, where Castle stops the movie just before the climax to invite the "cowards" to leave. Instead of the customary closure of the

Figure 4.2 Direct address in the opening of *House on Haunted Hill* (1959).

diegetic world, what we have is a certain fluidity between screen and audience, a collapse of the House on Haunted Hill and *House on Haunted Hill*, with the magisterial Price as our master of ceremonies.

House on Haunted Hill is all about a struggle of authorship, dominated by the question, "Whose party are we really at?" Loren and his wife Annabelle (Carol Ohmart) are among the least happy couples in cinema history ("Do you remember that fun we had when you poisoned me?"), and one of the film's most lasting pleasures is the sadomasochistic undercurrent to their deadly games of one-upsmanship. Each employs a set of quasi-cinematic devices in their attempts to kill the other. If there are real ghosts in the House on Haunted Hill, as Pritchard maintains to the last, we do not see any, just gimmicks rigged by the Lorens. In an early, tense conversation, the Lorens argue over the party itself. "This haunted house party was your idea," he says, but she counters with "The party was my idea until you invited all the guests. Why all these strangers—why none of our friends?" Loren explains the logic behind his invitation list: "I wanted kind of a cross-section: from psychiatrist to typist, and from drunk to jet pilot." (Is he describing the diversity of the cinematic audience?) Later, Loren says, "It's almost time to lock up the house, and then your party will really begin." His gaze subtly falling onto the audience, he adds, "I wonder how it'll end." Loren is both a diegetic character and our narrator, a character capable of breaching the closed internal world and addressing us directly, just like one of Méliès's magicians gesturing to show off a trick.

Fear is the weapon both Loren and Annabelle wield, in parallel to Castle. Most of the "supernatural" events crystallize around Nora Manning (Carolyn Craig), the youngest and most fragile of Loren's party guests, who is driven into an increasingly hysterical state by recurring shocks rigged by Annabelle. Midway through the narrative Annabelle seems to hang herself, and subsequently reappears as a ghost hovering outside Nora's window, noose around her neck. In the run-up to the film's climax, a further set of shocks send Nora into a hysterical fit, armed with one of the loaded guns Loren handed out as party favors. Insane with terror, she runs down to the wine cellar, where there is a pit of acid left over from an earlier murder in this very eventful house. When Loren comes down to investigate, Nora shoots him and he crumbles. This scenario was arranged by Annabelle and her secret lover, Dr. Trent (Alan Marshal). They faked Annabelle's suicide, scheming to drive Nora insane so she would shoot Loren and secure his inheritance for Annabelle. But Loren foresaw this scenario, and loaded Nora's gun with blanks. After killing Trent, he pulls a last trick on Annabelle (and Castle on his audience).

A fully intact skeleton emerges from the bubbling acid. It advances toward Nora. At this moment, *House on Haunted Hill* becomes a William Castle *gimmick* film, thanks to Emergo. To borrow John Waters' account:

Each theatre was equipped with a large black box installed next to the screen. At a designated point in the film, the doors to the box would suddenly fly open and a twelve-foot plastic skeleton would light up and zoom over the audience on a wire to the projection booth. Studio executives were initially skeptical when, at the first sneak preview, the equipment failed and the skeleton jumped its wire and sent a *truly* horrified audience running for cover.

After further testing, Emergo was perfected and installed in theatres all over the country. The kids went wild. They screamed. They hugged their girlfriends. They threw popcorn boxes at the skeleton. Most importantly, they spent their allowance and made the film a huge hit. Was this not the first film to utilize audience participation to an absurd length?[31]

Most accounts treat Emergo as wholly extra-diegetic spectacle (Brottman notes that it represents "an intriguing slant on the recently deceased 3-D process"[32]), but its narrative placement is key. The skeleton marches on Annabelle (Figure 4.3). "At last you've got it all, everything I had," says Loren's voice. "Even my life. But you're not going to live to enjoy it. Come with me, murderess." The skeleton's hand rests on her shoulders and she screams endlessly, hopefully cueing the audience to do the same, and finally teeters into the pit of acid. From behind a huge keg steps Frederick Loren, a device in his hand with which he has been controlling the skeleton (Figure 4.4). It is a fake, a gimmick, just like Emergo. He addresses his would-be

Figure 4.3 The skeleton walks in *House on Haunted Hill*.

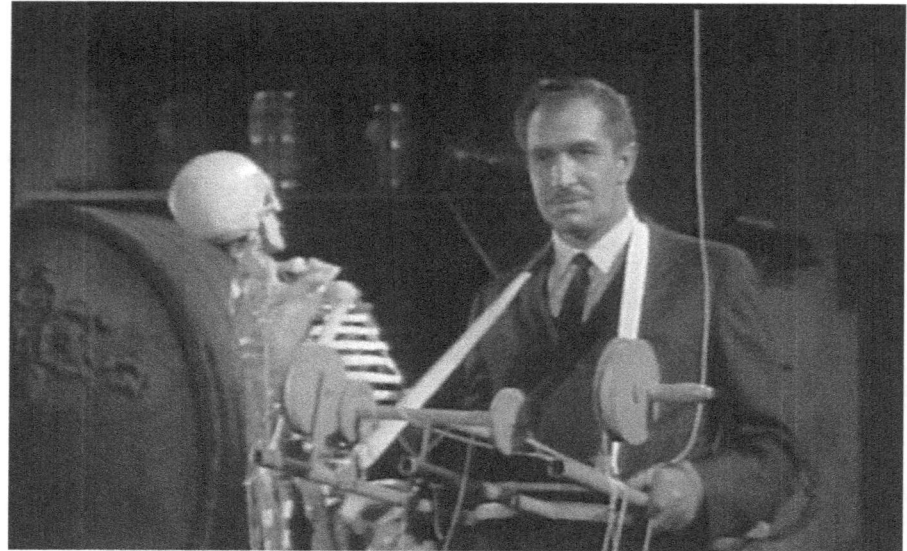

Figure 4.4 Frederick Loren (Vincent Price) is revealed as the puppet-master in *House on Haunted Hill*.

killers: "The crime you two planned was indeed perfect, only the victim is alive and the murderers are not. It's a pity you didn't know when you started your game of murder that I was playing too." In the game of authorship, Frederick Loren is the victor, Castle's proxy. Emergo is a signal of Castle's approval, the final merger between character and director, alike in both method (a phony skeleton) and intention (scaring a spectator).

The image of the skeleton recurs throughout Castle's later films, almost becoming his emblem. Scarcely common in horror cinema, walking skeletons are more often found in supernatural texts of a fantastical mode, like *The Skeleton Dance* (1929) and *Jason and the Argonauts* (1963). The skeleton, however, is important in proto- and early cinematic depictions of death and the supernatural, participating in a tradition reaching all the way back to the medieval Dance of Death.[33] The shows of Étienne-Gaspard Robertson's "Phantasmagoria" (circa 1797) would end with a projected image of a skeleton, "the fate that awaits us all,"[34] and a century later Georges Méliès would use skeletons frequently, most famously replacing his assistant Jehanne D'Alcy with a skeleton in his *ur*-trick film *The Vanishing Lady* (1896).[35] Castle's fondness for skeletons thus harks back to early cinema's iconography and that of the Phantasmagoria. The purest example of Castle playing Méliès[36] is the intro to *13 Ghosts* (1960; Figure 4.5). It takes place in Castle's "office," filled with hokey horror props and a skeletal secretary ("No more dictation today," he says, and she obligingly raises her pencil). Castle explains how to use the

Figure 4.5 Castle's introduction to *13 Ghosts* (1960).

special "ghost viewer," magically switching the screen from regular black-and-white to the special blue-tinted process for the film's gimmick, Illusion-O, and back again. Finally Castle says, "Shall we go?" to the female skeleton, and they both vanish! Here Castle, more obviously than ever, deploys a set of conventions from early cinema in order to position himself as a latter-day Méliès.

"THE ONLY WAY I CAN FRIGHTEN MYSELF IS TO MAKE IT REAL": THE TINGLER

The Tingler is Castle's film to have attracted the most academic attention, but even Mikita Brottman's admirable work on it fails to grant it much consideration in terms of its gimmick(s). Screenwriter Robb White reuses numerous plot elements from *House on Haunted Hill*, including a feuding husband and wife (two sets of them this time!), a gun loaded with blanks and the perennial Clouzot-derived plot device of someone trying scare a fragile person into hysteria.[37] Here Vincent Price plays a pathologist named Warren Chapin engaged in an unorthodox study of fear as a sideline to his job as medical examiner at a local prison. Following Castle's brief spiel on Percepto and the information that "a scream at the right time could save your life," the film opens, like *House on Haunted Hill*, with a scream. A set of screaming teenaged faces appears, an image of the audience. These dissolve into the face of an older man, also screaming. He is a murderer being led to the electric chair, the model for the film's major gimmick, the buttock-buzzing Percepto (a connection implied in some of the film's advertising, pairing a movie theatre seat with the challenge

"Are you brave enough to sit in this chair?"). In the prison's autopsy room, the murderer's brother-in-law Ollie Higgins (Philip Coolidge) meets with Chapin, who quickly discovers that the executed man's neck was broken, but not due to the electricity. Says Chapin: "I've seen this many times in people who were badly frightened just before they died. There's a force in all of us that science knows nothing about. The force of fear . . ." On Ollie's suggestion, Chapin names it "the tingler," saying "I wonder how many die *of* fear . . . Not on the death certificate," another reference to *Macabre*'s insurance policy gimmick by the increasingly self-referential Castle.

Chapin learns that Ollie lives above and operates a movie theatre devoted to showing silent films and even has a relic from a silent movie for a wife, all further evidence of Castle's strong interest in cinema's early decades. As the deaf-mute Martha Higgins, Judith Evelyn gives a jarringly effective performance right out of a silent melodrama, a mass of exaggerated tics. "Some of these old silents are just as good as the movies they make now," says Ollie. "Even with the sound and the color and the screens a block wide." Here we find Castle mildly mocking the new directions in cinema with a nostalgic reference to a time when cinema itself was sufficient gimmick to attract an audience. Dr. Chapin acquires a human subject for his experiments in his brazenly adulterous wife (Patricia Cutts). He scares her into fainting with a gun loaded with blanks and X-rays her while unconscious. On her spine he discovers a parasite: the tingler. It is a living alien body residing within all of us, says the film's ironclad science. It feeds on fear but is subdued and reabsorbed by the body upon screaming.

Chapin is anxious to experience the tingler's power for himself but does not think himself capable of being scared. To remedy this, he experiments with the new drug lysergic acid. If for no other reason, *The Tingler* finds its place in cinema history as the first film to depict LSD use, a decade before Roger Corman took *The Trip* (1968). Again, fear is at the heart of the narrative justification for this sensationalistic sequence. Chapin says that "Kids can scare themselves by lying in the dark and making ghosts out of chairs but we can't. The only way I can frighten myself is to make it real." He takes LSD to experience fear outside that of an imaginative (childlike) spectator—in short, beyond what an ordinary horror movie provides. His assistant Dave (Darryl Hickman) paints LSD as a horror film, again stressing greater "reality": "You're wide awake but you're having nightmares." Chapin plays the game of a mature audience member of a horror film—he wants to experience terror but not scream. The drug does what Castle hopes to do the audience: it breaks Chapin's defenses down, *forcing* him to scream.

The acid trip sequence makes reference to *House on Haunted Hill* as Chapin, coming apart as Vincent Price gnaws the scenery mightily, lurches into the skeleton hanging in the corner of his office. Only at this point does Castle depict Chapin's trip subjectively, blurring the skeleton and making it appear to walk forward. This triggers Chapin's final breakdown; as in *House on Haunted Hill*, the ambulatory skeleton marks the "real" terror, with Vincent Price now facing down the skeleton instead of pulling its strings. "Mustn't scream!" he murmurs, forcing his fist into his mouth, but he cannot control himself long, screaming and collapsing unconscious on a lab table. We flash forward to the roused Chapin lamenting "I broke down and screamed, didn't I?" with the now benign skeleton still prominent in the frame. It hovers in the background as Chapin says, "I don't think anyone could keep from screaming if they were really terrified."

The exception is a mute, and so Chapin drops in on Martha to give her a shot. The following sequence becomes puzzling on repeated viewings, since it is unclear whether she is hallucinating from an injection of LSD (as we initially think) or is being driven to hysteria by Ollie (as later events confirm). The shock imagery here is much like that which Nora encounters in *House on Haunted Hill*. A moldering corpse sits upright and comes at Martha with a knife. A hairy, grasping arm hurls an axe at her. A rocking chair moves by itself (as Heffernan notes, this image both echoes the electric chair in which Martha's brother died and references Percepto).[38] Voiceless but terrified, Martha flees into the bathroom, discovering a bathtub full of bright red blood against a black-and-white background, terrifying the phobic Martha as a gory arm reaches out of it. Again we have a ramping up of "reality," the sudden intrusion of color into a black-and-white film, associated with fear. The medicine cabinet swings open; inside is a completed death certificate with Martha's name and details on it. It reads "Cause of death: FRIGHT," the danger promised by *Macabre* fulfilled (Figure 4.6). She collapses on the floor.

Figure 4.6 Martha's fake death certificate in *The Tingler*.

Figure 4.7 Dr. Chapin extracts the tingler.

When Ollie brings her corpse to Chapin, Chapin performs an autopsy on the other side of a scrim. The scene casts Chapin in the director's part as Ollie watches Chapin conjuring up a giant tingler in shadow—when we see the tingler in silhouette again it will be explicitly associated with cinema (Figure 4.7). This tingler has grown to gigantic size because of Martha's inability to scream; the implausible monster, one of cinema's oddest, rather resembles a grotesque lobster.[39] Following an unsuccessful attempt by Chapin's wife to kill him using the tingler, Chapin decides that a moral law has been transgressed and that he needs to place the tingler back inside Martha's body. Back at Ollie's apartment, where Ollie is hiding her body, Chapin learns that *Ollie* terrified her to death with his bag of tricks ("She would've killed me if you could've," Ollie protests. "She tried, lots of times."). Meanwhile, the pesky tingler breaks free of its cage and crawls into the movie theatre, showing Henry King's melodrama *Tol'able David* (1921).

The sequence that follows "must be the ultimate direct audience address."[40] The tingler crawls along the floor amid the feet of the unsuspecting audience members, intercut with a fight scene from the movie and the rousing piano music. A woman looks down to discover the tingler grabbing onto her leg. She screams; paralyzed, it falls to the ground. Outside the theatre, Chapin throws a switch, shutting off the movie (*Tol'able David* or *The Tingler*? The distinction has ceased to matter). We now get a purely extra-cinematic interlude. Watching on DVD or television, we hear Price's voice (it seems more appropriate to name Price than Chapin here) say, "Ladies and gentlemen, there's no cause for alarm. A young lady has fainted. She is being attended to by a doctor, and is quite all right. So please remain seated. The movie will begin again right

Figure 4.8 The tingler is projected onto the screen.

away. I repeat, there is no cause for alarm."[41] For the cinematic audience of *The Tingler*, this was synchronized with an in-theatre stunt, a woman planted to faint and be taken away by phony physicians. Castle posted hearses and phony nurses outside of *Macabre*, but has now gone further, incorporating staged extra-cinematic activity into the film itself.

Shortly after the film resumes, the tingler appears in the projection booth and attacks the projectionist. Suddenly, *Tol'able David* disintegrates before our eyes, replaced with a completely white screen. The silhouette of the tingler crawls slowly across (Figure 4.8). Seven years before the projector broke in *Persona* (1966) and Woody Allen staged an erotic encounter in the projectionist's booth in *What's Up, Tiger Lily?* (1966), Castle gives us an unforgettable reminder of cinema's fragility. Another interlude, "the Scream Break," follows, with Price declaring: "Ladies and gentlemen, please do not panic! But scream! Scream for your lives! The tingler is loose in this theatre!" Screams are heard all over, both those on the soundtrack and hopefully those within the theatre, with a little help from Percepto. The exhibitor's manual for *The Tingler* calls for the projectionist to "'give two pushes in rapid sequence' to the vibrating motors under the seats."[42] "Scream!" yells Price. "Keep screaming! Scream for your life!" Recorded voices shout, "Look out, it's under the seat!" "It's over here!" "It's on me, it's on me!" Terror in the aisles. As Bob Burns describes it in the DVD extra "Scream for Your Lives: William Castle and *The Tingler*": "The theatre was just pandemonium for a few seconds, because it was totally in darkness. That's when they started hitting sporadically these little vibrators . . . and then finally a collective scream from about everybody. It's contagious!" Price finally says, "The tingler has been paralyzed by your screaming. There is no more danger. We will now resume the showing of the movie." When the film resumes, it is on the same image of Ollie and Chapin that it left, leaving no doubt this was truly an extra-diegetic "break."[43]

With the film's climax and the gallery of gimmicks done, the remainder of the narrative is obligatory anticlimax, with one last scare in store. As Ollie and Chapin find the subdued tingler in the projection booth, they hide it in a film canister, literalizing the association of the tingler with cinema (that is, the tingler with *The Tingler*) that echoes the House on Haunted Hill/*House on Haunted Hill* collapse. The projection booth carries a prominent sign warning against smoking, a reminder of the deadly fires from early cinema; cinema, we are being reminded, is dangerous. Chapin restores the tingler to its host vessel, Martha's corpse, and leaves, promising the electric chair for Ollie. But as Ollie is left alone, Martha is apparently reanimated by the tingler's strength. She approaches him (Castle gives us dramatic close-ups of her dead eyes) and he struggles to scream. Ollie suffers the fate the audience for *Macabre* fortunately avoided: death by fright. As Denis Meikle notes, "This was the stuff of 'ghost train' rides; as narrative it is pure piffle."[44] Despite his dismissive tone, Meikle has a point in alluding to the "attractions." *The Tingler* has passed to a realm beyond narrative, a realm of affect, the realm of terror, and it closes on this note, with a promise of effects outlasting the film: finally, over darkness, we hear Vincent Price's voice again, an echo of Castle's opening speech, "Ladies and gentlemen, just a word of warning. If any of you are not convinced that you have a tingler of your own, the next time you're frightened in the dark, don't scream."

(ARE WE EVER) BEYOND THE GIMMICK: ON THE LEGACY OF WILLIAM CASTLE

In "Film Form, 1900–1906," Barry Salt argues for a discontinuity between early trick films and narrative cinema: "It is my view that excessive attention has been devoted to early trick films . . . in view of the fact that they proved a dead end as far as the development of the cinema is concerned."[45] Despite what Salt says, the gimmick film represents a neglected line of continuity with the trick film, but now we face a parallel question—that of the influence of the gimmick film. Was it a dead end in itself? Castle found his gimmick films eventually losing the ability to attract audiences and abandoned his practices in all but minor ways. He distributed bloody cardboard axes to moviegoers for his Joan Crawford vehicle *Strait-Jacket* (1964), but describes this as more of a nostalgic lark than a serious marketing ploy.[46] Castle's postgimmick canon retains much consistency with his gimmick films, especially in themes of spectatorship and reflexive references to the cinematic experience of horror.

The Night Walker (1964), perhaps his most mature film, opens with a tumble of surreal images reminiscent of Dali's work for *Spellbound* (1945). A narrator intones, "What are dreams? What do they mean? What do you know about the secret world you visit when you sleep? Strange faces, strange creatures, faces that haunt our nightmares. Sometimes we watch them, and sometimes they watch us. Did you ever dream of being stared at?" The screen fills with staring eyes. Finally, a hand clutches a Daliesque eyeball and rams it forcefully toward the front of the screen, an image more jarring than any other in Castle's canon thus far but consistent with the logic of Emergo (or 3-D).

Castle eventually attained new legitimacy by co-producing *Rosemary's Baby* (1968),[47] but we should not overlook the legacy of his gimmicks. Late in his autobiography, he writes about the release of *Earthquake* (1974) with a gimmick (the word Castle uses) called "Sensurround" that accompanies action scenes with waves of high-decibel sound, "[giving] audiences the feeling of being part of the film."[48] The title of one of the subsequent films using the process, *Rollercoaster* (1977), speaks volumes about the persistence of the cinema of attractions where technical innovation is concerned. Perched just before the age of the blockbuster begins in earnest with *Jaws* (1975), it is tempting to say that this is the moment where the gimmick film re-merges with the logic of mainstream Hollywood. From there, we find the merging of narrative cinema and the funhouse mentality as the line between action/horror film and theme park rides blurs, while virtual reality continues a continuity from the stereoscope (a connection made by Mark Hansen)[49] through 3-D (itself experiencing a renaissance, including wedded to IMAX technology). Angela Ndalianis has stated that "Contemporary blockbuster special effects cinema and attractions owe a great deal to film spectacle of the 1950s,"[50] and we must acknowledge that this lineage goes far beyond Hollywood's prestige product, demanding space for a skeleton or two fluttering overhead, and a few seats that vibrate.

Tom Gunning famously wrote, "In some sense recent spectacle cinema has reaffirmed its roots in stimulus and carnival rides, in what might be called the Spielberg-Lucas-Coppola cinema of effects."[51] In 1999, filmmakers Joel Silver and Robert Zemeckis (both Spielberg collaborators) created Dark Castle Entertainment, a horror production house purportedly designed to keep Castle's style alive. Castle's daughter Terry has co-producer credits on the remakes of *House on Haunted Hill* (skeleton-free, it must be said) and *Thirteen Ghosts* (2001). Silver and Zemeckis are vocal about the impact of Castle on their careers, suggesting that we may understand Castle as a halfway house between the cinema of attractions and its funhouse roots and the effects hegemony of modern Hollywood. Joel Silver stresses continuity between Castle's film and the 1999 *House on Haunted Hill* with a gimmick of his own—"We're doing a big promotion over the weekend when the movie opens... [Castle] would park ambulances in front of the theatre and sell death insurance. We're going to give out a million dollars, which is essentially what the characters get a chance to do in the movie."[52] This symmetry between diegesis and gimmick echoes that in Castle's works, blurring the audience of the film with the partygoers of the narrative. Another sometime Spielberg collaborator, Joe Dante, paid Castle and the gimmick film fond tribute with *Matinee* (1993). Castle's influence was felt in exploitation filmmaking as well, and John Waters had written articulately about his love for Castle in *American Film* and in a foreword to the reissue of Castle's autobiography. "William Castle was my idol. His films made me want to make films," writes the inventor of Odorama. "In fact, I wish I *were* William Castle."[53] One expects the ritual cinema of *The Rocky Horror Picture Show* (1975) owes something to *The Tingler* as well.[54]

2009 saw a release of a box set of seven Castle films by Sony Pictures, also including the documentary *Spine Tingler! The William Castle Story* (2007), directed by Jeffrey Schwarz, which had previously had a successful festival run. Perhaps as significantly, La Cinémathèque Française in Paris (the French long being Castle's biggest supporters) ran a Castle retrospective from June 19 to August 2, 2009. This new attention to Castle's films seems appropriate for the age of *Avatar* (2009), in which gimmickry, spectacle and even the long-neglected 3-D achieve respectability and acclaim undreamed of by "the Master of Gimmicks." Castle, his name attached to *The Lady from Shanghai* and *Rosemary's Baby* as well as unapologetic B-movie fare, stands as an exemplar of the thin line between high and low, and as the history of Hollywood marches on, his stature only seems to grow.

NOTES

1. Tom Gunning, "An Aesthetic of Astonishment: Early Film and the (In)Credulous Spectator," *Art & Text* 34 (Spring 1989): 31–45.
2. For treatments of this issue, see Stephen Bottomore, "The Panicking Audience?: Early Cinema and the Train Effect," *Historical Journal of Film, Television and Radio* 10.2 (1999): 177–216; Martin Loiperdinger, "Lumière's *Arrival of a Train*: Cinema's Founding Myth," *The Moving Image* 4.1 (Spring 2004): 89–118; Thomas Elsaesser, "Archaeologies of Interactivity: Early Cinema, Narrative and Spectatorship," in Annemone Ligensa and Klaus Kreimeier (eds.), *Film 1900: Technology, Perception, Culture* (New Barnet: John Libbey Publishing, 2009), pp. 9–22.
3. Not all moviegoers were able to experience the gimmick. The cost belonged to the theatre, which was free to do it as well or as poorly as budget permitted, with some ignoring the gimmick altogether. *The Tingler* must have played *very* strangely to those in a Percepto-free theatre. In recognition of this problem, *13 Ghosts* played in two versions, one with Illusion-O (and a tongue-in-cheek first-person prologue by Castle) and one without.
4. Mikita Brottman, "Ritual, Tension and Relief: The Terror of 'The Tingler'," *Film Quarterly* 50.4 (Summer 1997): 2–10.

5. William Castle, *Step Right Up! I'm Gonna Scare the Pants Off America* (New York: G. P. Putnam's Sons, 1976), p. 134.
6. Tom Gunning, "The Cinema of Attractions: Early Film, Its Spectator and the Avant-Garde," in Thomas Elsaesser and Adam Barker (eds.), *Early Cinema: Space, Frame, Narrative* (London: British Film Institute, 1990), p. 57. For an excellent source on the affinities of the cinema of attractions and the horror film, see Adam Lowenstein, "Living Dead: Fearful Attractions of Film," *Representations* 110 (Spring 2010): 105–128.
7. Linda Williams, "Discipline and Fun: *Psycho* and Postmodern Cinema," in Christine Greenhill and Linda Williams (eds), *Reinventing Film Studies* (London: Arnold, 2000), p. 356.
8. Castle's autobiography also finds him replicating the silent film practice of playing music on set to get the cast and crew in the proper mood (*Step Right Up!*, p. 180).
9. David J. Skal, *The Monster Show*, revised edition (New York: Faber and Faber, 2001), p. 259.
10. John Belton, *Widescreen Cinema* (Cambridge, MA: Harvard University Press, 1992). See also Tim Recuber, "Immersion Cinema: The Rationalization and Reenchantment of Cinematic Space," *Space and Culture* 10 (2007): 315–30; Kimberly A. Neuendorf and Evan A. Lieberman, "Film: The Original Immersive Medium," in Cheryl Campanella Bracken and Paul D. Skalski (eds.), *Immersed in Media: Telepresence in Everyday Life* (New York: Routledge, 2010), pp. 9–38.
11. James L. Limbacher, *Four Aspects of the Film* (New York: Brussel & Brussel, 1968), p. 157.
12. Kevin Heffernan, *Ghouls, Gimmicks, and Gold: Horror Films and the American Movie Business, 1953–1968* (Durham, NC: Duke University Press, 2004), p. 18.
13. Surely the boldest of all taglines, linking the miracle of Christ's resurrection with the miracle of widescreen cinema.
14. Gimmick films of Castle's variety (contrasted with 3-D, which appeared in westerns, science fiction, and action-adventure movies; even pornography!) are mainly horror and related genres, at least until we find them merging with disaster and action films in the 1970s. Why horror? Pamela Thurschwell suggests that "early cinematic ghosts were created in part because the technology available motivated their production" (Pamela Thurschwell, "Refusing to Give Up the Ghost: Some Thoughts on the Afterlife from Spiritual Photography to Phantom Films," *The Disembodied Spirit* [Brunswick, ME: The Bowdoin College Museum of Art, 2003], p. 26); ghostly subject matter served as an appropriate context for trick shots and double exposures. Even ignoring the possibility of a direct continuity from the trick film to the gimmick film, I would suggest that, similarly, the generic character of horror lent itself readily to the trick film because of horror's central emphasis on spectatorship; Carol J. Clover has suggested that it is the most self-reflexive of genres because it so frequently thematizes looking (*Men, Women and Chain Saws: Gender in the Modern Horror Film* [Princeton: Princeton University Press, 1992], p. 168).
15. Ray Zone, *Stereoscopic Cinema & the Origins of 3-D Film, 1838–1952* (Lexington: University Press of Kentucky, 2007).
16. Qtd. in Heffernan, *Ghouls*, p. 24.
17. Harry Medved and Michael Medved, *The Golden Turkey Awards: Nominees and Winners—The Worst Achievements in Hollywood History* (New York: Perigee Books, 1980).
18. See Limbacher, *Four Aspects of the Film*, pp. 245–51 for an account of the fascinating rivalry between Smell-O-Vision and the competing process, AromaRama.
19. Castle, *Step Right Up!*, p. 155. This is not to say that Castle did not borrow egregiously from Hitchcock, especially in *Homicidal* (1961), but John Waters is bold enough to declare

"it was Hitchcock who ripped off Castle first, not vice versa" (Waters, "Whatever Happened to Showmanship?", *American Film* (December 1983): 57). It is pleasant to think of a reciprocal relationship between the Master of Suspense and the Master of Gimmicks. Though Hitchcock had often appeared briefly in his trailers since the 1940s, he did not begin making his trademark first-person trailers until after Castle had made similar ones. Hitchcock reacted with bemusement when James Brown asked him a question about his film *Homicidal* on *The Mike Douglas Show* in 1969.

20. "Columbia's *The Tingler*—You—And Your Audience—Play Important Roles in Percepto," *Motion Picture Herald*, September 19, 1959, p. 26, p. 25.
21. Waters, "Whatever Happened?", p. 56.
22. Wanting to make a 3-D version of Jules Verne's *From the Earth to the Moon*, he says he suggested the typically Castle-esque name SEE-A-VISION for the process (Castle, *Step Right Up!*, p. 121). 3-D would later inspire his slightly different optical trickery in *13 Ghosts* (1960).
23. Limbacher, *Four Aspects of the Film*, p. 161.
24. Heffernan, *Ghouls*, p. 31.
25. Ibid. p. 26.
26. Gunning, "The Cinema of Attractions," p. 56.
27. Tom Gunning, *D. W. Griffith and the Origins of American Narrative Film: The Early Years at Biograph* (Urbana: University of Illinois Press, 1991), p. 190.
28. Karen Beckman, *Vanishing Women: Magic, Film and Feminism* (Durham, NC: Duke University Press, 2003), p. 131.
29. Castle was not a paragon of honesty, and his autobiography should not be considered anything like an unbiased source. Rather, *Step Right Up!* is fascinating as Castle paints himself as a benign trickster, bluffing his way into success again and again.
30. In the trailer for *House on Haunted Hill*, the very same floating head introduces itself as Vincent Price and invites the viewer to "my party in the House on Haunted Hill."
31. Waters, "Whatever Happened?", p. 56.
32. Brottman, "Ritual, Tension and Relief," p. 4.
33. Tom Ruffles, *Ghost Images: The Cinema of the Afterlife* (Jefferson, NC: McFarland, 2004), pp. 12–14.
34. Erik Barnouw, *The Magician and the Cinema* (New York: Oxford University Press, 1981), p. 19. See also Mervyn Heard, *Phantasmagoria: The Secret Life of the Magic Lantern* (Hastings: The Projection Box, 2006), pp. 263–4.
35. For more on skeletons in Méliès, see Yuri Tsivian, "Media Fantasies and Penetrating Vision: Some Links Between X-Rays, the Microscope, and Film," in John E. Bowlt and Olga Matich (eds.), *Laboratory of Dreams: The Russian Avant-Garde and Cultural Experiment* (Stanford: Stanford University Press, 1996), pp. 81–99). Skeletons are also commonplace in the works of other trick filmmakers like George Albert Smith, Edwin R. Booth, and Émile Cohl, and even the Lumière brothers made an experimental stop-motion short called *Le sequelette joyeux* (1897). I explore the topic of skeletons in early cinema in more detail in Murray Leeder, *The Modern Supernatural and the Beginnings of Cinema* (Houndmills: Palgrave Macmillan, 2016), esp. pp. 135–72.
36. A 1960 article describes Castle as an "amateur magician" (John Kobler, "Master of Movie Horror," *The Saturday Evening Post*, March 19, 1960, p. 31).
37. The target of such "gaslighting" is usually a woman, but not in *Macabre*. For the high visibility of this theme in film noir, see Marlisa Santos, *The Dark Mirror: Psychiatry and Film Noir* (Lanham, MD: Lexington, 2010), pp. 139–64.
38. Heffernan, *Ghouls*, p. 102.

39. Castle remarked, "People won't be eating lobster for the next five years" (Castle, *Step Right Up!*, p. 150). No word on whether this attempt to create a new mass phobia took root.
40. Heffernan, *Ghouls*, p. 98.
41. The practice of using women as plants that scream or faint during horror films goes back to at least the 1930s. See Rhoda Berenstein, "'It Will Thrill You, It May Shock You, It Might Even Horrify You': Gender, Reception and Classic Horror Cinema," in Barry Keith Grant (ed.), *The Dread of Difference: Gender and the Horror Film* (Austin: University of Texas Press, 1996), pp. 117–42.
42. Heffernan, *Ghouls*, p. 103.
43. As Kim Newman notes, the reflexive scenario of the monster attacking a movie theatre is anticipated by *The Blob* (1958) and echoed in *Targets* (1968); see "Panic in the Cinema," in Leonard J. Schmitt and Brooke Warner (eds.), *Panic: Origins, Insight, and Treatment* (Berkeley: North Atlantic Books, 2002), pp. 221–8). Beth A. Kattelman notes that the idea behind Percepto may be borrowed from the midnight ghost or "spook" shows that were in decline around the time Castle made his gimmick films; see Kattelman, "Magic, Monsters, Movies: America's Midnight Ghost Shows," *Theatre Journal* 62.1 (2010): 28. Held in movie theatres and piggybacking on the success of horror movies, ghost shows mixed magic, stage spiritualism, spooky music and sound effects, and often built to a "blackout" akin to what we see in *The Tingler*. Doubtless, the carnivalesque atmosphere of the theatres where the gimmick films were shown owed more than a little to the ghost show.
44. Denis Meikle, *Vincent Price: The Art of Fear* (Richmond: Reynolds & Hearn, 2003), p. 59.
45. Barry Salt, "Film Form, 1900–1906," in Thomas Elsaesser (ed.), *Early Cinema: Space, Frame, Narrative* (London: British Film Institute, 1990), p. 40.
46. Castle, *Step Right Up!*, p. 174.
47. Even here Castle could not break from his showman roots, as he told *Variety*: "Instead of a tingler under the seat, a skeleton coming from the screen, or issuing a 'fright insurance' policy on viewers' lives, now I'm getting publicity by bringing over Vidal Sassoon to cut Mia Farrow's hair" (qtd. in Heffernan, *Ghouls*, p. 190).
48. Castle, *Step Right Up!*, p. 247.
49. Mark B. N. Hansen, *New Philosophy for New Media* (Cambridge, MA: MIT Press, 1994), p. 170.
50. Angela Ndalianis, "1990s Cinema of Attractions," in Vivian Sobchack (ed.), *Meta Morphing: Visual Transformation and the Culture of Quick-Change* (Minneapolis: University of Minnesota Press, 2000), p. 267.
51. Gunning, "The Cinema of Attractions," p. 61. This line led to decades' worth of scholarship applying the attractions model outside of early cinema, a trend that has reached its full flowering in the Wanda Strauven-edited collection *The Cinema of Attractions Reloaded* (Amsterdam: University of Amsterdam Press, 2006). Some scholars have expressed misgivings about the movement from using the phrase "cinema of attractions" to describe a historically specific mode of film style, to a more generic and transhistorical meaning; see Vivian Sobchack, *Carnal Thoughts: Embodiment and Moving Image Culture* (Berkeley: University of California Press, 2004), p. 57. See also Andrew Nelson, "Cinema from Attractions: Story and Synergy in Disney's Theme Park Movies," *Cinephile: The University of British Columbia's Film Journal* 4 (2008): 36–40.
52. Patrick Lee, "Joel Silver, king of the action movie, turns to horror," *Science Fiction Weekly* 132.2, <http://www.scifi.com/sfw/issue132/interview.html> (accessed March 25, 2009).
53. Waters, "Whatever Happened?", p. 56.

54. For more on Castle's legacy, see Ben Kooyman, "How the Masters of Horror Master Their Personae: Self-Fashioning at Play in the *Masters of Horror* DVD Extras," in Steffen Hantke (ed.), *American Horror Film: The Genre at the Turn of the Millennium* (Jackson: University Press of Mississippi, 2010), p. 198.

CHAPTER 5

Ghost Show Ballyhoo: Castle's *Macabre* Will Scare You to Death

Beth Kattelman

This chapter takes a look at William Castle's *Macabre* (1958), a film that is best known for a marketing campaign in which Lloyd's of London insured audience members against "death by fright" for the duration of their watching the film. It explores Castle's borrowing of ballyhoo techniques from the magicians who presented midnight spook shows and ghost shows throughout the early part of the twentieth century, and how his death-by-fright gimmick heightened audience apprehension by directly connecting the diegetic space with the audience space both synchronously and asynchronously. The paper also takes a brief look at the scientific evidence surrounding the phenomenon of psychogenic death, positing that the effectiveness of Castle's gimmick was bolstered by the fact that death by fright is a real phenomenon.

[Close-up of wall clock, accompanied by a voiceover] Ladies and Gentlemen. For the next hour and fifteen minutes you will be shown things so terrifying that the management of this theatre is deeply concerned for your welfare. Therefore, we request that each of you assume the responsibility of taking care of your neighbor. If anyone near you becomes uncontrollably frightened, will you please notify the management so that medical attention can be rushed to their aid. Please set your watches. It is 6:45 in the evening in a town called Thornton.

Thus begins *Macabre*, the first film from director William Castle and his newly formed production company Susina Associates. *Macabre*, released in 1958, is a black-and-white thriller that deals with the search for Doctor Rodney Barrett's (William Prince) three-year-old daughter, who has been kidnapped and is reportedly buried alive in a coffin. As the sinister voice on the telephone reports, the doctor has only a brief time in which to find her before the air runs out. The screenplay was by Robb White. William Castle both produced and directed. Even though *Macabre* is a rather low-quality film that contains a convoluted plot and uneven acting, it has not faded into oblivion like many other 'B' horror films of this era due to the famous promotional gimmick that Castle attached to it: each audience member who attended *Macabre* was insured for $1,000 against "death by fright" for the duration of their watching the film. With this ingenious bit of ballyhoo Castle turned a potential money-loser into an event sensation. *Macabre* made a three-million-dollar return on William Castle's original $90,000 investment in the film.[1]

The hucksterism employed by Castle on *Macabre* set him off on a career that would eventually lead to his becoming known as the master of the "gimmick film," a term that Murray Leeder appropriately defines as "a series of mainly horror and suspense films, beginning in the late 1950s, that introduced innovative tricks to attract audiences by addressing them more directly than Hollywood cinema is accustomed to doing."[2] And Castle certainly did find effective ways to directly address the audience. Throughout his career, he developed many now-infamous gimmicks designed to heighten the fun and to draw audiences into movie theatres at a time when movie attendance was experiencing increasing competition from television and other leisure-time activities. From offering insurance policies, to providing ghost viewers, to wiring seats with buzzers, Castle engaged audience members with techniques that made them feel (sometimes literally feel!) a part of the action. Castle recaptured the excitement that had been associated with attendance at carnivals and spook shows of bygone days, and by so doing, was able to capitalize on some second-rate films that would most likely have faded into obscurity had it not been for his crafty marketing ideas.

A VERY BRIEF BIO

William Castle was born William Schloss, Jr. in New York City in 1914. At the age of thirteen he went to see a production of the play *Dracula*, starring Béla Lugosi, and later described becoming enamored of scary entertainments, "I knew then what I wanted to do with my life—I wanted to scare the pants off audiences."[3] In his teen years, Castle dropped out of high school and worked in various positions in the legitimate theatre both on touring shows and on Broadway. At age twenty-three he relocated to California upon being hired by Harry Cohn of Columbia Pictures. Thus began Castle's career in the movie business. He learned all aspects of movie-making from Cohn and soon began directing low-budget B-pictures. He gained a positive reputation for his thrifty ability to complete projects quickly, a skill that was to come in very handy once Castle began producing and directing his own films.

In 1955, when Castle was already working on several films and producing a television series, he went to see the new French thriller *Les Diaboliques*, directed by Henri-Georges Clouzot. The film was getting rave reviews and people were lining up around the block to see it. Castle himself loved the film, and the hubbub that surrounded the thriller revived his desire to make scary entertainments: "I remembered how Karloff and Lorre used to pack the houses and I realized we hadn't had a good suspense film in nearly a decade. I sold out of the TV series, mortgaged my house, cleaned out my bank account, put everything I had—about $90,000—into making a movie . . ."[4] Ultimately Castle's attendance at *Les Diaboliques* led to the creation of his production company, Susina Associates, and its first film, *Macabre*.

SYNOPSIS

Robb White's screenplay for *Macabre* was based on the novel *The Marble Forest*, credited to author Theo Durrant. This is actually a pseudonym, however, for a group of twelve different authors who each contributed to the story. The name Theo Durrant was taken from a criminal who had been executed more than a century earlier for the murders of six women. It was chosen because one of the contributing writers had written a book about Durrant a few years prior to the *Marble Forest* project.[5] The film is set in the small town of Thornton. The opening scene shows Ed Quigley (Jonathan Kidd), the town undertaker, animatedly talking to police chief Jim Tyloe (Jim Backus) in front of the funeral parlor. He is explaining that a child's coffin has been stolen from the funeral home window, and he implores Jim to find the culprit quickly since he cannot afford the financial loss. It seems that Ed owes some deep gambling debts to many of the townspeople. Jim then sees the town doctor, Rodney Barrett (William Prince), pulling up outside his office and goes over to talk to him. It is immediately apparent that Jim is hostile toward Rod, and we soon learn that this stems from the fact that Jim was deeply in love with Alice, Rod's wife, and still blames the doctor for taking her away from him. The next scene takes place in the doctor's office, where we meet Polly, Rod's nurse (Jacqueline Scott). From her primping and flirtatious interactions with Rod, it is clear that she is in love with him. She tries to convince Rod to leave town and to take her with him, since the locals are now shunning him because they blame him for the recent death of Nancy Wetherby. By the end of these opening scenes we have learned most of the necessary exposition: Jode Wetherby (Philip Tonge), the richest man in town, had two daughters, Nancy (Christine White) and Alice (Dorothy Morris), who both died very suddenly. At the time of Alice's death three years ago, her husband Rod was not by her side, but was drunk and spending time with his girlfriend, Sylvia Stevenson, a mistake for which most of the locals have never forgiven him. Jode's other daughter, Nancy, has died suddenly just two days prior to the beginning of the film from circumstances that still remain unclear to the audience. Nancy's funeral is forthcoming and, for some unknown reason, Wetherby has scheduled his daughter's funeral to take place at midnight.

In the next scene, Rod and Polly go over to the doctor's house to take his three-year-old daughter, Marge, out for dinner. Rod's housekeeper, Miss Kushins (Ellen Corby), indicates that Marge is playing in her room, but no one is able to find her anywhere in the house. Rod leaves to see if Marge has gone over to Sylvia's, but while he is gone, Polly takes a phone call in which a sinister voice notifies her that Marge has been buried alive in a coffin and that the air will run out in approximately four or five hours. "Tell the doc that Marge's funeral has just taken place and now she's with the dead." From here on, at various points throughout the film, the camera cuts back to the funeral parlor clock so that the audience can track how much time little Marge has left before she will suffocate. When Rod returns to the house, Polly tells him about the sinister phone call. Convinced that the entire town is against him, Rod will not let Polly or Miss Kushins tell anyone else about Marge's predicament, not even her grandfather, Jode Wetherby: "Miss Kushins, you know his heart condition. Do you want to *kill* Mr. Wetherby? . . . Then I advise you not to tell him what has happened to Marge." Rod states that he and Polly will have to find Marge themselves, so they grab some shovels and head out to the graveyard. As soon as they leave the house, however, Miss Kushins runs over to Jode Wetherby's house and tells him what has happened.

When Rod and Polly arrive at the cemetery, they rush directly to Nancy's open grave because they believe that Marge might be buried at the bottom of it. Of course, they both immediately climb in and begin digging furiously. Then they hear someone walking up near the edge of the grave and see a rifle pointing down at them, "Who is that? What are you doing down there?" It turns out to be Hummel, the cemetery caretaker. Before he can do anything else, though, Hummel is hit over the head by an unseen assailant. Polly and Rod climb out of the grave and, as the doc checks Hummel, Polly is grabbed by a hand that slowly emerges from behind a tombstone—a typical horror film trope. The hand ends up belonging to Jode Wetherby, who has also rushed to the graveyard to try and find Marge. He explains that when he saw Hummel point the rifle down into the grave he thought Marge might be down there, so he decided to club Hummel with his cane. It turns out that Hummel has died from the blow. Still, Rod is convinced that no one else must know about Marge's predicament, so he decides that they must cover up Hummel's death. He sends Polly and Jode home while he conceals Hummel's body.

The graveyard scene among Jode, Polly and Rod is interrupted with a series of flashbacks that reveal Nancy Wetherby's story. Through them we discover that she was totally blind and was also quite self-destructive. We first see her speeding down the road in a sports car, flooring the pedal while her chauffeur, who is sitting right next to her, does his best to steer. The car is pulled over by Jim Tyloe. Nancy proceeds to flirt with Jim and ends up getting into his police car. The two then go to an out-of-the-way grain storage shed, where they have a tryst. Next we see Nancy in Rod's doctor's office, where he gives her the news that she is pregnant. She alludes to the fact that she wants him to perform an abortion, but he refuses. Then the film cuts to a scene of Rod answering the phone, getting the news that Nancy has been in a terrible car accident that ultimately turns out to be the cause of her death. As he rushes to the hospital the flashback ends. Later in the film we are also introduced to Rod's wife, Alice, through a flashback sequence. Here we see a very cold and unfeeling side of Rod as he complains to his mistress, Sylvia, about having to put up with his sick wife and her difficult pregnancy. This flashback also confirms that Rod was at Sylvia's house when Alice died in agony during childbirth (melodramatically calling out for him, of course)! This is the reason that the townspeople have held a grudge against him ever since. The rest of the film consists primarily of Polly, Rod and Jode running around town trying to find Marge: digging in the graveyard, looking in a large family tomb and inspecting coffins at the funeral home. Jim Tyloe also mysteriously shows up at several of these places to confront them.

The penultimate scene of the film takes place in the graveyard at Nancy's midnight (!) funeral. It has all the atmospheric trappings of a typical Gothic horror scene: swirling mist, a torrential rainstorm, thunder and lightning. After a brief eulogy, Jim, Rod, and Ed begin filling in the grave, when Rod's shovel hits a small child's coffin that has been concealed under the mound of loose dirt. Rod opens the coffin and looks horrified at what he sees there, which causes Jode to go over to also inspect the contents. The camera then reveals a gruesome, partially-decomposed small figure inside the coffin. Jode immediately has a heart attack and falls dead into Nancy's open grave. We then hear gunshots and see that Rod has been hit. The shots come from a pistol wielded by Ed Quigley. Ed yells, "He's crazy! I didn't do it! . . . Look in his pockets!" and pulls out a wad of bills and throws them in Rod's face. He then rushes to the small coffin and holds up the figure, showing that it is only a doll dressed in Marge's clothes. Ed then goes on to reveal the entire scheme. Rod had blackmailed him by promising to give him the money to pay off all of his gambling debts, as long as he would take a child's coffin from his funeral home, make a fake child's body to place in it and plant it at Nancy's midnight funeral. It turns out that Rod concocted the scheme in order to kill Jode Wetherby, whose heart he knew would surely give out from the stress engendered by Marge's abduction and by seeing what he believes to be his granddaughter's dead body at his daughter's midnight funeral. So it turns out that all along Rod intended to kill Jode Wetherby by frightening him to death. As Joe Quigley notes, "Doc never let up on the old man. Killing him with one shock after another."

Even though Rod has been shot in the gut, he insists that the police chief take him and Polly to his doctor's office instead of to the hospital. There, he reveals to Polly that he concocted the entire scheme to get Joe's money. With both daughters out of the way, Rod was next in line for the inheritance. At the doctor's office, Rod plays a tape that he used to create the phone call announcing Marge's abduction. Then he collapses dead on the office floor from his gunshot wounds. Polly rushes into the next room and discovers Marge sleeping on the examination table, safe and sound. The film ends with a shot of the clock, which reads 12:15, and another voiceover, "Ladies and gentlemen, please do not—I repeat—please, do not reveal the ending of this picture to your friends, as it will spoil their enjoyment of it." Finally, it is time for the credits to roll; and they also deserve mention, because the performers' names are superimposed over a whimsical animation that depicts a funeral procession led by caricatures of William Castle and Robb White. For each actor who played a character that died in the film, a cartoon horse and carriage drawing a coffin rolls by as the performer's name appears. Those actors who played characters that survived are depicted in caricature, walking in the funeral procession. It is a delightful bit of animation accompanied by bouncy upbeat music, thus signaling to the audience that the foregoing experience has been all in fun. After the credits, one final voiceover provides a humorous punctuation for the film: "We trust that there have been no casualties, and that you are all in the best of health."

GOTTA HAVE A GIMMICK

Castle completed the filming of *Macabre* in nine days. Although he was hoping for an effective thriller along the lines of *Les Diaboliques*, he quickly realized that there was little chance that this film would garner such a response. It did not have the artistry and dread-inducing style of *Les Diaboliques* and Castle knew it, so he decided that he would need to give it some help if he was going to recoup his investment: "When I'd finished I looked at it and recognized that a Clouzot I ain't. I had to have a gimmick to sell that movie."[6] Thus, through necessity, Castle came up with his first major marketing ploy, the "death-by-fright" insurance policy. Considering that *Les Diaboliques* was the inspiration for *Macabre*, it is not entirely surprising that the "death-by-fright" gimmick was the one Castle settled upon to try and sell his film. *Les Diaboliques*' plot centers upon a man and his mistress who kill the man's wife by scaring her to death. The pivotal scene is one in which the wife encounters her husband's supposed dead body rising from the bathtub, thus creating a moment so shocking that it forces her into fatal cardiac arrest. *Macabre*'s plot is based upon the same concept, wherein one character attempts to kill another by frightening him to death; but Castle took this idea one step further and expanded it beyond the screen. By warning the audience even before they set foot in the theatre of the possible physiological dangers that might befall them, Castle was able to mirror the action taking place on screen within the larger world of the audience.

Castle surmised that in order to really make his death-by-fright stunt work, he needed to engage the services of the largest, most recognizable insurance company in the world, so he traveled to the UK to negotiate a policy with Lloyd's of London: "They computed a table on the number of people who might drop dead during a viewing of *Macabre* and arrived at a figure of eight in the United States in a single year."[7] In order to hedge their bets, Lloyd's also included some coverage exclusions. The policy would not pay for any audience member who died by suicide, or for any usher or member of the theatre staff who keeled over in the performance of their duties; and most importantly, it was not valid for anyone with a known heart or nervous condition.[8] But even these exclusions did not dilute the impact of the buzz generated by the death-by-fright insurance policy. With this brilliant marketing move, Castle turned a second-rate picture into a first-rate success. It made such an impression that decades later, Stephen King still remembered the excitement *Macabre* generated, and acknowledged that it was the biggest "gotta-see" film of his grammar school days, even though many of his buddies had the title slightly wrong: "Its title was pronounced by my friends in Stratford, Connecticut as *McBare*."[9]

GHOST SHOW BALLYHOO

The main draw of *Macabre*, of course, was not the film itself, but everything else surrounding it. The whimsical, tongue-in-cheek tone created by the death-by-fright insurance policy and the opening voiceover in which audience members are prompted to "assume the responsibility of taking care of your neighbor" help to set a mood akin to a carnival funhouse. Audience members knew that they should just sit back and "go along for the ride." This was not a film to analyze or dissect.

In creating the movie-going experience of *Macabre*, the ballyhoo was most important: a fact that is also borne out by the press book for the film. In addition to the death-by-fright insurance policy, it suggests several other ideas that can be used to extend and enhance the buzz. It proclaims "PULL OUT ALL THE STOPS ON THIS ONE!: You Can't Over Sell It!" In addition to the traditional advertising cuts and prefab articles that are usually found in movie press books, it contains an entire page of ideas that exhibitors can use to hype the film. They include:

> For a most unusual lobby shocker . . . obtain the use of a department store manikin, male or female, and a real coffin! Place the "body" in the coffin and illuminate the display with an eerie green spotlight. To add to its effectiveness, buy or borrow a horror type mask (not a caricature), but a mask with hideous features . . . and place it over the manikin's face.
>
> Have [an] ambulance parked at the curb in front of your theatre.
>
> Have [a] uniformed "nurse" in attendance with a medicine cabinet containing a supply of "stimulants." Have her distribute envelopes containing ordinary candy drops which look like nerve-steadying pills.
>
> Plant "Screamers" [in the audience] on opening [night] shows.
>
> Offer a cash prize of $5.00 to any woman who will watch the picture at a midnite [sic] preview showing all by herself in a completely darkened theatre.
>
> Offer a pair of tickets to all young ladies who will walk through a cemetery after midnight ALONE! . . . Plan in advance to give your newspaper the opportunity to cover the stunt and get pictures and stories that should stress the fact that graveyards hold no terror for the modern teenager.
>
> Have your sign artist make up a sign with the following copy: *ATTENTION DOCTORS! Please let a theatre attendant know where you are seated. You may be needed during the showing of MACABRE.* Spot [the] sign near your box office for passersby to see. A special trailer clip with the same copy can be run immediately preceding picture title.[10]

With this list Castle demonstrates that his showmanship has a direct lineage to the techniques used by the magicians who presented midnight ghost shows throughout the first half of the twentieth century. These shows (also known as midnight spook shows, midnight horror shows, or spookers) were touring "twofer" performances that combined a live magic show with a film. They were performed at midnight and were accompanied by a great deal of gimmickry and hyperbolic advertising. When the midnight ghost shows began around 1929, they were primarily linked with the Spiritualism craze, offering a mock séance setting in which magicians would "conjure up" spooky ghosts and spirits. As the films featuring Universal Monsters such as Dracula, Frankenstein, the Mummy, and the Wolf Man became popular, the ghost shows morphed into horror shows featuring monsters and mad scientists. The effects in these horror shows were more gruesome than those in the earlier productions, often including illusions of violence and (sometimes) gore, such as sawings, decapitations, and immolations. The one thing the ghost shows and horror shows all had in common, however, was the inclusion of a blackout sequence in which the theatre would go completely dark and luminous ghosts, ghouls, and monsters would "fly" throughout the theatre. After this blackout sequence, the stage show would conclude and the film would begin.[11] Castle appreciated the tricks which these "ghostmasters" used to fill their theatres, a fact that he makes direct reference to in *Macabre*'s press book when he suggests that exhibitors open the film's engagement with a midnight performance and "sell it along the lines you would sell a Midnite Spook show."[12]

The stunts listed in the *Macabre* press book were indeed used to promote ghost shows, but they date back even further than that. Although some entertainment historians have speculated upon the first time that these types of gimmicks arose, it is impossible to directly pinpoint their origin since they have been in circulation throughout the entire history of popular entertainments—particularly magic and horror entertainments. In the early days of the "sawing a woman in half" illusion (circa 1921), for example, magician Horace Goldin would post a sign in front of the theatre reading "Don't Park Here—Reserved for Ambulance in Case Saw Slips,"[13] and in an even more lurid instance of gruesome ballyhoo, Goldin's rival Percy Selbit, who was also presenting a "sawing a woman" illusion, had the stagehands pour buckets of blood into the gutter in front of the theatre each night.[14] Thus, in offering a death-by-fright insurance policy, and by suggesting other possible stunts that exhibitors could use to promote his film, William Castle was following in the footsteps of a long line of showmen who were pragmatists as well as entertainers. These guys knew how to draw in audiences. They realized that ballyhoo and excitement helped to fill the seats more than any published critic's opinion ever did. And a full house was what helped to pay the bills.

PLOT, PERFORMANCE, AND ATMOSPHERE

In analyzing *Macabre* strictly in terms of its quality and efficacy as a horror film one must note that it suffers from many problems, including a weakly constructed plot, stilted dialogue, and overly melodramatic acting. At the time of its initial release, critical responses to the film were generally negative, such as this one by John Knobler of the *Saturday Evening Post*: "*Macabre* plods along from its opening scene in a funeral parlor to its denouement in a graveyard unimpeded by the faintest intrusion of good taste, literacy or sense."[15] And it is true that the plot is hard to follow, even upon repeated viewings. As one of the commenters on Amazon.com notes, *Macabre* contains a "what the hell just happened" plot.[16] Also, most of the characters are superficial and one-dimensional so the audience never gets a chance to really care about their plight; and the two Wetherby sisters are particularly undifferentiated. The fact that both Alice and Nancy died suddenly, are both introduced through flashbacks, were both love interests of Jim Tyloe, and that the town blames Rodney Barrett for both of their deaths, makes these characters' storylines confusingly tangled; the film never fully justifies the need for having two daughters whose profiles are so similar. Also, the narrative tries to set up too many characters as red herrings. By the end of the 73-minute film, almost every main character except Rod has been blamed for Marge's abduction, including Jim Tyloe, Miss Kushins, Ed Quigley, and even Polly. Most of the accusations against these characters do not seem credible, however, since they come directly from Rod, who is in a state of panic throughout the film. His suspicions are never fleshed out and are not supported by much in the diegetic world, so his numerous accusations only serve to muddy the narrative.

Another weakness in *Macabre*'s screenplay is the nonsensical and illogical actions of the characters. Many of the scenes are extremely contrived, and the characters do things that are so strange they make for some truly absurd moments. For example, Jim and Rod let Polly enter the Tyloe family tomb alone, even though up to this point Rod and Polly have been scouring the graveyard side by side, and in spite of the fact that the tomb is that of Jim Tyloe's family. Instead of accompanying her, they send her in unescorted; they remain outside, and do not rush in until they hear the bloodcurdling scream that is prompted by her encounter with Hummel's dead body. This is just one of numerous times that Jim Tyloe's actions, in particular, are totally absurd. One would think that, since he is the chief of police and since the tomb belongs to his family, he would be the one to lead the way, but instead, he remains outside until he hears Polly scream. As a matter of fact, Jim is one of the most poorly written characters in the screenplay. Throughout the entire film he continually does things that make absolutely no sense. It is a testament to Jim Backus's acting ability that he is actually able to enact this character and still retain some credibility in the performance. A lesser actor would have been unwatchable in the role. The scene in the graveyard in which Hummel is killed is another that is an unmotivated mess and raises numerous unanswerable questions. Why do Rod and Polly immediately assume that Marge has been buried at the bottom of a grave? Once Hummel has been clubbed to death, why do Rod and Polly charge out of the grave without fearing for their own lives since they do not know the identity or exact whereabouts of the club-wielding assailant? After clubbing Hummel, why does Jode retreat to behind the tombstone and then silently grab Polly without uttering a sound? Why do Jode and Polly so quickly go along with Rod's plan to cover up the murder and hide Hummel's body? If all these unanswered questions are prompted by just one scene in the film, one can imagine how many others are raised throughout the entire running time. Although the inclusion of some of these unmotivated moments might be excused by acknowledging that they reflect standard 1950s horror-film tropes, the sheer number of them foregrounds the haphazard narrative and questionable rationale of the characters.

The film is also rife with instances of overacting. While an exaggerated, melodramatic style of acting was a feature of many horror films of this period, there is no doubt that some actors were able to embody the style better than others. Jacqueline Scott, who plays the role of Polly, for example, comes off as rather "schlocky" with her melodramatic, over-the-top performance. This is perhaps not entirely her fault, given the fact that *Macabre* was her first film; prior to this she had only done a few bit parts for television. The majority of her acting experience was on the stage, and it is often true that performers who have spent most of their time on the legitimate stage are too demonstrative when seen through the lens of the movie camera. Film often requires a subtler performance because the exaggerated facial expressions needed to convey emotions to the spatially distant audience of the live theatre often do not read well when brought into the close-up view of the camera. In fact, Jacqueline Scott herself was quite surprised to learn that William Castle was considering her for the movie:

> Jacqueline Scott, who made her film debut in *Macabre*, recalled the day her agent phoned and informed her that Castle had seen her on live TV in New York and wanted her for his next movie. Scott's first reaction? Laughter! The actress was performing in summer stock in Ohio at the time, and the movies were the furthest thing from her mind; she just wanted to work on the stage.[17]

Likewise, William Prince, Philip Tonge, and Jonathan Kidd all have their moments of mugging for the camera. The performers who are best able to handle the heightened "horror style" without going overboard are Jim Backus (who has a real challenge here due to the fact that, as previously mentioned, his character has a huge number of bizarre, nonsensical moments to navigate), Christine White, and Ellen Corby (who would later become best known for playing Grandma Walton in the popular television series *The Waltons*).

Even though *Macabre* contains some questionable acting and a ridiculous plot, it does deliver a solid horror atmosphere thanks to some high-quality black-and-white cinematography by Carl E. Guthrie, which is supported by great chiaroscuro lighting reminiscent of the classic Universal horror films. Castle also makes effective use of fog to support the Gothic settings, and he does manage to create a few scenes that work very well in isolation, even though they do not make a lot of sense within the context of the narrative. One of these is when Polly stumbles upon Hummel's battered corpse. One would expect that the corpse would be lying on the floor, but this is not the case. Instead, it is propped up in the corner. This makes no logical sense, but it does facilitate the startling moment when Polly unexpectedly comes face-to-face with the figure and causes it to fall forward. Visually the scene is very effective, with the aforementioned chiaroscuro lighting, careful framing of Polly prior to her discovery, and a well-timed musical sting when the face of the corpse is revealed. Another effective moment occurs in the graveyard when the small gruesome figure in the coffin is shown, accompanied by a perfectly timed thunderclap and lightning flash. In fact, the sound effects and suspenseful music are another plus for the film. They effectively support the atmosphere and help to create some tension in scenes that otherwise would have none, a result that is often accomplished in horror films primarily through music and ambient sound effects.

CASTLE'S INTERACTIVE MARKETING

As the foregoing discussion demonstrates, as a film *Macabre* has its problems. However, one must remember that it deserves a place in film history not for its stellar plot, solid acting, or brilliant film-craft, but for allowing William Castle to show what an ingenious huckster he was: one who could turn a standard night at the movies into a much-anticipated event. His death-by-fright ruse elevated a run-of-the-mill B-film to a memorable one and marked a turning point in Castle's career, thus securing it a place in movie history. The success of *Macabre's* campaign led to a succession of gimmicks subsequently employed by Castle, each cleverly aligned with an element of its own film's narrative.

Macabre follows the model of the classical Hollywood style. Classical-style films employ a psychologically motivated narrative that revolves around a central enigma. They also contain a series of cause-and-effect events that reveal and resolve the enigma and eventually provide narrative closure. The classical film relays a sense of verisimilitude and is, therefore, the most comprehensible style for film-going audiences.[18] *Macabre* can be aligned with this style because its story is psychologically motivated, it revolves around an enigma, and it ends in narrative closure. Other than the opening and closing voiceovers that bookend the film, it follows a linear narrative. Also, the diegetic world is self-contained and there is no direct interactivity between the on-screen space and the audience space. The fourth wall remains intact. Or does it? By offering the insurance policy, Castle finds a way to penetrate the fourth wall without using traditional filmic techniques. Instead, he situates his address to the audience within the insurance policy. By having each audience member fill out the death-by-fright policy upon their arrival at the theatre, Castle is saying to the audience, "Now you have entered into an agreement to experience this film, and you are a part of this world of danger and death. Although the characters and settings are safely contained upon the screen, the events engendered by the film may not be. *Macabre* may be able reach right out from the screen and touch you by creating a deadly physical reaction in you or in one of your neighbors." This is how Castle interpolated audience members as active participants in a way that even the scariest horror films of the time did not. Even though *Macabre* did not employ gimmicks that directly broke the fourth wall—such as the flying skeleton of *House on Haunted Hill*, or the buzzing seats in *The Tingler*—it was an early example of a clever way in which Castle could add heightened emotional participation by psychologically and physiologically connecting audience members with the on-screen characters. As David Parkinson notes, Castle "delighted in blurring the line between the mise-en-scène and extra-frame space."[19]

Any horror film could have used the "death-by-fright" gimmick (and several later ones did), but the special thing about the way in which Castle employs it with *Macabre* is that the concept is central to both the diegetic world and the audience world. This ability to foreground the relationship between the spectators and the characters in a film was one of the unique qualities that made Castle so successful in the implementation of his marketing ideas. While other promoters only loosely connected their promotional gimmicks to the diegetic content, Castle embedded his. With the death-by-fright insurance policy he created a direct parallel between the film world and the real world, since—even though the audience does not know it for most of the film—the entire narrative is driven by Rod Barrett's desire to kill his father-in-law by scaring him to death. Wetherby is a surrogate for the audience, not just in a narrative sense, but in a physiological sense. As Barrett tries to scare Wetherby to death, he also tries to scare us. While it is standard that the scares in horror films are meant both for characters in the diegetic world and the audience in the theatre, by making the direct bodily parallel between Wetherby's heart and each audience member's heart, Castle animates interactivity that goes beyond the standard engagement an audience experiences when watching a film. As Catherine Clepper notes, Castle's death-by-fright gimmick "bridges the gap between the onscreen world and the off screen threat/risk."[20]

Castle also accentuated the effectiveness of the "death-by-fright" gimmick by repeatedly employing it in asynchronous time. In his wide-ranging advertising campaigns, Castle made sure to foreground the gimmick so that audience members attending the film would already be aware of the potential bodily harm it might cause. By warning the audience that the film might "scare you to death," Castle created an uneasiness that manifested prior to the direct encounter with the film. Even before the audience arrived at the theatre, they were already aware of how the film might affect them physically. The asynchronous fear that was engendered by the marketing campaign and the curiosity that the campaign fostered were instrumental in drawing audience members to an event for which their reactions had already been primed.

DEATH BY FRIGHT?

Castle's "death-by-fright" gimmick is particularly effective because there is some credibility to the idea that one can be scared to death. If the idea had been too outrageous audiences would not have responded; but most people believe that being frightened to death is within the realm of possibility, because they have heard anecdotes of those who have experienced a traumatic fright and then dropped dead on the spot. So even though they knew that it was highly improbable, some moviegoers went to *Macabre* on the outside chance that they would be there when a tragedy might occur. As filmmaker John Waters recalls, "Audiences fell hook, line, and sinker. Nobody talked about the movie, but everyone was eager to see if some jerk would drop dead and collect. Of course, no one died. But if they had, it would have been even better."[21]

So is there any actual evidence to suggest that one can die from being too scared? It turns out that death by fright (also known as "psychogenic death," "psychosomatic death," or "voodoo death") is actually a recognized occurrence that has been documented and researched by scientists. In 1942, for example, Walter B. Cannon published an article on a phenomenon that he called "voodoo death." In the article he examines reported cases of "primitive" people who died after being subjected to spells, sorcery, or "black magic." Cannon notes that, in these cases, death resulted from physiological changes brought about by a persistent and profound emotional state, and he concludes that "'voodoo death' may be real, and that it may be explained as due to shocking emotional stress—to obvious or repressed terror."[22] Another paper published in 2001 in the *British Medical Journal* reported the findings of a study that examined whether there is a link between stress and fatal heart attacks. The scientists analyzed statistics of death among Japanese- and Chinese-Americans on the fourth day of the month, since these populations consider four to be an unlucky number. The scientists found "a significant increase in Asian-American deaths on the fourth day of each month, especially among people with chronic heart disease, and consider these additional deaths due to stress." They named this phenomenon the "Hound of the Baskervilles effect" in reference to Sir Charles Baskerville, a character in the Arthur Conan Doyle story who dies from a stress-induced heart attack.[23] The phenomenon has also been studied extensively by Dr. Martin Samuels, a preeminent scholar on the topic, who also asserts that psychogenic death can occur. Samuels notes that "death by fright" is a misnomer for the event, however, because it is not just fear that can deliver a fatal blow to the nervous system; psychogenic death can be brought about by many types of physical stress: "There are people who have died in intercourse or in religious passion. There was a case of a golfer who hit a hole in one, turned to his partner and said, 'I can die now'—and then he dropped dead." [24] Stories and rumors of those who had died from fright were one of the reasons that Castle was able to make his marketing campaign all the more effectual. Audiences had heard of people being scared to death; and if it had happened before, it might just happen again.

ALL IN FUN

Perhaps when examined in relation to traditional standards of narrative cohesion and high-quality acting, *Macabre* will never be considered a great film. It can, however, be appreciated as a solid B-film that offered audiences excitement and fun, primarily due to its ingenious marketing campaign. It deserves recognition for setting William Castle off on a career that would lead him to create some of the most memorable film promotions of all time. Castle drew on the documented phenomenon of death by fright to create a clever gimmick that primed audiences for the experience he wanted them to have. His asynchronous reinforcement of the potential "danger" of the film enhanced the anticipation of the audience and helped him to generate excitement that could supersede the traditional standards by which films are often judged. Castle created more than just films, he created *events*. Although *Macabre* did not find favor among many professional film reviewers at the time of its original release, this was not the audience he was trying to impress. Castle catered to audience members who were not looking for a perfect narrative or renowned acting; he spoke to those who wanted to take part in a happening. First and foremost, he wanted moviegoers to play along and to have fun, and if they happened to have a good scare as well, that was even better.

NOTES

1. Cecil Smith, "Scaring Up Fans for TV Chillers," *Los Angeles Times*, May 3, 1972, p. 115.
2. Murray Leeder, "Collective Screams: William Castle and the Gimmick Film," *The Journal of Popular Culture* 44.4 (2011): 773.
3. William Castle, *Step Right Up: I'm Gonna Scare the Pants Off America* (Belvedere, CA: William Castle Productions, 1976), p. 13.
4. William Castle quoted in Smith, "Scaring Up Fans."
5. "12 Authors Wrote Film 'Macabre,'" *Daily Boston Globe*, April 20, 1958. In this article "Durrant" is incorrectly spelled "Durrand."
6. William Castle quoted in Smith, "Scaring Up Fans."
7. Philip K. Scheuer, "Fright Death Policy Issued," *Los Angeles Times*, March 3, 1958.

8. Ibid.
9. Stephen King, *Danse Macabre* (New York: Gallery Books, 1981), p. 192.
10. *Macabre* Press Book (Hollywood: Allied Artists, 1958), p. 5.
11. For more information on midnight ghosts see Beth A. Kattelman, "Where Were You When the Lights Went Out?: American Ghost Shows of the Twentieth Century," in Mary Luckhurst and Emilie Morin (eds.), *Theatre and Ghosts: Materiality, Performance and Modernity* (Houndmills: Palgrave Macmillan, 2014), pp. 96–110.
12. "Open Run With Midnite Show," *Macabre* Press Book, p. 5.
13. Anon., "Plenty of 'Halves' on All Circuits," *Variety*, November 11, 1921, p. 4.
14. Jim Steinmeyer, *Hiding the Elephant: How Magicians Invented the Impossible and Learned to Disappear* (New York: Carroll and Graf, 2003), p. 281.
15. John Kobler, "Master of Movie Horror," *Saturday Evening Post*, March 19, 1960, p. 31.
16. "Creepy and Atmospheric Fifties Style," *Amazon.com*, *Macabre* comments section, <https://www.amazon.com/Macabre-William-Prince/product-reviews/B009ZQG798/ref=cm_cr_arp_d_viewpnt_lft?ie=UTF8&reviewerType=avp_only_reviews&showViewpoints=1&sortBy=recent&filterByStar=positive&pageNumber=1> (accessed April 18, 2016).
17. Kim Luperi, "Tricks and Treats with William Castle and *Macabre*," *I See a Dark Theatre*, October 31, 2014, <http://www.iseeadarktheater.com/william-castle> (accessed March 31, 2016).
18. For an extended and detailed explication of the Hollywood style see David Bordwell, Janet Staiger and Kristin Thompson, *The Classical Hollywood Cinema: Film Style and Mode of Production to 1960* (New York: Columbia University Press, 1985).
19. David Parkinson, "Spine tingling came of age with William Castle," *The Guardian*, July 8, 2008, <https://www.theguardian.com/film/filmblog/2008/jul/08/spinetinglingcameofagewit> (accessed October 18, 2017).
20. Catherine Clepper, "'Death by Fright': Risk, Consent and Evidentiary Objects in William Castle's Rigged Houses," *Film History* 28.3 (July 2016): 66.
21. John Waters, *Crackpot: The Obsessions of John Waters* (New York: Vintage Books, 1987), p. 16.
22. Walter B. Cannon, "'Voodoo' Death," *American Anthropologist* 44. 2 (1942): 169.
23. David P. Phillips, George C. Liu, Kennon Kwok, Jason R. Jarvinen, Wei Zhang, and Ian S. Abramson, "The Hound of the Baskervilles effect: natural experiment on the influence of psychological stress on timing of death. (Beyond science?)," *British Medical Journal*, 323.7327 (December 22, 2001): 1443.
24. Dr. Martin Samuels qtd. in Coco Ballantyne, "Can a person be scared to death?" *Scientific American*, January 30, 2009, <https://www.scientificamerican.com/article/scared-to-death-heart-attack/> (accessed October 18, 2017).

CHAPTER 6

How to View *13 Ghosts*

Eliot Bessette

"I've always made shockers, not horror films. There's a difference. Horror films have no credibility. The shocker has real believability."— William Castle[1]

1960, which saw the release of *Psycho, Peeping Tom*, and *Eyes Without a Face*, is sometimes viewed as the year horror turned serious.[2] It was also a year of fun horror films. In 1960, William Castle released *13 Ghosts*, which at a superficial level depicts the shopworn story of a family that moves into a haunted house. But like many of Castle's films, it is unconventional in its utilization of a gimmick. Audiences were supplied with a special "ghost viewer" called "Illusion-O," which featured two colored filters they could look through during special tinted sequences. The film spawned a substantially more violent and frightening remake, styled as *Thir13en Ghosts* (2001). The remake was a box-office mediocrity, surely resulting in part from the lack of a ghost viewer.

The original *13 Ghosts* holds a special place in Castle's filmography. It is one of the most gimmick-reliant of all of his films, and its gimmick placed an unusual amount of agency in the audience. Unlike the Punishment Poll of *Mr. Sardonicus* (1961), which fatalistically resulted in the same ending no matter how the audience voted, Illusion-O could change the experience of the film in meaningful respects. Unlike the Fright Break of *Homicidal* (1961), it was not a singular episode at the climax of the film. Instead there were eight distinct times to use the ghost viewer. Furthermore, *13 Ghosts* emerged at a period of broader awareness of Castle, owing to his streak of box-office successes and gimmicky promotions. Castle was not a household name prior to his 1958 *Macabre*, but he released that film along with *House on Haunted Hill* (1959) and *The Tingler* (1959) in a remarkably quick ten-month span. In the theatrical trailer for *House on Haunted Hill*, there is no mention of the director. Rather, the disembodied head of Vincent Price introduces himself and the plot. Several months later, Castle introduces himself at the start of the trailer for *The Tingler* as the director of that film and previously *House on Haunted Hill*. Next year, in the trailer for *13 Ghosts*, a sonorous narrator instructs the audience: "Listen to William Castle, whom the *Saturday Evening Post* calls 'the master of movie horror.'" Then there is a variant of the film's prologue, in which Castle appears and alludes to the ghost viewer. Clearly he was growing more recognizable, and his films increasingly relied on his name.

In what follows, I seek to specify the uniqueness of *13 Ghosts* and explore modes of audience and critical interaction with the film. In the first section I offer a summary and analysis of *13 Ghosts* and its gimmick. I argue that we should reinterpret Castle's own account of Illusion-O and instead think of it as a form of spectatorial play that offers counterfactual views of the film. Next I assess the marketing and exhibition strategies of *13 Ghosts* alongside those of another gimmicky 1960 horror production, *Psycho*. Detailing their shared historical context and surprising cultural intersections, I propose we might view *13 Ghosts* as *Psycho*'s happy-go-lucky twin. Then I turn to period reviews in popular and trade presses to examine how critics frequently read *13 Ghosts* as a straightforward horror film, which in turn made it seem like a failure. I argue that this interpretive strategy is mistaken and offer reasons why the film has a more oblique relation to horror. In the final section I provide a solution to the conundrum of its genre. I read *13 Ghosts* as an amusing and defanged derivative of horror which I call "mock-horror." I believe this classification not only acknowledges the perspectives of 1960s and contemporary audiences, but also tracks the film's peculiar emotional project.

SEEING AND BELIEVING

The plot of the mostly black-and-white *13 Ghosts* follows the Zorbas, a handsome family of four, who inherit an old house from a recently deceased uncle Plato. Unfortunately for them the house is ridden with twelve ghosts. In addition to the property, the Zorbas receive special goggles that allow them to view the apparitions. Plato captured ghosts over his paranormal career through some combination of the ghost goggles and ultraviolet photography. Three of the four family members, father Cyrus (Donald Woods), mother Hilda (Rosemary De Camp), and older daughter Medea (Jo Morrow), all believe to varying degrees in the reality and threat of the ghosts, though their attitudes and beliefs are drastically inconsistent from scene to scene. Younger son Buck (Charles Herbert) is the only one who consistently believes in the ghosts, though he generally does not find them scary or threatening.

From the audience's perspective, there is no question that the house is genuinely haunted. An early scene is representative. Shortly after the Zorbas move in, they play with a Ouija board. They rest their fingers on the pointer and guide it, or let it guide them, to answers about the alleged ghosts in the house. At one point a heavy picture frame detaches from the wall and nearly falls on Buck. Perhaps it is a ghostly prank, perhaps just coincidence. Then Buck asks the board whether the ghosts will kill anyone in the family. At that moment the Ouija pointer levitates off the board, floats through the air, and descends into his sister's lap, in plain view of everyone. There is no possibility of a naturalistic explanation, yet the characters remain unalarmed. This evil omen turns out either to be a lie or an oversight on the ghouls' part, however, since Medea is never harmed and the threat is not mentioned again.

From that point forward, supernatural signs proliferate. Cyrus and Buck each get extended opportunities to observe the ghosts, which are only visible through the inherited ghost goggles. At other times tins of flour and bottles of milk levitate and upend themselves impishly in front of Cyrus and Hilda. There is periodic violence in the antics. One of the few ghosts to receive a name and backstory, Emilio the cuckolded chef, whacks his unfaithful ghost wife in the head with a spectral meat cleaver (which we see him do), and later hurls a real metal meat cleaver into the wall next to Cyrus (we only see the flying implement). The Zorbas lack Plato's capacity to control the ghosts through visual technology, yet despite all the domestic mischief, no one is hurt except Cyrus. The ghosts scorch the number 13 into his hand. The Zorbas engage in half-hearted discussion about leaving due to their twelve rambunctious housemates, yet they never actually move out.

Amidst the genuine hauntings come hoax hauntings and human villainy as well. Ben (Martin Milner), a former friend and legal aid to Plato, wishes to acquire the house himself along with Plato's hidden wealth. Ben believes in the ghosts, and at one point he dons a ghastly costume in the likeness of Plato's ghost in order to scare Medea and thereby drive the family out of the house.[3] We later learn that Ben murdered Plato by crushing him underneath an automated piece of bedding which can be raised and lowered with the turn of a hidden dial. Ben's trickery in no way casts doubt on the rest of the film's supernaturalism, however. By posing a threat to the still living Zorbas, Ben brings about his own demise at the hands of the supernatural. Buck inadvertently discovers Plato's trove of cash and guilelessly discloses it to Ben, who obtains the money. Ben then attempts to kill Buck, the only party who knows of his theft, in the same way he killed Plato. Meanwhile, the family has enlisted the housekeeper and spiritual medium Elaine (Margaret Hamilton) to conduct a séance to contact Plato.[4] Elaine summons the authentic version of Plato's ghost, the house's twelfth. Buck escapes the crusher bed, and Plato's ghost pins Ben underneath it, killing him in turn and creating the house's thirteenth ghost. In a brief, jovial final scene, the family decides to remain, and while it momentarily seems the ghosts have been dispelled by Plato's revenge murder, they all return for one last appearance.[5]

It takes effort to wrest coherence from the narrative. *13 Ghosts* is not one of the more cogently plotted Robb White scripts. Yet this hardly matters. The aesthetic focus of the film is not a mystery narrative or the accumulation of evidence for ghosts, but a frank presentation of ghostly spectacle and the implementation of the incredible gimmick, Illusion-O. Each audience member received a specially designed card with two rectangular openings cut out. A red cellophane filter covered one of the openings. A blue filter covered the other.[6] Bookending the narrative were direct addresses to the audience in which William Castle explained his gimmick.

In the prologue, a skeleton secretary opens a door to Castle's office.[7] We cut in to Castle at his desk, surrounded by bones, bubbling beakers, and portraits of the thirteen ghosts. He sets down the book he is reading, *13 Ghosts* by Robb White, and asks the audience, "Do you believe in ghosts? Some people believe in them. Others do not. Personally I do, and I feel sure that when you leave this theatre, you, too, will believe in ghosts." Castle then instructs viewers how to use the card, called a "ghost viewer." When the normally black-and-white image becomes tinted blue (often prefaced by the subtitle "use viewer," and often as a character puts on their own ghost goggles), audiences should look through their ghost viewers. Anyone who believes in ghosts is supposed to look through the red filter, while those who do not believe should look through the blue filter. The ghost viewer itself repeats these instructions. Framing the red filter are the phrases "This is a ghost viewer / To see them, look thru here." Framing the blue are "This is a ghost remover / To not see them, look thru here." Castle does not further elaborate how Illusion-O works, but audiences will see for themselves twenty-five minutes into the film. During the ghost scenes, human characters and material objects are tinted blue, while any ghosts appear red. Looking through the red filter would mute the blue background and intensify the red ghosts, whereas looking through the blue filter was supposed to screen out the red light so that the ghosts were not visible. The conclusion of a ghost sequence was marked by a return to black-and-white, often accompanied by the subtitle "remove viewer," at which point audiences were to put down their ghost viewers. Castle makes a plea that audience members explain Illusion-O to anyone who arrives late. Then he turns to his skeleton companion and—*poof!*—the two of them disappear, and the story proper begins.

Castle reappears in an epilogue for a parting word. He expresses his wish that the audience enjoyed the film, and he invites skeptical viewers to take their ghost viewers home and seek ghosts in the dark that night. This recalls the conclusion of *The Tingler*, when Vincent Price's character Warren Chapin invited audiences *not* to scream the next time they were scared to test whether the tingler did in fact exist and could kill them. In both instances a cinematic theme—and in some respects, the cinematic experience—overflows the temporal boundaries of the running time and the spatial boundaries of the screening area. The aesthetic spillage here mirrors the performative spillage in other contexts, where the screening spaces of Castle's films were raucous sites peopled with actors and audience plants rushing in and out.

In his autobiography, Castle attributes the genesis of Illusion-O to a fortuitous trip to the optometrist's.[8] He cycled through different corrective lenses. Most of them worsened his vision, but one crisply improved it. Substituting color filters for refractive lenses, he had his gimmick. As Castle tells it, his team spent "many months and thousands of dollars" to run forty different tests on the ghost viewers until finally hitting the mark—though, curiously, he misremembers the final product as "a simple pair of green and blue plastic lenses."[9] While the veracity and details of this story are suspect, as is much of Castle's autobiography, the anecdote is nevertheless instructive. The incorrect lenses were options he could reject, and indeed he would be foolish if he stuck with them. The correct lenses clarified the appearance of the world around him. Without those lenses the world and its inhabitants would persevere, impervious to anyone's vision. Illusion-O functions in much the same manner. The blue filter dulls features of the world. The red filter improves them and, once selected, is hard to reject in the long term. Still, people getting glasses or ghost viewers for the first time might amuse themselves by alternating between improved and worsened vision.

Nevertheless, the gimmick was not just superfluous fun. Illusion-O is essential to the experience of the film, just as its dichotomous modes of seeing and not seeing, believing and disbelieving, are essential to the plot. The ghosts reveal themselves to everyone except Medea, but the family does not behave predictably or sensibly given this fact. At one point Hilda admonishes the ghosts (which are invisible at that moment) for causing trouble in her kitchen, and she proposes that the family relocate before the children are hurt. But then she reacts nonchalantly to her son's story that he met a lion in the basement. Hilda seems to believe Buck is telling a boyish fib rather than reporting a supernatural encounter. Later she derides the "séance nonsense," although there is nothing to suggest it is any less real than the twelve spirits of the house. With the exception of Buck, who always believes in the ghosts, the attitudes of the Zorbas defy psychological realism and oscillate wildly from scene to scene.

The audience seems to mirror this behavior. Viewers armed with Illusion-O can fluctuate from scene to scene, and even moment to moment, in their attitude toward the ghosts as expressed by which filter they look through. Castle can be a paramount literalist in his gimmicks. As Catherine Clepper notes, *The Tingler*'s gimmick Percepto literalizes cinematic metaphors of touching or moving viewers.[10] *The Tingler* is really shocking! *13 Ghosts*, viewed in a certain light, externalizes audiences' psychological ability to endorse or refuse a narrative explanation. Suppose we take Castle at his word in the prologue. Looking through the red filter, a stance of belief, accepts a supernatural account of the hauntings and enhances the red-tinted ghosts that were already there. By contrast, looking through the blue filter, a stance of disbelief, insists on a naturalistic interpretation. If audiences believe in ghosts, then Illusion-O confirms their belief. If audiences disbelieve in ghosts, then Illusion-O confirms their disbelief. Yet as I have discussed, a naturalistic explanation is impossible. There are, after all, black-and-white scenes featuring supernatural occurrences, such as the floating Ouija pointer and the levitating milk bottle. The audience cannot change or reject these. Spectral whispers and roars are audible during tinted and black-and-white scenes. Furthermore, the default option of watching the film without the viewer leaves the ghosts on screen in a muted pinkish-red. Not even the blue filter can fully banish the ghosts. Shadowy remnants linger. Setting aside how Illusion-O might work in theory, in practice the ghosts are ineliminable.

However, we might understand looking through the blue filter not as a genuine expression or assumption of disbelief. We might not take Castle at his word. Instead we might view Illusion-O as a form of play: audiences can temporarily see an approximation of the film world and the film text *as if there were* no ghosts. Cyrus would cower against a door and scream for no reason. How silly that would seem! Scenes of Buck pacing back and forth in an empty basement would extend interminably. Even the basic cinematic syntax of shot/reverse shot would become inarticulate through reverse angles of empty rooms. Illusion-O affords a game of epistemic peekaboo. We play *now we see it, now we (mostly) don't*, while we pretend to play *now we believe it, now we don't*. Instead of narratively internalizing the ambiguity between the naturalistic and supernatural, the film settles on supernatural.[11] Yet through the gimmick of Illusion-O the audience can shuttle between actual and counterfactual versions of the film world and film text. Decoupling Illusion-O from belief also obviates the difficulty of explaining two features of viewers' conviction that would arise otherwise. The first has to do with volatility. Our beliefs do not really oscillate wildly with each dip or rise of the ghost viewer. Beliefs are not the sort of mental state that alternate that rapidly, and the fact that characters' beliefs do contributes to the film's amusing tone. The second problem has to do with volition. I take it that we cannot turn our beliefs on and off at will: we cannot choose to believe or disbelieve.[12] Our choosing to believe in the ghosts is doubly precluded by the nature of this film, and the nature of belief. It is unclear, however, whether the Zorbas' beliefs are supposed to be under their volitional control.

Before we venture too far into the philosophical weeds, we might remember that Illusion-O is fun. Much of the joy of watching *13 Ghosts* comes from rotating playfully among red and blue and neither filter.[13] Regrettably, certain audiences missed the full experience. Some theatres screened an Illusion-O-free version of the film, an entirely black-and-white print lacking Castle's prologue and epilogue and the subtitled instructions to viewers.[14] The gimmickless version presents the ghosts as black-and-white superimpositions on a black-and-white background. They seem paradoxically less integrated into their environment than when they are spectrally distinguished through red coloration. The lion ghost in particular looks like an accidental double exposure, or at least a spatial miscalculation, in black and white (Figure 6.1). Its scale relative to the basement, its location relative to Buck, and its motion relative to camera tracks are all jarringly inconsistent from shot to shot, none of which matters when viewers can busy themselves with the ghost viewer. Unlucky audiences of the fully black-and-white version were stuck with one version of the film world and film text, and they lacked any special means of participating in the cinematic experience. Worst of all, that version is less fun. As the gimmick goes, so goes most of the cinematic *raison d'être*. The lone advantage of the Illusion-O-free print is that audiences can see the whole film image more clearly. With Illusion-O, looking through the red filter obscures darker background details in blue at the expense of vivid red for the ghosts: what is clearly a shelf of books viewed through the blue filter or with the unaided eye becomes an indistinct dark rectangle through the red. And of course the blue filter largely screens out the red ghosts. But this hardly recommends the black-and-white version. Fortunately for audiences in 1960, anyone

Figure 6.1 The lion ghost appears spatially incongruous in the black-and-white version of *13 Ghosts*.

who missed out on Illusion-O could have found a gimmicky substitute across the street.

13 GHOSTS AND PSYCHO

William Castle draws frequent comparisons with Alfred Hitchcock. We find the clearest overlap in *Homicidal* and *Psycho*. The former film is indebted to the latter, from the broad storyline of a murderous transvestite character to such minor details as staging the second murder-by-knife at the top of a staircase. Both directors promoted their works with their recognizable names and images (or silhouettes). Like Castle, Hitchcock memorably addressed his audience in prologues and epilogues to episodes of his television series *Alfred Hitchcock Presents* (1955–62) and *The Alfred Hitchcock Hour* (1962–5). It is even possible to detect similar tones in their films. After all, Hitchcock called *Psycho* "fun."[15] Heretofore undiscussed are the connections between *13 Ghosts* and *Psycho*, both released in the summer of 1960. They were often presented as a horror-film double bill, with *Psycho* as the headliner and *13 Ghosts* as the secondary feature.[16] They complement each other more deeply than perhaps any other pair of the directors' works.

During the initial theatrical run of *Psycho*, Hitchcock demanded that movie houses admit no guest who arrived after the film had begun. He wanted to ensure an uninterrupted screening experience, so audiences had to line up in advance. Linda Williams has analyzed *Psycho*'s unique exhibition and how it retrained audience habits of strolling into and out of theatres with little care for start times. She argues that being controlled by marketing and exhibition practices—submitting to them—was pleasurable. Audiences relinquished power to Hitchcock and received heightened enjoyment and emotion in return. Promotional material designed for exhibitors promised that waiting in line would heighten guests' pleasure through anticipation, in the manner of a theme park ride. Williams argues that the film itself contains vertiginous drops and sensational swerves, like a roller coaster, that carry audiences through intense feelings and prevent them from being in control. These feelings were exacerbated by the sight of anguished people exiting previous screenings and by the air of secrecy shrouding *Psycho*. In trailers and print advertisements for the film, Hitchcock forbade audiences from revealing the "secret," which could refer to the murder of Marion, the psychosexual confusion of Norman, the preserved corpse of Mrs. Bates, or some combination of the above.[17]

Contrast these habits and pleasures with those of *13 Ghosts*. There is no narrative secret to hide. There is a mild twist in that Ben turns out to be a greedy villain, but that is telegraphed well in advance. There is a mild twist in that Ben turns out to be the thirteenth ghost, but that barely matters.

There is no further secret to the ghosts. They exist, as the title declares, and we never doubt it. Furthermore, instead of disciplining audiences into early and orderly attendance, the prologue of *13 Ghosts* promotes a very different screening space. William Castle anticipates that people will arrive after the start of the film. He encourages audience members to explain to latecomers how Illusion-O works. Instead of Hitchcock's rigorously prescribed start and finish times, *13 Ghosts* is an experience that can begin late and last long after the screening time proper, given Castle's final dare to use the ghost viewers at home. The only moments of discipline in *13 Ghosts* are the instructions to use and remove the ghost viewer, but as we have seen, these involve choice and the possibility of refusal. The pleasure of *13 Ghosts* is in ungoverned play, not discipline. Still, it maintains an emotional equanimity throughout, never foisting intense sensations upon the audience. It is more tram ride than roller coaster. And contrary to *Psycho*, audiences leaving screenings of *13 Ghosts* did not look pallid and devastated. One review of Castle's film reports, "few of the large preview audience emerged without a happy smile."[18]

About a month after that preview audience enjoyed the film, it debuted in Chicago, where *Psycho* had been selling out theatres for several weeks. *Psycho* had built anticipation from a series of announcements in the *Chicago Tribune* beginning ten days before its local premiere—the print analogue to waiting in line. This campaign began with a half-page, multi-paragraph advertisement on June 12th, 1960, in which Hitchcock discoursed unhurriedly about his creation, explained the no-late-admission policy, and asked that viewers not reveal its secrets.[19] The dominant features of this notice, and of the follow-up a week later, were wordiness, rules, and an image of Hitchcock. Conversely, the *Tribune*'s introduction of *13 Ghosts* was a large advertisement on July 28th, one day before its premiere, which was largely pictorial. It featured depictions of all the ghosts save for Ben, a full-sized reproduction of the ghost viewer, and an image of Charles Herbert holding another ghost viewer (which Buck never does, since characters in the film wear ghost goggles). The language used was punchier and eye-catching: "See the ghosts in ectoplasmic color!" and "The greatest thrill since 3-D."[20] Throughout their publicity campaigns, *Psycho* stressed the no-late-admission rule and the fact that it was a Hitchcock film, while *13 Ghosts* offered a broader variety of enticements: color, Illusion-O, a ghost viewer, ghosts, reminders of Castle's other films, and so on. Despite these differences, both films converged in their atypical strategy of threatening potential viewers. An August 4th *Tribune* ad for *13 Ghosts* promised of the ghost viewer: "It turns ghosts on ... It turns ghosts off ... If they turn on you!"[21] Viewers were of course not meant to take this threat seriously, yet the film does come packaged with the remedy to its own faux-danger. On the other hand, one week after his June 12th salvo of rules, Hitchcock warned regarding *Psycho*: "The manager of this theatre has been instructed, at the risk of his life, not to admit to the theatre any persons after the picture starts. Any spurious attempts to enter by side doors, fire escapes, or ventilating shafts will be met by force."[22] To be sure, Hitchcock's tongue is in his cheek here; yet there is a glimmer of menace to the suggestion, considering he hired Pinkerton guards to monitor the screening spaces.[23]

Regional variations in the marketing of *13 Ghosts* were at times puzzling and incoherent. On September 6th, the *Los Angeles Times* featured large side-by-side advertisements for *Psycho* and *13 Ghosts*.[24] *Psycho*'s ad featured a footnote next to an illustration of Hitchcock that said, "Please don't give away the ending. It's the only one we have." This was in the spirit of *Psycho*'s air of rigor and secrecy. As though in direct response, the *13 Ghosts* ad next to it blared, "Please don't reveal how your ghost viewer works!" Three days earlier the *Times* had run an even more histrionic ad imploring "Please, please don't ever reveal how your ghost viewer works!"[25] The secret would have to be kept till the grave. Or beyond. This is manifestly not in the spirit of *13 Ghosts*, and it is curious for several reasons. The *Times* published a review on September 2nd that explained how Illusion-O worked.[26] The Chicago advertisements and theatrical trailer had no compunctions about revealing the ghost viewer. In fact, early industry reports on the trailer announced that its very purpose was to entice audiences through an explanation of Illusion-O.[27] And as soon as the film begins, Castle explains how to use the ghost viewer. The most that could be said in favor of secrecy is that the prologue does not disclose precisely what viewers will or will not see with Illusion-O, and the theatrical trailer features black-and-white footage of the ghosts with just a tease of color in a red-and-blue title card. That readers of the *Los Angeles Times* were begged not to explain how Illusion-O works seems at once an attempt to mimic *Psycho* and a gimmick of reverse psychology. In a sense, it did not matter if one gimmick or advertising hook for a Castle film contradicted another. Anything that got people's attention would do.

Secrets notwithstanding, both films benefited from cultural pervasiveness and extensive word of mouth. For its part, *Psycho* balanced its mystique with ubiquitous visibility (from the advertising blitz to the lines of anxious guests outside theatres) and ubiquitous audibility (given the recordings of Hitchcock's various exhortations that played inside theatre lobbies).[28] Not all cinemagoers were charmed by this strategy, however. In a letter to the *New York Times*, one correspondent proclaimed himself "angry because of the salesmanship associated with 'Psycho'"; he felt Hitchcock's omnipresent instructions on how to view the film and what not to say about it amounted to an overbearing invitation "to become a member of a 'Psycho' club, initiation to which is the frightening and ugly film itself."[29] Many more potential guests gladly accepted the challenge and initiated themselves. As so often happened, Castle took a metaphor and literalized it. *13 Ghosts* had an actual club, the

William Castle Horror Advisory Board and Fan Club. In early 1960, young "gore-respondents" were "sinc-eerie-ly" invited to spread the news of the "Screamiere" of *13 Ghosts* to their friends.[30] In return, they were promised advance information on the film. Castle claimed that at their peaks his various fan clubs totaled over 250,000 members, all eagerly spreading the word about his newest gimmick.[31] One can only imagine how many ghost viewers must have circulated through schoolyards and playgrounds.

Often forgotten in discussions of cinematic gimmicks is the role individual theatres played in supplementing their own creative ballyhoo. One Texas theatre invited patrons to win tickets by writing a short essay "telling of their definition of 'Psycho.'"[32] Proponents of a sadomasochistic theory of Hitchcock's exhibition need look no further than the New York theatre that offered free handcuffs to audiences of *Psycho* and instructed them to cuff themselves to their seats so they could not run away in a peak of fright.[33] But the spirit of William Castle seemed to animate theatre owners even more powerfully. Over two days, one enterprising Ohio theatre hosted a contest to name the most films with "ghost" in the title, awarded free tickets for the first thirteen people in line, and collaborated with a department store to sell ice cream sundaes for thirteen cents; mannequins dressed as ghosts caught eyes in the lobby, and employees dressed as ghosts wailed up and down the aisles. Not to be outdone, a Louisiana theatre organized a citywide ghost hunt. Models in ghoulish makeup were hired to stalk the streets of downtown New Orleans for several days before and after the premiere of *13 Ghosts*. Louisianans were invited to photograph the ghosts in the wild and submit their sightings to a contest run by a local radio station, through which they might win free tickets to the film. The week culminated in a parade that fused Mardi Gras and William Castle.[34] Participants could recreate the playful and benign ghost-sighting of Illusion-O and imitate the ghost-capturing research of Plato Zorba, of whom one character in the film reports, "Dr. Zorba proved that if you could see a ghost, you could control it—to a certain extent." It is difficult to imagine a marketing scheme that more brilliantly and entertainingly dovetails with the film's paranormal themes.

To view *Psycho* or *13 Ghosts* in the context of their original exhibition is to view them in a forest of ballyhoo and theatrical exploitation. They had to contend for novelty and audience attention in a clamorous marketplace.[35] Both, moreover, are gimmick films. Although many viewers forget it today, the similarity was not lost on industry commentators at the time.[36] Castle himself concurred years later, referring to Hitchcock's no-late-admission rule as a "very unusual gimmick."[37] Yet the garish theatrical promotions have disappeared, and so has *Psycho*'s gimmick, since it was part of the exhibition and not part of the film text. Accordingly, *Psycho* has been able to shake off the low-cultural associations of gimmicks; Hitchcock's stature in film history also surely accelerated this process.[38] Castle's films, by contrast, remain indelibly connected to their gimmicks. While we can better understand *13 Ghosts* through an analysis of its original exhibition context, reviewers at the time often fell prey to considerable misunderstandings of its genre and tone.

CASTLE AND HIS CRITICS

Variety published a short piece during the theatrical run of *13 Ghosts* lamenting the disconnect between the critical appraisal of a film and its box-office success.[39] Some critical darlings were ignored by the public. Other films, like *13 Ghosts*, were the objects of critical dismissal but drew in crowds. Reviewers reached a broad consensus: *13 Ghosts* was a failure because it was not scary enough.[40] The *Chicago Tribune* titled its review "'13 Ghosts' Movie Just Isn't Spooky" and concluded that no audience member older than six would be scared.[41] *Variety* called it "a workmanlike, but not very frightening, horror film" and bemoaned the forthright presentation of the ghosts at the expense of eerie intimation.[42] Among the major outlets, the most measured review came from the *Los Angeles Times*. Though still critical, it praised the film's reliance on visual storytelling in lieu of the wordy screenplays of *House on Haunted Hill* and *The Tingler*, both also written by Robb White. The review noted the default presence of ghosts with neither filter and the lingering spectral traces even with the blue filter, setting up the piece's punch line: "Those wishing to blot the whole thing out must close their eyes. Or see an adult film instead." But most interestingly, it articulated why the film was not frightening:

> Mr. Castle has, curiously, decided to telegraph all his ghost apparitions. He starts the film with an amiable prologue which gives everything away. And then, well in advance of his ghosts, he gives the black and white screen a bluish tinge. He caps it all by actually flashing on the screen the words "Use Viewer" so that the audience can laugh and get comfortably ready to be "surprised." Curious.[43]

The film drastically undercuts its ability to scare most audiences by removing surprise. The tinted ghost scenes, moreover, lack startles or much attempt to frighten viewers at all. Nothing really *happens* in several of the lengthy Illusion-O sequences, and with few exceptions, the ghosts never harm or even endanger the Zorbas. So what to make of an ostensible horror film that does not try to elicit fear?

In one way or another, critics had to deal with the conundrums of what genre the film belongs to and what tone it has. Reviewers by and large converged in classifying *13 Ghosts* as a horror film or holding it to a standard of frightening audiences as a horror film would. This genre-interpretive pattern held for Castle's other work from 1958–61. In fairness, critics may have allowed his previous three films—what Clepper calls "Castle's 'death-by-fright' trilogy"—to shade their reading of *13 Ghosts*.[44] Critics tended to associate *13 Ghosts* tonally with Castle's other work. *13 Ghosts* and its predecessors *The Tingler* and *House on Haunted Hill* were all "horrific films" and instances of the "macabre."[45] Later, *13 Ghosts* would by affiliated with *Homicidal* and *Mr. Sardonicus* as Castle's "usual format of the macabre mixed with terror"; these were contrasted with the forthcoming mirth of *Zotz!* (1962).[46] On paper there may be a difference between a silly word that causes hijinks and a haunted house filled with murderous ghosts. But in practice, is there any?

BoxOffice magazine was a rare exception to the tendency to read *13 Ghosts* as a straightforward horror film. Since it was an industry publication designed for exhibitors, *BoxOffice* may have had a better sense of regular audience responses. According to its reviews, *13 Ghosts* was a "horror comedy," whereas *House on Haunted Hill*, *The Tingler*, and *Mr. Sardonicus* were "horror," and *Homicidal* was a "horror mystery."[47] There is undoubtedly more art than science to these attributions, but *BoxOffice* appeared to read *13 Ghosts* differently than its gimmicky counterparts.[48] It sensed there was a generic departure from Castle's previous films—even *The Tingler*, which is shot through with levity. Apart from *BoxOffice*, there are only glimmers of tonal acuity in the other major publications. While *Variety* thought *13 Ghosts* was a failed horror film, it was the most reliable source in finding humor in Castle's other work. It felt *House on Haunted Hill* successfully alternated screams and laughs: "There is some good humor in the dialog which not only pays off well against the ghostly elements, but provides a release for laughter so it does not explode in the suspense sequences."[49] Of the Fright Break in *Homicidal* it opined, "It's good for laughs, probably intended by Castle and White, a good mood piece and showmanship which builds to even greater suspense."[50] It is puzzling why so few critics saw *13 Ghosts* in similar humorous terms.

Children suffered no such generic confusion. The *Chicago Tribune* noted that no one in the audience was scared, yet "when the various spooks started their wailing on the sound track the youngsters in the audience wailed right back."[51] In the documentary *Spine Tingler! The William Castle Story*, John Waters recalled, "The critics thought he was ridiculous and kids thought he was great."[52] Children understood not to construe *13 Ghosts* as straightforward horror, just as they did when they brought slingshots to aim at the in-theatre skeleton released during *House on Haunted Hill*'s Emergo.[53] Castle vacillated on whether *13 Ghosts* was designed especially for children, but he affirmed they were a crucial part of his audience.[54]

There is meager content in *13 Ghosts* to foster a reading as a straight horror film. Plato's ghost does look creepy as he pins Ben under the crusher bed, the lone incident that frightens Buck—yet ten seconds after this ghost sequence, we fade to a happy scene the next morning, lest the mildest fear linger. There are some moderately startling visual moments, such as the sudden appearance of a telegram delivery man at the Zorbas' house, the reveal of Ben dressed as Plato from behind a curtain, and the quick cut to Buck wearing a ghost-of-Plato mask pilfered from the recently murdered Ben.[55] Most of these are accompanied by a cymbal crash and a jolt of strings to surprise the audience, though there is never any violence during the jump scares. These moments lend some credence to Castle's self-description as a creator of "shockers, not horror films." But compared with the rest of his output from 1958–61, the shocks, violence, and gruesomeness are attenuated significantly. There is nothing like the surprising cut to the dead girl doll in *Macabre*, the bloody knife attacks in *Homicidal*, or the torturous experiments in *Mr. Sardonicus*.

Looking at the film now it is hard not to see goofiness and lightheartedness at every turn, a mixture of the intentional and unintentional, of aesthetic decisions and budgetary constraints. There is the utterly phony fly that electrocutes itself in Ben's office, with the string holding it up plainly visible. There is Cyrus's cross-eyed appearance through the goggles, and his exaggerated screaming as the flaming wheel does nothing to him. There is the fact that the ghost goggles are too big for any character's head, in particular Buck's; they slip down one side of his face as he watches the lion, which, along with his slackened jaw and non-response to two ghosts, makes him look narcotized (Figure 6.2). We can add to this Hilda's sardonic remarks, Castle's dialogue with the skeleton secretary, and a myriad of other performance cues. *13 Ghosts* should not be taken seriously as horror, or very seriously at all.

Figure 6.2 Buck and the goggles: Buck, avid ghost viewer.

A moment late in the film has a unique role in securing an upbeat and nonthreatening tone. When Elaine tells Buck the ghosts have gone into abeyance but will return, Buck beams, "Real soon, I hope!" Many horror films with happy endings, like *Macabre*, imply the future will be benign and safe. *13 Ghosts* offers as much through the destruction of Ben, but it goes further than a standard happy ending. Buck's gleeful desire to re-encounter the ghosts implies the *past was* benign and safe. Buck, the smallest, most vulnerable, and most reliable character, casts a retroactive agreeableness on the action that preceded. If the film somehow managed to upset any very young audience member, Buck's enthusiasm serves to quash any lingering discomfort.

Attempts to label *13 Ghosts* as a horror film are now and have always been inadequate. But that still leaves unanswered how we ought to categorize it. We saw in the last section how Linda Williams excavated a lost interpretive context for *Psycho*. In the final section, I offer a genre-interpretive strategy for *13 Ghosts* that circumvents dead-end expectations of frightfulness and encompasses its fun, humor, relative emotional quietude, and horror-adjacency.

PRETENDING TO SCARE

Certainly it would be a critical improvement, and fairer to Castle's films, to read many of them as successful horror-comedies rather than failed horror, as Murray Leeder urges.[56] But I argue we need a further way to differentiate the ubiquitous goofiness and lack of serious threat in *13 Ghosts* from the at least intermittent scares of Castle's other shockers. Horror-comedies are often distinguished by the type and degree of emotions they wish to engender. They elicit screams of fear and bursts of giggles to puncture tension, "inducing laughter alongside perfectly complementary chills."[57] A scene may appear to build to a scare but instead culminate in a gag. In other cases a scene may juxtapose a developing scary threat and an incongruously humorous character reaction. Horror-comedies typically sustain a high pitch of emotional intensity as well. William Paul describes a horror-comic scene in *Carrie* (1976) as inducing a galvanic and invigorating effect in the audience.[58] Significantly, horror-comic fear and laughter are real reactions. We do not merely feign to be scared or amused. Successful horror-comedies elicit genuine high-energy sensations in us, even if we cannot stipulate in advance whether they will manifest nearer to the horrific or comic poles in a given viewer.

We know from the rest of William Castle's body of work that he can elicit both laughter and screams. It is within his power to craft an authentically, unironically scary scene. But can we honestly say *13 Ghosts* elicits complementary chills, or is that just a polite conceit we may adopt when discussing the film? And does it ever rise out of a rather muted emotional level? The utterly unfrightening character of nearly the whole of *13 Ghosts*, amidst the trappings of a haunted house horror film, invites a different response and an acknowledgment that our reaction of "fear" is altogether dissimilar from the fear we feel in response to a horror film like *Peeping Tom* (1960) or a horror-comedy like *Dead Alive* (1992). With no attempt to frighten, neither "horror" nor "horror-comedy" will suffice for *13 Ghosts*.[59] "Comedy" is also an imperfect fit. While there are funny moments, humor is not central to the narrative and formal aims of the film. Instead, the gimmick is the structuring principle. Illusion-O, ghostly spectacle, and high-spirited audience participation organize the film, and they animate the climax during the séance and murder of Ben. The dominant emotional features are the conspicuous absence of fear most of the time and the near-instantaneous evaporation of shock or mild fear, whenever they are elicited, through a comforting scene or a dissolve from nighttime to morning.

Given the film's tonal idiosyncrasy, its generic misconstruals, and the legacy of William Castle, I propose we classify *13 Ghosts* as a "mock-horror" film. In the same way that the mockumentary *This is Spinal Tap* (1984) mimics documentary aesthetics but knowingly lacks an essential component (something like the fact that "the author intends the audience to believe the content of the text"), so *13 Ghosts* mimics horror aesthetics but knowingly lacks an essential component (the fact that the author intends the audience to be scared).[60] Mock-horror does not dissimulate about the "reality" status of scary content, as *The Blair Witch Project* (1999) did. It dissimulates about the *scary* status of "scary" content. There is even some contemporaneous support for this notion. The *BoxOffice* review suggests *13 Ghosts* "provides a good deal of delightful spoofing at the horror idea."[61] The film stands outside "the horror idea," instead adopting an amusing and deflationary stance toward fear.

If Castle had intended his audience to be frightened, but *13 Ghosts* did not accomplish this, then critics would have been correct that it was a failed horror film. But *13 Ghosts* only *acts* like it wants to scare us. It has the right set-up to be scary—ghosts in a haunted house, periodically attacking good human characters—but there is no real attempt to elicit audience fear. All of the promotional materials *boast* that the film will scare us. The theatrical trailer announced the film was "Happily created by William Castle . . . to scare the living daylights out of you!" As we have seen, certain newspaper ads threatened the ghosts might "turn on" audiences, and other ads invited comparisons with *Psycho*. Moreover, in a speech before the film's release, Castle revealed the "secret" gimmick, yet his account of Illusion-O differed from the one he gives in the prologue; he explained the blue filter was an option for viewers who were too frightened to continue watching, as though audiences could not handle the film.[62] I have previously argued that Illusion-O lets audiences shuttle between supernatural and naturalistic versions of the film text and film world. Now we can add that it lets audiences shuttle between not-too-scary and intolerably scary versions of the film text. The intolerably scary version is just as fanciful as the naturalistic.

There are two ways to take this boastful rhetoric. We might read it, following David Sanjek on carnival barkers and exploitation filmmakers, as a cynical tactic "that treads a fine line between obfuscation and outright deceit."[63] However, falsehood of this sort would not work twice for a recognizable name like Castle's. And the firsthand reports we have give no indication that general audiences felt misled or shortchanged. Rather, they loved the product and came back for more next year with *Homicidal* and *Mr. Sardonicus*. We can instead characterize the film as *pretending* to scare us. *13 Ghosts* takes the same faux-serious attitude with respect to genre as it did with respect to the importance of keeping its "secret."

If all films invite their own kind of "cooperative viewers," those "who allow the film to do its intended emotional work," then the uncommon emotional work of *13 Ghosts* may invite an uncommon style of cooperation.[64] At a minimum, viewers can participate with the ghost viewer (if they have one), and they might ignore the shadowy remnants of the ghosts when looking through the blue filter. They can react to the pretense of terror with amusement.[65] And exceptionally cooperative viewers, those willing to meet the film more than halfway, might pretend to be scared in return.[66] Children seemed to do this most readily. Such exceptional cooperation might take the form of willfully, playfully overreacting to the ghost sequences—wailing along with the soundtrack, as the *Tribune* observed—or even screaming along with Cyrus, despite not feeling authentic fear. (Elsewhere, viewers might cooperate with the mock-horror of *Homicidal*'s Fright Break by pretending they are in for something really ghastly.)[67] In ways large and small, viewers can give themselves over to the mock-horrific conceit in exchange for more spectatorial pleasure, just as audiences of *Psycho* could submit to Hitchcock's discipline for more pleasure.

Psycho, as many critics have observed, is in one respect a horror film about horror spectatorship: it explores at the level of form and content themes such as voyeurism, violence and transgression, and the rupture of expectations. *13 Ghosts* is likewise in one respect a mock-horror film about horror spectatorship: it explores at the level of form and content themes such as belief, hiding and revealing, and the paradoxical pleasure of being scared. In another respect *13 Ghosts* is a standout instance of gimmickry and ballyhoo from a different era of exhibition, and in yet another it is a peculiar and delightful film in its own right. However we view it—whichever filter we adopt, or whether we choose no filter at all—the sublime silliness shines through.

NOTES

For thoughtful feedback during earlier stages of this work I would like to thank Kristen Whissel, as well as attendees of the 2015 SCMS conference, in particular Chuck Kleinhans. Thanks also to Cliff Galiher for his incisive and generous commentary on a draft.

1. Charles Champlin, "Castle Operates Chilling Business," *Los Angeles Times*, August 30, 1965, p. C21.
2. This owes in large part to the colossal impact of *Psycho*. Robin Wood dates 1960 as the beginning of a paradigm shift in American horror cinema toward horror located in the family. He views this as the dominant genre trope for the next twenty years and an opportunity for more trenchant cultural critiques. Wood awards primary responsibility for this tendency to *Psycho*. See *Hollywood from Vietnam to Reagan* (New York: Columbia University Press, 1986), pp. 83–4. In a different vein, Andrew Tudor credits *Psycho* and *Peeping Tom* as inaugurating a trend of insanity-based horror that traffics in distrust of self rather than distrust of supernatural interlopers. He, too, stresses 1960 as a dividing line. See *Monsters and Mad Scientists: A Cultural History of the Horror Movie* (Cambridge, MA: Basil Blackwell, 1989), pp. 47–8, 186–8.
3. Presumably Ben must have seen Plato in ghost form to recreate his appearance faithfully.
4. There is a running joke that Buck calls Elaine a witch, implicitly referencing Margaret Hamilton's role as the Wicked Witch of the West in *The Wizard of Oz* (1939). Whether she is a witch is never proven, though at the end of the film Elaine picks up a broom and smiles toward camera.
5. Fourteen ghosts appear in farewell succession. The addition is the flaming wheel, which is not a distinct ghost but a fusion of the flaming skeleton and a few others.
6. Reviews of the film and Castle himself refer to the red and blue parts of the ghost viewer as "lenses," but "filters" is more accurate, since Illusion-O does not refract light.
7. In the estimation of Murray Leeder, this prologue features Castle most pointedly channeling Georges Méliès. See "Collective Screams: William Castle and the Gimmick Film," *Journal of Popular Culture* 44:4 (2011): 783.
8. William Castle, *Step Right Up! I'm Gonna Scare the Pants Off America* (New York: G. P. Putnam and Sons, 1976), p. 162.
9. Ibid.
10. Catherine Clepper, "'Death by Fright': Risk, Consent, and Evidentiary Objects in William Castle's Rigged Houses," *Film History* 28:3 (2016): 55.
11. For a discussion of genuine indeterminacy between the naturalistic and supernatural in horror films, see Noël Carroll, *The Philosophy of Horror, or: Paradoxes of the Heart* (New York: Routledge, 1990), pp. 144–57.
12. Whether we can choose to believe a proposition has attracted a richer philosophical literature than I am giving it credit for, reaching through Pascal and Descartes and beyond. For an influential account challenging the notion that we have much volitional control over belief, see Bernard Williams, "Deciding to Believe," in *Problems of the Self: Philosophical Papers 1956–1972* (New York: Cambridge University Press, 1973), pp. 136–51.
13. Leonard Maltin confirms this style of viewing in *Spine Tingler! The William Castle Story*, dir. Jeffrey Schwarz (U.S.A.: Automat Pictures, 2007).
14. Today's audiences also have limited access to Illusion-O. Certain home releases feature the tinted version and include a ghost viewer. Others feature the tinted version with no ghost viewer. And some feature only the black-and-white version.
15. Quoted in numerous sources, including Linda Williams, "Discipline and Fun: *Psycho* and

Postmodern Cinema," in Christine Gledhill and Linda Williams (eds.), *Reinventing Film Studies* (London: Arnold, 2000), p. 353.
16. As one of the year's biggest box-office hits, *Psycho* was the more standalone work of the two. It could play as a screen's sole feature multiple times per evening. Yet when it was packaged with another film, it was frequently with *13 Ghosts*. Castle's film, on the other hand, was uncommonly flexible in its exhibition. Sometimes *13 Ghosts* served as the bottom half of a double bill with *Psycho*. In some theatres it played as a standalone feature. And intriguingly, Castle's fame was such that it could function as the top half of a double bill. In these cases it was often paired with *The Electronic Monster*, which debuted in 1958 in the UK under the title *Escapement* but was not released in the United States until the summer of 1960 ("'13 Ghosts' Haunt Today," *Los Angeles Times* August 31, 1960, p. B9). For a discussion of the cultural and economic context of horror film double bills around this time, see Kevin Heffernan, *Ghouls, Gimmicks, and Gold: Horror Films and the American Movie Business, 1953–1968* (Durham, NC: Duke University Press, 2004), pp. 64–8.
17. Williams, "Discipline and Fun," pp. 356–8, 362–6.
18. Review of *13 Ghosts*, *BoxOffice* June 27, 1960, p. 111. All issues of *BoxOffice* cited are the Southeast Edition; the pagination is irregular and sometimes absent, so some page citations involve my best inferences.
19. *Chicago Tribune*, June 12, 1960, p. D13.
20. *Chicago Tribune*, July 28, 1960, p. E15.
21. *Chicago Tribune*, August 4, 1960, p. G15.
22. *Chicago Tribune*, June 19, 1960, p. D13.
23. One suburban drive-in tempted fate by recasting Hitchcock's rule as "no one admitted 3 minutes after 'Psycho' starts." *Chicago Tribune*, August 13, 1960, p. W_A9.
24. *Los Angeles Times*, September 6, 1960, p. C11.
25. *Los Angeles Times*, September 3, 1960, p. A6.
26. Charles Stinson, "'13 Ghosts' Attempt Co-Op in Old Mansion," *Los Angeles Times*, September 2, 1960, p. 26.
27. "Trailers for '13 Ghosts,'" *BoxOffice*, May 30, 1960, p. 15.
28. Seth Friedman, "Misdirection in Fits and Starts: Alfred Hitchcock's Popular Reputation and the Reception of His Films," *Quarterly Review of Film and Video*, 29:1 (2012): 92.
29. James H. Schwartz, letter to the editor, *New York Times*, July 24, 1960, p. X7.
30. These details are related, third-hand and grumpily, in "An Irishman's Diary: Lament," *Irish Times*, January 5, 1961, p. 6. A version of this letter also appears in *Spine Tingler! The William Castle Story*.
31. Castle, *Step Right Up!*, p. 159.
32. "Public Is Lapping Up 'Psycho' and Its Admission Gimmick," *BoxOffice*, September 19, 1960, p. 149.
33. "Handcuffs Go to Patrons in Advance of 'Psycho,'" *BoxOffice*, October 3, 1960, p. 157.
34. "'13 Ghosts' Boxoffice Zooms, With Hoopla and Prizes Contests Added on the Stage," *BoxOffice*, September 19, 1960, p. 148.
35. In one week in 1960, a South Dakota theatre ran a "Name the Puppy" contest and puppy giveaway (for *A Dog of Flanders*); a Louisiana theatre featured a live python, tarantula, and lizards in its lobby (for *Congo Jungle*); an Ohio theatre released three hundred partially inflated helium balloons, each with an attached ticket (for *A Visit to a Small Planet*); a Wisconsin theatre held a beauty contest exclusively for tall women (for *Tall Story*); and a Michigan theatre scattered shrunken heads, love potions, and roving live guitarists

throughout the neighborhood, displayed impaled and bleeding voodoo dolls in its lobby, and hired a "Voodoo Queen, who rode around town in a coffin in a transparent hearse with appropriate banners, followed by a band on a flattop truck playing lugubrious music" (for *Macumba Love*). These promotions were reported in the "Showmandiser" section of *BoxOffice*, May 30, 1960, pp. 85–7; the quote comes from "Spotlight on Voodoo for 'Macumba Love,'" p. 87.

36. "Selling-the-Sell Continues Salient," *Variety*, August 10, 1960, p. 7.
37. Castle, *Step Right Up!*, p. 155.
38. For a survey of the changing critical fortunes of the film, see Williams, "Discipline and Fun," pp. 352–3.
39. Gene Arneel, "New Hard Look at Film Critics and Their Relationship to B.O.," *Variety*, August 10, 1960, p. 3.
40. Critics found other things to fault as well. The *New York Times* wearied of Illusion-O and all of Castle's gimmicks, wishing he "would forget all the monkey business" and make conventional thrillers instead. The *Washington Post* published a satirical review in which their columnist imagines taking a three- and four-year-old to see *13 Ghosts*. Afterwards the children, characterized as vastly more mature than the film, disparage Castle and his cynical money-grubbing as they drink martinis and make witty banter about Margaret Mead. Howard Thompson, "Screen: Haunted House '13 Ghosts' Arrives at Forum Theatre," *New York Times*, August 6, 1960, p. 9; Richard L. Coe, "One on the Aisle: A Square Born Every Minute," *Washington Post*, September 17, 1960, p. B14.
41. Mae Tinee, "'13 Ghosts' Movie Just Isn't Spooky," *Chicago Tribune*, August 1, 1960, p. B13.
42. Review of *13 Ghosts*, *Variety*, June 29, 1960, p. 9.
43. Stinson, "'13 Ghosts' Attempt Co-Op," p. 26.
44. Clepper, "'Death by Fright'," p. 77.
45. John L. Scott, "Robinson Wins Big Role in 'My Geisha': Star Will Play Studio Chief; Castle Buys 'Old Dark House,'" *Los Angeles Times*, November 4, 1960, p. A7.
46. "Castle Turns to Comedy," *Los Angeles Times*, June 13, 1962, p. C10.
47. Review of *13 Ghosts*, *BoxOffice*, June 27, 1960, p. 111; "Review Digest," *BoxOffice*, October 26, 1959, p. 173; "Review Digest," *BoxOffice*, October 26, 1959, p. 174; "Review Digest," *BoxOffice*, March 26, 1962, p. 120; "Review Digest," *BoxOffice*, March 26, 1962, p. 120. Industry reviews of *13 Ghosts* were typically kinder than reviews in the general press.
48. It assigned the genre "horror-comedy" sparingly. Two of the only other films around that time to receive it were *A Bucket of Blood* (1959) and *The Little Shop of Horrors* (1960). Review of *A Bucket of Blood*, *BoxOffice*, November 9, 1959, p. 185; review of *The Little Shop of Horrors*, *BoxOffice*, October 3, 1960, p. 165.
49. Review of *House on Haunted Hill*, *Variety*, December 3, 1958, p. 6.
50. Review of *Homicidal*, *Variety*, June 21, 1961, p. 20.
51. Tinee, "'13 Ghosts' Movie Just Isn't Spooky," p. B13.
52. *Spine Tingler! The William Castle Story*.
53. Clepper, "'Death by Fright'," p. 75.
54. In one interview he characterized *13 Ghosts* as "a horror story for children," while in another he predicted the film would have more appeal for adults than his previous work. Eugene Archer, "2 Top Stars Cast in Major Movies: Olivier to Be in 'Nuremberg' and Audrey Hepburn in 'Breakfast at Tiffany's,'" *New York Times*, May 25, 1960, p. 42; "Straight-From-the-Shoulder Selling Essential in Today's Market: Castle," *BoxOffice*, May 9, 1960, p. 10.

55. The appropriation of a mask in the likeness of a murder victim, previously worn by his murderer, now himself a murder victim, could be a disturbing moment in another film, but it is presented as a harmless boyish prank. Nothing serious sticks to *13 Ghosts*.
56. Murray Leeder, "The Humor of William Castle's Gimmick Films," in Cynthia J. Miller and A. Bowdoin Van Riper (eds.), *The Laughing Dead: The Horror-Comedy Film from Bride of Frankenstein to Zombieland* (Lanham, MD: Rowman & Littlefield, 2016), p. 90.
57. Ibid. p. 89.
58. William Paul, *Laughing Screaming: Modern Hollywood Horror and Comedy* (New York: Columbia University Press, 1994), p. 410.
59. Very young viewers might be frightened by the film, but criticism cannot be held hostage to the reactions of five-year-olds. Otherwise we would have to classify kindergarten and asparagus as horrific.
60. Noël Carroll, "Fiction, Non-Fiction, and the Film of Presumptive Assertion: A Conceptual Analysis," in Noël Carroll and Jinhee Choi (eds.), *Philosophy of Film and Motion Pictures: An Anthology* (Malden, MA: Blackwell, 2006), p. 162. For approaches to mockumentaries that proceed from different assumptions about documentary's relation to reality, see Alexandra Juhasz and Jesse Lerner (eds.), *F is for Phony: Fake Documentary and Truth's Undoing* (Minneapolis: University of Minnesota Press, 2006).
61. Review of *13 Ghosts*, BoxOffice, June 27, 1960, p. 111.
62. "Castle Film Slated for Summer Bookings," *Motion Picture Daily*, 16 May 1960, pp. 1–2. See also "Now You See Ghost; Now You Don't in Castle Film," *BoxOffice*, May 23, 1960, p. 30.
63. David Sanjek, "The Doll and the Whip: Pathos and Ballyhoo in William Castle's *Homicidal*," *Quarterly Review of Film and Video* 20.4 (2003): 252.
64. Carl Plantinga, *Moving Viewers: American Film and the Spectator's Experience* (Berkeley: University of California Press, 2009), p. 97.
65. They can also react with boredom or irritation, particularly if they wanted a horror film, but that would be uncooperative.
66. The language of my argument here rubs up against the terminology of Kendall L. Walton in "Fearing Fictions," *Journal of Philosophy* 75:1 (1978): 5–27, though we have distinct modes of audience reaction in mind. On my model, viewers of *13 Ghosts* can pretend to be scared (that is, willfully overreact or deliberately feign fear) because they lack the genuine fear experienced by normal viewers of successful horror films. Viewers who pretend to be scared in my sense will not experience common physiological horror-film reactions like sweaty palms or racing heart rates; nor will they feel an interior mental sensation of fright. Walton seeks a much wider ambit with his terminology. He contends that audiences of horror films are *never* scared and feel no real emotions in response to fictions. Instead they feel "quasi-fear" or "make-believe fear," which does entail fearful-seeming physiological symptoms like sweaty palms and racing heart rates; however, quasi-fear is not a real emotion because it lacks belief in the reality of the threat. On Walton's model, viewers who are quasi-afraid pretend to be scared (that is, they exhibit fearful-seeming symptoms and report they are afraid as part of an adult game of make-believe) because it is essentially impossible that they should ever be genuinely scared by a film. I think that this will not do as a general theory of horror spectatorship. Besides the incongruity with my felt experience of fear while watching horror films, there are numerous philosophical reasons to doubt Walton's account, summarized in Carroll, *Philosophy of Horror*, pp. 68–79.
67. I am unaware of another Castle production that fully deserves to be called mock-horror. *13 Ghosts* is unusual even within his eccentric filmography. Yet we find scattered

mock-horrific moments in his other work. *Homicidal* can elicit genuine fear with its bloody murders, while the Fright Break's terrified thudding heartbeat, meant to approximate our own, is an amusing overstatement, a pretense that at the moment the film is scaring us much more than it is.

CHAPTER 7

Chaos Made Flesh: *Mr. Sardonicus* (1961) and the Mask as Transformative Device

Alexandra Heller-Nicholas[1]

"My name was not always Sardonicus, and I did not always wear a mask."

The cult reputation of exploitation icon William Castle in large part stems from gimmicky commercial strategies such as Emergo, Percepto, and Illusion-O. Yet his 1961 horror film *Mr. Sardonicus* stands apart from many of the horror films he directed during this period in a crucial way. While it still contained a signature gimmick in the form of the Punishment Poll, the film relied less on Castle's lo-fi "technological" promotional attractions than on an artifact imbued with hugely potent cross-historical, social, and cultural value: the mask. This chapter explores the mask as itself a kind of technology or device central to *Mr. Sardonicus*, arguing for its knowing deployment as an object with an extraordinary capacity to evoke simultaneous anxieties and fascinations in Castle's audience. If masks are, as Georges Bataille has suggested, "chaos made flesh,"[2] the transformative potential embedded into the object itself (and related acts of masking and unmasking) in *Mr. Sardonicus* contains a symbolic aspect of transgression active within the film far darker and more complex than its more novel aspects might at first suggest.

Based on the 1961 short story "Sardonicus" by Ray Russell, the film follows London-based paralysis specialist Sir Robert Cargrave (Ronald Lewis), who is summoned to the fictional central European region of Gorslava by his ex-lover Maude (Audrey Dalton). Now Baroness Sardonicus, Maude requests Cargrave's presence on behalf of her husband, Baron Sardonicus (Guy Rolfe), but a note of desperation in her invitation causes concern for the doctor, who still has feelings for her. Traveling from the train station to the Baron's castle, Cargrave is simultaneously disturbed by his bleak surroundings and shaken by the nervousness of the stationmaster when Sardonicus's name was mentioned previously. Upon arrival, Cargrave is struck by both the barbaric experimentation with leeches that Sardonicus's assistant Krull (Oskar Komolka) enacts on a terrified servant girl, and by Maude's unusual behavior—and meeting the masked, abrasive Baron does little to assuage his suspicions. Sardonicus finally tells Cargrave his story: as an innocent, well-meaning yet poor man called Marek, he was desperate to appease his greedy wife Elenka (Erika Peteres). She demanded he exhume his dead father Henryk (Vladimir Sokoloff) to retrieve a winning lottery ticket from his waistcoat pocket. On doing so Marek was so traumatized by the shock of seeing his father's decomposed face that his own facial muscles contorted into a state of paralysis, freezing in a gruesome, terrifying imitation of a smile. Wishing to help Maude, and defaulting to his professional dedication to applying his specialist medical knowledge for the benefit of others, Cargrave agrees to help Sardonicus, but his experiments at first prove fruitless. After Sardonicus threatens Maude with harm if the doctor does not succeed, Cargrave tricks the Baron: while making a great display of continuing his medical experiments, he simply injects Sardonicus's face with water as a placebo and makes him face his father once again. Knowing that Sardonicus's paralysis was psychosomatic, Cargrave acts quickly and leaves for London with Maude after the cured Sardonicus happily agrees to an annulment. At the station they are stopped by Krull, who tells them that Sardonicus's face has now completely frozen and he is unable to open his mouth, with starvation imminent. Cargrave tells Krull this is easily solved: The Baron merely needs to be told that the condition was all in his imagination. Upon returning to the castle, Krull does not pass on this information to his abusive master, instead telling Sardonicus that he did not get to see the doctor in time. The film ends as Krull feasts merrily in front of Sardonicus, who, terrified, waits to starve to death.

The mask is a central motif in terms of both the construction of narrative and the creation of spectacle in *Mr. Sardonicus*. Castle had previously utilized the object in earlier films to varying degrees, suggesting a long-held, intuitive understanding of the mask's cultural impact that manifests most centrally in this film in particular. A fright-mask provides one of the many memorable scares in his legendary horror film *The Tingler* (1959), but he had much earlier utilized a lion mask to great effect in the opening scene of his film noir *When Strangers Marry* (1944). Although hardly ubiquitous across his filmography, Castle's use of masks is nonetheless typical of his palette of horror iconography: from the skeletons of *House on Haunted Hill* (1959) to the ethereal wailing she-spirit of *Thirteen Ghosts* (1960), Castle's *mise-en-scène* springs forth from a child's Halloween imaginary. "I have always been interested in horror ever since I was a kid," Castle told John Brosnan. "I think it started when I was about 6 years old."[3] As a ubiquitous ritual of the North American experience of childhood, Halloween and its symbols have long been associated with the social and cultural mechanics of mask-wearing, leading Jack Santino to designate Halloween as a key contemporary example of "public masquerade."[4] This chapter considers how these traditions of masks and mask-wearing manifest in *Mr. Sardonicus* as a transformative device, with particular emphasis on how it relates to the construction, and collapse, of identity, power, and morality.

BEYOND THE PUNISHMENT POLL

According to Castle himself, the inspiration for *Mr. Sardonicus* struck while on holiday in Hawaii with his family when he read Russell's story in the January 1961 issue of *Playboy* magazine. He immediately purchased the film rights to the story and hired Russell to write the screenplay.[5] The film and original story deviate in only a few ways: Joe Jordan suggests that the new addition of the death of Sardonicus's mother was a reference to the recent passing of Castle's own mother,[6] the only other major difference being in the figure of Krull, a combination of a number of nameless characters in the original story.[7] Filming in Hollywood on Columbia's sound stages, Castle sought to replicate the European mood of the film by hiring a British cast, building a set that was "a Gothic re-creation" and relying heavily on dry ice for foggy atmospherics.[8] Following the film's premiere in New York City on 18 October 1961, Howard Thompson's *New York Times* review was less than complimentary, although Jordan has noted that, "*Mr. Sardonicus* . . . and the Punishment Poll were a hit with the American public."[9]

It is the gimmick of the Punishment Poll for which, like most of Castle's films from this era, *Mr. Sardonicus* is most readily remembered. As Dana Harris noted, "for Castle, every movie meant a gimmick";[10] Todd McCarthy and Charles Flynn even christened him in 1975 "Mr. Gimmick," as "a trick device of some sort was invariably the key to the promotional campaigns for his horror films of the late 1950s and early 1960s."[11] Critical reappraisals of Castle's work tend to not only privilege his gimmick-centric films,[12] but also approach these gimmicks as a blanket, singular whole, the Punishment Poll tending to fall under the same taxonomical umbrella as Emergo in *House on Haunted Hill*, Percepto in *The Tingler*, and the "ghost viewer" glasses that were given to audiences of *Thirteen Ghosts*.[13] But there is some suggestion that by 1961, Castle's relationship to his gimmick-heavy brand was beginning to falter. Joe Jordan suggests that it was when discovering Russell's short story on holiday that the idea "to implement yet another creative gimmick" came to Castle,[14] but according to Castle himself the allure of gimmick-based films was starting to wear thin:

Besieged with the same question from theatre owners and audiences—"What's your next idea?"—and now being crowned "King of the Gimmicks," I decided it was time to try to abdicate my throne.

With *Mr. Sardonicus*, however, he stated: "the abdication was short."[15] After *Mr. Sardonicus*, this feeling returned when he moved onto his next project, *Strait-Jacket* (1964): "Having to create a new, fresh gimmick for each picture was becoming tiresome. Critics were now starting to attack, claiming the only reason my films were successful was the gimmicks, and I was unable to make an important thriller without one."[16] With the star power of Joan Crawford, Castle found a new draw card.

Castle's shift away from the gimmicks that had brought him so much success becomes apparent when considering the production history of *Mr. Sardonicus*: despite the close relationship of the Punishment Poll to the film in popular memory, the decision to include it was significantly made *after* the film's final cut.[17] Unlike Percepto in *The Tingler*, which was closely aligned to the film in both its sensorial experience and narrative logic, in *Mr. Sardonicus* the Punishment Poll is comparatively random: it could feasibly apply just as easily to *any* film with a villain. A similarly interactive idea of audience-as-jury had been deployed earlier by the popular 1940s radio series *Crime Doctor*, syndicated across the United States on CBS.[18] By his own account, Castle came to the idea of the Punishment Poll only *after* a falling out with Columbia:

Columbia had seen the final cut of the picture and demanded that I reshoot the final scene, which they cautioned would be unacceptable to audiences. In the scene in question, Sardonicus, unable to eat or drink because of his frozen grin, goes insane as he slowly and agonizingly dies. Columbia wanted a more palatable ending and insisted I let Mr. Sardonicus live. I refused adamantly, and just as adamantly they demanded another ending. During the stalemate, I suddenly realized that Columbia had unknowingly given me the gimmick for the picture. I would have two endings—Columbia's and mine—and let the audience decide for themselves the fate of Mr. Sardonicus.[19]

Consciously seeking to replicate "the thrill-hungry Roman crowds in the Circus Maximus,"[20] Castle appears near the film's conclusion and invites the audience to cast their final judgment. While Castle himself insisted that "contrary to some opinions (just in case the audience voted for mercy), we had the other ending,"[21] as Murray Leeder notes, this was all part of the Castle mythology: "the appearance of agency on the audience's part is a fiction: there was only one ending, for Castle knew no one would ever want him to live."[22] Suspending the privileging of the Punishment Poll as the central factor that drives audience engagement with *Mr. Sardonicus*, then, this chapter instead looks at the different ways the film engages with masks and masking in the context of the horror genre.

UNCANNY TRANSFORMATIONS: MASKS AND HORROR

The mask in horror cinema is a continuation of a multifaceted historical trajectory that continues the ritualistic and myth-making capacities linked to power, ideology, and identity for the many cultures across space and time that have a recorded history of privileging this object. A cursory consideration of the function of the mask in horror prompts associations with identity and anonymity that contain a function intrinsically narrative in nature. This logic reduces the utility of the horror mask to simply one of revelation and occlusion: a given villain is disguised until the mask is removed and their identity is revealed. While not wholly untrue, it is worth flagging from the outset that often in horror we know the identity of the mask wearer, and *Mr. Sardonicus* is a perfect example. A simplistic evaluation of the power of the mask in horror as one merely of an anonymity device elides the symbolic power of the object itself.

Numerous writers have emphasized the etymology of the term.[23] For Elizabeth Tonkin, it is significant that the English word "person" has its origins in the Latin term for mask, "persona."[24] For John W. Nunley and Cara McCarty, its origins can also be traced to the Arabic term *maskhara* (meaning to transform or falsify), while in Ancient Egypt the word *msk* specifically referred to leather as a kind of "second skin."[25] As Laura Makarius has noted, it is common for subjects of the Rorschach test to identify the random inkblots as masks, suggesting that human masks are an integral aspect of the collective human consciousness.[26] The very word "mask" doubles as both a verb and a noun: as the former, it pertains to what N. Ross Crumrine has identified "as the ritual transformation of the human actor into a being of another order."[27] In the case of Castle's film, this masked transformation from Marek to Baron Sardonicus is marked by a series of dramatic, narrative-propelling oppositions: wealth/poverty, villainy/innocence, abused spouse/abusive spouse.

In their status as faces-that-are-not-faces, there is at the most cursory level something fundamentally uncanny at play in the act of mask wearing. This notion is an important one when considering why the mask is such a strong tradition in horror: defined in Sigmund Freud's foundational essay "The Uncanny" as "that class of the frightening which leads back to what is known of old and long familiar,"[28] in practical terms, uncanny imagery in Gothic horror manifests in phenomena such as "repetitions, returns, *déjà vu*, premonitions, ghosts, doppelgangers, animated inanimate objects and severed body parts."[29] Like Gothic novels before them, masks in horror films in particular are riddled with the uncanny, "simultaneously frightening, unfamiliar and yet also strangely familiar."[30] The mask in horror, in its varied, diverse, and often aggressively perverse dual replication and replacement of the human face, fits precisely this model. For Bataille, the act of masking and unmasking contains both threat and danger: "that which is communicated by way of open faces is the reassuring stability of order, founded on the serene surface of the ground between men," he says. "But when the face is closed and covered by a mask, it no longer participates in stability or the ground." For Bataille, "the mask communicates incertitude and the menace of unexpected changes, unforeseeable and as insupportable as death. Its irruption liberates that which had been enchained for the maintenance of stability and order."[31]

Sardonicus's mask typifies its transgressive status as a face-that-is-not-a-face, marked by a broader uncanny quality of the object that, as Efrat Tseëlon observes, provokes a key tension, "a mixture of fascination and avoidance."[32] Masks are from this perspective the perfect subject for horror, as they strategically provoke dual, contradictory responses of captivation and repulsion. The manner in which Tseëlon articulates this tension reveals that it shares fundamental points of interest with horror cinema: "The mask stands in an intermediary position between different worlds," she says. "Its embodiment of the fragile dividing line between concealment and revelation, truth and artifice, natural and supernatural, life and death is a potent source of the mask's metaphysical power."[33] In the case of *Mr. Sardonicus*, through these binaries the mask physically demarcates the precise lines that split Marek from the Baron. As the manner by which he chooses to hide the disfiguring paralysis caused by his moral transgression (the defilement of his father's grave), an act thoroughly out of keeping with his past character, the Baron's mask acts as a complex transformative device. While superficially disguising his paralysis, it also marks his ethical deterioration, a symbol of his corrupted morals and the total change in personality from the innocent, browbeaten Marek to the evil, violent, and cruel Sardonicus. The mask, if not possessing him as such, stands as a physical symbol of his transformation into the monstrous. "The mask is simultaneously animated and inanimate, living and dead: an expressionless mass transformed into expressive being," says Tseëlon. "On its own it is a lifeless piece of matter . . . But as soon as the mask is worn . . . they come to life." She continues, "human interaction infuses them with spirit. The effect of the mask on the wearer is a well-known phenomenon in theatre and ritual: the wearer wishes to be identified with the mask they wear."[34]

This notion of identity is fundamental to *Mr. Sardonicus* and its construction of horror through the mask. That the film's power relations are so heavily governed by the bodily transformations of Marek/Sardonicus through the mask itself emphasizes just how closely related identity is to the face. For W. Anthony Sheppard, "the human face is the center of personal identity and expression," and he notes that "four of the five senses are centered on the face and much of both verbal and visual communication emanates from this region of the body."[35] Elizabeth Tonkin places a similar emphasis on the face as a fundamental communication interface, suggesting that it "is the main point at which human identity is communicated."[36] But the close physical relationship between the mask and the face should not belie the broader dynamics of how masked communication manifests. For Tseëlon, "when the face is covered, awareness shifts to the body and different registers are used. The lifelessness of any mask becomes strangely animated when the body moves."[37] It is in precisely in this manner that Baron Sardonicus's monstrosity is constructed, and the revelation of his distorted, grotesque face acts merely to confirm (in a visually explicit, spectacular manner) this reading of his character, rather than to be the sole basis for it.

The mask in *Mr. Sardonicus* is thus a transformative device that is fundamental to the film's thematic and narrative trajectory and, through acts of masking and unmasking, provides many of its key horror spectacles. Castle's film is not unique in this way, nor is this utilization of the mask in horror as a transformative device specific to earlier cinematic genre traditions. As horror writer and filmmaker Clive Barker notes in the introduction of Doug Bradley's book *Sacred Monsters: Behind the Mask of the Horror Actor*, when wearing a mask "the man disappears, and a creature of mythic proportions replaces him: some demon or divinity, a terrible intelligence."[38] As an actor and writer, Bradley (renowned for playing the iconic Pinhead in Barker's *Hellraiser* franchise) noted that this process of transformation is part of the very functionality of the object itself: "any person who picks up even the simplest mask and places it over their face has become something new," he says. "If that person now animates themselves and speaks through the mask, it is no longer him or her that we respond to, but this new character created by the mask."[39] Through his deployment of the mask, Castle actively mines the vast cross-cultural and historical potency of the object, one whose power in the context of the horror genre stems back (at least) to Edgar Allan Poe, the Grand Guignol theatre, and Lon Chaney's famous performance in *The Phantom of the Opera* (1925). Aware of these traditions and the inherent power contained therein, Castle deployed the mask as a central visual motif in *Mr. Sardonicus* with full force to form the foundations for a complex range of conceptual negotiations with issues of identity and duplicity, as we shall now see.

BEHIND THE MASK

Mr. Sardonicus opens as Big Ben chimes. For audiences missing the geographical reference, text appears on screen designating our time and place: "London

1880." Footsteps are heard through the foggy London night as ominous silhouettes rush about. William Castle passes the camera, approaching us in another frame as he tries to light a cigarette: "Confounded fog, makes the matches so damp, you know." We are, instantly, in on the joke: it's not London, it's not fog, but we're happy to go with it, the twinkle in Castle's eye all the invitation needed to play along. He knows we know the game, reminding us immediately, again, where we are supposed to think we are, and of his previous horror film: "this of course is London and I am William Castle . . . good to see you again, my homicidal friends." The Punishment Poll is not mentioned here, but Castle has something just as important to tell us as he introduces a story of a "different kind . . . an old-fashioned story, full of gallantry, and graciousness, and ghouls." The historical nature of the film to follow is marked by Castle himself in his cameo as a deviation from the predominantly contemporary contexts of his previous horror movies, but the "old-fashioned story" he wishes to tell is one he rushes to jokingly frame as essentially primal, defining the figure of the ghoul as he reads from a dictionary ("an evil being who robs graves and feeds on corpses") and joking, "ah yes, just an old-fashioned story!"

Historical horror films like *Mr. Sardonicus* were in vogue at the time of its release, notably Roger Corman's Edgar Allan Poe cycle; the opening credit sequence of *Mr. Sardonicus* is formally comparable to those films.[40] Cutting to Cargrave in his clinic, the film picks up its narrative action immediately after Castle's introduction and these opening credits. Upon arriving at Sardonicus's isolated castle, the film's central motif of facial disfigurement is foreshadowed by Cargrave's discovery of the servant girl Anna (Lorna Hansen) being tortured, leeches applied to her face as she screams in a macabre, medieval medical experiment undertaken by Krull on Sardonicus's orders. Despite his later claims to believe in science and the supremacy of the scientific intellect, this image of Anna belies Sardonicus's civilized claims: before he is even introduced, he is marked by a fundamentally violent barbarism. Further grand gestures continue to mark Sardonicus as inherently superstitious even before he is introduced: as Cargrave looks around Sardonicus's home, he is struck by the empty frames on the stairwell. "The Baron has disowned his forefathers in one magnificent gesture," Krull explains admiringly, the removal of the portraits yet again another foreshadowing of Sardonicus's corrupt obsession with faces, history, and identity.

This dynamic, of course, manifests most explicitly in the object of the mask. Castle shrewdly builds tension toward the revelation of Sardonicus's face by introducing the figure himself slowly and with great fanfare: The Baron is first shown (wearing the mask) at roughly the 25-minute point, the uncanny nature of the object emphasized by the striking contrast of his unmoving, blank visage with the sound of a voice emanating from underneath. Ten minutes later he is shown from behind, lying in bed, the plain white mask hanging from the end of the bed. While this is a simply constructed shot, its tension-building mechanics are important—the image acknowledges the presence of what is still currently absent, and thus effectively unimaginable: Sardonicus's face, something understood as so terrifying that it needs to be hidden. Indeed, the reveal of Sardonicus's face behind the mask occurs a whole fifty minutes into the film, the shock of which in large part hinges as much on the heavy make-up and prosthetics applied to actor Guy Rolfe as it does the precision with which the build-up to the revelation is made.

Importantly, Marek's face is shown in flashback before Sardonicus's face underneath the mask is revealed. As he tells Cargrave his story, Marek is presented as a notably contrasting figure to Sardonicus: he is sympathetic, desperate, and clearly the victim of his greedy wife. Surrendering to her insistent demand that he retrieves the winning lottery ticket from his father's buried corpse, Sardonicus confesses: "that night, Sir Robert, I became . . . a ghoul." Much is made within the film of the revelation of the father's corpse, particularly the deterioration of its face—again, continuing a fascination that builds tension and anxiety around the film's core enigma: what lies underneath Sardonicus's mask? The opening of his father's coffin itself acts as a kind of unmasking: a gesture privileged within the narrative that leads to a spectacular (horrific) reveal. Sardonicus describes the look on his father's decomposed face: "the dead lips drawn back in . . . a soul-shattering smile." As he goes home to his wife with the ticket, this same description can also apply to his now disfigured face. With Elenka having killed herself at the shock of his deformity, Marek cashes in the ticket, buys the title of Baron and invests in the best medical attention he can find, learning to speak again but achieving no success with his facial paralysis. Out of desperation he turns to folk remedies, and finally to Maude's ex-lover.

Much attention is paid in the film to Cargrave's experiments, initially through massage and then through elaborate procedures with animals and seemingly complex laboratory trials. Injecting Sardonicus with water and locking him in a mysterious room with the corpse of his father—"my nemesis, my demon," says the Baron—Cargrave's cure is fundamentally psychological as he tells his patient we "are going . . . into your past, Baron. Into your youth." After Cargrave and Maude's departure, the film is briefly interrupted with the bureaucracy of Castle's Punishment Poll, with the film then concluding with Krull's return to the Baron, ending with his joyful feasting as the terrified, frozen-faced Sardonicus prepares to starve to death. Liberated from the confines of his mask, the symbolic distortion of Sardonicus, now with his face returned to its previous aesthetic status, has remained – his ethical disfigurement stains his very notion of self. Although seemingly "cured," he is marked in his return to his previous appearance by lingering guilt at his own transgressions, beginning with the ghoulish exhumation of his father's corpse and amplified by his viciousness and violence not only to Krull, Anna, and Maude, but to what is suggested to be a parade of beautiful, unsuspecting young female villagers who also fall prey to his sadism. The mask off, the face restored, *Mr. Sardonicus* concludes with a sense that the transformative power of the object has transcended its materiality, its sustained power drilling deep down into the Baron's own subconscious and sense of self. His desperation to transcend physical ugliness has destroyed his very humanity.

DUPLICITY, TRANSFORMATION, AND HUMANITY

It is in this sense of the mask in *Mr. Sardonicus* as a transformative device that the film engages with an enduring fascination across Castle's horror films with doubling and duplicity—not merely in the films he directed during this period, but of course also in Roman Polanski's *Rosemary's Baby* (1968), which Castle famously produced. For David Sanjek, "a curious kind of surrogate appears in virtually all of Castle's self-produced feature films in that a character or set of characters within the narrative attempts to deceive other individuals in order to accomplish a particular (and often deadly) end." He continues, "the charades perpetuated by the characters turn out to be, like Castle's press campaigns, either hollow or successful only insofar as they bring about a limited and predetermined end."[41] *Mr. Sardonicus* from this perspective complicates the notion of duplicity through the centrality of the mask: the object itself, as a covering of the Baron's 'true' appearance, is of course a disguise, a deception. The doubling in the film hinges around the transformation of Marek into Sardonicus, one that the film's conclusion suggests is irreversible: the personality changes that occurred alongside the necessity of wearing the mask have outlasted on a psychosomatic level the physical disfigurement the mask was at first employed to conceal. It is perhaps ironic, then, that Sardonicus is ultimately revealed as ultimately not being capable of *any* return to an ethical status quo: the mask may be a symbol of his transformation, but the act of *un*masking (when the need to conceal is no longer necessary) is rendered ultimately futile. As Cargrave notes, the cause of the physical alteration was in Sardonicus's head all along.

Mr. Sardonicus destabilizes the relationship between the face and identity in other ways beyond the Baron's mask. Most notable of these is in a nightmare Cargrave has after his first meeting with Sardonicus on his first night in the castle, featuring what Jordan calls a "phantasmagoric series of floating heads."[42] Different characters' disembodied heads appear floating in a black space above his bed, speaking of young women and medical experiments, combined with the privileged repetition of Maude's phrase that Cargrave's visit is "most urgent to my wellbeing." As Jordan observes, "the order in which the heads are displayed is noteworthy,"[43] beginning with the stationmaster (Charles H. Radilak and his puzzling statement to Cargrave of his fear of the Baron that "You would not understand. You are young. You do not yet have daughters." Next is Anna and her hope that the gruesome medical experiments to which she has been a victim will cease. Third is Krull, reiterating his devotion to his master; then the sequence returns again to Anna, this time screaming in pain, before cutting to Maude. The final disembodied head shown before Cargrave awakens is, significantly, Sardonicus himself: as the character who most literally renders a disruptive disconnection between face and self, it is his appearance that shakes Cargrave the most.

The horror of the Baron, and of *Mr. Sardonicus* more broadly, is explicitly linked to this transgressive disconnection between face and identity. Of all the kinds of masks Castle could have selected, that he chose a blank white mask cannot be underplayed. One can reasonably speculate that it was in some part at least inspired by Georges Franju's *Eyes Without a Face* (*Les yeux sans visage*, 1960), released the previous year, but in the context of *Mr. Sardonicus* itself it makes perfect sense: from the Noh mask of Japanese theatrical traditions to that of Michael Myers in the *Halloween* (1978–) series, the blank mask offers a space bereft of meaning, a receptacle or canvas ready for inscription. Through gesture, action, and performance, the blank mask acts as an interface that defies traditional ways of "reading" faces, challenging our reliance upon the interpretation of faces as a mode of communication. Rather, the very emptiness of the blank mask, in horror in particular, speaks of the dreadful possibility that there is nothing *to* be read; that the mask reflects nothing but a hollow, emotionally barren and fundamentally inhuman emptiness. Through the mask, it is ultimately the very notion of humanity itself that lies at the heart of *Mr. Sardonicus*: the loss of it, the search for it, and its profound and inescapable connection to identity and a sense of self.

NOTES

1. The author would like to acknowledge support received for this chapter through an Australian Government Research Training Program Scholarship.
2. Georges Bataille, "The Mask," *LVNG* 10 (2002): 63–7.
3. John Brosnan, *The Horror People* (New York: St. Martin's Press, 1976), p. 137.
4. Jack Santino, "Flexible Halloween: Longevity, Appropriation, Multiplicity, and Contestation," in Hugh O'Donnell and Malcolm Foley (eds.), *Treat or Trick?: Halloween in a Globalising World* (Newcastle: Cambridge Scholars, 2009), p 12.
5. William Castle, *Step Right Up! I'm Gonna Scare the Pants Off America* (New York: G. P. Putnam's Sons, 2010), Kindle edition, p. 131.
6. Castle, *Step Right Up!*, p. 392.
7. Joe Jordan, *Showmanship: The Cinema of William Castle* (Albany, GA: Bear Manor Media, 2014), 271.
8. Castle, *Step Right Up!*, p. 131.

9. Howard Thompson, "*Five Golden Hours* and *Mr. Sardonicus* in Multiple Openings," *The New York Times*, October 19, 1961, <www.nytimes.com/movie/review?_r=1&res=9402E2D6113DE733A2575AC1A9669D946091D6CF&partner=Rotten%2520Tomatoes> (accessed October 19, 2017).
10. Dana Harris, "Castle: The King," *Variety*, November 4–10, 2002, p. 90.
11. Todd McCarthy and Charles Flynn (eds.), *Kings of the Bs: Working Within the Hollywood System: An Anthology of Film History and Criticism* (New York: E. P. Dutton, 1975), p. 287.
12. Marc Olivier, "Gidget Goes Noir: William Castle and the Teenage Phone Fatale," *The Journal of Popular Film and Television* 41.2 (2013): 41–52.
13. See, for example, David Sanjek, "The Doll and the Whip: Pathos and Ballyhoo in William Castle's *Homicidal*," *Quarterly Review of Film and Video* 20.4 (2003): 247–63 (254).
14. Jordan, *Showmanship*, p. 269.
15. Castle, *Step Right Up!*, p. 131.
16. Ibid. p. 133.
17. Ibid. p. 132.
18. Jordan, *Showmanship*, p. 409.
19. Castle, *Step Right Up!*, p. 132.
20. Ibid.
21. Ibid.
22. Murray Leeder, "Collective Screams: William Castle and the Gimmick Film," *Journal of Popular Culture* 44.4 (2001): 774–96.
23. See, for example, Simon Shepherd and Mick Wallis, *Drama / Theatre / Performance* (London: Routledge, 2004), esp. pp. 179–84.
24. Elizabeth Tonkin, "Mask," in Richard Bauman (ed.), *Folklore, Cultural Performances, and Popular Entertainments: A Communications-Centered Handbook* (Oxford: Oxford University Press, 1992), p. 225.
25. John W. Nunley and Cara McCarty, *Masks: Faces of Culture* (New York: Harry N. Abrams, Inc., 1999), p. 15.
26. Laura Makarius, "The Mask and the Violation of Taboo," in N. Ross Crumrine and Marjorie Halpin (eds.), *The Power of Symbols: Masks and Masquerade in the Americas* (Vancouver: University of British Columbia Press, 1983), p. 201.
27. N. Ross Crumrine, "Masks, Participants, and Audience," in N. Ross Crumrine and Marjorie Halpin (eds.), *The Power of Symbols: Masks and Masquerade in the Americas* (Vancouver: University of British Columbia Press, 1983), p. 1.
28. Sigmund Freud, "The Uncanny," in *The Standard Edition of the Complete Psychological Works of Sigmund Freud, Volume XVII (1917–1919): An Infantile Neurosis and Other Works* (London: Hogarth, 1919), p. 219.
29. Helen Wheatley, "Television," in William Hughes, David Punter, and Andrew Smith (eds.), *The Encyclopedia of the Gothic* (Malden: John Wiley & Sons, 2016), p. 667.
30. John Bowen, "Gothic Motifs: Discovering Literature: Romantics and Victorians," *British Library*, n.d., <http://www.bl.uk/romantics-and-victorians/articles/gothic-motifs#sthash.LaaeSoS4.dpuf> (accessed October 19, 2017).
31. Bataille, "The Mask," p. 265.
32. Efrat Tseëlon, "Reflections on Mask and Carnival," in Efrat Tseëlon (ed.), *Masquerade and Identities: Essays on Gender, Sexuality and Marginality* (London: Routledge, 2001), p. 20.
33. Ibid.
34. Ibid. p. 21.

35. Anthony W. Sheppard, *Revealing Masks: Exotic Influences and Ritualized Performance in Modernist Music Theater* (Berkeley: University of California Press, 2002), p. 27.
36. Tonkin, "Mask," p. 226.
37. Tseëlon, "Reflections on Mask and Carnival," p. 22.
38. Doug Bradley, *Sacred Monsters: Behind the Mask of the Horror Actor* (London: Titan Books, 1996), p. 8.
39. Ibid. p. 12.
40. Corman's Poe cycle ran from 1959 to 1964 and was made up of eight films, seven of which starred Castle's collaborator on *The Tingler* and *House on Haunted Hill*, Vincent Price: *House of Usher* (1960), *The Pit and the Pendulum* (1961), *The Premature Burial* (1962), *Tales of Terror* (1962), *The Raven* (1963), *The Haunted Palace* (1963), *The Masque of the Red Death* (1964), and *The Tomb of Ligeia* (1964).
41. Sanjek, "The Doll and The Whip."
42. Jordan, *Showmanship*, p. 275.
43. Ibid.

PART 3

Castle, Authorship, and Genre

CHAPTER 8

A Sick Mind in Search of a Monstrous Body: William Castle and the Emergence of Psychological Horror in the 1960s

Steffen Hantke

BEYOND THE GIMMICK: WILLIAM CASTLE'S DUBIOUS SUCCESS

While William Castle helped to create a model for the horror film that would move horror during the 1960s from its technological Cold War anxieties to a psychological foundation with broad appeal and lasting cultural relevance, he is doomed to be remembered for something else. His fondness for surrounding his films with gimmicks (and, in turn, the fondness of his fans for that fondness) has come to dominate the perception of Castle's films to a degree that, for the longest time, critical assessment based on attentive close reading was the exception to the rule of Castle scholarship. Granted, Castle's inventiveness remains impressive when taken on its own terms. Peter Hutchings has compiled a list of some of the more memorable of Castle's gimmicks, among them "insuring against anyone dying from fright during screenings of his 1958 film *Macabre*"; and "a plastic skeleton suspended on wires being pulled across the front of the auditorium at a climactic moment [of *House on Haunted Hill* (1959)]."[1] For *The Tingler* (1959), a film about "the search for the physiological origins of fear,"[2] Castle devised a device he called "Percepto": "In what must be the ultimate direct audience address, the monster is turned loose in a movie theater at the film's climax as the actual theater seats begin to vibrate from small motors installed under many of the seats."[3] When the film's eponymous creature is announced to have escaped in the theatre, "a planted female in the auditorium screams in sync with the woman in the film, and the projectionist turns up the house lights as the image goes black ... ushers run down the aisles and place the 'fainted' woman onto a stretcher."[2] As tactical efforts of self-consciously positioning films in the marketplace, these gimmicks are not to be underappreciated. Aside from Hutchings' own observations about the interplay between horror and humor as a model of spectatorship in general,[5] Joan Hawkins has commented on the "Bakhtinian marketplace mood" that surrounds much of horror cinema as a cultural phenomenon,[6] while Ben Kooyman has shown how Castle constructs and cultivates a star persona on a par with those generated for actors and actresses within the Hollywood star system.[7]

Opposed to this appreciation of Castle's sheer inventiveness, however, critical consensus has it that Castle was, at best, a mediocre director. His films do not measure up on their cinematic merits to those produced and directed by his contemporaries working in the same or adjacent genres, like Robert Aldrich and Henri-Georges Clouzot. This is especially obvious in direct comparison with Alfred Hitchcock, with whom Castle shared a penchant for showmanship and self-stylization. Unlike Hitchcock, whose precarious connection to horror was to elevate the genre, Castle is said to have contributed to its decline in the 1950s by turning horror into "a despised teenage exploitation genre wielded like a blunt instrument."[8] In his memoirs, Robert Bloch, author of the novel *Psycho* and scriptwriter for Castle's *Strait-Jacket* (1964), calls Castle "a sort of Minor-league Alfred Hitchcock."[9] Accusations of this type against Castle cite particularly the gimmicks in support of their claim that his taste ran toward the garish. Similarly insistent is the criticism that Castle is derivative. Joseph Maddrey considers Castle's *Homicidal* (1961) "a shameless rip-off of *Psycho*," and points out that the "murder-by-fright plot [of Castle's *Macabre* (1958)] was modeled on [Clouzot's] *Diabolique* [1955]."[10] Kevin Heffernan goes back even further in tracking down Castle's shameless plundering of sources: "The motif of the silent theater and the terrified, mute heroine [in *The Tingler*] was 'borrowed' by screenwriter White from *The Spiral Staircase* (1946)."[11] Peter Shelley, in his discussion of *The Night Walker* (1964) ("silly but fun"), quotes Phil Hardy's condemnation of the film as "ludicrously contrived" and "shoddy," and dismisses its maker for "once again trying to be Hitchcock."[12] Instead of critically interrogating the influences that cross back and forth among these directors, the critical consensus has little appreciation for Castle as a creative mind. From broad plot contrivances to specific scenes, Castle is supposed to have helped himself freely from superior work by his contemporaries, distracting from, or making up for, the lack of originality by wrapping the films in gimmicks that would garner more attention than the films themselves.

Assuming that the critical consensus about the lack of originality in Castle's work is correct, an analysis of his films as mere cultural artifacts would still do justice to Castle's contribution to a larger historical transformation, a paradigm change, within the horror film between the late 1950s and early 1960s. The period of William Castle's work that marks this paradigm change begins with *Macabre* and then continues, in tight sequence, with the series of films including *The Tingler*, *House on Haunted Hill*, *Thirteen Ghosts* (1960), *Mr. Sardonicus* (1961), *Homicidal*, *The Old Dark House* (1963), *Strait-Jacket*, *The Night Walker*, and *I Saw What You Did* (1965). In all of these films, Castle's derivativeness would be an asset to the critical project of reading him as a representative figure of horror's paradigm change during this period. It would exactly be his lack of originality that would place him, without an overly idiosyncratic auteurist style muddying the critical waters, among directors like Hitchcock, Aldrich, and Clouzot, who are driving forward this change. Looking at Castle's membership among their ranks would help to identify a set of shared thematic and stylistic characteristics in the horror film at that moment, just as Castle's career as director and producer would align itself with a larger internal rearrangement of modes within the horror genre during which the historical dominant of the previous period was yielding to a new model. As in the genre at large, this paradigm shift in Castle's work does not present itself as a neat sequence in which one model replaces the other as a clearly discernible singular event. Instead, Castle plays to the different paradigms simultaneously, serving both residual and emergent audiences and their tastes at the same time. Despite these complex historical permutations, however, an overview of Castle's films during this period reveals how as a producer and director, Castle works through the available models of the horror film and, in the process, helps to zero in on what was to become the dominant model of the horror film for its next cycle. To trace the progress of this transition is one of the goals of the following discussion; to describe the emergent dominant of horror for the 1960s, the psychological horror film, is another.

Assessing Castle's gimmicks is an important part of this project. Since Castle's reputation seems doomed to rest on his creative use of gimmicks, the discussion will return to these devices in its final turn. The goal here will be to demonstrate that Castle, as a filmmaker with a high degree of auteurist autonomy, is conscious of the paradigm change within the horror genre, and that his deployment of gimmicks is consciously addressing the implications of changing paradigms. Underlying this contention are two aspects of Castle's work recurring across a variety of films from the period: the films' thematic engagement with the question of how abnormal psychology is concretely embodied, and the use of devices that break the fourth wall for the audience yet still reflect the same question of embodiment the films themselves are dealing with. In this manner, the gimmicks that made Castle famous and have endeared him to his fans to the present day function not as a matter of camp or cult, or as the means of authorial self-representations, but as critical reflections on an integral problem of the psychological horror film, both at the moment of its emergence as a historical dominant in the 1960s and for its lasting heritage to the present day.

CASTLE AROUND 1960: WORKING THROUGH THE HORROR FILM

The period immediately preceding Castle's peak of production was dominated by a paradigm from which all 1960s horror tried to distance itself as the old paradigm was collapsing under the weight of prolonged exposure, overfamiliarity, creative exhaustion, and growing topical irrelevance. This paradigm is characterized by the merging of horror and science fiction, as Cold War anxieties are manifested in contemporary settings, both domestic and political (and frequently military), in the form of monstrous mutations.[13] This old paradigm makes one final appearance in Castle's films around the turn of the decade with *The Tingler*. Vincent Price plays a scientist whose private research attempts to locate the physical origin of fear in the human body. This leads to the discovery and liberation of a creature wrapped around the spine and concealed within the human body. The film is driven by a sense of the crucial importance and vague menace of technology, its eponymous creature a physical manifestation of pharmaceutically enhanced human emotions. Though this central metaphor of externalized and embodied anxieties already announces Castle's reliance on psychology as a site of the monstrous, the film works perfectly as an example of 1950s technohorror in retaining its emphasis on the physical embodiment of abjection in the form of the monstrous creature elicited by science gone haywire. While the creature itself, framed unequivocally within the discourse of science, recapitulates the previous cycle of horror films, as does the film's contemporary urban and suburban setting, Vincent Price's scientist reaches back even further, beyond the paradigm of institutional 1950s technoscience. A throwback to the mad scientists of the 1930s and 40s, Price's character, Dr. Warren Chapin, is operating in isolation from institutional and politicized frameworks, a mad loner fearlessly experimenting on himself. In these respects, *The Tingler* is an oddity among Castle's films from the period—a farewell to the previously dominant tropes and concepts as Castle, and other directors and producers at the time, are searching for the next thing in horror.

Alongside the farewell to 1950s technohorror with *The Tingler*, Castle's films from the late 1950s and early 1960s also revisit the true and tested Gothic trope of the haunted house, with *House on Haunted Hill*, *Thirteen Ghosts*, and *The Old Dark House*. The films make various efforts to transfer this trope from its European origins into the historical present. The mansion in *Thirteen Ghosts* is a specimen of California Gothic in glorious decay, much like the Bates house in Hitchcock's *Psycho*, just as the building in *House on Haunted Hill* harks back to the radical American modernism first glimpsed in Edgar Ulmer's *The Black Cat* (1934). *The Old Dark House* is an actual remake of James Whale's original classic (1932), and its basic formula refers back even further to *The Cat and the*

Canary, earlier adapted by Paul Leni in 1927 and by Elliott Nugent in 1939, and other early proto-horror films in which genre conventions have not fully settled yet. The farcical humor and generic impurity in these early horror films, which ironically fracture the abject imagery and undercut the affective immersion necessary for achieving horror as an emotional response in the viewer, is congenial with Castle's understanding that the Gothic trope is too dated for straight dramatic appropriation. Whale and Ulmer, and even more so Leni and Nugent, do not trust the trope of the haunted house in its traditional Gothic manifestation quite yet; Castle does not any more.

In all three of Castle's films, the tropes of horror are quite self-consciously bracketed as citations. The films frame the central plot contrivance, the overnight stay in the haunted house, as a game, staged and supervised by an eccentric millionaire as an absent author akin to the films' director. *The Old Dark House* traffics largely in clichés of British eccentricity, placing a hapless American character at the center of the overfamiliar family plot and its accompanying murders and mayhem. *Thirteen Ghosts* revisits the classic ghost story's trope of the supernatural detective (as in Algernon Blackwood or William Hope Hodgson), rewarding the scientific investigation into the supernatural haunting with the revelation that, yes, there really *are* ghosts, but that the greedy lawyer, willing to murder a child in exchange for grabbing the fortune hidden in the house, is the real monster of the film. Castle's choice of collaborators underscores this ironic revisiting of the horror genre: the opening credits to *The Old Dark House* are designed by Charles Addams, famous creator of the *Addams Family* cartoons, just as the eccentric housekeeper in *Thirteen Ghosts* is, quite self-consciously, cast with Margaret Hamilton (of *The Wizard of Oz* [1939] fame), her character referred to by others in the film simply as "the witch."

The casting of Vincent Price, perhaps the most crucial actor in horror films at that moment, in *The Tingler* and *House on Haunted Hill* also links Castle's films to the larger cycle of horror films revisiting classic 1930s Universal horror at the start of the 1960s. Starting with *House of Usher* (1960), Price was to become the face of a series of Poe adaptations by director and producer Roger Corman, which marked the turning away from contemporary settings in favor of Gothic extravaganza.[14] Lending themselves to camp readings, Price's overwrought performances were to complete the films' conspicuous antiquarianism, which manifests itself in vaguely European locations and historical settings, and the claptrap that had been a staple of horror since its Gothic beginnings in the late eighteenth century. Corman's films gleefully embrace all of it, from the castles, the portraits with the moving eyes, and the brooding aristocratic Byronic heroes, to the pathetic fallacies of dark and stormy nights and the supernatural chestnut of the family curse. Castle's haunted house films profit from this brief resurgence of traditional Gothic tropes as much as Corman's do. But between the two, it is Castle whose treatment of the trope shows a more self-conscious acknowledgment that viewers who have lived through the 1950s can hardly take these tropes seriously any longer.

Ironically enough, the film that marks the transition from historicizing Gothic horror to contemporary psychological horror is a film with a historical setting: *Mr. Sardonicus*. Much like Hammer horror films and Corman's Poe adaptations throughout the 1960s, *Mr. Sardonicus* reaches back to the nineteenth century, moving from enlightened Victorian England to the far reaches of Europe as its physician protagonist travels to meet his former love, now married to the film's eponymous Byronic hero. In Ray Russell, author of the film's source material, Castle found a collaborator similarly uninterested in contemporary settings. "There was something about this latter half of the Twentieth Century," Russell's narrator in the novella "Sagittarius" complains, "with its sports cars and television and nuclear bombs and cold wars—that just did not jibe with the flamboyant alchemy, the mysterious powders. The exotic elixirs, the bubbling, old-fashioned retorts and demijohns of Dr. Jekyll's and Mr. Hyde's."[15] As Russell's transition into an archaic, picturesque, and arcane vocabulary in the latter half of this statement suggests, there is an argument to be made for an audience no longer stirred by the anxieties of industrial modernity or the Cold War (or at least tired with hearing them discussed in literal representational terms). Unlike Castle's three "haunted house" films, however, *Mr. Sardonicus* is ultimately in pursuit of something beyond the claptrap of exhausted Gothic conventions. It approaches its subject matter with dramatic seriousness, and it is against the backdrop of this seriousness that Castle's transition to psychological horror unfolds.[16]

Mr. Sardonicus illustrates that in the transitional phase during which psychological horror was to emerge as a historical dominant, it would prove itself compatible with the waning historicizing Gothic model. To the extent that Corman's and the Hammer Studios' films would share the psychological horror film's interest in "psychological disturbance" and investment in a "vague psychoanalytic explanation locating the cause of madness in [a] character's earlier developing sense of sexual identity,"[17] the two subgenres would exist peacefully. Regardless of its historical setting, *Mr. Sardonicus* would first move Castle into the dark territory of the human mind.

THE TURN TO PSYCHOLOGICAL HORROR

Psychological horror, as defined by Hitchcock and Castle, is based on a concept of horror that locates the site of anxiety and abjection within the human mind. It foregoes the technophobia that had driven the cycle of techno-horror films that dominated the 1950s, just as it foregoes the supernatural, even though it remains interested in the possibilities of generating uncanny ambiguity and uncertainty from both the supernatural and the technological. Monstrosity and abjection, to the degree that they are located within the human mind, potentially move horror from the margins or the outside the community, i.e. from a clearly demarcated space of the other, into the space of the self or the heart of the community, continuing a long cultural tradition of detecting and conceptualizing the insanity and derangement that may conceal themselves beneath the surface of normality. With Alfred Hitchcock's *Psycho* ("the film that lent the most legitimacy to horror in the 1960s")[18] as the cycle's initiating event, America in general, and California in particular, would quickly become the epitome of this bright contemporary normality, and thus simultaneously of its dark psychological underbelly. Abandoning the archaic in favor of the modern, psychological horror can insist on the bright daylight of the contemporary world. Monstrosity, once the deceptive ordinariness and normality are stripped away from the human body in which it hides itself, poses the problem of how best to represent itself. The psychological horror film is driven by finding creative solutions to this representational problem.[19]

The plot in *Mr. Sardonicus* revolves around a surgeon, Sir Robert Cargrave (Ronald Lewis), summoned to cure the facial disfigurement of the film's eponymous villain (Guy Rolfe), a rictus reminiscent of that modeled famously by Conrad Veidt in *The Man Who Laughs* (1928). At first glance, the film is very much preoccupied with this hideous deformity as well as other material trappings of the Gothic: the Gothic mansion not unlike those haunted houses in other Castle films, the main character's cruelty toward his wife and physical torture of the innocent designed to coerce the surgeon into compliance, and so on. It is on this level that the film appears to relapse into those Gothic tropes that Castle's haunted house films had already ironically dismissed. On closer inspection, however, *Mr. Sardonicus* transfers its interest from these external aspects to the psychological dimension of the characters. In this dimension, the material reality of the body and the less immediately accessible dimension of the mind perform an odd pivot. As it turns out, the origins of Sardonicus's facial disfigurement are located in an Oedipal trauma triggered by having witnessed the abject spectacle of his father's decaying corpse (glimpsed during the act of grave robbery that laid the foundations for Sardonicus's present wealth). It is, by common parlance, a psychosomatic ailment, and thus beyond both the grasp of allegorical morality (as in the classic Gothic) and pharmaceutical technology (as in the 1950s horror-film cycle). The final disambiguation, which pulls the narrative firmly into the realm of the psychological, reassures viewers that there are natural explanations for past events mistakenly assumed to be supernatural; that there are, in other words, psychological explanations for phenomena easily mistaken to be purely physical, bodily, or technological. In the film's final plot twist, the surgeon installs a new trauma at the core of his villainous patient, condemning him to a miserable, short life in agony as revenge for the suffering he used to inflict on the woman for which both characters have been competing. While Cargrave demonstrates that his science, wielded cruelly and immorally, commands just as much the power of abjection as the spectacle of the decaying corpse, Sardonicus is turned into the abject spectacle of being a walking corpse himself.

As ingeniously as the film moves the conventional Gothic into the realm of psychological horror, Castle's first psychological horror film with a genuinely contemporary setting, *Homicidal* (1961), confirms to what critics have criticized as his indebtedness to Hitchcock. Whether driven by crass commercial purposes or testifying to admiration for the "master of suspense," the similarities between *Homicidal* and Hitchcock's work well beyond *Psycho* are striking. *Homicidal* features a cool blonde (by the 1960s, a signature trait on Hitchcock's part) who reacts in a moment of sexual panic (not unlike the one to come in *Marnie*) to the attempts of a man to kiss her with a violent murder (reaching as far back as *Blackmail*). During her escape from the murder scene, she erroneously assumes herself to be pursued by a police car (*Psycho*). Arrived back at her house, she ascends a long staircase reminiscent of the one in *Psycho* where insurance investigator Arbogast comes to a grisly end. And, not surprisingly, there is a demanding older woman in that house whose inertness in a wheelchair and muteness conjures up Norman Bates's mother.[20]

As *Homicidal* works its way through permutations of the Hitchcockian formula, Castle sets up character configurations reminiscent of *Psycho*. Miriam Webster (Patricia Breslin) and Karl Andersen (Glenn Corbett) function as the model of heteronormativity akin to Sam and Leila in *Psycho*, while Warren/Emily (both played by "Jean Arless") provide the grotesque other akin to Norman/Mrs. Bates (with that inquisitive policeman thrown in to fill the role of Arbogast). Based on these characters, *Homicidal* lays out a murder plot that revolves around Warren/Emily and his/her gender confusion, and the deliberate and strategic deferment of its revelation to the audience, as much as *Psycho* does. The final wrap-up and belated explanatory exposition, in which the police officer does the job of the psychiatrist at the end of *Psycho*, reveals a plot twist in which the film differs from *Psycho* and returns to Castle's preference for the relativization or even demystification of the seemingly supernatural. Unlike *Psycho*, which focuses on the psychological to the complete exclusion of any pragmatic cause of violent crime, *Homicidal* ultimately hinges on Warren's plans to inherit his father's estate—the exclusive prerogative of the male heir to the estate. Emily, as it turns out, is merely a pragmatic construct invented by Warren, who needs a front for committing the murders necessary to clearing the path to the inheritance.[21]

The cross-dressing by which the murderous Emily transforms into Warren is carefully concealed in two complementary scenes in which both characters are seen undressing, both presented in a long shot through a door frame which

Figure 8.1 Jean Arless contemplating the fluidity of gender roles in *Homicidal*.

pretends to provide visual evidence but, in reality, carefully conceals it. Each scene is aborted before the body is fully revealed lest it give away its subject's true sex. But in the scene that shows Emily undressing, we hear Warren speak from the bed, where he is visible only as a vague shape. In the closing credits there is a brief scene designed as a dramatic reveal in which Warren and Emily come out and, in a seamless split-screen shot creating the illusion of a single continuous space, take a simultaneous bow. Both characters are identified as having been "played by Jean Arless." The fact that behind this pseudonym is the actress Joan Marshall playfully continues the gender confusion, undercutting the revelatory power of the breaking of the fourth wall (Figure 8.1). As much as the film's inheritance plot pulls back from the pathology of cross-dressing and murder, these gestures return the audience to the psychological dimension of the film, most notably to their own interest in or fascination with observing the ambiguously gendered performance.

While most of Castle's maneuvering around the true identity of Warren/Emily depends on the management of visual information, the film's crucial dimension is auditory. In a number of scenes, Castle shoots Warren from behind, obscuring his face as he "speaks," or has Warren speak from off screen as Castle moves the camera around or reframes to bring him into the shot. Apart from withholding visual information, the effect of this peculiar blocking strategy is strangely uncanny, separating the dubbed-in male voice even further from the female body that is performing Warren in drag. At first glance, Castle's interest in the auditory, his separation of Emily/Warren's voice from the actual body of the actress, is, as much else in *Homicidal*, reminiscent of the way Hitchcock handles the double identity of Norman Bates and his (late) mother in *Psycho*. But while this maneuvering around the sources of sound and their authenticating power fails to return in Hitchcock's work as a pervasive theme, Castle's interest in the dissociation of voices from their originating bodies comes across as a preoccupation beyond the confines of this single film.

The eponymous character in *Mr. Sardonicus*, for example, initially comes across as a speaking voice from behind the mask he wears to conceal his hideously deformed face. The mask covers that part of his face afflicted directly by the rictus—the mouth. Once the surgeon has healed his psychosomatic ailment, the character is plunged into silence as soon as the medical procedure allows him to remove the mask. The narrative of the entire film traces the development by which Sardonicus goes from being a voice without a body to being a body without a voice. Another version of this theme appears in *The Tingler*. Critic Kevin Heffernan has pointed out that the "performance of Judith Evelyn as Martha is the centerpiece of the film, and her neurotic pantomime [as her deaf character attempts in vain to articulate her state of terror in a liberating scream] (screenwriter White gives her a full range of obsessive and phobic tics) sets her off from all of the other characters in the film." Her distinguishing feature, Heffernan suggests, is her connection to sound by way of her voice: "She is, in the words of film critic Tim Lucas, 'truly a silent character in a sound movie', and her association with the silent-movie theater establishes a narrative justification for both her ultimate death by fright and her tingler's eventual 'escape' into the theater to set up the Percepto stunt."[22]

The earliest film in the cycle, *Macabre*, already anticipates this thematic preoccupation. Its plot hinges on a phone call—this one made by a kidnapper who has abducted a little girl and buried her alive, leaving the father and a number of ancillary characters to find her in time before, presumably, she runs out of oxygen and suffocates in her buried coffin. The film's central plot twist—a plot twist construed as so surprising and crucial that the film ends with a tagged-on address to the audience asking them not to reveal the ending to anyone who has not yet seen the film (a device imitated by Hitchcock two years later in the ad campaign for *Psycho*)—is that this phone call is a doubly disembodied voice. The kidnapper's voice is mediated once by the telephone and once by tape recorder, by which the voice turns out to have been recorded and played back. The dissociation of the voice from the body is mostly a matter of technology (this is, after all, the earliest film in the cycle, and thus still beholden to the technological paradigm of 1950s technohorror), but it already announces the theme in its later iterations.[23] Befitting Castle's commitment to the demystification of Gothic conventions, all this machinery is set in motion to disguise the fact that girl's father is the kidnapper, and that the kidnapping has been staged merely to terrorize the girl's grandfather into a heart attack, which would leave the father with a sizable inheritance (Figure 8.2).

The second remarkable feature of *Macabre*, one which ties the film to

Figure 8.2 The power and terror of the disembodied voice on the phone in *I Saw What You Did*.

Psycho but distinguishes it from Hitchcock's other films, is Castle's invariable commitment to the visual representation of abjection (this is perhaps the crucial distinguishing mark between Castle as a director of horror and Hitchcock as a director of thrillers). With its key trope of the kidnapped child buried alive, *Macabre* revolves around an abject body, a hideous corpse akin to the one that twists Sardonicus's face into a hideous mask. Unlike the mummified corpse of Mrs. Bates in *Psycho*, this body never makes a direct appearance in the film yet is constantly evoked, announced, and prefigured.[24] Given the transgressive potential inherent in the visual representation of a violated child, these strategies of oblique reference are understandable simply as a matter of restraint, even for a low-budget film operating below the radar of an already attenuated Production Code. Still, the idea is horrific enough to function as part of the film's exploitation strategy of promising sights hitherto considered taboo, but not so horrific that the simple announcement of the trope would suffice. Not only does the film place this concrete yet abject body into the center of the narrative; it also imagines that body by showing other character's responses to its imaginative evocation. The call from the mysterious kidnapper causes an emotional response in the woman who picks up the phone that is so dramatically overplayed, so histrionically overwrought, that the actress's screams already model the emotional range appropriate to a murder that has not yet occurred. Clearly, this is a performance reminiscent of the one Kevin Heffernan places at the center of *The Tingler* (or the ones delivered by the notoriously histrionic Joan Crawford in *Strait-Jacket* and the usually more restrained Barbara Stanwyck in *The Night Walker*). The disproportion between the diegetic causes for emotional distress and the performative response modeled by Castle's actresses serves as yet another means to separate body and mind from each other. While the actress's screams are not literally separated from her performing body, they take on an abstract quality in proportion to their lack of psychological verisimilitude. Several such scenes of dramatically overplayed horror disproportional to their diegetic cause are scattered throughout *Macabre*, each one signaling an unspeakable locus of abjection projected systematically off screen by the film's narrative.

Knowing that the discovery of the child alive and well in one of the final scenes of the film will be both a relief and a disappointment to the audience, Castle also mobilizes other instances of abjection that have no other discernible function in the film than to substitute for this unspeakable central one. In a prolonged sequence in a cemetery, the two main characters are searching for the buried child at the bottom of a freshly dug grave; here the location alone is sufficient to evoke, if not the child's body, then some other corpse brought into horrible proximity with the characters in the enclosed space at the bottom of the grave. With similar diegetic randomness, the cemetery scene also features the accidental shooting death of a groundskeeper, which produces a bloodied corpse that will make an appearance later when its surprising discovery and horrific sight produce a substitute for exactly that horror which the film denies its audience with the perpetually withheld murdered child.

Enacting these strategies of framing psychological monstrosity by projecting it away from its actual embodiment and onto abject bodies, Castle's *The Night Walker* (1964) takes an intermediary step toward the more fully developed *Strait-Jacket* a year later. As in *Strait-Jacket*, Castle's casting is rife with intertextual significance. Barbara Stanwyck reprises her iconic star persona by playing a woman menaced or abandoned to peril by the men around her, established in *Sorry, Wrong Number* (1948) and repeated in *Witness to Murder* (1954). Stanwyck's pairing with her ex-husband Robert Taylor, playing the lawyer scheming to drive her insane so that he can inherit her late husband's estate, adds another layer to Castle's intertextual play. None of the psychological monstrosity in the film is, however, projected onto Stanwyck's aging body; in fact, the film downplays the star treatment, capitalizing instead on the skills of its leading lady as a character actress. Monstrosity, following Castle's earlier formula, is embodied by the walking corpse of Stanwyck's dead husband, disfigured by the fire that killed him and brought into uncomfortable proximity to Stanwyck's character and Castle's camera (and thus the audience). That horrific face, worn literally as a mask by Taylor's character, stands in for that character's murderous actions and, by extension, the actions of his two criminal co-conspirators (both framed by the narrative as especially young and beautiful).

Like *The Night Walker*, the final entry into the 1960s cycle of psychological horror films, *Strait-Jacket*, features similar scenes of abjection, this time in the form of decapitation and corpses placed next to characters in bed to be discovered upon waking up. And as in *The Night Walker*, it is again in the realm of casting where Castle conceptualizes psychological monstrosity by projecting it onto abject bodies and actions. Twisted minds concealed behind normal appearances again determine the plot; the return, after twenty years, of a murderess from a mental asylum and her reunification with her daughter precipitate a series of new murders. But it is the casting of Joan Crawford as the lead that anchors the psychological plot twist of the film. Bringing aging female stars of the classic Hollywood period back to the screen coincides with the rise of psychological horror in this period. Neither was this Castle's doing alone, nor was *The Night Walker* the first of these films. Together with Robert Aldrich's *Whatever Happened to Baby Jane?* (1962, featuring Crawford and Bette Davis) and *Hush, Hush Sweet Charlotte* (1964, with Bette Davis and Olivia de Havilland), and Walter Grauman's *Lady in a Cage* (1964, featuring de Havilland), Castle's major contribution to the so-called hagsploitation (or "psycho-biddy") film cycle would be *Strait-Jacket*. As in other Castle films, it turns out that an ostensibly "normal" character, in this case Crawford's on-screen daughter, played by Diane Baker, is the subject of psychopathological grotesquery. Until this revelation, though, it is Crawford's on-screen presence that draws to itself associations of the abject. In one of its incarnations, Crawford's character visually revisits her lost youth, resulting in an assembly of costuming, hairdressing, and make-up that turns Crawford herself into a frightful spectacle.[25] Though the film's plot grants Crawford's character an alternate persona, in which the actress is, somewhat paradoxically, "made to" look her actual age and perform in a toned-down, more naturalistic register, it is the wild fluctuation between both of these personae, played by the actress at a high emotional pitch, which re-affixes the abject connotations to Crawford herself just as soon as her look and performance as the character's "normal" or "sane" self might have stripped them off. Much like the other actresses who figure prominently in this hagsploitation cycle, Crawford's bodily presence is marked by the implicit comparison between her former youth and beauty and her present diminished state—a comparison which, yet again, produces abjection as it separates and then plays against each other aspects of embodiment coded as parts of individual subjectivity and identity.

While Hitchcock's films, with the deliberate exception of *Psycho*, steer consistently and tastefully clear of such spectacles of abjection (the tactfully implied severed head buried in the flower patch in *Rear Window* [1954] is as carefully managed as the corpse concealed in a chest in *Rope* [1948]), Castle's films abound with the imagery of abjection.[26] From the corny skeletons in *Thirteen Ghosts*, the rubbery parasitic creature in *The Tingler*, and the grotesque facial rictus in *Mr. Sardonicus*, to the casting of specific actors and actresses and their specifically coded performance style; all these elements signify, and problematize, the embodiment of a monstrosity which grows all the more difficult to visualize the more deeply the horror film moves into the realm of psychology. Castle's films demonstrate a steady engagement with this inherent problematics of psychological horror, mapping out this new terrain by working through different permutations of the cinematic possibilities.

After *I Saw What You Did*, the films Castle was to direct would move away from horror just as Castle would become a director of lesser commercial significance. His parting gift to the genre would be the masterpiece of psychological horror he was never going to direct but only to produce, *Rosemary's Baby* (1968), a critical and commercial mainstream success. Given Castle's proclivities as a director, Roman Polanski can be credited with steering the film past the explicit tropes of abjection Castle was so fond of, leaving the audience only with the unsettling and unsentimental reminder that pregnancy is an abject state, and with that brief glimpse of the demonic child's abnormal eyes in the closing scene. Despite its most masterfully accomplished realization of psychological horror without the classic Gothic tropes of abjection, *Rosemary's Baby* would, ironically enough, have little to do with what would turn out to be Castle's lasting influence on the horror film: to develop a cinematic language that renders psychological monstrosity visible by obliquely linking it to the traditional Gothic signifiers of abjection.

The influence that Castle's model was to have on horror film is, yet again, best measured in the comparison between Castle and Hitchcock. Film historian David Cook is correct in pointing out that Hitchcock's seminal work in psychological horror points forward to a rich vein of psychological horror films that include the slasher film cycle of the 1970s and 80s, and later on the serial killer film cycle during the 1990s and beyond;[27] especially the serial killer film, in which the absence of abjection is a constitutive marker of otherness and monstrosity, owes more to *Psycho* than to any film of Castle's. But Castle's influence is felt most strongly elsewhere. With its steady commitment to the visual tropes of abjection and their deployment as spectacle for its own sake, Castle's 1960s psychological horror films prefigure the later cycle of so-called neo-horror, a cycle in which directors like George Romero, Wes Craven, and David Cronenberg were celebrated as much as special effects experts like Tom Savini, Chris Walas, and Stan Winston. It would be in their films that the interest in psychological monstrosity and physical abjection would be sustained in a precarious balance.

A BRIEF AFTERWORD: CASTLE'S GIMMICKS RECONSIDERED

In light of Castle's significance in moving the horror film from 1950s technohorror, past the trappings of a more traditional Gothic, and into 1960s psychological horror, as well as Castle's idiosyncratic negotiation between the disembodiment of psychological horror and the return of the abject body as a mainstay of Gothic horror, it is time to return, once again, to what more than anything else had earned Castle his reputation—his fondness for gimmicks. Even if Castle is recognized as an auteurist filmmaker with a coherent aesthetic vision, working through the urgent aesthetic and philosophical problems inherent in his chosen medium, it is difficult to get past the effect that his penchant for gimmicks can have on the appreciation of his work. At their moments of greatest complexity, Castle's films are as haunted by these gimmicks as the ramshackle mansions within them are haunted by corny special-effects ghosts. As I mentioned at the start of this discussion, these gimmicks have been read primarily as devices, tactics, and strategies for authorial self-fashioning, as latter-day versions of the carnival barker standing in front of the carnival's sideshow tent. While these readings are valuable for understanding horror cinema's grasp of its own affective aesthetics, I would like to finish with a few speculations about these gimmicks that consider them part and parcel of Castle's overriding thematic concerns throughout the 1960s psychological horror film cycle.

In the middle of *Homicidal* Castle has inserted what he calls a "fright break." The film pauses and we see an insert of a clock accompanied by the sound of a beating heart (note that, again, this is primarily a sound device). This, we are told, is our chance to leave the auditorium—in case we are too frightened to see what comes next—before "we go into the house." In terms of conventional Gothic elements, this would be the moment in every horror film when we finally catch a glimpse of the abject spectacle the advent of which we both dread and desire. The idea that the film could physically overwhelm its audience is also raised explicitly in Castle's direct address to the audience at the beginning of the film, in which he encourages audience members to monitor the person they are sitting next to, looking out for signs that "anyone near [them] is becoming uncontrollably frightened," then to notify the management so that "medical attention can be rushed to their aid." While these gimmicks play on the moment before the anticipated loss of the viewer's self-control, the "Percepto" gimmick of wired theatre seats for *The Tingler* aims at the tilting over into the viewer's loss of self-control as the scream by one audience member, planted or spontaneous, encourages the rest of the auditorium to join in. Needless to say at this point, sound plays a more prominent part in this gimmick than vision (the theatre lights have gone down at this moment).

What these two examples suggest is that Castle's gimmicks function as a continuation of the film's thematic preoccupations with extreme mental states and their embodiment. In regard to *Psycho*, Linda Williams has given one of the best accounts of the ways in which especially psychological horror aligns itself with the subjective experience of individual and collective identity being constructed. The audience of a film like *Psycho*, Williams argues, "has acquired a new sense of itself as bonded around certain terrifying sexual secrets. The shock of learning these secrets produces both a discipline [what Williams calls a 'docile' audience], and, around that discipline, a camaraderie, a pleasure of the group that was both new to motion pictures and destabilizing to the conventional gender roles of audiences."[28] Castle's gimmicks, I would argue, are not extraneous to this project. While the films thematically enact the (visual, auditory, cinematic) representation of psychological monstrosity by shifting it from the inconspicuous, normative, and seemingly normal bodies of the monstrous characters to the conventional Gothic signifiers of abjection, Castle's gimmicks replay this search for the encounter with the abject by aiming for the bodies of the viewers. They still play on the collective experience of the audience in the theatre, as Williams and other critics have remarked. But they also enlist these viewers in the encounter with the abject as an experience beyond the very rationalization that abjection threatens to undermine. Ever optimistic about what cinema can accomplish, Castle gimmicks extend the promise of a concrete embodiment of what Williams sees as new subjectivities by producing bodies in theatre seats laughing and screaming, alone with their anxieties, united in their pleasures.

NOTES

1. Peter Hutchings, *The Horror Film* (Harlow: Pearson, 2004), p. 80.
2. Ibid. p. 98.
3. Kevin Heffernan, *Ghouls, Gimmicks, and Gold: Horror Films and the American Movie Business, 1953–1968* (Durham, NC: Duke University Press, 2004), 89.
4. Ibid. p. 103.
5. Hutchings, *The Horror Film*, pp. 80–2.
6. Joan Hawkins, *Cutting Edge: Art-Horror and the Horrific Avant-Garde* (Minneapolis: University of Minnesota Press, 2000), p. 76.
7. Ben Kooyman, *Directorial Self-Fashioning in American Horror Cinema: George A. Romero, Wes Craven, Rob Zombie, Eli Roth, and the Masters of Horror* (Lewiston, NY: Mellen Press, 2014), p. 19.
8. David A. Cook, *Lost Illusions: American Cinema in the Shadow of Watergate and Vietnam 1970–1979* (Berkeley: University of California Press, 2000), p. 221.
9. Robert Bloch, *Once Around the Bloch: An Unauthorized Autobiography* (New York: Tor, 1993), p. 294.
10. Joseph Maddrey, *Nightmares in Red, White and Blue: The Evolution of the American Horror Film* (Jefferson, NC: McFarland, 2004), p. 45, p. 39.
11. Heffernan, *Ghouls*, p. 101.
12. Peter Shelley, *Grande Dame Guignol Cinema: A History of Hag Horror from* Baby Jane *to* Mother (Jefferson, NC: McFarland, 2009), p. 75, p. 80.
13. For a detailed description of this technohorror hybrid, see Steffen Hantke, *Monsters in the*

Machine: Science Fiction Film and the Militarization of America after World War II (Jackson: University Press of Mississippi, 2016), pp. 8–10.
14. Hammer Production's cycle of horror films beginning with *Dracula* (1958).
15. Ray Russell, "Sagittarius," in *Haunted Castles: The Complete Gothic Stories* (New York: Penguin, 2016), p. 107.
16. It is worth noting that Castle's sense of humor will continue to find its way into his work even in the most serious of films. The closing credits of *Strait-Jacket*, for example, feature an image of the Columbia logo with her head removed and placed at her feet (the film features several decapitations).
17. Barry Keith Grant, "Introduction," in Barry Keith Grant (ed.), *The Dread of Difference: Gender and the Horror Film* (Austin: University of Texas Press, 1996), p. 2.
18. Cook, *Lost Illusions*, p. 222.
19. For a full discussion, see Hantke, "Monstrosity without a Body: Representational Strategies in the Popular Serial Killer Film," *PostScript: Essays in Film and the Humanities* 22.2 (Winter/Spring 2003): 34–55.
20. Far more specifically, Castle's debt to Hitchcock, and specifically to *Psycho*, makes a stunning appearance fifteen minutes into *I Saw What You Did* (1965) in a scene in which a woman walks into a bathroom where her boyfriend is currently taking a shower. For diegetic reasons that are not entirely clear—the woman herself takes it as a sign that her boyfriend is crazy—the bathroom has been smashed up and a knife has been left stuck into a toppled piece of furniture. Angered by her boyfriend's anger, she steps up to the glass door of the shower, holding the knife, when that door opens and she is dragged forcefully into the shower. With the showering man's nudity carefully obscured, Castle starts the following sequence with an overhead shot in which the woman is pushed into a corner. Then it cuts to a close-up of her screaming face, transformed from fear to pain as Castle cuts to a medium close-up reverse angle shot of the man attacking her, alternating a few times between the man's arm thrusting forward and the woman's upper body registering the impact of what we presume to be the knife she brought into the shower with her. Eventually, Castle cuts to a close-up of the showerhead raining water down on the couple, albeit in a shot that steers clear of the object in the frame to avoid technical problems arising from the running water. The next shot shows the glass door of the shower from the outside, framing in silhouette the struggle inside. Three shots later—all shots so far occupying roughly the same two to four seconds: fast but not bewilderingly so—Castle shows us the legs of the two figures as blood runs down the drain between them. The woman then slides down the white-tiled bathroom wall, slumps on the floor, and is picked up by the man, who pulls her up and pushes her through the glass door. The sequence ends with several reverse angle shots of the man looking down on the woman on the floor outside the shower, and the woman herself from his point of view. Instead of Hitchcock's slow wind-down of the scene, Castle begins to cross-cut quickly to two other series of events—the teenagers and their prank call, and the man's neighbor entering the apartment. While Hitchcock transitions smoothly from the shower scene to the subsequent cleanup, Castle returns quickly to the thick of narration, event, and plot.
21. There is also the much-discussed superimposition of the grinning skull on Norman's face during the final dissolve of the prison cell scene, which, even when not read as a signifier of the supernatural, steers *Psycho*, in this microscopic instance, away from a mimetic to an expressionistic agenda. *Homicidal*'s rather mundane inheritance plot, by contrast, grounds it in a world of rational self-interest as a motive for murder.
22. Heffernan, *Ghouls*, pp. 100–1.
23. *I Know What You Did* features another disembodied voice on the phone, which returns as

an embodied agent to the origin of the phone call; this reciprocal exchange of agency replays in the auditory register the dynamic Hitchcock had been exploring in the visual realm in *Rear Window*.
24. Hitchcock's films may vary in their handling of the corpse's visibility, from *Rope* on one end of the spectrum to *The Trouble with Harry* (1955) on the other, but disavow abjection more consistently (whether through humor or concealment) than they embrace it in the single instance of *Psycho*.
25. By contrast, *The Night Walker* features a similar opportunity by making Barbara Stanwyck's character the owner of a beauty salon; while her interaction with this business and its employees raises interesting questions about age and beauty as standards of femininity, the film handles these questions by restraining the sensationalistic gaze at Stanwyck that enjoys free reign in *Strait-Jacket* when directed at Crawford.
26. For brevity's sake, this is obviously an oversimplified account of Hitchcock's work; as later films like *Frenzy* or *Torn Curtain* (1966) would demonstrate (both for the thriller and for psychological horror), Hitchcock would move increasingly from elegant ellipses toward more explicit cruelty and abjection.
27. Cook, *Lost Illusions*, p. 222.
28. Linda Williams, "Learning to Scream," in Mark Jancovich (ed.), *Horror: The Film Reader* (London: Routledge, 2002), 165.

CHAPTER 9

"What a Wicked Game to Play?": Playfulness, Generic Hybridity, and Cult Appeal in Castle's 1960s Films

Michael Brodski and Caroline Langhorst

William Castle's cinematic output may undoubtedly be counted among the most versatile and creatively playful body of work in American cinema. While Castle had grown up with and learned his craft in the studio system, embarking upon his film career at Columbia, he nevertheless sought a way to escape the narrow confines of major productions that were, at least during the heyday of the classical Hollywood era, cautiously guarded and controlled by the Production Code (1930–68). The flourishing terrain of exploitation production, on the other hand, turned out to be less restrictive. Accordingly, Castle's enthusiastic and recurrent exploration of stylistic, generic, and thematic boundaries was further facilitated by a certain artistic freedom that was simultaneously enabled by his repeated double role as both director and producer of his films. Moreover, his free-spirited manner and outspoken penchant for generic hybridity seem to find particular expression in several of his 1960s films: Castle's individualist stance was further supported and echoed by the decade's significant cultural transformations, its emphasis upon youth culture and juvenility, and its related shift toward a more liberal approach to formerly taboo topics that originated from the postwar era. Deviating from classical studio fare, Castle's films of the time are particularly multilayered and innovative, seemingly bursting with playfulness, generic hybridity, and cult appeal. At the same time, they comment upon central contemporary themes such as the generational conflict between the parent culture and the younger generation, the allegedly affluent society, the American nuclear family, and American middle-class values, as well as the shift in gender roles. This chapter endeavors to examine the aforementioned aspects in selected key texts of the stated period such as *13 Ghosts* (1960), *13 Frightened Girls* (1963), *Let's Kill Uncle* (1966), and *The Spirit Is Willing* (1967). These are paradigmatic examples of Castle's affinity for generic hybridity, deliberately merging, for instance, comedy with Gothic horror, thriller elements, and children's and youth film. They also exemplify the reflexive use, transformation, and playful subversion of genre conventions as well as the previously hinted at, strongly pronounced playful attitude (on both the directorial level and in terms of character interaction), and the resulting immense cult potential. In this regard, particularly the dominant conflation of various, and at times even seemingly contrary, generic patterns and the films' respective inherent metadiegetic commentaries shall be considered and linked to a complex (cult) mode of reception. The latter seems to be of specific relevance due to Castle's explicit consideration of the audience. This chapter is divided into several subchapters: First, *13 Ghosts* and *The Spirit Is Willing* will be investigated via a comparative analysis of the stated aspects. The following subchapter also serves as a further elaboration of the chosen methodological framework. Subsequently, *Let's Kill Uncle* and *13 Frightened Girls* will be analyzed in a non-chronological order, given the similarities between the former and *13 Ghosts* and *The Spirit Is Willing* concerning the fusion of the haunting motif and a commentary upon American domestic life.

"HAPPY HAUNTING"?: *13 GHOSTS* (1960) AND *THE SPIRIT IS WILLING* (1967)

Although released seven years apart, *13 Ghosts* and *The Spirit Is Willing* are connected by similar themes and stylistic patterns such as the combination of an American middle-class family dealing with a financial crisis and the coming of age of their children, and a temporary or more permanent change of scenery—the old haunted Gothic mansion in *13 Ghosts*, and the slightly decayed and similarly haunted vacation house in *The Spirit Is Willing*. The former was produced after the two Vincent Price vehicles, *House on Haunted Hill* (1959) and *The Tingler* (1959), and may be seen as occupying a transitional space between Castle's former films and the even more playful and colorful 1960s output. *The Spirit Is Willing*, in turn, was released in the watershed year, 1967, that saw different seminal productions subvert the Hays Code, such as Arthur Penn's *Bonnie and Clyde* and Mike Nichols's *The Graduate*. Like *13 Ghosts*, *The Spirit Is Willing* is clearly a product of its time, and its hyperbolic, comic yet menacing playfulness mirrors the mid-1960s yearning for the playful expansion and exploration of new perceptive and sexual dimensions and alternative lifestyles, its colorful psychedelic patterns, and the impending change of mood toward the increasingly violent and disillusioned end of the decade.

13 Ghosts sets in with a metadiegetic cameo appearance and introduction by

Castle himself. By this means, cinema's artificial disposition is self-consciously underscored and the audience is invited to partake in a tale of haunting as the director/producer ends his introductory remarks on ghosts and the use of the two-colored (red and blue) ghost viewer, witnessed by his skeleton companion, with a teasing "happy haunting" before suddenly vanishing into thin air. At the same time, however, Castle's own persona is playfully brought to the fore. In contrast to, for instance, Alfred Hitchcock's often diegetic and nonverbal cameos, Castle not only directly addresses the spectator, explaining one of his newest gimmicks, but also exhibits his constructed artistic persona as director/producer with apparent relish. As Ernest Mathijs and Jamie Sexton highlight, he is a "self-conscious cult auteur"[1] with a decidedly entrepreneurial strain. Discussing Castle and Dwain Esper, they state that, "it is in the realm of showmanship that they have really gained their cult reputations." Underlining the relevance of Castle's gimmicks such as "(fangs, special viewing glasses, cardboard axes), while arriving in a hearse for the premiere of *Macabre* and then placing himself in a coffin,"[2] it is important to note that such (albeit commercially oriented) "tactics are still different from the 'norms' of mass-marketing."[3] As a result, "[s]alesmanship here combines with a fiercely individualist belief in standing out from the crowd via outlandish behavior."[4]

Furthermore, such a paratextual introduction by the director/producer himself also seems to have the explicit aim of sensitizing the audience right from the beginning. The viewer is therefore invited to watch the film aside from the generic fear and suspense-evoking patterns of a ghost horror movie with a conventional and known structure. Instead, the tongue-in-cheek advice given to use the ghost viewer when a color change occurs on the screen enables the audience to participate in an ironic and knowing role, which no longer solely consists of the pleasure of fear. For Torben Grodal, for instance, such distancing methods situate the film spectator in a quite playful and game-like position by means of:

> the blending of explicitly coded narratives and thematic formulas with "metafictional" markers of distance to roles and patterns. The markers of distance show that the "obsessional" pattern repetition (and the occasional complete violation of pattern rules) is performed voluntarily (and therefore allows the addressee in a transitional role to consume the fictions "as a game").[5]

Acknowledging such markers, the film viewer seems to be taking part in the film reception in a less immersive and more knowingly playful way. The films' distinctive cult appeal, which arises from the playful manner and the related conflation and subversion of generic conventions, will be analyzed in the following via a close examination of the selected key films. Additionally, the chapter sets out to examine how this outspoken playfulness is repeatedly linked to the infantile or adolescent perspective, whether it be the vivacious ten-year-old Buck (Charles Herbert) in *13 Ghosts*, the puberty-ridden, almost sixteen-year-old Steve (Barry Gordon) in *The Spirit Is Willing*, the young and precocious Candace/Candy (Kathy Dunn) in *13 Frightened Girls*, or the child protagonists in *Let's Kill Uncle*. On top of this, each film explicitly comments upon turning everyday situations into highly artificial game-playing, either encouraging it or, at one point, claiming that the time for games is over (e.g. as stated by the adult spy and object of Candy's adolescent/womanly desire, Wally Sanders [Murray Hamilton] in *13 Frightened Girls*).

In *13 Ghosts*, which marks a stated transitional moment in Castle's body of work, the conflict between old and new is played out on different levels. On the extra-diegetic level, the film's dominant black and white is occasionally infused with the color-animated spectral shadows that ought to be perceived through the ghost viewers. On the diegetic level, present and past are repeatedly interwoven and juxtaposed with each other: the financially struggling paleontologist Cyrus Zorba (Donald Woods), who works in the L.A. county museum and accordingly spends his professional life dwelling on the past, unexpectedly inherits his uncle's old mansion with its "old-fashioned furniture." Similarly, the superstitious belief in otherworldly spirits and a witch-like housekeeper are set against and fused with the supposedly modern world of postwar American life and the Zorba family's children, Buck and his older sister Medea. The latter's quaint first name with its mythological implications and the deceased uncle's coexistence as scientist and advocate of rational thought, as well as the scientific scrutiny of supposedly irrational paranormal phenomena, demonstrate the intricate and complex nature of this conflict. Similarly, specific generic patterns are employed and juxtaposed: the popular American motif of the haunted house and its newly arrived tenants, in this case the almost-destitute Zorba family, are conflated with the greedy downside of human nature as often displayed in noir thrillers. The seemingly charming yet morally depraved young lawyer Benjamin "Ben" Rush (Martin Milner) serves as a scheming and ruthless antagonist figure. In the course of the film it becomes clear that he is prepared to transcend every moral threshold for the sake of enormous financial wealth.

In the following, the haunted mansion motif will be further explored in relation to the ghosts and its intersections with domestic family life. Whereas the landscape of European Gothic is littered with numerous derelict haunted castles, "the tale of the haunted house, while rooted in the European Gothic tradition, has developed a distinctly American resonance; since Poe first described the House of Usher in 1839, the motif of the haunted house has assumed an enduring role in the American tradition."[6] This specific significance also partly results from the house's symbolic role as indicator of social status and economic success, as the supposed manifestation of the American Dream's "from rags to riches" ethos, and as the center of American middle-class domesticity.[7] Distinguishing the haunted house story from the strain of (often psychological) American nineteenth-century ghost fiction by writers such as Henry James and Edith Wharton and its focus on ontological ambiguity, the former places its emphasis upon the antagonistic force of the house itself and not the otherworldly spirits that restlessly roam its many rooms.[8] While *13 Ghosts* adheres to the haunted house tale in that its main protagonists, the Zorba family, experience the increasing menace that seemingly emanates from the house, which is further alluded to as being cursed by the housekeeper Elaine (Margaret Hamilton)[9] and the ghosts, this conventional pattern is suddenly disrupted as the uncle's lawyer and Medea's crush Ben turns out to be the actual culprit. Ironically, he plans to strike when the family members—apart from little Buck, who is sent to sleep but who sneaks downstairs to catch a glimpse of the event—are holding a séance with Elaine as the medium, summoning the ghost of Zorba to question him about his strange death. By this means, both generic patterns are playfully juxtaposed and continued. At the beginning of the film, Ben mischievously attempts to gain the family's trust by pretending to care for their actual wellbeing: he gives advice to the sudden heir, Cyrus, courts Medea, and tells Buck that they are friends and must help each other, ultimately and unscrupulously taking advantage of Buck's trust to get hold of Zorba's hidden fortune. He even dresses up as Zorba's ghost and frightens Medea, thereby trying to scare the family away, as he wants to be left alone with the treasure. His greedy and evil character is gradually exposed in the course of the narrative, culminating in the ice-cold attempted murder of Buck that is simultaneously supposed to echo Zorba's death by suffocation in his bed. Yet the murderer is subjected to his own heinous weapon as Zorba's ghost takes revenge on him. Despite Ben's incarnation of human evil, Zorba's collected ghosts are by no means harmless or gone. On the contrary, as the witch-like housekeeper tells Buck smilingly, they and their playful yet potentially dangerous shenanigans are likely to come back, since the diegetic psychological explanation of the ghosts' existence is grounded upon their being "unhappily earthbound because of unresolved problems," and only Zorba's "problem" has been resolved by the film's ending. Unlike in other narratives, the house is therefore not destroyed in order to restore social order. Whereas it certainly assumes a relevant narrative function as the ghosts' various actions are accentuated by their interaction with the house and its distinctive atmosphere, equal attention is paid to both before the disruptive element of the greedy human murderer occurs. Moreover, as Rebecca Janicker claims with regard to haunted house fiction, the motif occupies a liminal space.[10] This liminal space is then further linked in the film to the liminality of the child's (Buck's) perspective. In *The Spirit Is Willing*, the liminality of the haunted vacation house is fused with Steve's adolescent point of view and his impending coming of age.

The ghosts are represented in playful and unusual ways. One of the first playful and ironic deviations from conventional representations of ghosts in horror movies occurs in a scene in which the viewer can observe the ghosts engaging in a lively discussion. On the auditory level, their incomprehensible conversation is reproduced as an unintelligible and chaotic mumble of voices with a funny falsetto intonation, resembling the imitation of speech in silent comedy movies. Besides, Castle constructs an interesting kind of body humor, which he will later also reintroduce in *The Spirit Is Willing*. Katherine A. Fowkes significantly observes with regard to the manifold physical constitution of ghost figures that "their manifestations and physical capabilities can be conveniently adapted to fit the needs of story."[11] Consequently, the ghost bodies occur not only in frightful circumstances, but also in a variety of humorous interventions that depend on their subordination to different laws and plausible possibilities from living characters (e.g. invisibility and bawdy exaggeration). Castle introduces such an amusing interpretation, for instance, by referring to the ghost body's sheer immortality and its resulting indestructability. Accordingly, it is precisely shown as being undead. One example would be the Mediterranean-tempered man, presumably a former cook, with an absurdly big moustache, who stabs a meat cleaver into the head of a female ghost during an impulsive outburst. As long as the meat cleaver is still stuck in her head, she keeps reacting to it.

Another important sequence shows Buck as witness to a bizarre interplay between two ghosts, a menacingly roaring circus lion and his tamer. Since this lurid attraction primarily consisted of the tamer putting his head between the animal's open jaws, the spectator can easily conclude the circumstances of his death, especially given his ghost's lack of a head and his search for it inside the lion's mouth. At the same time, the apparently angry animal tries to get rid of his old partner by hitting him with his pranks. Buck witnesses the entire spectacle fearlessly, with a genuine interest and a characteristic infantile curiosity. Of all the film's characters, the child seems to be the only one who interprets the spectral incidents as an attractive and exciting form of play. In this regard, his reaction seems quite plausible as he impassively tells his mother that he has encountered a lion and a man without a head. As Christian Stewen states, the child figure in ghost horror films often functions as a kind of medium, able to perceive things that adults cannot. Thus, the child has "the power and ability to question ways of perception, to open up new reflective spaces and to mediate meaning. In fact, the child works as the medium of knowledge and visibility."[12] Although the ghosts can be recognized by the viewer and by all the family members, only Buck realizes their joyful potential in such a medium-like way. As the audience also occasionally shares his point of view, thereby perceiving the ghosts in an ironic and playful manner, it is exactly the child's specific perspective that strengthens the film's cult potential. As Timothy Corrigan aptly stresses: "[C]ult movies map a place for the viewer where she or he can act out simultaneously the vision of child and adult."[13]

As previously indicated, the child's perspective is replaced with the adolescent's point of view in *The Spirit Is Willing*, which also presents an even stronger interaction with the ghosts. The coming of age in *13 Ghosts*—evident in Medea's crush on Ben and her contradictory behavior, which ranges from trying to act like a mature adult (e.g., her reprimanding remarks about Buck's roller skating or sliding down the banister) and outbursts of adolescent curiosity (e.g., the moment she and Buck keep questioning the Ouija board when the adults have given up such "irrational" endeavors)—becomes the central conflict in *The Spirit Is Willing*. Even before the Powell family arrive at their vacation residence, son Steve relishes establishing his image as the wayward and misunderstood teen, telling his confused and upset parents that he has a right to feel miserable and that he has had a dreadful life so far. He even delivers the classic comment that he did not ask to be born in the first place. Thus, the ideal of the American nuclear family—particularly 1950s small-town domesticity—is exposed from the start, before eventually collapsing completely. It quickly becomes clear that the long-deserved vacation is just a desperate escape attempt from the family's multiple problems. Steve's parents, Ben (Sid Caesar) and Kate (Vera Miles), are not only confronted with their private troubles—e.g., their son's impending puberty, which, in his father's words, makes him "a stranger walking down the stairs"—but on top of that, Ben has professional struggles as he loses his job and seems to undergo a midlife crisis. His wife does not know how to deal with her son's and husband's respective struggles. Moreover, both parents seem to have been very young when they married and settled down, as was quite common at the time. The generational divide between Steve's parents, who had to mature rather early, and Steve himself, who spends his childhood in late 1950s and 1960s American society, is played out throughout the film. Apart from acting the miserable and lonely teenager part with almost ironic relentless conviction, endlessly moaning about everything—and thus echoing Marlon Brando's famous reply as the delinquent biker leader Johnny in *The Wild One* (1953) to the question "What are you rebelling against?", "Whadda you got?"—Steve actually benefits from postwar cultural changes, including the new role of youth culture, the emergence of a counterculture, and a related downright articulation of dissatisfaction, alienation, and anger. As Catherine Driscoll states, referring to David Considine's examination of the period, a youth market and cinematic representations of youth had already been central to 1930s and 40s American cinema.[14] Yet as Thomas Doherty remarks in his seminal examination (1988), in 1950s American exploitation cinema the youth market was catered for to a higher degree than before.[15] Filmic portrayals of youth included, for instance, "the 'juvenile delinquent' film, the rock'n'roll teenpic, the 'clean' teenpic, and the 'weirdies',"[16]—that is, mainly horror and science-fiction productions. Drawing upon Doherty's observations, Mathijs and Sexton then take a closer look at the cult appeal of youth-related exploitation films, highlighting that 1950s teenage culture underwent a transformation into youth culture that became "a state of mind"[17] and thus elevated earlier forms of teenage alienation to a new level. They also briefly mention Castle's films in this regard as one of the pivotal emerging independent production companies alongside AIP (American International Pictures) and other cult figures such as Roger Corman who attracted a certain cult following.[18] Furthermore, they claim that the films were especially popular with young audiences:

> ... they were being lapped up by younger viewers in particular, and could therefore be considered cult because they were appealing primarily to a "deviant" subculture who believed these films were communicating with them. Of course, much of the status of "delinquent youth" was constructed through exaggerated press reports, but this nevertheless led to *perceptions* of deviant groups consuming deviant films.[19]

In *The Spirit Is Willing*, Castle employs different dominant youth-related tropes (coming of age, the misunderstood and rebellious teenager, the juvenile delinquent), and also references the popular combination of youth and horror as depicted in films such as *I Was a Teenage Werewolf* (1957). At the same time, his tongue-in-cheek mode wittily comments upon the above-mentioned medially constructed nature of the recurrent moral panic surrounding juvenile delinquency and its morally and socially disruptive potential, which was mainly a catalyst for profound cultural anxieties about the sociocultural changes, the growing criticism of the Vietnam War, increasing protests against racial and gender inequality, and the ongoing Cold War conflict that left American society in a state of uncertainty and conflict. Steve's attempt at juvenile rebellion, with occasional hints at delinquency (e.g., his parents' false assumption that their son has wrecked the kitchen), then, is treated playfully and ironically; his character seems troubled yet lacks, for example, Brando's potentially menacing corporeality. Instead, it rather echoes Jim Stark's (James Dean) inner and domestic conflict with a weak father figure in Nicholas Ray's seminal *Rebel Without a Cause* (1955). As if that was not enough, Steve's wealthy uncle George (John McGiver) comes to visit and repeatedly interferes with their life. Consequently the family conflict reaches a higher scale, as Uncle George cannot stand the sight of his sister's husband. The two men embody entirely different and almost opposite forms of masculinity—the uncle is a tough and self-assured businessman who unhesitatingly seizes an opportunity when he sees one, whereas the father often appears rather weak-willed, passive, and out of his depth. The domestic strife at times takes on an albeit humorous and deliberately over-exaggerated melodramatic tone, and the youth-related tropes are then confronted with and further expressed via the supernatural haunting motif and encounters with spectrality. Contrary to the earlier *13 Ghosts*, however, *The Spirit Is Willing* was produced when the television landscape was populated with new serial narratives such as *The Addams Family* (1964–6), *The Munsters* (1964–6), and *Dark Shadows* (1966–71), which fused domestic family life, melodrama, and supernatural/horror elements, thereby presenting alternative family models and lifestyles as opposed to the patriarchal and heteronormative nuclear family. This tendency is also mirrored in Castle's film to a certain extent.

Accordingly, *The Spirit Is Willing* employs a ghost subplot to build up an ironic and metareflexive counterbalance to the stated patterns of family drama and juvenile delinquency. Already the film's exposition, which deals with the backstory of the three house ghosts' genesis, enriches their appearance with amusing intertextual undertones: A jealous wife murders her unfaithful husband and their housemaid (with whom he was having an affair) with a meat cleaver, and is in turn simultaneously murdered by her spouse. Their knowingly exaggerated acting and the comic background music playfully expose the scene as being reminiscent of a similar scene in Castle's *Strait-Jacket* (1964). The ghosts function less as individual characters; instead, they may be read as symbolic embodiments of the films' central conflicts, and their main emotional cores are exposed in a tongue-in-cheek manner. Since the former housemaid Jenny's activity lies almost entirely in the seduction of all the men she encounters (in the end, even the inexperienced Steve succumbs to her charms), while the virgin Felicity (Cass Daley) craves her first intimate experience with a man (even killing several candidates for this purpose), they over-exaggeratedly embody the sexual undertone of the film's principal conflicts. Analyzing the American screwball comedy *Topper* (1948), Fowkes suggests that the liminal role of ghosts' bodies as both present and absent enables a subversion of production code policies—for instance, through the suggestion of an invisible body being naked.[20] *The Spirit Is Willing* undoubtedly follows such a classical Hollywood tradition, but since it was produced in the midst of the decline of code policies during the 1960s, it exploits the possibility of the ghostly body in a more extensive way: it turns the spectral beings into purely affect-driven entities that mechanically follow their inner drives. As a result, the stated discourses of the nuclear family and of juvenile delinquency are heavily ironized by such a blunt exposure of real, basic needs. Apart from their sexual alignment, such urges also become manifested in childlike and carnivalesque play instincts as the three ghosts try to resolve their conflicts by throwing all kind of things at each other. As they smile while harmonically performing picturesque and dancelike moves, everything is presented as a kind of game instead of a serious confrontation. Contrary to generic ghost narratives, no strict rules for the ghosts' bodily appearance seem to apply; they can sometimes be touched by the living, but are at other times so transparent that they cannot even hurt each other. The latter quality also serves as a source of several humorous moments. Correspondingly, Castle shows that he is more interested in a funny trope than a serious interrogation of the genre; instead, he attaches his undead figures to different humorous ideas. For example, the jealous Felicity sometimes appears in a cloud of red drizzle, and even grinningly approaches the camera directly in one scene while slowly becoming invisible.

"TRY TO THINK OF IT AS A KIND OF GAME": *LET'S KILL UNCLE* (1966)

The adaptation of *Let's Kill Uncle* seems to be an attempt to structurally adhere to the considerable heterogeneity of Rohan O'Grady's eponymous novel (1964). Its multifarious nature was further described as "the most readable blend of humor, horror, chills and child psychology since *High Wind in Jamaica*."[21] In this context, the film can be considered an apotheosis of Castle's stated excessive play with various heterogeneous tropes and patterns. Right from the beginning, he presents a surplus of highly ramified backstory information concerning the diverse characters, which is not actually crucial to the plot's further development. Besides, the audience continually faces rapidly alternating insertions of children's film, horror, adventure, melodrama, and crime cinema devices. The film introduces two main child protagonists, Barnaby (Pat Cardi) and Chrissie (Mary Badham), who share traumatic backstory wounds. The setting is a mysterious island that consists of an exotic jungle with ancient ruins and a gloomy abandoned hotel, including a swimming pool with a shark in it. Moreover, a scar-faced and crippled inhabitant is introduced through a shocking close-up, and the children later come across a medallion with a hypnotizing effect. These are only some examples of the narrative's chaotic hybrid fusion. More precisely, *Let's Kill Uncle*'s diegesis repeatedly and mischievously attempts to evoke specific expectations in the supposedly generically experienced viewer by at least temporarily employing certain conventional patterns. In the next moment, however, these may be dropped or subverted entirely. As a result, *Let's Kill Uncle* never achieves a semantic closure for the audience. For instance, the film's opening shows the allegedly accidental death of Barnaby's father. Initially, one can observe a severe car crash as well as a bloodstained, apparently dead male body. According to the common narrative laws of classical Hollywood style, the spectator would expect this to be crucial to the unfolding narrative. Within Castle's diegetic universe, however, this is not the case. Instead, this incident only serves to construct more inconsistencies, since the second protagonist, Barnaby's title-giving uncle Kevin (Nigel Green), a former major and heroic World War II veteran, is indirectly suspected of having staged his brother's death in order to take over his property. Yet there is no actual proof, not to mention the smallest clue, he could have been involved. In the same way, Barnaby receives a murder threat from him: "Try to think of it as a kind of game, Barnaby!" Kevin tells the astonished boy, while proposing different rules. For example, he declares the house as a neutral, violence-free zone and explains that his nephew's death shall look like an accident. Indeed, a real kind of cat-and-mouse game emerges between the two and later expands to involve Chrissie, since the main characters seemingly try to murder each other. Once again, Castle uses child protagonists in an innovative and disruptive way. As Dominic Lennard analyzes, in normative representations of child figures, including children's films, their innocence and need for adult protection tend to be underlined, given the child's general subordination to adult knowledge and power. Implicitly preserving such normative ideas of childhood, evil child figures in horror films are thus denied the status of proper children, constructed rather as unchildish, monster-like entities.[22] Instead, Barnaby and Chrissie appear to occupy a liminal space that is positioned between children's film and horror film conventions. As they attempt to kill Uncle Kevin by serving him poisoned mushrooms or putting a spider in his bed, the children indeed develop a great lust for cruelty. This pronounced survival instinct, however, is primarily a response to the permanent threat of death. By this means, they subvert Kevin's adult-marked threat without being portrayed as inhuman monsters. On the contrary, the interaction between adult and child appears to be a more playful kind of power relation which also manifests itself in different comic-relief moments: In one scene, Kevin supposedly tries to burn the children alive, but they are incidentally rescued by a sudden thunderstorm. While they celebrate their survival with exaggerated dance moves, their uncle is left downtrodden and soaking wet.

In the end, Kevin declares that everything was only a kind of play and leaves the island on his plane, with Barnaby saying that he will definitely miss him. Was everything only an attempt to resolve the boy's trauma by engaging him in a supposedly deadly but in reality just playful situation—or was there a real killing intended? The film simply refuses to offer any explanation, thereby irritating the viewer with so many loose ends. Such usage, mixture, and nevertheless non-fulfillment of genre expectations can affect the viewer's emotions in quite a significant way. While, according to Peter Wuss, the recipient's genre anticipations condition a "stable emotional climate,"[23] their disruption, occurring also through the stated fusion of different patterns, can result in different emotive turns and a corresponding instability in the viewer's reaction. Moreover, this can be regarded as a catalyst for the film's cult appeal. Consequently, Justin Smith's definition of cult movies, placing the audience in a "dialectical relation to texts which display a double articulation of visual pleasures through strategies of engagement and distancing, of abandon and control,"[24] seems quite fitting.

Although it would be tempting to regard a certain lack of directorial as well as authorial skill and production values as the main reason for such a loosely connected bricolage, the film's quality seems to transcend the screenplay's common framework, which is typically based upon narrative coherence in Hollywood films. Instead, it seems rather to be a metareflexive commentary upon the structure of classical Hollywood works in general. As Janet Staiger notices in contrast to various other genre theories that strive for a clear separation, most movies of the classical "Fordian" Hollywood era (1917–60) can be attested a certain degree of impurity and conflation of their generic categories. Staiger considers audiences' reactions to film releases and their respective multiple traits; accordingly, comic, dramatic, action, and suspense qualities, for example, may be ascribed to such a multilayered cult text as *Casablanca* (1942).[25] *Let's Kill Uncle* encourages such thinking in an even more exaggerated way, and could be read as a retrospective consideration of its cinematic predecessors, as it tends to sublimate such genre impurity in an ironic and self-consciously explicit manner.

"SO SMALL THAT NOBODY WOULD NOTICE HER": *13 FRIGHTENED GIRLS* (1963)

With his 1963 production *13 Frightened Girls*, Castle enters a ghostless terrain, despite the title's potential evocation of frightful horror images and its echoing of *13 Ghosts*.[26] Although *13 Frightened Girls* shares the other examples' playful manner and relish in generic hybridity, it differs from them in specific, significant aspects. Its narration is situated in Europe, with early 1960s London being the main setting; its central characters are teenage diplomat daughters who attend an international boarding school called "Miss Pittford's Academy for Young Ladies" in a picturesque part of Switzerland; and the story is told by the central protagonist, the young American "Candy" Hull herself, from a first-person point of view.[27] While the plot seemingly takes place in the realm of high politics, with its focus on the world of espionage at the peak of the Cold War just shortly after the Cuban Missile Crisis of 1962, it presents, like the other films, a detached microcosm—in this case, the high society life of the diplomatic elite—that is as remote from reality as 007's screen adventures (which had been launched the year before with *Dr. No*). In the following, the film's hybrid generic concoction of spy-thriller elements and the youth film's coming-of-age theme will be scrutinized.

At the beginning of *13 Frightened Girls*, the young students are sent on vacation. Before they even arrive at the airport, calamity strikes when Candy, the proud winner of the Latin vocabulary prize, is allowed to drive the bus. Her over-enthusiastic and daringly reckless driving style, and the unexpected appearance of a spider, cause the vehicle to crash. As with the films discussed earlier, a seeming idyll (in this case of innocent girlhood) is unmasked right from the start. At the same time, the death of the spider and the shattered glass are employed as a humorous bad omen and a foreshadowing hint at Candy's nemesis: a highly dangerous killer operating under the codename "Spider," who ironically happens to be her father's chauffeur, Mike (Charlie Briggs). Furthermore, Candy's double life as Agent Kitten is the incidental result of her adolescent crush on her father's colleague Wally, who is already engaged to another spy called Soldier (Joyce Taylor). Sixteen-year-old Candy's still girlish features are repeatedly juxtaposed with Soldier's more mature, womanly appearance. Like the amorous Medea in *13 Ghosts*, she attempts to act like an adult, telling the surprised Wally as she clumsily tries to seduce him that she is "older than [her] age" and "now a woman." Because she feels neglected, not taken seriously, and bored, she sets her mind on helping Wally after she sneakily overhears a confidential conversation between him and her father on the limousine's shielded back seat. Upon learning that her father and Washington have been dissatisfied with Wally's work lately, and are therefore questioning his professional competence, she is shocked.

Agent Kitten's first mission is prompted by another accidental overhearing: an initially innocent visit to her Chinese friend Mai-Ling (Lynne Sue Moon) turns into an espionage voyage when the highly sought Kaganescu is murdered by Mai-Ling's uncle and his henchmen and deposited in the meat chamber with her father's letter opener. The girl engages in a dangerous hide-and-seek game using a food elevator, and succeeds in escaping with the device that was intended to cause a political scandal by wrongly accusing her father of murder. While Kitten's subsequent missions are planned beforehand, her self-assured, cheeky, and brave yet endearingly naïve way of handling the ensuing situations remains the same. As her verbal exchange with Wally demonstrates, she projects her unrealistic and romantic notions of love onto the sphere of espionage. Wally, in turn, jokingly tries to tease her by telling her that phrases like "master spies" have been considered obsolete since 1918. This, however, does not wake her from her romantic dream of exciting adventures in spy wonderland. Neither does it stop her from reading the book *Methods and Training for Modern Espionage 1918*—especially since she has also heard Wally say that spying is only a game and a poker play. In the following scenes, she too treats it as a game. As in *13 Ghosts*, secrecy is pivotal, yet Candy (not unlike Buck) has difficulty behaving unobtrusively due to her unwavering enthusiasm. When she attempts to follow the book's advice that the "female agent must know all the powers of her sex" by seducing the Russian leader of the student party posing as the Dutch Peter van Hagen (Garth Benton), her espionage methods are so clumsy and conspicuous that she is effortlessly exposed and drugged by her target. This scene marks a narrative turn toward a darker tone which is, however, counterbalanced by *13 Frightened Girls*' overall playful manner, its 1960s pop aesthetic, and its comic moments. Candy's amateurish yet successful behavior, daring attitude, and charming *naïveté* are further accentuated by the accidental codename "Kitten" and its playful and slightly infantile signature trademark of cat footprints. Another example of the playful directorial approach is the shot of Candy's actual cat, signifying Agent Kitten, marching in front of a moving globe that serves as a humorous visualization of the spy's increasing omnipresence.

While Candy enters a primarily masculine-connoted, patriarchal territory (apart from her agent status, for instance, Soldier is confined to the decoding room), she applies its methods to her juvenile environment, mainly spying at dancing parties or receptions at her various friends' respective embassies. She feigns amorous interest in young men who are affiliated with one or more of her friends (such as Peter van Hagen) in order to get hold of secret information, or eavesdrops on conversations between adult diplomats at parties. The social interaction sequences with the other girls repeatedly combine the espionage element with that of the youth film which is, in this case, the coming of age of young girls and their first encounters with men. At the same time, it is mainly via the girls' interactions and competitions (e.g., a tennis match between the American Candy and the Russian Natasha [Gina Trikonis]) that political conflicts such as the Cold War are articulated. The film therefore playfully presents different girlhoods that are tied to different political systems and mindsets (e.g., Mai-Ling likes to listen to "imperialistic" American music), while at the same time maintaining its tongue-in-cheek manner. Politics are otherwise only discussed vaguely through remarks such as "break codes, new codes" concerning the Cold War conflict, or the expression of nostalgic lament for bygone espionage techniques.

Castle made *13 Frightened Girls* at the peak of the British spy boom, which extended to literature, television, and cinema. It set in at the beginning of the 1960s with television series such as *Danger Man* (1960–2, 1964–6), starring Patrick McGoohan—who would later become famous for his unique hybrid cult television series *The Prisoner* (1967–8), combining a dystopian Orwellian narrative with a playful pop aesthetic. The spy boom reached its height with Bondmania, the filmic adaptations of Len Deighton's Harry Palmer novels starring Michael Caine,[28] the rather nihilistic John le Carré adaptation *The Spy*

Who Came in from the Cold (1965) with Richard Burton as disillusioned Agent Leamas, and television series such as *The Saint* (1962–9) or *The Avengers* (1961–9). While Candy—to the amazement of her political enemies—operates on her own as an autonomous amateur spy in order to assist the American intelligence service, the narrative contains—even if portrayed in a playful and generically disruptive manner—the spy/secret agent thriller's generic "manner of cloak-and-dagger intrigue (spying, sabotage, espionage, counter-espionage, theft of state or industrial secrets, political assassination)."[29] Moreover, *13 Frightened Girls* combines elements of what James Chapman defined as the action-based "sensational" thriller (e.g., the Bond series) and occasional moments echoing the "realist" thriller in the vein of le Carré or *Danger Man*, which reflects "the moral ambiguities and uncertainties of the spying game and questions the values of patriotism and duty that are so prominent in the sensational thriller."[30] Whereas the narrative does not display much in the way of physical violence or Bond-echoing action spectacles, the episodic plot structure nevertheless moves along quickly from one mission to another. The generic convention of spectacular physical combat is replaced by an emphasis upon Agent Kitten's changing costumes, ranging from a black turtleneck sweater and green tartan skirt to dance dresses. This is in keeping with the focus on the dress codes of other female agents (professional or amateur) of the fashion-conscious 1960s, such as Modesty Blaise,[31] *The Avengers*' combat-experienced Mrs. Peel (Diana Rigg), or Doris Day's two amateur spy roles in the Frank Tashlin comedies *The Glass Bottom Boat* (1966) and *Caprice* (1967). Notwithstanding, the aforementioned mode of cult reception that is characterized by a double articulation of incongruity and excess comes to the fore in this case on account of the film's excessive attention to fashion and playfulness while the plot becomes more and more incongruous, thereby making an ironic commentary upon the potentially elusive and confusing narrative of spy thrillers. The repeated infantilization of Candy's character by the films' adult characters, and her youthful appearance, also foreshadow the prominent mid-1960s shift in female body images and fashion. As Heike Jenss remarks, for instance, the female body tended to be infantilized in the 1960s on account of the predominant focus on youthfulness and a tendency toward unisex dress codes and a more androgynous appearance, as paradigmatically personified by Twiggy.[32] Highlighting the (late) 1950s' and 1960s' contradictory atmosphere of progressive and reactionary tendencies, particularly with regard to notions of gender, everybody naturally assumes that Agent Kitten must be male.

As previously hinted at, *13 Frightened Girls* is embedded within 1960s culture and thus displays a distinctive pop aesthetic that is "a product of the social and cultural changes of the 1960s and revolves around the themes of modernity and consumerism."[33] According to Chapman, "the spy/secret agent genre became the 'dominant fictional form of the pop ethic.'"[34] He further cites

David Buxton: "[i]nextricably linked to patriotism and the overcoming of class divisions, the spy genre becomes additionally coded with discourses pertaining to tourism, conspicuous consumption and sexual pleasure, an ideal terrain on which to confront and explore the tension between duty to a higher authority (the state) and the individualism produced by the new consumer culture."[35] The consumerist strain is further accentuated by the film's American-centered perspective and Candy's naïve idealization of Americanness. As she proudly tells her Russian friend and competitor Natasha, "in my country, our place is face to face with man." This stance is, however, disrupted in the end. Most crucially, in one comparatively "realist" moment, the unrelenting harshness of the job and the likeness between both sides are exposed when Candy's father, unaware that he is addressing the fate of his own daughter, suggests trading Kitten in for the kidnapped Soldier, since Kitten has become too hot to handle and thus expendable. The ongoing hunt for Candy, which turns into a playful distraction scene in which all the girls engage in a hide-and-seek game with the intruders, and the eventual exposure of the chauffeur as the cold-blooded killer—a common crime trope, ironically employed as such—further underscore the underlying absurdity of it all.

CONCLUSION

As the preceding analysis has demonstrated, William Castle's 1960s films display a hybrid concoction of his earlier styles and themes, sociocultural issues of the postwar era (in particular the 1950s and 1960s), and a plethora of diverse generic elements. These different elements are playfully fused and to a certain extent interconnected with each other. Moreover, the self-conscious, tongue-in-cheek use and subversion of generic patterns requires a very attentive and active audience, as spectators' expectations are repeatedly built up and then undermined, often resulting in a blurring or eventual breakdown of generic structures.

In *13 Ghosts*, the monstrous Other/innocent victim binary model is subverted, as the actual threat emanates from an evil human who takes advantage of the haunted Gothic mansion's notorious reputation for entirely selfish purposes. In *Let's Kill Uncle*, normative constructions of childhood are abolished while classical Hollywood's stylistic hybridity is underlined. In *13 Frightened Girls*, the heteronormative model of the male spy is ironically turned upside down. As Donald Woods Winnicott suggests, "in playing, and perhaps only in playing, [one] is free to be creative."[36] Castle's films seem to equip the audience with such a condition. In the selected key texts, game-playing is also reflexively referenced as a central aspect of the films' narratives. Additionally, it is repeatedly associated with the liminal position of either an infantile (*13*

Ghosts, Let's Kill Uncle) or an adolescent (*13 Frightened Girls, The Spirit Is Willing*) point of view. By this means, and given Castle's individualist stance and remarkably creative impulse, his films display an enormous and lasting cult potential.

NOTES

1. Ernest Mathijs and Jamie Sexton, *Cult Cinema: An Introduction* (Malden: Wiley-Blackwell, 2011), p. 72.
2. Ibid.
3. Ibid. pp. 73–4.
4. Ibid. p. 74.
5. Torben Kragh Grodal, *Moving Picture: A New Theory of Film Genres, Feelings, and Cognition* (Oxford: Oxford University Press, 1999), p. 226.
6. Dale Bailey, *American Nightmares: The Haunted House Formula in American Popular Fiction* (Madison: University of Wisconsin Press, 1999), p. 6.
7. Ibid. p. 8.
8. Ibid. pp. 5–6.
9. The deliberate casting of Margaret Hamilton in this role is also a humorous metadiegetic reference to her famous role as the Wicked Witch of the West in *The Wizard of Oz* (1939).
10. Rebecca Janicker, *The Literary Haunted House: Lovecraft, Matheson, King and the Horror In Between* (Jefferson, NC: McFarland, 2015), p. 1.
11. Katherine A. Fowkes, "The Bawdy Body in Two Comedy Ghost Films: *Topper* and *Beetlejuice*," in Murray Leeder (ed.), *Cinematic Ghosts. Haunting and Spectrality: From Silent Cinema to the Digital Era* (New York: Bloomsbury Academic, 2015), p. 162.
12. Christian Stewen, "Childhood, Ghost Images, and the Heterotopian Space of Cinema: The Child as Medium in *The Others*," in Debbie Olson and Andrew Scahill (eds.), *Lost and Othered Children in Contemporary Cinema* (Lanham, MD: Lexington Books, 2011), p. 272.
13. Timothy Corrigan, "Film and the Culture of Cult," *Wide Angle* 8.3–4 (1986): 93.
14. Catherine Driscoll, *Teen Film: A Critical Introduction* (Oxford: Berg, 2011), p. 28.
15. See, for instance, Chapter 3 on the teenage marketplace, 32–53, Chapter 4 on rock'n'roll teenpics, 54–82, and Chapter 6 on horror teenpics, 115–44, in Thomas Doherty, *Teenagers and Teenpics: The Juvenilization of American Movies in the 1950s* (Philadelphia: Temple University Press, 2002).
16. Mathijs and Sexton, *Cult Cinema*, p. 148.
17. Ibid. pp. 149–50.
18. Ibid. pp. 148–9.
19. Ibid. p. 150.
20. Fowkes, "The Bawdy Body," p. 164.
21. See Martin Rowson, "Let's Kill Uncle drew me into a deliciously horrible adult world," *The Guardian*, August 8, 2013, <https://www.theguardian.com/commentisfree/2013/aug/07/lets-kill-uncle-martin-rowson> (accessed October 19, 2017).
22. See Dominic Lennard, *Bad Seeds and Holy Terrors: The Child Villains of Horror Films* (New York: State University of New York Press, 2014), pp. 4–6.
23. Peter Wuss, *Cinematic Narration and Its Psychological Impact: Functions of Cognition, Emotion and Play* (Newcastle upon Tyne: Cambridge Scholars Publishing, 2009), p. 143.

24. Justin Smith, *Withnail and Us: Cult Films and Film Cults in British Cinema* (London/New York: I. B. Tauris, 2010), p. 109.
25. See Janet Staiger, "Hybrid or Inbred: The Purity Hypothesis and Hollywood Genre History," in Barry Keith Grant (ed.), *Genre Reader IV* (Austin: University of Texas Press, 2012), p. 212.
26. The film also references *Homicidal* (1961).
27. There exist several versions of the film with a differing national focus.
28. The trilogy consists of *The Ipcress File* (1965), *Funeral in Berlin* (1966), and *Billion Dollar Brain* (1967).
29. James Chapman, *Saints & Avengers: British Adventure Series of the 1960s* (London: I. B. Tauris, 2009), p. 20.
30. Ibid. pp. 21–2.
31. The character's origins lie in a 1963 comic strip that was turned into a flamboyant yet utterly cynical film version by Joseph Losey in 1966, starring Monica Vitti as Modesty.
32. See Chapter 3 on "Icons of Modernity: Sixties Fashion and Youth Culture" in Heinke Jess's *Fashioning Memory: Vintage Style and Youth Culture* (London: Bloomsbury, 2015), pp. 37–64.
33. Chapman, *Saints & Avengers*, p. 14.
34. Ibid.
35. David Buxton, *From* The Avengers *to* Miami Vice*: Form and Ideology in Television Series* (Manchester: Manchester University Press, 1990), p. 77.
36. Donald Woods Winnicott, *Playing and Reality* (London: Routledge, 2005), p. 71.

CHAPTER 10

"Where Did Our Love Go?": The Case of William Castle's *The Night Walker*

Michael Petitti

"How do you tell a genuine director from a quasichimpanzee?"—Andrew Sarris, "Notes on the Auteur Theory in 1962"

"I was unique... My ideas were all my own... It's something that you either have or your don't. And I have ideas. I'm an idea man."—1974 interview with William Castle from *Kings of the Bs: Working with the Hollywood System: An Anthology of Film History and Criticism* (1975)

What is the problem with *The Night Walker*? To start, it's important to clarify that *The Night Walker* has never been considered William Castle's finest film. At the time of its release in 1964, the Castle thriller was savaged. Mike McGrady, writing for *Newsday*, labeled *The Night Walker* "a rotten picture,"[1] while *The Globe and Mail*'s Frank Morriss called it "a second-rate film that might not get by even on the late, late, late TV show."[2] Bosley Crowther, the notorious film critic for the *New York Times*, was restrained in his assessment, calling Castle's film a "creaky gimcrack thriller,"[3] though Clifford Terry, at the *Chicago Tribune*, overcompensated for his peer's composure, declaring, "Barbara Stanwyck and Robert Taylor, once a couple in real life, have been paired in only three motion pictures throughout their long careers. The first two were produced in 1937. Now comes the third, 28 years later. They should have waited a little longer."[4] Still, seeking contemporary plaudits, when considering a William Castle film, is a fool's errand.

The dubious distinction of "the best William Castle film" might be applied to his debut gimmick film, the histrionic *Macabre* (1958), or his now-acknowledged camp classic *The Tingler* (1959)—a film John Waters has called a "masterpiece."[5] Perhaps the case for excellence could be made for *Homicidal*

(1961), Castle's playful and menacing *Psycho* (1960) rip-off, and a film that scholar David Sanjek notes is able to "scare one's pants off but also brings a tear to one's eye."[6] Or, one might rush to the defense of *Mr. Sardonicus* (1961), Castle's almost stately Mario Bavaesque chamber nightmare. Regardless, debates of the sort (i.e., "Best William Castle Film?") never seemed to matter to the filmmaker. Castle was not a critical darling, and he evidently reveled in a self-effacing manner in the responses of his harshest critics. For example, during a sneak preview for *House on Haunted Hill* (1959), Castle recalls asking an elderly man to quit "fidgeting." He continues, "Turning to me, he whispered back, 'The biggest piece of shit I've ever seen.' With that, he brushed past me and left the theatre."[7] Nevertheless, Castle knew the exact worth of his films: they were exploitable commodities. As illustrated in the anecdote from his autobiography, Castle never took his work too seriously. When asked by a critic once how he could "produce such trash," Castle responded, "When I've made enough money, I'll make better pictures."[8] *The Night Walker*, however, proved also to be a commerical failure, which was something Castle could not abide.

In William Castle's autobiography—one should consider throwing quotation marks around that term—*Step Right Up! I'm Gonna Scare the Pants Off America*, the filmmaker joined critics in espousing an equally cold view of *The Night Walker*, but not for its hoary setup or flawed performances. Instead, Castle recounts the failures of his postgimmick films, including *13 Frightened Girls* (1963) and *The Old Dark House* (1963), in quick succession in order to allocate considerable space for touting his association with *Rosemary's Baby* (1968), a film he produced. As such, Castle's recollection about *The Night Walker* has nothing to do with reuniting the formerly married Stanwyck and Taylor, or getting Robert Bloch, the *Psycho* scribe, to write the screenplay, or responding to the critical vitriol the film elicited. Rather, Castle recalls that the film was a box-office disaster, stating, "I felt the declining box office on my next picture, *The Night Walker*, costarring Robert Taylor and Barbara Stanwyck, both big stars that I felt would be strong enough to pull customers in. The picture played to almost empty theatres."[9] Therefore, in two banal sentences, Castle conflates *The Night Walker* as indistinguishable from his other flops of the period, including *I Saw What You Did* (1965) and *The Spirit is Willing* (1967). In this way, Castle implies the critical response to *The Night Walker* was validated by its commercial irrelevance, a notion that appears to be endorsed by the ensuing critical silence around the film.

The Night Walker has not received academic reappraisals or critical attention similar to that foisted upon other Castle films in recent decades. Murray Leeder's comment about *The Night Walker*, that it was "perhaps [Castle's] most mature film,"[10] is telling. Specifically, Leeder's comment, coupled with the relative silence surrounding *The Night Walker*, illustrates the fact that maturity is rarely what one seeks in Castle's work. As indicated by Castle's pithy dismissal of the film in his autobiography, disinterest in *The Night Walker* has a long history. In fact, during a career retrospective interview with Linda May Strawn from 1974, Castle doesn't once mention *The Night Walker*. Again, we feel compelled to ask: what is the problem with *The Night Walker*? Castle's film was, in manifold ways, mature, but it was also critically maligned and a box-office failure, making it ripe for reevaluation. So what has staunched interest in *The Night Walker*? In part, the answer is located within the film's narrative.

Critics likely responded unfavorably to *The Night Walker* because William Castle had been considered a showman instead of an auteur, and the film is "creaky". But, logical as such attitudes might have seemed at the time, they also enhance what is interesting about the film; something that can only be realized by considering *The Night Walker* as a synthesis of Castle's auteurist tendencies. *The Night Walker* struggles to emerge as a cohesive work of art given its narrative concerns with conscious and unconscious states of being, dream life versus waking life, and issues of sight or blindness. Castle and screenwriter Robert Bloch assumed the film's narrative would provide keys to its analysis, but its narrative merely scratches the surface of what's genuinely fascinating about *The Night Walker*. I wish to argue that what Leeder identifies as maturity in *The Night Walker* is its latent content: a pervasive assault on capitalism by way of a critique of American marriage. This, as I will show, is not an incidental theme of *The Night Walker*, but the elongation of Castle's cinematic fascination with this particular theme. In other words, this aspect of capitalist critique is sustained throughout Castle's oeuvre, finding its fullest voice in *The Night Walker*. Ultimately, I will argue *The Night Walker* should be reconsidered as a keystone work in the career of William Castle—a film that suggests Castle was an auteur whose overriding feature was a genuine disdain for the American capitalist ideology.

GLASS CASTLE

At the time of his 1974 interview with Linda May Strawn, William Castle must have recognized he was at the twilight of his career—three years after the interview, Castle would be dead from a heart attack at 63.[11] Throughout the interview, Castle offers sober insights about his career. For Castle, the only path to success as a filmmaker was to target the youth. Making the shock films he was known for, Castle notes, "you are appealing to a younger element and if you can try to figure out what that younger element wants, you're in business."[12] And, during the late 1950s and early 1960s, business was good for Castle. The filmmaker's successful run of gimmick films coincided with a moment of great change within the film industry. As scholar Catherine Clepper notes, Castle was able to take advantage of the industry-wide rift created by the fallout from the Paramount Decree, the splintering of film audiences due to television, and the rise of the economically viable teenager. So, though Castle wasn't too different from prior exploitation filmmakers, his circumstances were, and the "sudden self-reliance and/or corporate unmooring of exhibitors gave Castle access to a broader audience and industrial network than that available to a slightly older generation of cinematic hucksters."[13]

The late 1950s may have represented a tumultuous period for the American film industry, but William Castle found success by targeting the young with the gimmicks he deployed for these early features.[14] In these films, Castle's gimmicks and narratives coalesce to form a peculiar tension. For example, we can see how such incongruous combinations manifest in *House on Haunted Hill*, a film whose gimmick (Emergo) clearly appealed to youngsters who would otherwise struggle to discern the finer points of its marital drama.[15] Such tensions only grew sharper with Castle's postgimmick work, where the gimmicks (when applicable) were subtler, diverting the focus, as in the case of *The Night Walker*, to the film's mature content. Furthermore, at the time of that film's release, the leads (Barbara Stanwyck and Robert Taylor) were in their fifties, and their former marriage—the film's chief gimmick—would have been more interesting to the parents of young moviegoers. Therefore, as the 1960s progressed, the industrial quirks Castle capitalized on during his gimmick run were outmatched by narrative content that alienated his young audiences.

In his interview with Strawn, Castle acknowledged that gimmickry had changed, though he remained committed to it spiritually, arguing, "You've got to have some little hook, whether it's perfume, whether it's incense, or whether it's a flamethrower. But you've got to have something."[16] Of course, Castle is not wrong, and there's a substantial history of American film and exploitation. In fact, presold material, bankable stars, and stunt casting were sanctioned versions of gimmickry utilized by major Hollywood studios throughout film history. Castle's comment suggests that he wished to view his postgimmick career as maintaining the carnival atmosphere of his gimmick run, but the truth is he struggled to maintain his creativity with his gimmicks. In 1963, *The Old Dark House* represented a creative nadir for Castle, who seemed to believe teaming up with Hammer studios to remake a cult classic would be gimmick enough to promote the film. Castle's comment to Strawn sought to retcon his postgimmick career, which had flagged due to creative exhaustion induced by his constant workflow.

A true sign of the creative impoverishment informing William Castle's ensuing promotional approaches can be read in his reliance on multiple gimmicks per film. With the exception of *Mr. Sardonicus*, whose "Punishment Poll" seems to be its sole gimmick, and the aforementioned absent gimmickry of *Old Dark House*, Castle's postgimmick films evince a grab-bag approach. The roadshow nature of Castle's initial gimmick run allowed for exhibition practices like Percepto or Emergo, which required custom labor, but the same could not be expected for Castle's more widely distributed 1960s films. As a result, Castle settled on cost-effective ways to integrate gimmicks into these films. For instance, *Homicidal*'s flagrant theft from *Psycho* maintains that one of the subtler gimmicks for Castle's film was his self-conscious deconstruction of the well-known narrative of Hitchcock's film. Hitchcock's famously strict screening procedures for *Psycho*—"set show times, closely spaced screenings, elimination of cartoons and short subjects and patient waits in lines"[17]—provided Castle with his "central gimmick," which appears as *Homicidal* nears its climax and Castle's voice announces a "fright break"[18] for audience members who wish to flee before the film's climatic standoff.[19] Elsewhere, *13 Frightened Girls*, a.k.a. *The Candy Web* (1963), offers an example of Castle's layered gimmickry. The press material for Castle's campy spy picture hyped up its cast of international young female stars who had won contests for roles (gimmick #1), while, in its theatrical release, Castle provided introductory and concluding remarks informing viewers that the card they received as they entered the theatre might, when wet, reveal they were prizewinners (gimmick #2). Lacking in ambition compared to Emergo or Percepto, Castle still hoped to maximize the exploitative potential for each film. Evidence can be found in the case of Castle's proto-slasher *Strait-Jacket* (1964), released the same year as *The Night Walker*. *Strait-Jacket* offered up the casting of Joan Crawford, including multiple in-person appearances at screenings of the film (gimmick #1) as its primary draw, and, supposedly, also provided audience members with cardboard axes (gimmick #2). Regardless, *The Night Walker* was released in the wake of such creative fervor and fatigue.

The critical and commercial failure of *The Night Walker* had less to do with the blasé quality of its gimmick and more to do with the ramifications of enacting such a casting gimmick. The easiest way to parse what Castle dredged up with *The Night Walker* is to understand that his duality as "Shock-Meister"[20] and auteur collided to generate a film with a ferocious ideological critique that was metastasized by the decision to cast Barbara Stanwyck and Robert Taylor. Such alchemy is the extension of a career upending American capitalist ideology, something that was likely unknown to Castle as he created his merry assortment of B-grade horror fare. Yet, first, one must make the case that William Castle was an auteur.

THE AUTEUR FORMERLY KNOWN AS WILLIAM SCHLOSS

In what seems an oversight, Andrew Sarris, in his expansive categorizing of American film auteurs, *The American Cinema: Directors and Directions 1929–1968*, does not include William Castle. The volume sets as its central project a comprehensive categorizing and sorting of all the auteurs working in American film. As such, Sarris creates a panoply of divisions that manage to encompass almost every conceivable director working during his timeline, including outliers in his sections "Expressive Esoterica," "Oddities, One-Shots, and Newcomers," "Subjects for Further Research," and "Miscellany." Considering fellow B-filmmakers Roger Corman and (at the time) Francis Ford Coppola merit inclusion in Sarris's "Oddities, One-Shots, and Newcomers" section,[21] and that André de Toth, director of the 3-D *House of Wax* (1953), and dark card émigré Edgar G. Ulmer both received inclusion in "Expressive Esoterica," the exclusion of William Castle is baffling. It's hard not to interpret Castle's omission as evidence of a pronounced bias, particularly in critical circles, against the filmmaker at the time (see: the opening of this chapter). Unless, perhaps, Sarris was operating from the notion that Castle was more of a producer than an auteur, but even then the incorporation of incidental or infrequent directors ("One-Shots") presents solid counterevidence given Castle's prodigious directorial output. As punctilious as he could be, Sarris didn't tend to distinguish between auteurs who aspired to art versus those who exploited film form when populating his categories, apparent in the inclusions of Jacques Tourneur and Samuel Fuller. In order to understand the auteur responsible for *The Night Walker*, however, it's important to interrogate why Andrew Sarris omitted William Castle from the rank of auteurs, and, in turn, make the case for his inclusion.

For one thing, William Castle possibly wore too many hats to fall within Sarris's purview. When he began his film career at Columbia, Castle was under what he later dubbed a "seven-way contract," where he could be expected to perform the roles of "actor, dramatic coach, dialogue director, film cutter, assistant director, director and producer."[22] If it seems unlikely Sarris would focus his sights on Castle based on the thirty-nine B-movies he made for Columbia, the question becomes: why would Sarris ignore Castle after his iconic gimmick run? Perhaps the fact that Castle was not a credited writer on any of his iconic projects may have tipped the scale against him. Castle co-wrote *Bug* (1975), his final film as producer, with novelist Thomas Page, but received writing credits for nothing else during his major gimmick and postgimmick run. For his part, Page viewed Castle as a total auteur, stating, "I can attest Bill Castle knew more about the process and business of producing movies than any other person I have ever met. From the germ of an idea in his head, to costing a script, purchasing raw stock, hiring actors, wardrobe, directors, lighting equipment, Castle had the numbers in his head and time worked out to the second."[23] Being a writer-director auteur is far from essential for Andrew Sarris's conceptualization, and several of his notable "Pantheon Directors," including Hitchcock and Ernest Lubitsch, wrote little of their most recognizable work. Therefore, it seems Castle's biggest failing to being deemed an auteur, paradoxically, was not taking enough credit (on screen, at least) for his work.

Homicidal, however, presents a fascinating case study for William Castle as the total auteur. During preproduction for the film, Castle seized authorship of the project, much to the chagrin of screenwriter Robb White. In fact, White blames Castle for the film's explicit theft from Hitchcock's *Psycho*. In describing the preproduction process for *Homicidal*, White makes it clear that Castle's input in the finished product extended beyond his producer-director byline, claiming, "Bill gave me the idea for *Homicidal*, and when I started to work on that screenplay he worked on it more than I did—more than he had on any other script that I did for him. It just felt very funny to me, that he was helping out so much, and that he wanted it exactly this way and that way and so on."[24] Meanwhile, in his autobiography, Castle describes the production of *Homicidal* as his "most fun,"[25] aided by the fact the film received "great reviews," gloating, "I consider it one of the most original of my motion pictures."[26] Confirmation that Castle had indeed arrived as an auteur could be seen in the fact that *Time* decided to include *Homicidal* in its ten best films of 1961. Despite the film's artistic plagiarism, *Time* argued, "[Castle's film] was obviously made in imitation of Hitchcock's thriller," yet *Homicidal* "just as obviously . . . surpasses its model in structure, suspense, and sheer nervous drive."[27] Or, as Castle saw it: "I was becoming a star."[28]

Another link between Castle and sanctioned auteurs can be located in his economic approach to his productions, bringing to mind Hitchcock in the 1950s or Robert Altman in the 1970s. Like those confirmed auteurs, Castle recycled personnel throughout his gimmick and postgimmick runs. Prior to Castle's tampering with *Homicidal* severing their professional relationship, William Castle and Robb White "cofounded Susina Associates, a short-lived but highly profitable independent film production company"[29]; Susina Associates would become William Castle Productions, allowing Castle to make distribution deals with Columbia, Universal, and Paramount for the remainder of his career. Before striking those deals, however, Castle and White collaborated on the filmmaker's major run of gimmick films: *Macabre, House on Haunted Hill, The Tingler, 13 Ghosts*, and *Homicidal*. After White's departure, subsequent screenwriters took on multiple assignments with Castle, including Ray Russell (*Mr. Sardonicus* and *Zotz!*), Robert Dillon (*13 Frightened Girls* and *The Old Dark House*), Ben Starr (*The Busy Body* [1967] and *The Spirit is Willing*), and Robert Bloch (*Strait-Jacket* and *The Night Walker*). Castle also had productive, long-term relationships with cinematographer Harold E. Stine, who worked on four Castle films beginning with *The Night Walker*, and editor Edwin Bryant, who was responsible for cutting twelve of Castle's features throughout his gimmick and postgimmick periods. Additionally, the majority of the music for Castle's features from the era was composed by Von Dexter (gimmick run), Van Alexander (postgimmick), and Vic Mizzy (postgimmick, including the carnivalesque score for *The Night Walker*). And, of course, there was Castle's cadre of actors.

Acting has emerged as the most transparent sign of an auteur's commitment to maintaining quality and tone across projects. Throughout the 1950s and 60s, William Castle recast Vincent Price (*House on Haunted Hill*, *The Tingler*), Tom Poston (*Zotz!*, *The Old Dark House*), Jim Backus (*Macabre*, *Zotz!*), Sid Caesar (*The Busy Body*, *The Spirit is Willing*), and Joan Crawford (*Strait-Jacket*, *I Saw What You Did*) to evoke a preferred sensibility for each film; Price and Crawford provided a camp presence while Poston and Caesar were clowns. In many instances, auteurs work with the same actors for multiple projects because of quality control, personal attachment, or the development and stability of a particular vision. Castle, however, often worked with similar personnel, in rapid succession, for more budgetary purposes. Castle doesn't do much to contextualize the production process for his films in his autobiography, and the fact he often blurs his films together, from paragraph to paragraph, or within chapters, is telling. The same manic energy can be seen in Castle's recycling of the cast and crew for successive films, sometimes within the same year. Screenwriters Ben Starr and Robert Bloch each made two movies a year with Castle, just as Sid Caesar starred in both *The Busy Body* and *The Spirit is Willing* in 1967, and then there was producer Dona Holloway. Holloway had an active hand in all of Castle's films from 1959 (*The Tingler*) to 1968 (*Rosemary's Baby*), and not merely as an investor: "Whenever Castle had an idea for a film, Holloway was usually one of the first to hear about it. Her feedback was important, and she had enough influence to reject a proposal if she deemed it unsuitable for motion picture production."[30] Whatever Castle's purpose for reusing personnel, the finished films generate stylistic and thematic continuity that are indicative of his predilections. The resulting films provide a cohesive vision due to the repetition of faces, or similar writing, editing, and musical styles. If the work of an auteur illuminates "[t]he author is present in the text as a cinematic effect,"[31] Castle's signature is emblazoned across his work.

Teasing out the critical premises that illuminate Andrew Sarris's auteur theory might elucidate what prevented Castle's inclusion. For Sarris, "the first premise of the auteur theory is the technical competence of a director as a criterion of value."[32] Technical competence may be easy to overlook regarding Castle, but runs counter to the evidence. As someone who cut his teeth as a jack-of-all trades (or, at least, seven trades) for Harry Cohn at Columbia Pictures, Castle is, quite simply, no Ed Wood. It's worth recalling Thomas Page's adoring comment about the filmmaker's acumen, or considering the films themselves for further evidence. In Castle's films, boom microphones do not drop into shots and camera shadows are not crowded into frames—in fact, the actors and the camera are often in harmony. Much of the negative critical commentary surrounding William Castle's work conflates the sometimes overwrought, sometimes inept acting in his films with his own technical style. This means a scene-chewing turn by Vincent Price or Joan Crawford is read as evidence against Castle's otherwise discernible technical style (a style that can improve, as we will see with *The Night Walker*, if the material and cast are especially strong), creating a critical trap.

Andrew Sarris's second premise for auteurs is that "the distinguishable personality of the director" serves "as a criterion of value."[33] A cursory perusal of this collection reveals there are few cinematic personalities more forceful or pronounced than William Castle, an auteur who literally put himself into his films, as master of ceremonies (*Mr. Sardonicus*), droll jester (*Homicidal*), or critical commentator (*The Tingler*). In this sense, the gimmicks of Castle's films of the late 1950s and early 60s *are* the distinguishable personality of William Castle. As Sarris notes, for an auteur "recurrent characteristics of style ... serve as his signature,"[34] and Castle's bookend on-screen interjections or gimmick-heavy narratives serve this function. Lest one suspect Sarris isn't implying an auteur's signature is their actual presence in their films, it's worth remembering his canon includes Hitchcock, Charlie Chaplin, John Cassavetes, and an entire comedy cohort of actor-auteurs (Jerry Lewis, W. C. Fields, Harold Lloyd, The Marx Brothers, and Mae West) in his collection.

Sarris's third and final premise, "interior meaning," is a more abstract concept, and one that exists as a "tension between a director's personality and his material."[35] The tension between William Castle as corporeal presence and William Castle as curator of terrible tales is visible throughout Castle's work. Collections like this help separate the content, and its critical implications, of Castle's films from his gimmickry. Castle may have presented himself as a ham, but even his films pitched for children, like *Zotz!*, *13 Frightened Girls*, *Let's Kill Uncle*, or *Shanks* (1974), exhibit a subliminal desire to investigate topics such as nuclear war, murder, divorce, and child abuse. As I will show with my reading of *The Night Walker*, Castle's gimmicks are capable of representing the outflow of his oversized personality without obfuscating his critical concerns.

Regardless of how he slots into Andrew Sarris's conception of the auteur, William Castle was an auteur. And, it should be noted, Castle's canonization as auteur is not, as Dudley Andrew suggests about the democratizing of the concept, a mere effect of trendy "canon-bashing" that allowed "new auteurs to climb into the pantheon ... at deflated value."[36] As we have seen, even working from the antiquated premises of Sarris's famed theorization of the auteur, Castle passes muster. Peter Wollen argues that auteurs "must be defined in terms of shifting relations, in their singularity as well as their uniformity."[37] The Castle of the gimmick period, a singular figure, is impossible to comprehend without also considering William Castle, the hired hand for Columbia Pictures. Castle's singular auteur status also coexists with the fact that he was only a producer for the two most historically significant films in his canon,

The Lady From Shanghai (1947) and *Rosemary's Baby*. For Wollen, the auteur theory is only as strong as the critic, arguing, "The auteur theory, as I conceive it, insists that the spectator has to work at reading the text."[38] Therefore, it seems the only genuine way to validate Castle's auteur authentication is to examine his work. Dudley Andrew's auteur argument about "struggles of faith in an atheist world" is duly applicable for auteurs like Castle: "With the disappearance of God we are left with the body of the world: so, with the disappearance of the author, we are left with the material body of the text."[39] In which case, let's examine the bodies.

THE RULING IDEAS OF THE MISERABLE CLASS

At this point, it's necessary to provide a complete list of William Castle's gimmick and postgimmick work (his films from 1958–74), as a kind of legend for readers to follow for the remainder of this chapter: *Macabre, House on Haunted Hill, The Tingler, 13 Ghosts, Homicidal, Mr. Sardonicus, Zotz!, 13 Frightened Girls, The Old Dark House, Strait-Jacket, The Night Walker, I Saw What You Did, Let's Kill Uncle, The Busy Body, The Spirit is Willing, Project X* (1968), and *Shanks*. Surveying these films allows us to trace thematic consistencies in the content of Castle's films. The gimmicks behind Castle's films often distract viewers and critics alike into ignoring his narrative preoccupations, particularly the one paramount to *The Night Walker*: an assault on American capitalist ideology through the institution of marriage.

Robin Wood argues, in "Ideology, Genre, Auteur," that film criticism must "interpenetrate" Hollywood films through a sort of blended critical approach, which he calls "synthetic criticism,"[40] in order to analyze the latent intentions of filmmakers. Wood claims that classical Hollywood films circulated around concepts culled from the "American capitalist ideology," which can then be discerned in the work of auteurs (Wood focuses on Alfred Hitchcock and Frank Capra) who prominently reveal "values and assumptions so insistently embodied in and reinforced by the classical Hollywood cinema."[41] As is Wood's wont, he articulates these concepts of American capitalist ideology found in classical Hollywood films as a list. The list itself is fascinating, but what is of particular interest for William Castle and *The Night Walker* is Wood's thesis that from this list "emerge logically two ideal figures."[42] For Wood, classical Hollywood cinema circulates American capitalist ideology around these two figures: "The Ideal Male: the virile adventurer, potent, untrammeled man of action" and "The Ideal Female: wife and mother, perfect companion, endlessly dependable, mainstay of hearth and home."[43] Anyone who has even a passing familiarity with classical Hollywood films can instantly recall several examples of films that express the untenable alliance between the ideal male and ideal female; perhaps most famously exhibited in *Casablanca* (1942). Of course, Wood recognized this too.

The primary reason Robin Wood concerns himself with the "ideological oppositions" of the Ideal Male and Ideal Female in classical Hollywood cinema is that these figures represent "a complex interlocking pattern" most "profitably examined" through genre films helmed by auteurs.[44] It's here where William Castle comes back into view: our misunderstood auteur made genre films released by classical Hollywood studios (Columbia, Universal, and Paramount). And, examining Castle's films, we find manifold variations on classic Hollywood's Ideal Male (adventurer) and Female (domesticated)— prominent examples can be found in *House on Haunted Hill*, *The Tingler*, *13 Ghosts*, *Zotz!*, *13 Frightened Girls*, *Let's Kill Uncle*, and *The Spirit is Willing*. The incongruity between these traditionally gendered figures, however, is a concern for Wood (and, as we will see, Castle). That is, Robin Wood's Ideal Male and Female may be the logical figures embodying the other concepts of the American capitalist ideology ingrained in classical Hollywood films, such as the work ethic, marriage, and success/wealth, but they form a union of "quite staggering incompatibility."[45] In order to resolve this tension, classical Hollywood cinema offers up two "shadow" figures: "The settled husband/ father, dependable but dull" and "The erotic woman (adventuress, gambling lady, saloon 'entertainer'), fascinating but dangerous, liable to betray the hero or turn into a black panther."[46] As we return to Castle's work to locate these four figures, the Ideal Male and Female and settled husband/father and erotic woman, the filmmaker's interest in destabilizing and critiquing American capitalist ideology becomes more pronounced. The difference between Castle and Hitchcock and Capra, the other genre auteurs Wood examines, is that Castle's default critique of American capitalist ideology resolves itself in wryer, more cynical ways.

One of the key features of Castle's early gimmick films is his complicating of the foursome of the Ideal Male and Female and their shadow selves— whereas auteurs like Hitchcock and Capra worked within approved patterns. For instance, in *House on Haunted Hill*, Castle presents a central couple that should make for an ideal match: the Ideal Male and erotic woman. Instead, Frederick Loren (Vincent Price), a "potent, untrammelled" millionaire, must constantly work to satisfy his (fourth) wife Annabelle (Carol Ohmart), who he implies is as an "erotic woman" even as audiences view her as an Ideal Female with reasonable trepidation about her husband since his other wives have died or mysteriously disappeared. Castle's major reveal, however, is that Annabelle actually is the erotic woman, and she and her lover fake her suicide while planning Frederick's murder. This seems to upend Wood's conception because, as Ideal Male and erotic woman, Frederick and Annabelle should have been a match. Instead, viewers are left to assume Frederick was not the adventurous ladykiller implied in the film's opening scenes, but instead the "settled" and "dull" husband. As such, the marriage between Frederick (settled husband) and Annabelle (erotic woman) becomes a classic case of an incompatible pairing. *House on Haunted Hill* also offers a romantic subplot involving a pilot, Lance Schroeder (Richard Long), and polite, working-class office drone, Nora Manning (Carolyn Craig), who are meant to represent the actual Ideal Male and Female (assuming the "perfect companion, endlessly dependable" is more integral to the equation than Wood's "wife and mother," since the couple are not married). Remarkably, Castle allows the Lance-Nora subplot to fizzle out (so much so that their foreshadowed romance scans as willful misdirection), overshadowed by Frederick and Annabelle's drama. Nevertheless, in just his second gimmick feature, we see how William Castle was attuned to and defiant of the classical Hollywood conventions Robin Wood located in the work of Castle's peers.

Similarly playing against type, in his first gimmick film, *Macabre*, Castle sets up Dr. Rod Barrett (William Prince) as the settled father (he is a widower), only to reveal him to actually be the film's devious mastermind. The unease between Barrett and his wife's family in *Macabre*, who despise how he handled the death of both of their daughters, can be read in conjunction with Barrett's actual villainy, emphasizing Castle's inherent cynicism about the American capitalist ideology regarding marriage and family. Throughout most of its runtime Barrett is painted as a victim, making the revelations about him more distressing to viewers. This persistent cynicism about American families and marriages sours further in Castle's work, so that by the time he releases *Strait-Jacket* in 1964 there can be little expectation of how Castle will handle domestic matters beyond the fact that it will involve a devastating twist. Therefore, in *Strait-Jacket*, the Ideal Female figure is initially presented as Carol Harbin (Diane Baker), the sweet daughter of former axe-murderer Lucy Harbin (Joan Crawford). In the film, Carol is set to wed the dull and dependable Michael Fields (John Anthony Hayes). The opening of *Strait-Jacket* depicts Lucy axing her ex-husband and his mistress to death in a fit of rage, making it evident she is the "dangerous" woman. The major twist of *Strait-Jacket*, however, is that Carol has been working to frame Lucy, who has been released after being putatively reformed. Instead, Carol is revealed to be Wood's "black panther," an axe murderer who has been annihilating various characters in order to frame her mother. Therefore, *Strait-Jacket* presents yet another curious inversion by Castle. This time, the seemingly dangerous woman turns out to be an Ideal Female (a dependable mother), while her apparently placid daughter has been corrupted into the dangerous woman through her mother's past actions. The gleeful frequency of William Castle's execution of these character shifts provides concrete evidence of his delight in perverting the American capitalist ideology.

William Castle's recurrent diversions from Robin Wood's simple formulations of the marital dis/harmony critique within classical Hollywood cinema make for critically rich films, which have often been overshadowed by his gimmicks. For example, *The Tingler* offers several iterations of ideological critique, but this is all but rendered obsolete by the cult canonization of the film. (For years, Los Angeles's Cinefamily screened the film with Percepto for Halloween.) The Percepto gimmick glosses over the fact that *The Tingler*'s narrative exemplifies the American capitalist ideology as lousy with "hopeless contradictions and unresolvable tensions."[47] In the film, Dr. Warren Chapin (Vincent Price) is a scientist who represents an "untrammeled man of action" (the Ideal Male); specifically, the action of locating and identifying the "tingler," an arthropod-like creature triggered by fear. Meanwhile, Warren's wife Isabel (Patricia Cutts) despises her husband because his work has made him inattentive and withdrawn, so she actively courts other men as an "erotic woman." In fact, Isabel's first scene shows her passionately kissing a lover on the lawn as Warren watches through the window, visually illustrating the gulf between them. Throughout the film, Isabel attempts anything that might "betray the hero," but, unlike *House on Haunted Hill*, there is no eventual reveal that Warren and Isabel were miscast as the Ideal Male and erotic woman. Because *The Tingler* is not intent on reassembling the union between the two into something that could explain their tumult, it instead doubles down on featuring one of the most unpleasant depictions of marriage found in William Castle's work. That is, until *The Night Walker*.

What makes *The Tingler* notable within Castle's critique of American capitalist ideology, beyond extending the tension between Warren and Isabel, is the way in which Castle presents and undoes multiple variations of coupling throughout the film. For example, Dave Morris (Darryl Hickman), Warren's understudy, and his fiancé Lucy Stevens (Pamela Lincoln) represent a perfect pairing (in development, as they are not yet married). Lucy is the Ideal Female, a "perfect companion," and, though he is chided for putting in too much time in the lab with Chapin, Dave is presented as the Ideal Male (his initial scene is showing up tardy for a date with Lucy because he was chasing a black cat down an alley) in the midst of a willing transformation into the settled husband. Their union is presented as natural, and Warren advocates for it by telling Dave to take time away from the lab and threatening Isabel, who despises the pairing. Dave and Lucy's pairing makes for an odd sighting in Castle's work from the era: an almost saccharine domestic coupling. One of the only other examples is that of loving parents Cyrus Zorba (Donald Woods) and Hilda Zorba (Rosemary De Camp) from *13 Ghosts*.[48] What is fascinating about *The Tingler*, however, is that the film offers up another couple as a twist on the animosity of the Chapins: Martha Higgins (Judith Evelyn), a mute, and her husband, Oliver (Philip Coolidge), who run a silent-movie theatre. The couple appear to be a genuine match until Martha's death from fright shines new light on things, revealing that Oliver—the ideal female and settled husband—actually killed Martha for financial gain.

Strangely enough, a murderous, ill-willed male figure is not accounted for in Wood's analysis of ideology in classic Hollywood film, which means Castle needed to create unique figures to complete his cynical vision of the American marriage. Martha's murder is financially motivated in a way that indicts Wood's other categories of capitalism ("Success/wealth" and "Money isn't everything"),[49] suggesting they can pollute certain unions as the tendrils of capitalism mercilessly wrapping themselves around Martha and Oliver's marriage like a tingler, choking out the vestiges of love, respect, and unity. Taken as a grouping, William Castle's gimmick and postgimmick films show him to be interested in toppling the American capitalist ideology of ideal pairings and marriages—something many other classical Hollywood films seek to reify.

If William Castle's status as auteur was ever in question, his thematic interest in destabilizing the American capitalist ideology should cement it. Robin Wood argues the ideological tensions found in classical Hollywood cinema are "not . . . a reliable evaluative criterion" without "the presence . . . of an individual artist."[50] Therefore, only through an auteur can "ideological tensions come to particular focus."[51] Further analysis of Castle's work indicates that he exhibited an interest in deconstructing other attributes of Wood's American capitalist ideology, including "capitalism," "the work ethic," "America as the land where everyone actually is/can be happy."[52] Evidence of such critiques are constant in Castle's films; in *Macabre*, a small town becomes the stifling environment supporting sordid drama; in *The Tingler*, a suburban house and small movie theatre become scenes of chaos; unease and rampage upset the faux-Dutch community of Solvang, California (including its defenseless flower shop) in *Homicidal*; a farm and bedroom closet are rendered into execution chambers in *Strait-Jacket*; and *I Saw What You Did* infuses terror into the rural homestead and the telephone ("technology"[53] being another of Wood's categories).

Robin Wood spotlights Frank Capra and Alfred Hitchcock because their films, particularly *It's a Wonderful Life* (1946) and *Shadow of a Doubt* (1943), critique the influence of American capitalist ideology on small towns, quaint communities, and families in order to illustrate, as a "central ideological project," a "reaffirmation of family and small-town values."[54] Conversely, William Castle's films attempt no such reclamation project. Even when order is restored in a Castle film, it is often at the cost of various lives or with the understanding that things have drastically changed—even in his lighter fare. For instance, at the culmination of *The Spirit is Willing* the domestic turbulence between the parents is resolved, but deep fissures of instability remain (illustrated through the visible presence of ghosts, some recently made during the course of the film). Nevertheless, William Castle's apocalyptic approach to the American capitalist ideology is best exemplified by his most "mature" film: *The Night Walker*.

WAKING LIFE

On the set of *The Night Walker*, a spectator observing Barbara Stanwyck and Robert Taylor act together for the first time in decades declared, "Bill Castle . . . may have the hottest combination here since Frankie Avalon and Annette Funicello. Hotter, even, than Elvis and Ann-Margret."[55] In promotional interviews surrounding the production, both Stanwyck and Taylor were chipper about the prospect of reuniting on screen. From the moment Castle approached Stanwyck with his idea of reuniting the pair, the actress claims she was thrilled, stating, "I said I thought it was a hell of a good idea, but that he'd better ask Bob."[56] Taylor was similarly effusive, stating, "Anybody who would turn down a chance to work with Barbara is crazy."[57] Overall, there was no public fallout during the production of *The Night Walker*; Taylor was struggling with the lung cancer that would kill him in five years, which may have assured there was no acrimony on the set. In fact, the only intrigue associated with *The Night Walker* comes from a promotional column where actress Ursula Thiess, Taylor's current wife, was asked if she approved of the pairing: "'Not necessarily,' she said, smiling enigmatically."[58] For all the milquetoast press surrounding *The Night Walker*, the subtle rancor between Thiess and Stanwyck, to say nothing of the inspired decision to cast former married Hollywood stars in a feature that savagely devalues the institution of marriage, hints at what is remarkable about *The Night Walker*.

In some ways, what William Castle managed with *The Night Walker* was a sort of precursor to what Stanley Kubrick accomplished with *Eyes Wide Shut* (1999). For his film, Kubrick pitched Tom Cruise and Nicole Kidman, a married Hollywood couple at the time, into a nightmare scenario that would have particular resonance following the actual dissolution of their marriage soon after. Castle, however, used *The Night Walker* to bring together a formerly married Hollywood couple in a film suffused with nightmares, spotlighting the caustic mind games that can develop from a rotten marriage. Both *Eyes Wide Shut* and *The Night Walker* play with the idea of public marriage, investing their turbulence with a patina of Freudian psychology, but what's especially interesting about Castle's film is the way the psychological aspects of his film represent a feint, obfuscating the filmmaker's actual concerns. As I stated previously, Castle, the auteur, had a particular interest in generating narratives that challenged marriage under the American capitalist ideology, and *The Night Walker* provided him with a unique opportunity to do so.

The Night Walker opens with a "tumble of surreal images":[59] a woman falling through a variety of abstract backdrops, a *Twilight Zone*-esque image of outer space, a screen that fills up with disembodied, blinking eyeballs, as a male narrator (Paul Frees) inquires, "What are dreams? What do they mean?" This fantastical opening culminates with an eyeball tucked into a fist, as the camera zooms in, something that has been identified as "an image more jarring than any other in Castle's canon thus far."[60] The narrator's dramatic declaration, "When you dream you become . . . a night walker," then initiates the actual narrative of the film. This abstract beginning of the film seeks to present *The Night Walker* as concerned with dreaming and waking states and other issues of pop psychology . . . which it is. But there is a marked difference between Castle's desired purpose and the film's latent content. As such, it's essential to highlight that what follows Castle's artsy opening for *The Night Walker* is a scene of marital discord.

The proper narrative of *The Night Walker* begins with Howard Trent (Hayden Rorke), a blind man, standing over his wife, Irene (Stanwyck), as she tosses in bed muttering, "Hold me close" and "I need you." Castle focuses his camera primarily in a medium shot on Howard's tortured expression, his milky white eyes being a particularly ghoulish touch commented on in many reviews at the time, as his wife appears to gyrate in rapture with a phantom lover. Therefore, within the first minute of its actual narrative, *The Night Walker* acknowledges its core grief: the tortured and tawdry aspects of the American marriage. As Howard departs the couple's bedroom to enter his palatial study, savvy viewers will recognize that Howard, like Frederick Loren in *House on Haunted Hill*, is another of Castle's wealthy, dissatisfied men. Just like Frederick Loren, Howard's profession, or the source of his wealth, is never noted, though Barry Morland (Taylor), his attorney, will declare he's "a very rich man." Immediately after eavesdropping on his wife, Howard kibitzes with Barry in his study about his blindness, his legacy, and Irene. Howard explains to Barry that he assumes Irene's dreams are admissions of her infidelity, so he has wired his estate to catch her with her lover, stating, "I've had to create a new world for myself, a world of sounds." Robin Wood notes that in classical Hollywood cinema "the homestead is built for the Woman" so that "civilized values"[61] can be sustained and embodied through the children. In *The Night Walker*, however, Castle makes it clear that Howard has turned his house into a trap for his wife, and the couple is locked into a distrustful, broken marriage represented by the lack of progeny. For the convenience of the plot, Howard confesses to Barry that he has bugged Irene's room because he suspects that she and Barry, based on what Irene says in her sleep, are lovers. Here is where Castle's larger purpose starts to come into view.

The meta-textual implications of Taylor (i.e., Barry), the former spouse of Stanwyck (i.e., Irene), being her lover in *The Night Walker* present a fascinating approach for analyzing Castle's film. For instance, as Howard confesses his espionage of Irene to Barry, his wife has been observing her husband's accusations from the doorway, something Barry observes but does not comment upon. Barry does attempt to defend Irene, calling her "a wonderful woman" who "appears to be . . . dedicated to your welfare." The play on sight, blindness, and misrecognition, a theme throughout the film, is picked up here, as Howard bellicosely shouts at Barry, "*Appears* to be!" After Howard leaves his study, Barry is again confronted, this time by Irene, in a perverted repetition of his previous encounter. Although Barry has defended Irene as she watched, she decides that her husband's suspicions have provided her with a loophole and Irene implies she will blackmail Barry based on Howard's suspicions. As Irene pulls Barry close to her, she asks, "Don't you want to kiss me, darling?" Instead of continuing the embrace, which would imbue the opening moments of *The Night Walker* with a particular meta-textual resonance, Castle has Irene break down, incapable of committing to the charade and cheating on Howard. Irene pardons Barry from the mess of her marriage, though, as we later find out, Castle makes it clear that such kindness is unwarranted and unwise. Nevertheless, bringing Irene and Barry together to share secrets and, nearly, an indiscretion is a calculation on the part of Castle to overlap his gimmick with the film's narrative.

On the staircase, Howard confronts his wife for being dressed to go out at a late hour. Howard's blindness has made his hearing extrasensory, and so he reads the signifiers of Irene (her shoes, the sound of her dress) as confirmation bias for these suspicions. As with many of Castle's films, the implication about the inherent jealousy bred within the American marriage is positively acerbic, and Howard's reproach of Irene quickly becomes atomic. Howard levels accusations of infidelity at Irene, from a position above her on the staircase, and the staging of the scene implies generic positions of power within the household (Figure 10.1). In truth, Howard's placement is meant to offset his blindness and provide him with some advantage in the ensuing standoff. During the exchange, Irene attempts to defend herself, responding to Howard's accusations in increasingly agitated ways before exploding, "Here's the truth: my lover is only a dream but he's still more of a man than you!" What's interesting is that prior to this eruption, Irene has edged past Howard to seize a dominant position above him on the staircase (Figure 10.2). This is fortuitous, since her comment makes Howard's rage boil over and he attempts to assault Irene with his cane. In this brief encounter, Castle has visually signaled the shift in the power dynamics within Howard and Irene's marriage, with Irene winning the pushing match by forcing Howard to the ground and fleeing to her bedroom. Castle also uses the narrative opening of *The Night Walker* to hint at thematic concerns by bringing Irene and Barry together under awkward circumstances and putting a premium on Howard's jealousy. Defeated, Howard leaves his

Figure 10.1 Howard Trent, the patriarchal figurehead, assumes his position of power in *The Night Walker*.

Figure 10.2 Irene Trent physically upsets the capitalist ideology underwriting her marriage.

battle with Irene and somberly marches upstairs to his laboratory, a space that implies, inscrutably, how Howard may have accrued his vast wealth, only to have the room explode shortly thereafter. In a moment that represents physical force, but implies much more, Castle focuses his camera outside Howard's laboratory door in a medium shot where an adjacent window shatters with the force of the explosion. If there were a sole image that encapsulates *The Night*

Figure 10.3 Castle depicts the Trent house torn asunder by Irene's disturbance of the ideological order.

Walker's fascination with the rupturing of the American marriage, this would be it (Figure 10.3).

Subtlety not being Castle's style, the scene immediately following the laboratory explosion features an arson detective, Frank Malone (Jess Barker), informing Irene, "In an explosion like this, the heat is so intense it would destroy anything." At this moment, viewers must dispel any hope that *The Night Walker* will reinforce Robin Wood's concepts of marriage or the homestead in American capitalist ideology like other classical Hollywood films. *The Night Walker* works to destabilize such categories for the opening portion of its runtime and, following Howard's death, hunkers down to examine its real thematic concern: the disintegration of the American family. After Howard's death, *The Night Walker* becomes concerned with Irene's dreams and nightmares. In his iconic essay on American horror films of the 1970s, Wood notes that dreams and nightmares in horror films commonly represent a return of "repressed desires, tensions, fears" that elevate "seemingly innocuous genre movies."[62] In *The Night Walker*, Howard, now a hideously scarred figure, returns to Irene on the night of his death as a nightmare. The nightmare return of Howard, which culminates in his charred laboratory, is meant to haunt Irene, suggesting her attempts to eschew capitalism or circumvent its ideology, unwitting or not, were futile. It's worth noting that prior to her nightmare, Detective Malone warned Irene, "Stay out of that room." Therefore, Howard's reappearance as a nightmare only reinforces Irene's failure to maintain the American capitalist ideology in her marriage and her homestead.

Invariably, William Castle's ambition for *The Night Walker* was no different than any of his films: financial success. *Strait-Jacket*, which directly preceded Castle's Stanwyck-Taylor vehicle, featured more blood (including several decapitations) than any previous Castle films. Only *Homicidal*, with one particularly bloody attack and one decapitation, could be in the same conversation. Nevertheless, Castle offered a candid response to *Strait-Jacket*'s success, stating, "I made a fortune from it, but I feel I did go too far."[63] Unfortunately, Castle's candor is thrown into question when put into context with his followup comment about whether he would tone it down for *The Night Walker*, claiming, "If the audience buys this, then I've proven I can make this kind of film successfully . . . But if not, then by God, I'll go right back to chopping off heads."[64] It's been well established that Castle's "mature" approach for *The Night Walker* failed, and, when examined in contrast to *Strait-Jacket*, we see can see why. As Castle told Linda May Strawn in 1974, successful filmmaking was about appealing to the young and realizing that "an audience wants to be entertained."[65] As such, it's not surprising that the bitterly adult *The Night Walker* missed the mark, and that transcends its on-screen content.

One might assume that Stanwyck and Taylor's aged reunion was responsible for the financial failure behind *The Night Walker*, but Castle had a solid track record at the box office with films that prominently featured older performers, including Vincent Price and Joan Crawford. However, at the time of their work with Castle, Price and Crawford also had traction within the horror genre. This was not the case for the formerly married Hollywood stars of *The Night Walker*, which can especially be gleaned from Stanwyck's strained turn as a "scream queen" during the film's opening sequence. After the dream sequence featuring Howard's return, Castle required Stanwyck to scream, repeatedly, and the result could generously be labeled a coarse, fractured bellow. Stanwyck's excessive screaming throughout the film (Figure 10.4), something of a trademark in Castle's gimmick and postgimmick work, was a topic of interest in both promotional and critical material surrounding *The Night Walker*. One critic went as far to state, "Stanwyck's biggest problem [on *The Night Walker*] was the fact that she had to scream continuously throughout the feature."[66] Nevertheless, Stanwyck's overall performance is easily the strongest in the entire film, and she appeared gamely committed to Castle's project. In fact, in an interview after the release of *The Night Walker*, Stanwyck claimed she was hoping to do "another suspense shocker"[67] with Castle, *The Possessors*, a film that never materialized. Interestingly, Stanwyck would never star in another feature film, moving into television instead, and Castle's next two features, *I Saw What You Did* and *Let's Kill Uncle*, opted for adolescent protagonists.

Returning to *The Night Walker*, proof that the veneer of the American capitalist ideology has been cracked, vis-à-vis the explosive conclusion of Irene and

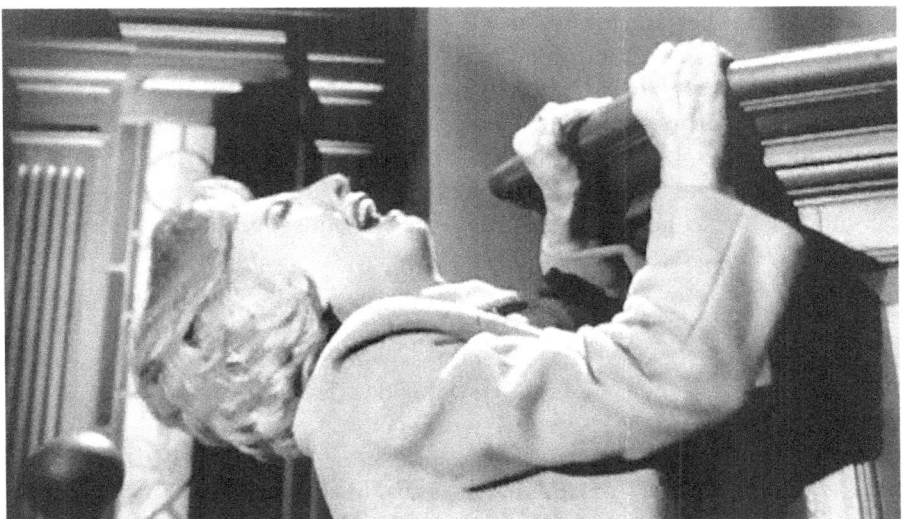

Figure 10.4 Barbara Stanwyck, unlikely scream queen.

Howard's marriage, can be located, counterintuitively, in the fact that Irene seeks to suture her situation by reclaiming financial agency from her past. After Howard's death, Irene moves out of her palatial estate, the homestead, and into an apartment at the back of Irene's, her beauty shop. Irene's shop represents a space of productive capitalism outside of the marriage, which Irene makes a point of noting when she states she "owned and operated" Irene's before she married Howard. Capitalism dictates "the right of ownership, private enterprise, personal initiative,"[68] but in classical Hollywood cinema that often applies to men or, if it connects to a woman, it is surrendered once she commits to marriage. That Irene returns to this space following the literal destruction of her marriage is telling. It's a drawing back inward (after all, the establishment is named after her), hinting that only capitalism can smooth the ruptures discord generates.

Even if we operate under the assumption that Castle, in attempting to tell a spooky story, is unconscious in his critique of the American capitalist ideology, the filmmaker goes out of his way to establish Irene's as a productive, restorative space for Irene Trent. Rather than making it an incidental space, Castle includes several shots throughout *The Night Walker* of Irene's as an active space: there are two interactions with customers wearing mud masks and hair-curlers, there are after-hours shots of vacant drying chairs and waiting lounges, and there's a late-night shot of the shop sign as a cat traverses the street. Many of these shots contribute nothing to the narrative beyond mood, but the cumulative result of their presence is to underscore Irene's domain and capital. Irene embraces her move back to the shop, telling Barry it's a necessary "escape" from her situation with Howard, and Barry concurs, assuring her that the move to Irene's will put her "back in the real world." Unlike her stalled, miserable life with Howard, Irene views her return to Irene's as progressive, especially in contrast to her formerly regressive homestead. When Joyce (Judi Meredith), an employee of Irene's, rushes to apologize to Irene about the cramped nature of her new apartment, Irene quickly corrects her, stating, "You have no idea how good it looks to me." By this point in his career, made clear by *House on Haunted Hill*, *The Tingler*, *Homicidal*, *Strait-Jacket*, and *The Night Walker*, Castle has a tendency toward depicting the homestead as a space of enslavement under capitalism. What's fascinating is that in *The Night Walker* Castle further reveals himself to be skeptical of any return to normalcy, and, as such, he rapidly goes about destabilizing the illusion that private enterprise might be an effective response.

Once Irene moves back into her beauty shop, *The Night Walker* becomes more illegible as Irene's dream life and actual life overlap, with Castle providing purposeful misdirection for both. After Howard's nightmarish return, Irene begins to be visited and romanced by a handsome young man, credited as The Dream (Lloyd Bochner), who takes her out on the town and, eventually, to a surreal chapel to be wed; the chapel is populated by a priest, organist, and a couple of wedding spectators who are all life-sized wax figures. During her preliminary encounters with the Dream, viewers might sense a strange bit of déjà vu as Irene's dream life mirrors what Howard overheard at the beginning of the film. Alarmed by such vivid dreams, Irene attempts to enlist Barry to help her investigate whether she is dreaming or not, and together the two of them seek out the locations from her dreams. Not only do they discover that the apartment complex from Irene's dreams does exist, but it's revealed that Howard owned the building, further cementing his role as the capitalist paterfamilias. At this moment in *The Night Walker* there is a surreal confluence of events that occur and overlap. Robin Wood claims our dreams "are also escapes, from the unresolved tensions of our lives into fantasies. Yet the fantasies are not meaningless; they can represent attempts to resolve those tensions in more radical ways than our consciousness can countenance."[69] For Irene, her life and dreams merge to construct radical attempts to resolve the tensions inherent to the American capitalist ideology—of the ideal mate, homestead, profession, and so on. William Castle forces his narrative to purposefully imbricate dreams, fantasies, nightmares, and reality in a way that expresses the impossibility of absolute resolution for Irene.

Fittingly, *The Night Walker* concludes in convoluted fashion in Howard's demolished laboratory. Irene returns to the homestead, finding it to be Wood's "Terrible House," which "stems from a long tradition in American and Western capitalist culture" where such a house "represents an extension or objectification of the personalities of the inhabitants."[70] In this final scene, the entire cast of *The Night Walker* returns either as themselves or counterfeits. Entering Howard's laboratory, Irene undergoes a series of encounters, the first one with Barry, who reveals he was posing as Howard's charred corpse in order to drive her mad so he could get "Howard's money"; Barry, taking advantage of Howard's blindness, wrote his own name as beneficiary. The Dream, however, turns out to have been a real private investigator, George Fuller, hired by Howard to spy on Irene and Barry. Instead, after Howard's death, George and Barry strike a deal to split the estate after Irene's untimely death. Meanwhile, Barry has killed Joyce, George's wife, in the previous scene, forcing the grieving husband to shoot Barry as he advances on Irene. After George believes he has killed Barry, he admits to Irene he must kill her, confessing, "I never intended murder, but now there's no choice." His method of execution keeps with Castle's theme of disintegration. George starts pumping gas at Irene, threatening, "There'll be another fire here tonight, and nothing will remain." Instead, Barry, still alive, rushes after George and the two men engage in a struggle that results in their deaths as they drop through the open chasm in the floor. With Howard, Joyce, George, and Barry deceased, two marriages shattered, and Irene alive but reasonably unnerved, *The Night Walker* ends with Castle's camera slowly zooming out from the carnage, in an inversion of the film's opening zoom into the mayhem (i.e., eyeball). Fittingly, the final sounds of *The Night Walker* are Irene crying as she stares into the chasm at two dead men. Castle zooms out to reveal that Irene is boxed in Howard's laboratory with the words "pleasant dreams" scrawled across the screen. Castle allows Irene, in the final seconds of the film, to turn away from the wreckage and open the door back into the Terrible House and an uncertain future.

The resolution of *The Night Walker* is chilling considering how frequently the narrative posited itself as the story of Irene's struggle for redemption and happiness following her abusive marriage to Howard. In many ways, the confined, dangerous space of the laboratory, as well as the Terrible House, serve as metaphors for Irene's situation. Recall that Malone, the arson detective, after padlocking the door to the lab, warned Irene, "Stay out of that room," but that Barry, who would not let her sell the house ("No danger in living there"), forces her back into it. Barry, played by Stanwyck's real-life estranged partner, draws Irene back into her unpleasant past—just as Castle had with Taylor and Stanwyck. For Irene, the home represents Howard's control of her, "an extension of the ownership principle to personal relationships . . . in a male-dominated society,"[71] so the insistence by various males throughout the film that she return either to the home or marriage is especially cruel.

In assorted ways, *The Night Walker* symbolizes the extended struggle between Irene and the men in her life. For example, the film's centerpiece "dream sequence" (a scene that, as viewers eventually understand, actually occurred) is the one featuring Irene and the Dream entering the chapel filled with wax figures for their wedding. Irene is demonstrably uneasy about the entire scenario, particularly the Dream's proposition of marriage, and her questions ("Where are we going?" "Where are we?") receive only evasive replies ("Some place, somewhere"; "Some place you'll never forget"). In a sense, Irene's struggle during the marriage ceremony should be read as demonstrating her fierce reaction against the American capitalist ideology—Irene does not wish to find another partner, a settled male to complement her (the Ideal Female). In the scene, Irene struggles to maintain the agency she is working to establish. After the Dream states his assent to their union, Irene says nothing (forgoing the ubiquitous "I do"), yet the Dream insists on placing a ring upon her finger. Running away from the horror-show scenario, Irene attempts to open the chapel door, only to be greeted by the burned corpse of Howard (Barry in costume). In this moment, William Castle depicts Irene's possible escape as another dead-end into patriarchy. The entrapped nature of this sequence magnifies the implications of Irene's ossification at the film's conclusion, within Howard's laboratory. In *The Night Walker*, Castle implies that the American capitalist ideology, through marriage or the "work ethic: the notion that 'honest toil' is in itself and for itself morally admirable,"[72] is a trap. Like many of Castle's films, *The Night Walker* interpolates viewers into its narrative, which, considering its critique, is unsettling. In fact, Castle believed the film was expressly interactive, asserting, "When Miss Stanwyck screams—one shriek after another—she's screaming in your place. 'The Night Walker' may seem mad, but there's logic in the plot."[73]

At the opening of this chapter, I asked a pointed question: What is the problem with *The Night Walker*? By now I hope it's obvious that various circumstances stacked up against the film. There's the gimmick that doesn't transcend the text, aging stars playing outside their preferred genre, and then there's the film's nasty, pummeling assault on the American capitalist ideology, particularly the institution of marriage, all framed within the deliberately "mad" logic of Castle's "mature" narrative. The rampant meta-text of the film, beyond even the casting of formerly married Hollywood stars, also doesn't help. As Joe Jordan notes, *The Night Walker* contains a preponderance of allusions to other Castle films:

> Approximately one hour into the narrative, Morland tells Irene, "When you were married to Howard, you lived in his world of darkness." His declaration is reminiscent of *Macabre* . . . Lucy Harbin, of *Strait-Jacket*, undergoes her cosmetic makeover at a place called Irene's Beauty Salon . . . Furthermore, particular scenarios of *The Night Walker*, similar to what is depicted in *House on Haunted Hill* and *Homicidal*, indicate that Morland is not the antagonist.[74]

The subterfuge and allusions, combined with its sustained assault on American capitalist ideology, demonstrate that *The Night Walker* is clearly the work of an auteur. Robin Wood argued that "[l]ike all the greatest American films," work by an auteur "transcends its director and would be inconceivable without him."[75] As we struggle to decipher what prevents *The Night Walker* from being a great film (maybe its B-movie qualities, the subpar acting beyond its leads, its incomplete storyline), exactly because the film fosters discord about the American capitalist ideology in a way that transcends William Castle's role while simultaneously embodying the apogee of his talents.

Ultimately, *The Night Walker* is a unique offering in William Castle's canon, and a work of intoxicating intrigue. The film is inextricable from its mischievous auteur: who else could manage such a severe critique of American capitalist ideology in a pop psychology package without softening its dire conclusions? At the climax of *The Night Walker*, before Barry attacks her, the malicious attorney notes with a hint of genuine admiration, "You're a truly remarkable woman, Irene." This line has meta-textual reverberations, calling to mind Jordan's claim that "Stanwyck and Taylor played their parts convincingly, perhaps drawing upon experiences of the past in order to establish an added sense of realism for their roles."[76] And, as we viewers take in the depiction of the ex-husband of a classic Hollywood star, himself the paterfamilias of Hollywood's communist-bating "Red Scare," adoring and threatening his former spouse in the same moment, reeling in the insinuations manifested by such levels of meta-commentary with churlish delight, we can see that William Castle, too, was truly remarkable. What's the problem with *that*?

NOTES

1. Mike McGrady, "Let's Give Him the Ax for 'Night Walker' Flop," *Newsday*, January 21, 1965, p. 2C.
2. Frank Morriss, "Castle's New Film Cheap and Shoddy," *The Globe and Mail*, January 29, 1965, p. 13.
3. Bosley Crowther, "Screen: Somnambulists," *New York Times*, January 21, 1965, p. 22.
4. Clifford Terry, "Film Reunites Stanwyck, Taylor—Too Soon," *Chicago Tribune*, March 17, 1965, p. A5.
5. John Waters, "Whatever Happened to Showmanship?" *American Film* 9 (1983): 56–7.
6. David Sanjek, "The Doll and the Whip: Pathos and Ballyhoo in William Castle's *Homicidal*," *Quarterly Review of Film and Video* 20 (2003): 248.
7. William Castle, *Step Right Up! I'm Gonna Scare the Pants Off America* (Los Angeles: William Castle Productions, 1976), p. 62.
8. John Kobler, "Master of Movie Horror," *Saturday Evening Post*, March 19, 1960, p. 97.
9. Castle, *Step Right Up!*, p. 195.
10. Murray Leeder, "Collective Screams: William Castle and the Gimmick Film," *The Journal of Popular Culture* 44.4 (2011): 788.
11. With only one more film credit, as producer and co-writer on *Bug* (1975), to his name.

12. Linda May Strawn, "Interview with William Castle," in Todd McCarthy and Charles Flynn (eds.), *Kings of the Bs: Working Within the Hollywood System: An Anthology of Film History and Criticism* (New York: E. P. Dutton, 1975), p. 291.
13. Catherine Clepper, "'Death by Fright': Risk, Consent, and Evidentiary Objects in William Castle's Rigged Houses," *Film History* 28.3 (2016): 56.
14. It feels odd to write of Castle's directorial career as though it began in 1958. William Castle directed thirty-nine features (Joe Jordan labels them "The Thirty-Nine Steps") before 1958.
15. Clepper points to the distracted nature of the juvenile viewing experience, noting that many youngsters in the audience awaited the appearance of Emergo during screenings—where a skeleton on a pulley was dragged over the crowd—as an opportunity to test their slingshots.
16. Strawn, "Interview with William Castle," p. 298.
17. Linda Williams qtd. in Sanjek, "The Doll and the Whip," p. 257.
18. Sanjek, "The Doll and the Whip," p. 259.
19. Castle's "fright break" was coupled with the Coward's Corner: a designed space for those who fled *Homicidal* to sit in shame/promotion. Though one might infer similar effort went into the Coward's Corner as Emergo or Percepto, its setups required no more effort than the ubiquitous lobby displays of films from the era.
20. Al Cohn, "Barbara's Old Enough Now for Castle Film," *Newsday*, January 20, 1965, p. 3C. Apparently, the German press gave Castle this designation.
21. A section where both John Wayne and Marlon Brando are included based on their sole directorial efforts at the time, *The Alamo* (1960) and *One Eyed Jacks* (1961) respectively.
22. Kobler, "Master of Movie Horror," p. 100.
23. Thomas Page, "Introduction," in Joe Jordan, *Showmanship: The Cinema of William Castle* (Albany, GA: BearManor Media, 2014), p. ix.
24. Sanjek, "The Doll and the Whip," p. 257.
25. Castle, *Step Right Up!*, p. 173.
26. Ibid. p. 174.
27. Schoell qtd. in Sanjek, "The Doll and the Whip," p. 259.
28. Castle, *Step Right Up!*, p. 174.
29. Clepper, "'Death by Fright'," p. 58.
30. Jordan, *Showmanship*, p. 323.
31. Dudley Andrew, "The Unauthorized Auteur Today," in Toby Miller and Robert Stam (eds.), *Film and Theory: An Anthology* (Malden, MA: Blackwell Publishers, 2000), p. 26.
32. Andrew Sarris, "Notes on the Auteur Theory in 1962," in Leo Braudy and Marshall Cohen (eds.), *Film Theory and Criticism* (New York: Oxford University Press, 2009), p. 452.
33. Ibid.
34. Ibid. Sarris's definitions are gendered.
35. Ibid. p. 453.
36. Andrew, "The Unauthorized Auteur Today," p. 22.
37. Peter Wollen, "The Auteur Theory," in Leo Braudy and Marshall Cohen (eds.), *Film Theory and Criticism* (New York: Oxford University Press, 2009), p. 465.
38. Ibid. p. 469.
39. Andrew, "The Unauthorized Auteur Today," p. 27.
40. Robin Wood, "Ideology, Genre, Auteur," *Film Comment* 13.1 (1977): 46.
41. Ibid. p. 46–7.
42. Ibid. p. 47.

43. Ibid.
44. Ibid.
45. Ibid.
46. Ibid.
47. Ibid.
48. Even still, the Zorbas also elected to name their daughter Medea.
49. Wood, "Ideology, Genre, Auteur," p. 47.
50. Ibid.
51. Ibid. p. 48.
52. Ibid. p. 47.
53. Ibid.
54. Ibid. p. 48.
55. Nancy Anderson, "Reunion of Barbara Stanwyck and Robert Taylor," *The Atlanta Journal and the Atlanta Constitution*, October 18, 1964, p. SM8.
56. Frank Morriss, "Barbara Stanwyck Deplores Movie Trend," *The Globe and Mail*, January 12, 1965, p. 13.
57. Anderson, "Reunion," p. SM8.
58. "Party Honors Divorcees in Filmland," *Florence Times*, May 9, 1964.
59. Leeder, "Collective Screams," p. 788.
60. Ibid. p. 789.
61. Wood, "Ideology, Genre, Auteur," p. 47.
62. Robin Wood, *Hollywood From Vietnam to Reagan . . . and Beyond* (New York: Columbia University Press, 2003), p. 70.
63. Cohn, "Barbara's Old Enough," p. 3C.
64. Ibid.
65. Strawn, "Interview with William Castle," p. 291.
66. John Law, *Scare Tactic: The Life and Films of William Castle* (San José: Writers Club Press, 2000), p. 133.
67. Morriss, "Barbara Stanwyck Deplores," p. 13.
68. Wood, "Ideology, Genre, Auteur," p. 47.
69. Wood, *Hollywood*, p. 70.
70. Ibid. pp. 81–2.
71. Wood, "Ideology, Genre, Auteur," p. 47.
72. Ibid.
73. Marjorie Adams, "William Castle: Terror-Stricken Audiences Have Made Him a Millionaire," *Boston Globe*, February 16, 1965, p. 27.
74. Jordan, *Showmanship*, p. 325.
75. Wood, "Ideology, Genre, Auteur," p. 49.
76. Jordan, *Showmanship*, p. 327.

PART 4

Castle's Legacy

CHAPTER 11

Homo/cidal:
William Castle's 1960s
Killer Queers

Peter Marra

"Homo/cidal" argues that director William Castle's 1960s thrillers made under the immense commercial and artistic influence of Alfred Hitchcock's *Psycho* (1960)—*Homicidal* (1961), *Strait-Jacket* (1964), and *I Saw What You Did* (1965)—advance important thematic and stylistic trends in twentieth-century American horror. It contends that (1): The films develop the figure of the killer queer, a persistent figure in horror with historical roots at least as far back as the early twentieth century whose non-normative gender and sexuality are linked by cinema to murderousness, and (2): that figure's historical trajectory is tied to the expanding national visibility of gay Americans in the 1960s and the increasing conception among gay Americans and straight Americans that "gay" signified a collective identity rather than discreet sexual behavior. "Homo/cidal" considers Castle's films from a contemporary queer perspective and articulates stylistic, narrative, and thematic features of his work with queer resonance. It addresses the historical context of these films at a transitional moment in the gay rights movement between the relative conservatism of gay rights organizations such as the Mattachine Society and Daughters of Bilitis in the 1950s and more radical gay rights politics following the Stonewall riots in 1969. From a genre studies perspective, "Homo/cidal" posits that the killer queer's increased prominence following Stonewall responded to rising gay visibility and that this response significantly influenced the popular slasher cycle of 1978–86. Thus I argue here Castle's redeployment of *Psycho*'s style and themes, often deemed derivative, actually progresses crucial trends that lead to the slasher. While the slasher has been largely studied as a subgenre bearing the influence of Hitchcock's *Psycho*, it has hardly, if ever, been studied as a subgenre bearing the influence of William Castle. In reinstating Castle's importance as a genre pioneer I hope to refocus attention on his contributions to twentieth-century American horror as a director who progresses the killer queer figure, and who shapes conventions of the popular slasher cycle.

THE RISE OF GAY VISIBILITY IN THE 1960S

By the arrival of *Homicidal* in 1961, gay visibility in America was significantly rising and advocacy for gay rights was taking shape. In the 1950s, gay rights organizations such as the Mattachine Society and Daughters of Bilitis made the first major pushes to unite gay and lesbian Americans socially and politically to achieve positive advancement. One of the primarily goals of Mattachine in the 1950s was to encourage gay Americans to recognize themselves as a part of a collective gay community. This concept was relatively new and had been fostered by the homosocial communities developed during World War II. Michel Foucault famously articulated the roots of this shift based in nineteenth-century medical science as the transition from an understanding of sodomy as a sex act to homosexuality as a "personage . . . a type of life, a life form."[1] "The sodomite had been a temporary aberration," he remarks; "the homosexual was now a species."[2] This new understanding of homosexual as an identity was formed around the idea of gender inversion, "a hermaphrodism of the soul."[3] Christopher Nealon describes this shift as the "inversion" model versus the "ethnic" model. Or rather, the notion of an identity indicated by inverse gender (e.g. a woman in a man's body) that dominated the earlier half of the twentieth century versus homosexuality as distinguishing "peoplehood" as was developed more popularly in the latter half of the century.[4] Mattachine, in its inciting manifesto, calls for the fair treatment of gay people with the expectation that they, as a society, might convince straight America that "homosexuals can lead well-adjusted, wholesome, and socially productive lives."[5] This more assimilationist gay politics radically differed from the post-Stonewall gay liberation movement, which called for the annihilation of normative society and the rebuilding of an alternatively queer country.[6]

Another crucial factor in the nation's collective cultural reconsideration of sexuality at the time were the publications of Alfred Kinsey's studies on male sexuality in 1948 and female sexuality in 1953. These reports garnered national attention for, among many other things, survey-based data that suggested homosexual sex was far more common than social norms might suggest. Kinsey subsequently theorized that such behavior might increase should the penalties discouraging homosexuality be removed. A key outcome of Kinsey's work was to suggest that homosexuality was far less abnormal than believed, and that it was instead an "inherent physiologic capacity."[7]

Despite historic advancements in destigmatizing queer sexuality, reactionary attitudes were highly prevalent. Notably, these objections were (as they have often been) framed around concern for the wellbeing of children and, in the case of national political visibility, framed as issues about children's corrupted sense of knowledge about sexuality. In the 1959 race for mayor of San Francisco between Russell L. Wolden and the incumbent George Christopher, Wolden famous raised homosexuality as a major issue facing the city. In a public radio broadcast he claimed the city had become "the national headquarters of organized sex deviates."[8] The city itself had recently become chronicled in national news when San Francisco police raided the City Lights bookstore in June of 1957 and arrested its owner, Lawrence Ferlinghetti, on charges of selling obscene literature. The text in question was gay poet Allen Ginsberg's poem *Howl*, which featured vivid details of homosexual sex.[9] Ultimately, the court ruled against the prosecution. In a biography of Mayor Christopher published soon after these events in 1962, George Dorsey laments, "And San Francisco parents were uncomfortably alone among the fathers and mothers of America that fall in having to field such questions from eleven- and twelve-year olds as, "Daddy, what is a homosexual?"[10] Thinking of Castle's movies as parallel to this reactionary panic to queer influence, particularly on children, makes evident the historical stakes of Castle's queer representations.

WHAT IS QUEER ABOUT CASTLE?

My use of the phrase "queer" here draws on the complex and intersectional work of scholars such as Michael Warner and Cathy J. Cohen. In his introduction to *Fear of a Queer Planet*, Michael Warner sets out to describe a new queer politics which, "no longer content to carve out a buffer zone for a minoritized and protected subculture, has begun to challenge the pervasive and often invisible heteronormativity of modern societies."[11] Here and throughout the introduction he argues that queerness contests such normative concepts as the "the family," "class identity," and "racial and national fantasy." Warner contends that "queer" is more than just vernacular for LGBTQ and instead signals connections between non-normative gender/sexuality and broader political and social positions that similarly question normativity. His approach to queer theory and queer politics is carried forward in Cathy J. Cohen's characterization of "queer" as a category more complex than merely oppositional to "straight." Cohen considers the role of power in the restricted experiences of gender and sexual minority groups, and advocates for "queer" to unite these groups with others marginalized by race, class, etc. She describes an investment in "examining the concept of 'queer' in order to think about how we might construct a new political identity that is truly liberating, transformative, and inclusive of all those who stand on the outside of the dominant constructed norm of state-sanctioned white middle- and upper-class heterosexuality."[12] Both authors situate queerness within a political project to transform oppressive structures rather than tethering the term exclusively to a gender or sexual identity. In this spirit, when I look at what is queer about the killer queer figures of Castle's cinema, I seek not to ascribe LGBTQ identifiers retroactively to characters but to assess what queer resonance these characters might have. How are they positioned as non-normative along the lines of gender and sexuality, but additionally how might they work against heteronormative ideologies more generally throughout the films?

Building on these queer representations, Castle's relative incoherence as a B-movie filmmaker lends itself to a decidedly queer feeling in his features. The director has often been criticized for making films with absurdist plots, cheap novelties, and limited formal innovation. A review of *I Saw What You Did* in the *Los Angeles Times* makes a case against Castle's effectiveness by citing his weakness in achieving filmic continuity: "William Castle is sufficiently a moviemaker to be able to photograph one scene, photograph another scene and paste the two together, and the mechanics of moviemaking are such that two scenes viewed consecutively can cause a certain amount of apprehension to be generated in the onlooker."[13] It goes on to critique the contrived and non-sequitur plot, the unbelievable sights and sounds, including stilted and implausible performances. The review concludes, in an interesting turn of phrase, "Castle doesn't so much make a movie as play around with it."[14] Indeed, Castle is perhaps best known for the popular interactive gimmicks used in films such as *The Tingler* and *13 Ghosts*. *Homicidal* features one such gimmick, a popular point of dismay in reviews: a "Fright Break" at the film's climax, in which a ticking stopwatch appears on screen and offers patrons the option to flee the theatre if they are too scared to stay for the ending. This interactivity and novelty suggest that Castle is at play in his films. This discordance with classical Hollywood continuity—in which a sealed diegesis is the norm and films commonly intend to make seamless their editing from shot to shot and scene to scene—invites a different audience interaction that can be said to function in a queer capacity.

As Eve Sedgwick phrases it, one way to think about queerness is as a failure for everything to "line up." A normative gender and sexual identity presumes that a number of features about a person will neatly line up: their chromosomal sex, gender, masculine or feminine traits per your sex and/or gender, the perceived gender of a partner, the chromosomal sex of that partner, the masculine and feminine traits of that partner per their sex and/or gender, etc. Queerness then is disjuncture from this normative line-up of things. It refers to "the open mesh of possibilities, gaps, overlaps, dissonances and resonances, lapses and excesses of meaning."[15] It poses the significant question, "What if the richest junctures weren't the ones where *everything means the same thing*?"[16]

Conceivably, then, what has earned Castle the ire of film critics (disjunctive filmmaking, lacking cohesion and with convoluted plots, stilted performances, and incoherent dialogue) might also be said to make Castle's work decidedly queer, open to a multiplicity of meanings and interpretation, not "lined up."

POLYSEMY, MEANING, AND MURDER IN *HOMICIDAL*

The potentially queer qualities of character and narration converge in interesting ways in the first Castle title of note here: *Homicidal*. The film's central queer character displays a noted inconsistency about his/her/their gender and sexuality. Likewise, the film's confused plot allows queer viewers to structure a story in more fluid ways.

In an opening scene, we are introduced to a children's playroom, filled with gendered toys—boxing gloves and trains for a boy, dolls for a girl. The room is organized spatially such that the camera begins in the "boy" section of the room and slowly pans right toward the "girl" section. A young girl is shown having a tea party with a doll. A boy enters behind her and watches her play. He snatches her doll away and she cries. "No, Warren!" The camera pushes in on his hands clutching the doll. At first glance the scene suggests a young girl being teased by a boy peer, possibly a sibling. The stealing of the doll seems a sneaky gesture designed to upset. However, what the film develops from this point forward raises questions about this perception of the scene, including the genders of the characters, the gendered relations between them, and the motivations that guide their actions. We learn to question if Warren is being purely mischievous here or if, indeed, he merely lusts after the coded "girl" side of the room from which he is spatially and socially segregated.

The film turns next to a visceral and bluntly satiric scene of marriage. A mysterious woman checks into a hotel under the name Miriam Webster. She offers the bellhop $2,000 to marry her at midnight on the sixth of September and he agrees. At midnight on the sixth, "Miriam" and the bellhop drive to the Justice of the Peace, Alfred S. Adrims, wake him from his sleep, and offer to pay double for his services at such a late hour. The Justice extracts an additional fee from the eager couple for the performance of accompanying wedding music despite his wife's harried objections that it will disturb the neighbors. "Play soft," he barks at her.

The wedding is a tepid by-the-numbers exercise comprising the couple in plain clothes and the Justice of the Peace and his wife in robe and nightgown. When the groom is asked if he takes the woman as his wife, he replies "I guess so." When Justice Adrims announces his intention following the ceremony to kiss the "little lady," the camera cuts to an extreme close-up of the woman's enraged eyes. She removes a knife from her purse and stabs him to death.

The childhood spat and gruesome marriage scenes open *Homicidal* to discourses on gender and normative gender relations that color the entire film. As with the scene of Warren possibly coveting a baby doll, the marriage sequence depicts a dissonant relationship to a set of gender norms and cultural rituals. It first reduces heterosexual marriage to a cash-in-hand ploy, then shreds any semblance of niceties by using the wedding as the site for a bloody murder. Moreover, the sequence of events suggests that Justice Adrims's attempt at kissing the bride inspires and/or expedites Miriam's plan of murder. Her refusal of his patronizing and gender-specific affection, kissing the bride whom he calls "little lady," is a grand and violent display against her heteronormative role in marriage as a customary object to be kissed.

Homicidal consistently presents characters who bristle with gender norms and/or are incompatible with a binary logic of gender. These representations function queerly by raising the audience's awareness of such norms of gender and sexuality and visualizing disjunctive relations with such norms that provide queer resonances. This queer characteristic is crucial to the core character drama of the film, which requires some elaboration to clarify.

Following the wedding murder, "Miriam" returns home. We learn she is here called Emily. She is caretaker to Helga, a wheelchair-bound mute woman. Emily's relationship with Helga appears caring in public scenarios, but in private Emily is verbally abusive and threatens Helga's safety. Emily, we learn, returned home with Warren (the owner of the estate) and Helga, following a stroke Helga had while she and Warren were in Denmark. Warren visits sporadically to check on Helga. Warren's sister, the real Miriam Webster, grows increasingly suspicious of Emily's odd and threatening behavior toward her. This includes breaking into Miriam's flower shop, threatening to kill her, and, of course, using her name to murder Adrims, which is revealed to Miriam late in the film. When Miriam finally convinces her brother Warren that Emily is unsafe, the two return home to aid Helga, who has been left alone with Emily. Miriam enters the house to find Helga decapitated. Emily then reveals to Miriam that she is, in fact, also Warren. Emily/Warren explains that he/she/they mean to kill Miriam and frame "Emily" for the murder. Emily/Warren cuts herself/himself/themself with a knife and means to be discovered as a wounded "Warren." However, a family friend, Dr. Jonas, interrupts and tussles with Emily/Warren. During the fight, Miriam shoots Emily/Warren, leaving her/him/them seemingly dead.

In a final scene reminiscent of *Psycho*'s ending, Lt. Miller, who has been investigating the Adrims murder, emerges to explain the story of Emily/Warren. He explains that Emily/Warren's seemingly misogynist father wanted a son as heir to his estate. When Emily/Warren was born biologically female, he/she/their mother along with Helga, who delivered the baby, and Justice Adrims, who was County Clerk at the time, conspired to enter the sex as "male" and to raise Emily/Warren as a son. Otherwise, the family inheritance would go directly to Emily/Warren's older sister by another marriage, Miriam. Emily/Warren's father died believing that "Warren" was his son. Then, in a subtle remark, the investigator notes following his death, Helga took Warren to Denmark and "what happened there, we don't know." Following Helga's stroke, he continues, "Warren" returned with "Emily," using "Emily" to kill those who knew of the deception and/or could stand in the way: Adrims, Helga, and Miriam. This narration of events is purely subjective. It is delivered by Lt. Miller with the corroborating documents of William Webster's will and Warren Webster's birth certificate. There are no visual or audio clues to suggest Emily/Warren survived his/her/their gunshot wound and no indication anyone has spoken to Emily/Warren to extract the details of this story. This, of course, raises the question: Where do the details of this story come from? It is a particularly puzzling question since the story purported here claims that all who would know these details are deceased: Adrims, Helga, Emily/Warren. Here Lt. Miller produces a story that it is impossible for him (or anyone) to know. In *Psycho*'s comparable ending, a psychiatrist emerges having spoken to Norman as "Mother" and relays what Mother has told him about the events depicted in the film. Here there is no suggested conversation with Emily/Warren, who, as best the audience knows, died from Miriam's bullet.

This leaves the audience with a number of polysemous plot points, of which the narration of Emily/Warren's story by Lt. Miller is one. There is the potential to read the film according to the narrative provided and indeed Lt. Miller's story does seem a reasonable and not totally disprovable story pieced together from the plot of the film. However, what if we take Lt. Miller's story as a heteronormative rationalization for a gender non-normative body? If Lt. Miller, Dr. Jonas, and others perceive "Warren" as a man with a vagina, this might lead to speculation. How can one normalize this body? The film's decision not to have an objective narration close the film leaves open myriad possibilities to consider the multiply queer resonances of the Emily/Warren dilemma.

In *Hollywood Androgyny*, Rebecca Bell-Metereau notes how even the subsequent credits continue the uncertainty around gender. As the androgynously named actor Jean Arless is given screen credit for the dual roles of "Emily" and "Warren," the film shows us Arless simultaneously in both character costumes, thus sustaining the ambiguity of even the performer's gender. In fact, the actress Joan Marshall played the two roles and the pseudonym Jean Arless was never credited again. Interestingly, Bell-Metereau demonstrates the kinds of fluid viewing experience with gender and sexuality I describe such a film as affording its audiences. She contextualizes *Homicidal* in a section on transvestite and drag movies like *Some Like It Hot* (1959), and though she maintains that Arless's gender is unknowable she nonetheless remarks that "Jean Arless is a totally convincing woman" and "the entire plot of *Homicidal* relies on the completely undetectable female impersonation performed by Jean Arless."[17] However, Marshall identified as a woman, meaning her screen performance is actually an impersonation of a man. Nonetheless, this slippery uncertainty is wholly conducive with the kinds of gender play the film encourages in the viewer.

One generative path to consider as an undercurrent in Emily/Warren's non-normative gender identity and expression is the period's emerging awareness of trans identities. A connection to this history seems implicitly suggested with the curious references made to Emily/Warren's time in Denmark.[18] *Homicidal* was released in 1961, about nine years following the national news story profiling Christine Jorgensen, who famously received her gender confirmation surgery in Denmark and emerged as a point of public interest in December of 1952 with a *New York Daily News* headline reading "Ex-GI Becomes Blonde Beauty." Jorgensen went on to stage a successful nightclub act and make frequent public appearances on television and radio.[19] In 1959, shortly before the release of *Homicidal*, Jorgensen's story became a renewed subject of national interest when she announced that she intended to marry Howard J. Knox, a statistician who worked in Washington, D.C. Jorgensen was famously denied a legal marriage because she could not legally prove her sex as female. Howard J. Knox lost his job following the news coverage of the incident and terminated his engagement to Jorgensen soon after.[20]

This period was also deeply affected by a darker news story that drew conversation to the concept of non-normative gender identities: the murders, grave robberies, and bodily mutilations of serial killer Ed Gein. In 1957, news broke of Gein's Wisconsin "house of horrors," which was decorated with remnants of corpses, including those he had sewn into furniture. Gein was ultimately found guilty of murdering two women and robbing nine graves.[21] It is not entirely clear how Gein's mutilation of women's bodies began to become narrativized as the actions of a frustrated transgender person, but this seemingly mythic characterization grew quickly in popularity. Harold Schechter, author of the Gein biography *Deviant*, offers details about a possibly influential *Milwaukee Journal* article crediting an "unidentified investigator" who attended Gein's interrogation. The source described Gein as having a ritual that "gave him great satisfaction" in which he would don a mask and vest made of women's skin and wear them around his farm. The source tied this to Gein's supposed desire to become a woman, stating Gein "considered inquiring about an operation to change into a woman and even thought of trying the operation upon himself, but did nothing about such plans."[22] *LIFE* magazine published similar uncited details in an eight-page photo spread that promised an inside look at Gein's farm. The magazine reported that, "He often wished, he said, that he were a woman. Psychiatrists studying his actions believe he is schizophrenic, or split personality."[23] These two sentences closely link possible non-normative gender with mental illness. Screen representations of Gein, or inspired by Gein, seemed to pick up on this unverified crossdressing or transgender aspect of his story and develop it to their own ends, often also conflating it with mental illness and a murderous pathology. Robert Bloch's 1959 novel *Psycho* and the 1960 Hitchcock film of the same name both heavily fictionalize the story of Gein in the form of mother-obsessed effete crossdresser Norman Bates. As the impact of *Psycho* loomed heavily over *Homicidal*, Gein's story may also have affected how audiences understood Emily/Warren's non-normative and inconsistent gender presentation.[24]

One pivotal and emotional scene for Emily/Warren features "Emily" breaking into Miriam's flower shop and vandalizing her floral wedding displays, including figures of brides and grooms in conventional white dresses and tuxedoes respectively. She picks a groom figurine from a display and rips its head off. Then she picks up a framed photo of "Warren" and shatters it. This scene is not given much context or addressed at any other point during the film. One possible interpretation is that Emily/Warren is repressing romantic and/or sexual feelings for Carl, the local druggist and paramour of Miriam with whom she flirts briefly at the pharmacy just one scene earlier. In this case Emily/Warren is stifling an attraction to avoid the social impropriety of the appearance of a homosexual attraction by "Warren" toward Carl. Most clearly, the scene signifies Emily/Warren's discomfort with gender norms and the heteronormative representations of marriage suggested by the gender coded bride and groom figures. Emphasis is placed on tearing off the head of the groom, and destroying Warren's portrait, perhaps showing Emily/Warren's anger at the need to perform a masculine persona. This sentiment is echoed throughout the film in scenes where Emily/Warren expresses outrage over her/his/their upbringing. In one scene Emily/Warren revisits the children's playroom of the opening scene along with Miriam, both adults now. They reminisce in a melancholy tone about their childhood, how Helga kept the two of them apart to make "Warren" more of a man. How their father paid neighborhood boys to start fights with "Warren" to toughen him. How Helga beat "Warren" with a switch at his father's orders. The scene emphasizes the exhaustive work of making "Warren" into an acceptably masculine persona. Scenes like these resonate with the personal experiences of femmes, trans women, and transfeminine people, feeling socially pressured to accomplish a correct and socially recognizable masculinity, to be toughened and masculinized through violence, to be separated from femme things like girl toys. The film's final shot shows the doll Emily/Warren once stole from Miriam, the one Helga tried to keep away, fall forward and land atop the switch Helga used to beat Emily/Warren into a "man," visually suggesting an opposition to the binary which plagued Emily/Warren as it does many queer people.

QUEER DESIRE AND SUBJECTIVE NARRATION IN *STRAIT-JACKET*

Strait-Jacket, like *Homicidal*, offers a fiscal motive for murder but nonetheless dwells more complexly on the psychological motivations of the killer, which supersede the practical rationale for the act. In *Strait-Jacket*, Lucy Harbin, described as a self-assured, sexual, and confident woman, returns home to find her husband in bed with another woman. She is so emotionally affected by this sight that she decapitates her husband and his lover in their sleep. Her young daughter, Carol, watches the events transpire from her bed. Twenty years later, Lucy is released from the mental asylum. Lucy, played by Joan Crawford, is now a more mature, gray-haired woman in drab clothes, whereas at the time of the murder she had been shown in a bold print dress with a stylish hairdo and gaudy bangle bracelets. She returns home to the care of her now adult daughter Carol. Carol takes an odd interest in restoring Lucy to her former aesthetic, leading her on a shopping spree that returns her visually to her exact style and appearance at the time of the murders. Not long after returning home, Lucy appears to experience audio and visual hallucinations. She hears children chanting a Lizzie-Borden-inspired schoolyard rhyme ("Lucy Harbin took an ax/Gave her husband forty whacks") and finds a bloody ax and severed heads in her bed. Eventually, murders begin again, and Lucy suspects she is responsible. A shapely figure with brown hair and bangle bracelets is seen committing the crimes. Ultimately, it is revealed that Carol has been committing the murders while dressed as Lucy (including a custom rubber mask) to frame her mother. Part of Carol's plan was to murder her fiancée's parents, a wealthy couple who did not approve of Carol. With the couple gone and Lucy in prison for their murders, Carol and her fiancée could marry and avoid scrutiny.

While this financial motivation stands as a logical possibility at film's end, the film itself develops more complex connections between Carol and her mother that suggest it does not fully explain these events. Carol's obsessive need to recreate her mother as she appeared during her childhood conveys a non-normative attachment not only to her mother, but to a specific aestheticized version of her mother. Her rebuilding of Lucy into her former self echoes the obsessive need of Scottie in Hitchcock's film *Vertigo* (1958) to return Judy back into the aestheticized vision of Madeline, down to her grey suit and pinned-up blonde hair. Here Carol has her mother wear a dark wig, a bright patterned dress, and clanking bangle bracelets again. Scotty's need to refashion his lover in *Vertigo* has often been analyzed as a sign of sexual domination and obsessive attachment. Here Carol exhibits a queer affection and physical obsession with her mother.

The scene of Lucy's first murders emphasizes the link between Lucy and her daughter Carol. Following the decapitations, the camera cuts to a shot of Carol watching. Footage of Lucy in a strait-jacket shouting "Leave me alone! I'm not guilty!" is superimposed over Carol's image. It appears Lucy is being removed from the scene and taken to an asylum. The disturbing superimposed footage of Lucy in restraints persists as the underlying footage alternates between Lucy bringing down the ax and Carol's shocked expression. In this way, Carol is filmically interwoven into the scenes of Lucy's murders and their aftermath. The camera pushes in to an extreme close-up of young Carol's eyes as she watches the murders. The shot of young Carol's eyes dissolves into a shot of adult Carol's eyes, visually informing the viewer that this new actress, Diane Baker, takes on the role of Carol. While this technique importantly cues the audience to recognize the character as performed by a new actress, it also suggests something more sinister: that young Carol's trauma shapes her as an adult. A sound-bridge of sirens and Lucy's screaming carries over into the shot of adult Carol, emphasizing this connection.

This sequence is revisited following the revelation that Carol, posing as Lucy, has committed the recent murders. Carol alternatingly shouts "I hate you!" and "I love you!" as she clutches and sometimes punches the mask of her mother's face she wore to kill. Her screaming image is then superimposed over the extreme close-up of young Carol's eyes in a direct echo of Lucy in her strait-jacket at the film's start. It continues to be superimposed over footage of Lucy swinging the ax twenty years ago, and the footage of Lucy screaming in her strait-jacket. At points their screaming faces and wide open mouths lie nearly exactly one over the other in temporary moments of graphic match. The implication that the early trauma carried into Carol's adulthood, suggested at the film's beginning, comes to fruition here as the screaming adult Carol is now enfolded into the series of terrifying images.

Carol's role as killer also complicates her subjective narration. The opening flashback detailing Lucy's ax-murders of her husband and lover are narrated by an adult Carol as told to her fiancée on the eve of her mother's return. Thus, the narration the audience is given about Lucy's actions relies solely on the subjective perspective of Carol, already entwined in a murderous plot to frame her mother for additional murders. Like *Homicidal*, it raises interesting questions about the reliability of the narration provided and instead suggests a multiplicity of stories able to be assembled from available plot. For example, could Carol's manipulation of her mother extend even further back than the present? How might the narrative be different when told by Lucy, or another subjective narrator? Hitchcock's *Stage Fright* (1950) very famously featured a so-called "false flashback," in which a character relays the details of a murder in a manner that demonstrates his innocence. The film seems to visually reinforce this narration through representational images of what the character describes, suggesting a return by the film's plot to an earlier point in the story (a flashback). However, by film's end we learn these images were representations of a character's subjectivity; the events visualized as told by the character were untrue and he was guilty. The trappings of Carol's narration similarly suggest an objective filmic flashback by returning the audience visually to this moment. Her voiceover is an impersonal one with no reference to her identity. It is not until the end of the alleged flashback, when the film cuts to adult Carol in the present, that it becomes clear this is a subjective diegetic narrator.

Gerard Genette describes these qualities of narrations using the term "focalization," a contraction referring to the "focus of narration." The opening scene of *Strait-Jacket* appears to be an omniscient narration not told from a character's point of view but by a third-person, non-character narrator. Genette's categorization would describe this as nonfocalized or zero focalization, meaning the film does not rely on any one character's perspective to convey the story to the audience. However, with the dissolve and the graphic match of Carol's eyes from childhood to adulthood we come to learn that indeed the scene is internally focalized, relayed exclusively from Carol's restricted perspective. Genette's model is helpful as it allows for shifts in narrator and changes from zero to internal focalization, including shifts between different internal focalizations. For example, in a reversal of the opening scene in which Carol speaks for Lucy, Lucy closes the film with her own internally focalized narration of Carol's murderous plan.[25]

SEEING AND KNOWING IN *I SAW WHAT YOU DID*

Perspective plays an important role in director William Castle's *I Saw What You Did* (1965) since, as the title suggests, the film foregrounds subjectivity and limitations of sight. In it, Libby Mannering invites her friend Kit to visit while she babysits kid sister Tess. The three girls decide to amuse themselves by making "crank" calls and whispering the phrase "I saw what you did . . . and I know who you are." Posters and promotional materials often marketed the film using the complete tagline *I Saw What You Did and I Know Who You Are*, which fittingly expresses a core concern of the film with both *seeing* and *knowing*—two acts that work in tandem, though neither encompasses the other. The relationship between the two, particularly the potential misunderstandings about what has been seen and what is known, make up a significant amount of the tension in the film. "I know who you are" explicitly shifts its emphasis from an action to an identity. Not "I know *what you did*," where the seeing confirms the action, but "I know *who you are*," where the action seen confirms a deeper truth of the receiver's identity. At the level of plot, this suggests vulnerability for the characters on the receiving end. To be known and identified allows for criminal prosecution. However, the line moves fundamentally beyond the fear of being identified superficially, by one's legal name, address, and phone number. Instead it focuses on the instability of knowable identities. The three girls pick a name and number from the phone book: Steve Marak. They know who he is on the page. Yet his presumption is that they have seen and known something far more intimate about him.

During the first third of the film, the prank phone calls remain a facile ploy. They give the girls voyeuristic access to strangers' personal lives, suggesting a fun engagement with worlds beyond their own. Notably, the film plays with the sexual dimensions of other, older people's lives, which appear to titillate the seemingly novice protagonists. The girls adopt breathy faux-sexy voices and call various men, stringing along hostile wives and bemused couples with innuendo about sexual liaisons. The calls playact exaggerated heteronormative roles as the girls each manufacture flirtatious personas of similar affectation and tone. Such repetition emphasizes the cultural construction of gender roles and the functions of playacting in adolescent explorations of heterosexuality. When the girls switch to their "I saw what you did . . . and I know who you are" calls, the accusations continue to be tinged with sexual implications. One call reaches a man and woman kissing in bed illuminated only by the dim light through a windowpane. The man answers the phone and presumes the girls refer to his current sexual encounter. "You did?" he asks. "Nothing is sacred."

In the instance of Steve Marak, the initial breathy mistress call is met with a cold indifference by Marak's wife, who insists the caller must be mistaken. The wife enters the bathroom to find it violently torn apart. She shouts at Steve through the shower door, "You wonder why I'm leaving you? You're not jealous. You're not that normal. You're insane!" He then pulls her into the shower and stabs her to death in a sequence that vividly recalls the shower scene in *Psycho*, including imitative shot compositions and editing techniques. Unable to get a response, the girls hang up. Meanwhile, Steve disposes of his wife's body. Later in the evening, the girls call back to prank him again and this time whisper "I saw what you did . . . and I know who you are." Unlike the typical heteronormative implications of sexual indecency and extramarital affairs, Marak's call instigates paranoia about totally unexpected aspects of his identity that the teen girls do not, perhaps cannot, even conceive: Steve as murderer. Moreover, unlike with other calls, Steve's life seems unmarked by heteronormative attitudes toward sex and romance. He is married, but displays no emotion or affection for his wife, whom he murders. His neighbor Amy (Joan Crawford) spends the film making romantic advances toward him that he coolly ignores. When he eventually murders her, he stands stone-faced while she desperately leans in to kiss him as she falls to the floor, deceased. Though Steve certainly inhabits a heteronormative world he appears characteristically at odds with, or indifferent to, its pleasures.

Steve's noted disinterest and detachment from heteronormativity coupled with an immense anxiety over the discovery of a non-normative identity by his mystery caller speaks to deeply held fears of being "outed" which are persistent in queer culture, but especially potent in the film's more conservative time of release. More overtly queer films of the time such as *Victim* (1960) and *The Children's Hour* (1961) dramatized the persecution of gay characters by gossip and blackmail. *I Saw What You Did* ultimately reflects a desire to understand and distinguish individuals based upon limiting discursive categories of identity, what Michel Foucault calls the "will to knowledge." Such a desire is intimately linked to the invention of the homosexual as an identity category after which the homosexual was, in Foucault's words, not just a person but also "a past, a case history, and a childhood . . . a secret that always gave itself away."[26] *I Saw What You Did* dramatizes a cultural desire to know secrets, investigate people's sexual interests and identities, and very literally *see* what they do and *know* who they are. The very first shot situates us as voyeurs while Libby and Kit talk on the phone. Each character is enclosed within a respective almond-shaped "eye" frame. A perspective for the eyes is never established. We never know who is looking at them, besides us. Moreover, it is a composite perspective, as each character is suggested to be in a different home, making it impossible for them to be seen by any left and right eye at the same moment.

Just as the voyeuristic opening joins improbable spaces, *I Saw What You Did* tonally creates an odd composite of two incompatible genres whose formal conventions clash against one another. The picture is decidedly a teen babysitter movie at some point and at other points a *Psycho*-ish thriller. This contrast results in dissonant cuts between shots of Steve violently murdering his wife and those of young girls laughing about prank calls while eating peanut butter and jelly sandwiches. The two narratives present a heavy contrast in tone that disrupts the continuity and plausibility of plot for the viewer. The most importantly mismatched scene is when Kit and Libby finally reach Steve Marak to deliver their "I saw what you did . . . and I know who you are" line. Steve's character occupies a world of murder and paranoia. Thus the prank line evokes an intense response in him. The girls, whose world consists of light-hearted teen antics and the rife potential for heteronormative romance, mistake his serious reaction as flirtation. "He's playing along," Libby proclaims excitedly. When Steve asks with chilling intentions, "Who is this?" she giggles and breathily coos "Suzette." When he presses, "Where are you calling from? Where can I reach you?" she shrieks, "What a swinger!" The girls hang up, laughing casually, while Steve registers their call as a sincere threat.

The disruptive mismatch in tone is echoed musically throughout the film in composer and bandleader Van Alexander's score. The young girls' central theme—a bubbly horn melody with a bouncy 4/4 time signature—sharply juxtaposes Steve's musical cues, which comprise sharper and moodier string sounds reminiscent of Bernard Hermann's score from *Psycho*. At least one review noted this, stating, "one thing particularly disturbing about this film is the soundtrack. Its tendency for abrupt and ill-timed changes in mood become very distracting."[27]

Here the tonally, visually, narratively, and sonically disjointed qualities of the film develop its queer themes. Each of these features exaggerates the high contrast between Steve and the girls to the extent that words have different meanings in their respective contexts. Most importantly, where the girls play around in a sandbox of heteronormative desire, likely acquired from media and imagination, Steve wholly misunderstands this display of sexuality. He is, in fact, the only call recipient that night to do so. His distinct and singular difference from the rest of the characters in the film develops a theme of queer detachment from heteronormative society. Further, he dramatizes something deeply profound about the fear of discovery for queer people. By 1965, "gay" as a sexual identity had relative hold and the idea that one could be detected would make cogent sense. Where *Homicidal* and *Strait-Jacket* play with queer desire and gender identity, *I Saw What You Did* evokes the queer experience of the closet and the fear of exposure.

SHAPING THE SLASHER THROUGH QUEER REPRESENTATIONS

The killer queer remains a significant character moving forward into 1970s cinema, both in queer cinema—for example, the murderous drag persona of Divine in the films of John Waters—and in mainstream cinema, whose legacy I would argue offers queer resonance—such as the Ed Gein-inspired killer androgyne Leatherface in *The Texas Chainsaw Massacre* (1974). Castle's work in the 1960s, though mostly considered derivative of Hitchcock's *Psycho*, meaningfully develops the killer queer seen in Norman Bates across the decade to its pinnacle of historical popularity—the slasher cycle, 1978–86. Castle progresses themes of gender non-normativity and sexual difference as intrinsic features for understanding the killer queer. His films touch on gender fluidity, queer desire, and feelings of stigma. Their structural oddness and narrative incoherence expand the queer potential of these works as queerness itself defies normative structures. Ill-explained characters—Emily/Warren—and oddly disjointed narratives—prank calls/murders—all speak to a potent failure to produce "coherence" as it is culturally constructed—a queer feat.

Castle's *I Saw What You Did* expands the peeping tom moments of Norman

Bates leering at Marion Crane in *Psycho* with a significant thematic examination of voyeurism. It is showcased in the opening scene of Kit and Libby as objects of sight and in the plot where Kit and Libby become voyeuristic audio spies prying into the private sex lives of their neighbors by telephone. *I Saw What You Did* also grows the role of the telephone as a vessel for sexual voyeurism that would become even more crucial in the slasher. Consider the lewd calls made to the sorority in *Black Christmas* (1974), the call from inside the house that terrorizes Carol Kane in *When A Stranger Calls* (1979), or the tongue of Freddy Krueger licking Nancy through the telephone in the dream-world slasher *A Nightmare on Elm Street* (1984).[28] *I Saw What You Did*'s parallel narratives of teen babysitters and a psycho killer also strongly prefigure this common setup for the slasher. In Castle's film the dramatic climax occurs when Steve Marak follows Libby and Tess to their home and terrorizes them on their property. This deeply echoes the plot of John Carpenter's 1978 film *Halloween*, commonly cited as the first "true" slasher. While much of 1960s horror mimicked *Psycho* in some way or form, the choice to merge *Psycho*'s key traits with a teen movie appears to be Castle's own very important contribution to this lineage leading toward the slasher.

CONCLUSION

William Castle has often been thought of as a critically maligned novelty filmmaker, but his 1960s thrillers, however repetitive of Hitchcock's work, are rife with radically queer potential. In thinking of Castle's work from a queer perspective, the emotionally queer resonances of a person struggling with gender identity (Emily/Warren) or facing a threat of being "outed" and socially stigmatized (Steve Marek) come to the fore. Moreover, what has made him a critical target speaks positively to the film's queer qualities. Queer theory helps to show how Castle's polysemous plots, sometimes called muddled or incoherent, speak to queer multiplicities of meaning and inconsistencies with cultural norms, including the "continuity" of classical Hollywood. Reflecting on queer culture of the 1950s and 60s allows one to recognize aspects of political and social discourse about queer lives that existed in the background of the increasingly popular *Psycho*-ish thrillers of the 60s. These films commonly built themselves around killer queers whose increasing popularity with moviegoers mirrored the increasing visibility of queer people in America. That the stylistic elements of *Psycho*, including the killer queer, only escalate further in popularity in the 1970s and 80s with the slasher picture makes logical sense through this framework as a continued cultural response to queer visibility seen at a new peak after the 1969 Stonewall riots. While Castle was only one filmmaker participating in this larger trend, his work is outstandingly rich with queer emotion and normative dissonance, offering us new ways to consider this important director's unique contributions to queer cinema and horror cinema.

NOTES

1. Michel Foucault, *The History of Sexuality, Vol. 1: An Introduction* (New York: Vintage Books, 1990), p. 43.
2. Ibid.
3. Ibid.
4. Christopher Nealon, *Foundlings: Lesbian and Gay Historical Emotion before Stonewall* (Durham, NC: Duke University Press, 2001), pp. 1–8.
5. Harry Hay, *Radically Gay: Gay Liberation In The Words Of Its Founder* (Boston: Beacon Press, 1996), p. 131.
6. For a detailed history of Mattachine and pre-Stonewall gay politics see John D'Emilio, *Sexual Politics, Sexual Communities* (Chicago: University of Chicago Press, 1983). For a historical account of early twentieth-century gay culture see George Chauncey, *Gay New York: Gender, Urban Culture, and the Making of the Gay Male World, 1890–1940* (New York: Basic Books, 1994).
7. D'Emilio, *Sexual Politics*, pp. 33–4.
8. George Dorsey, *Christopher of San Francisco* (New York: Macmillan, 1962), p. 187.
9. D'Emilio, *Sexual Politics*, p. 178.
10. Dorsey, *Christopher*, p. 88.
11. Michael Warner, "Introduction: Fear of a Queer Planet," *Social Text* 29 (1991): 3.
12. Cathy J. Cohen, "Punks, Bulldaggers, and Welfare Queens: The Radical Potential of Queer Politics?" *Sexual Identities, Queer Politics* (Princeton, NJ: Princeton University Press, 2001), p. 204.
13. Philip K Scheuer, "Phone Film That Fails to Ring Bell," *Los Angeles Times*, September 2, 1965, p. 12.
14. Ibid.
15. Eve Kosofsky Sedgwick, *Tendencies* (Durham, NC: Duke University Press, 1993), p. 8.
16. Ibid. p. 6.
17. Rebecca Bell-Metereau, *Hollywood Androgyny* (New York: Columbia University Press, 1993), pp. 134–7. See also Denise Noe, "Can A Woman Be A Man On-Screen?" *The Gay & Lesbian Review* 8.2 (2001): 21–2.
18. The possible allusion to a "sex change" via the dialogue about Denmark is also observed in David Sanjek, "The Doll and the Whip: Pathos and Ballyhoo in William Castle's *Homicidal*," *Quarterly Review of Film and Video*, 20.4 (2003): 247–63.
19. Joanne Meyerowitz, "Transforming Sex: Christine Jorgensen in the Postwar U.S.," *Magazine of History* 20.2 (2006): 16, 18–20.
20. "Bars Marriage Permit: Clerk Rejects Proof of Sex of Christine Jorgensen," *New York Times*, April 4, 1959, p. 20; "Engagement Off, Christine Is Told," *The Washington Post*, September 9, 1959, p. D9.
21. For full details on Ed Gein's crimes and arrest see Robert H. Gollmar, *Edward Gein: America's Most Bizarre Murderer* (New York: Pinnacle Books, 1989) and Harold Schechter, *Deviant: The Shocking True Story of Ed Gein, the Original Psycho* (New York: Pocket Books, 1989).
22. Schechter, *Deviant*, p. 132.

23. Anon., "House of Horror Stuns the Nation," *LIFE*, photographs by Francis Miller and Frank Scherschel, December 2, 1957, pp. 24–32.
24. For a detailed study of Gein's influence on screen killers see K. E. Sullivan, "Ed Gein and the Figure of the Transgender Serial Killer," *Jump Cut* 43 (2000): 38–47.
25. Gerard Genette, *The Narrative Discourse: An Essay In Method* (Ithaca, NY: Cornell University Press, 1983), p. 189.
26. Foucault, *The History of Sexuality*, p. 43.
27. Raymond Robinson, "'I Saw What You Did' Is Too Long, Too Dull," *New York Amsterdam News*, July 31, 1965, p. 23.
28. For a study of *I Saw What You Did* as a slasher precursor and "phone film," see Marc Olivier, "Gidget Goes Noir: William Castle and the Teenage Phone Fatale," *The Journal of Popular Film and Television* 41.1 (2013): 31–42.

CHAPTER 12

The Cinematic Pandemonium of William Castle and John Waters

Kate J. Russell

SHOWMANSHIP, GIMMICKS, AND MAYHEM

In 1983, John Waters wrote an ode to William Castle that reads as a eulogy for a cinema that privileged outrageous marketing stunts, gimmicks, and a carnivalesque theatrical experience over the critical evaluation of a singular film text. His essay, which decries a film industry in which the term showmanship "seems to have disappeared from movie moguls' vocabulary," rewrites cinema history as a history of the cinematic experience.[1] He denigrates Sergei Eisenstein and Jean-Luc Godard for not utilizing appropriate gimmicks for the promotion of their films, facetiously asking if either of them would have dared to turn up in a battleship or a crashed car at their premieres.[2] In their place, he elevates Castle for his immersion in his promotional campaigns, as he arrived in typically ghoulish style (in a hearse, jumping out of a coffin) for premieres of his first independent horror film, *Macabre* (1958).[3] Waters positions Castle as the pinnacle of a lineage of publicity masters, which he traces from Kroger Babb's exploitation of titillation masquerading as sex education for William Beaudine's film *Mom and Dad* (1945), to the producers of *The Worm Eaters* (1977), who did exactly as the title states to generate hype at Cannes Film Festival. Despite these stellar competitors, Waters declares that, "Without a doubt, the greatest showman of our time was William Castle."[4]

Waters' emphasis on Castle as showman as opposed to director indicates the centrality of the paratextual in Waters' understanding of cinema.[5] This understanding of cinema as the cinematic experience, an experience that begins with the anticipation generated by a film's attendant promotional materials and marketing ploys that precede the viewing, places the cinematic text as secondary to the social institution of the cinema. Waters' cinema privileges the communal space of the theatre as a social environment and an outlet for pleasure where anticipation explodes into riotous screams, laughter, and retches. This pleasure is not predicated on absorption in, and value judgments of, the film text. In what follows, I discuss Waters' relationship to Castle through the use of gimmicks, which assist in recreating the cinematic space as a carnival where rambunctious reactions are encouraged. I examine how Castle and Waters exploit the emotions of fear and disgust in tandem with comedy, and how these emotions are ripe for generating a chaotic cinema. I outline the exploitation-style publicity stunts used by both directors, foregrounding the paratextual in creating a cinematic experience that extends beyond the theatre space. Finally, I explore how tactics of direct address used by both directors break down the barrier between screen and audience by hailing the spectator and rupturing narrative absorption, thus transforming the theatrical space into a fairground where showmen and spectators interact.

The collective experience of the theatre is essential to Waters' reading of Castle. Waters regurgitated Castle's ethos of entertaining through fear into a debased and revolting comedy in an attempt to recreate the anarchic cinematic experience of Castle's gimmick films. Castle and Waters enthusiastically enticed and entertained audiences through pleasure in the negative emotions of fear and disgust respectively, cultivating the cinema as a space in which spectators respond viscerally to moments of spectacle. Castle most effectively achieved such responses through gimmick films, which are aptly defined by Murray Leeder as films that "introduced innovative tricks to attract audiences by addressing them more directly than Hollywood cinema is accustomed to doing."[6] A typical Castle gimmick involved an extensive promotional campaign and an element that could not be recreated outside the theatre, which directly solicited audience participation or response. For his film *13 Ghosts* (1960), for example, Castle introduced the gimmick "Illusion-O," which involved handing out "ghost viewers" to the audiences. These "ghost viewers" were spectacles that gave the audience the choice of whether or not they wanted to see the ghosts, depending on how scared they were. Castle's other most memorable gimmicks were *House on Haunted Hill*'s (1959) "Emergo" and *The Tingler*'s (1959) "Percepto." "Emergo" involved a plastic skeleton emerging from a box beside the screen at the same moment that the eponymous haunted house's millionaire host (Vincent Price) pulled a skeleton from a vat of acid, while "Percepto" buzzed viewers' seats at moments when the tingler—a creature that resides at the base of one's spine, grows when one is frightened, and may be subdued by screaming—affected characters on screen.

Castle began his career in theatre, claiming to have dropped out of high school at the age of fifteen to work as the assistant stage manager on a Béla-Lugosi-fronted production of *Dracula*.[7] It was in the theatre he first developed his predilection for gimmicks via an elaborate publicity stunt involving Adolf Hitler, whom he credited with launching his career in Hollywood.[8] This publicity stunt occurred when Castle was at the helm of the Stony Creek Theatre in Connecticut, the former home of Orson Welles' Mercury Players. Castle made a deal with a young German actress, Ellen Schwanneke, to star in his first foray into theatre production. However, Castle soon came up against the Actors Equity board, which informed him that during peak season, American actors must be given preference unless the role is specifically tailored to suit a foreign star. Castle claims that he then wrote a play titled *Das Ist Nicht Für Kinder* for his German actress and had his tailor's son translate it into German.[9] His ploy worked, and his German pseudonym, Ludwig von Herschfeld (misspelt as Ludwig Hirschfeld) was listed in the press as the original playwright.[10] In Castle's own exaggerated account, he exploited his German leading actress's invitation to return to Germany, allegedly from Adolf Hitler himself, to generate publicity for the play by sending a telegram to Hitler and Joseph Goebbels refusing the invitation, and then leaking the story to the press. He even claimed to have smashed the theatre's windows and daubed swastikas on the walls when the story about the telegram to Hitler failed to sell out the show. The vandalism, however, did the trick.[11] Newspaper reports on Ellen Schwanneke suggest that she fled Europe after snubbing Hitler, which contradicts Castle's account.[12] But the truth of his story is less important than how he employed it, as he recounted it to the press in order to position himself as a legendary prankster and showman with a sharp knack for publicity.[13] His claim that this stunt led to the play being a roaring success demonstrates his propensity for "ballyhoo and subterfuge" even when staging theatrical plays, as David Sanjek notes.[14] Waters was also inspired by Castle to begin a theatrical career of sorts in his childhood, when he created haunted houses to entertain the neighbourhood children.[15] He was also hired to perform puppet shows at birthday parties, and, as his brother remembers, emulated Castle by performing a puppet version of *The Tingler*, with his brother and friend dispatched underneath seats to grab the children's legs at the appropriate times.[16]

The gimmick film has a precedent in early cinema, in which films were exhibited to showcase images in motion as the attraction, as opposed to the narrative content of the film. In Tom Gunning's work on early cinema's spectator, he counters apocryphal accounts of panicked spectators running from theatres terrified that the locomotive on screen would burst through it, and posits instead that viewers were astonished by the movement of the photographic image itself, as "an unbelievable visual transformation [was] occurring before their eyes."[17] This spectator was not absorbed in a narrative, but acutely "aware of the act of looking, the excitement of curiosity and its fulfillment."[18] Gunning's cinema of attractions imagines an audience that is reacting to the film as an attraction—as a gimmick—in itself, conscious that they are viewing a moving picture that directly solicits their attention, and directly addresses them as spectators. In Gunning's outline, as narratives began to evolve in films, spectacles did not disappear, but rather could "still be sensed in periodic doses of non-narrative spectacle."[19] Examining the transitional era, Charlie Keil disrupts a "binaristic model of spectatorial address" that positions the attractions-era pleasure in "shock and confrontation" against classical-era "comfort" in narrative absorption.[20] Keil argues that spectacles in the transitional era were often used to develop a narrative, rather than merely astonish the spectator. Similar to Keil's conception of integrated attractions, Leeder convincingly argues that William Castle's horror repertoire makes spectacular use of attractions in his films, but that these attractions are intrinsically related to the narrative, revealing a "nonseparation between narrative and trickery."[21] Waters constructs wild narratives that are punctuated with moments of particularly obscene outrageousness and repulsive spectacles, but these diversions also either augment or further the narrative. For example, the plot of *Pink Flamingos* (1972) is constructed around two factions of people competing to be the filthiest person alive, and so the vignettes of protagonist Babs Johnson/Divine (Divine) urinating in public and shoplifting a steak by hiding it in her crotch aid narrative development in addition to attempting to leave the spectators "gagging in the aisles."[22]

While Castle and Waters both meld spectacle with narrative, and employ spectacle to augment the narrative, in the moment, the spectacles nevertheless override the "diegetic absorption" that Gunning cites as the goal of narrative-driven film.[23] At screenings of Castle's films, his audience was well prepared for the disruption of the narrative through extra-filmic events or gimmicks, and therefore had a heightened awareness of the theatrical experience. Castle's first gimmick was an insurance policy that insured audience members against death from fright for his film *Macabre*. Each audience member was given a life insurance policy to sign that would enable his or her beneficiary to collect $1,000 if he or she died from fright during the exhibition of the film. Naturally, those with pre-existing medical conditions and those who committed suicide were exempt. For Waters and his peers, the thrill lay in the potentiality of real horror in the theatre, real death, as "Nobody talked about the movie, but everyone was eager to see if some jerk would drop dead and collect."[24] Waters would later channel this fascination with death in the theatre into the climax of *Female Trouble* (1974), during which disfigured protagonist Dawn Davenport (Divine) culminates a maniacal performance by demanding to know, "Who wants to die for art?" A man yells, "I do!" and she promptly shoots him dead. The theatre erupts into bedlam as the panicked crowd scramble over one another to escape as more shots ring out. Peter Bürger theorizes that the historical avant-garde's major intervention was to "reintegrate art into the praxis of life," the most radical version of which is to die for art.[25] Waters also revisits the notion of death in the theatre in his film *Cecil B. Demented* (2000), which follows a group of renegade filmmakers seeking "death to mainstream cinema." Each member of the cast and crew, known collectively as the "Sprocket Holes," has a tattoo of a different director's name. Fidget (Eric M. Barry), the costumer, has "William Castle" tattooed on his chest, and Castle is later lauded in a rousing speech by the director and leader, the titular Cecil B. Demented (Stephen Dorff), for his "unashamed exhibitionism." At the beginning of the film, these underground filmmakers infiltrate the Baltimore premiere and benefit gala for Hollywood star Honey Whitlock's (Melanie Griffith) film *Some Kind of Happiness* to kidnap the actor at gunpoint. In the ensuing fracas, the charity's chairperson (Mink Stole) has a heart attack on stage and later dies in hospital. The underground filmmakers force Whitlock to star in their own film, which breaks the barrier between fiction and everyday life through their advocacy of a form of "cinema terrorism." They perform scripted scenes with unsuspecting members of public, using scare tactics to generate an authenticity that they believe is lacking in commercial film. In one scene, they storm into the Baltimore Film Commission's lunch and trick Honey Whitlock into throwing a live grenade into the assembled film world luminaries. While Waters incorporated the reintegration of everyday life (and death) and art into the plot of these films, Castle capitalized on the collapse between the film text and everyday life by invoking death by fright as a very real possibility in the space of the theatre during *Macabre*.

House on Haunted Hill's "Emergo" and *The Tingler*'s "Percepto" coincided with pivotal moments in the narrative, collapsing the distinction between the diegetic world on the screen and the space of the theatre. One scene in *The Tingler* effects the collapse of the on-screen movie theatre and the actual movie theatre particularly well, when the tingler breaks loose during the screening of a silent film. In the film *The Tingler*, a woman screams, at which point a plant in the audience also screamed and was subsequently carried out of the theatre on a stretcher. The house lights were turned on as the screen went black, and Vincent Price's voice, emanating from additional speakers positioned at the rear of the cinema, reassured patrons that normal service would soon resume. The tingler then appeared to knock both the silent film and *The Tingler* off the projector, as its shadow crawled across the blank white screen, merging the screen of the silent film theatre with the screen of the theatre showing *The Tingler*. Kevin Heffernan notes that this sequence "must be the ultimate direct audience address," as it was at this point that the "Percepto" gimmick of buzzing seats was unleashed, which was the cue for spectators to start screaming in tandem with the characters on screen.[26]

At the beginning of the film, Castle appears as himself to forewarn the audience that "a scream at the right time may save your life," and he implores his viewers to relinquish their inhibitions and shriek for all they're worth. Such uninhibited screams and yells of terror and delight are more usually heard at the fairground or amusement park, where thrill-seeking patrons ride roller coasters and ghost trains to vocally demonstrate their excitement mingled with fear. Noël Carroll suggests that "the emotive responses of the audience, ideally, run parallel to the emotions of the characters," but that the responses are not supposed to exactly replicate those of the characters.[27] Castle, however, used his gimmicks to attempt to forge a more visceral connection between the characters on screen and the viewers in the theatre. Rather than the characters' reactions pointing to the appropriate reaction for the viewer, the gimmicks "Emergo" and "Percepto" invade the actual space of the theatre and rupture the distinction between fiction and non-fiction, causing the viewer to jump, shudder, or scream at the same time as the character on screen. Castle conceived of the exhibition space as one of live theatre through such audience interaction with the film, transforming it into a space more like the fairground or amusement park. At the end of the film, Price dared any remaining doubters of the tingler to refrain from screaming the next time they are scared at night, a "parting shot" which Heffernan likens to the showman's final taunting words "as the shaken fairgoer leaves the darkened tent and makes her or his way back to the open air of the carnival midway."[28]

GAG REFLEX: DISGUST, HORROR, AND COMEDY

Waters followed in Castle's footsteps with his film *Polyester* (1981), for which he created a gimmick called Odorama that enabled viewers to smell what the characters smelled. Some of Waters' previously most vehement critics called *Polyester*, which follows hapless housewife Francine Fishpaw's (Divine) descent into alcoholism after a series of unfortunate events, "rather tame and conventional" by Waters' standards, with his "fabled shock tactics . . . toned down."[29] In lieu of the shocking and the grotesque, Waters employed Odorama, which he said was his "homage to Castle" and, in the spirit of Castle's humor, "a ludicrous joke."[30] This humor, as we shall see, was also an essential aspect of the theatrical experience in the Castle-Waters mode. *Polyester* was not the first film exhibition to harness the much-underused sense of smell in cinema. Around the same time that Castle was pioneering his own gimmicks of "Emergo," "Percepto," and "Illusion-O," Walter Reade Jr. inaugurated "AromaRama" for *Behind the Great Wall* (1959), which sprayed seventy-two scents into the audience. This foray into scent was followed by Michael Todd's *Scent of Mystery* (1960), which employed thirty different odours through "Smell-O-Vision."[31] Jets underneath seats in the theatres pumped the scents into the audience for *Scent of Mystery*, but some critics had reservations about this new sensory experience. One stated that it was "not the answer to the film makers' search for that missing dimension," while another expressed relief at the fresh air during intermission.[32] The relief at fresh air does, however, suggest it was more effective than "AromaRama," which had to have subtitles added to the film to inform viewers what scent they were supposed to smell.[33]

While "Smell-O-Vision" was linked to the audio track to automatically release the scents, Waters' "Odorama" involves the viewer scratching a number on a card to release the scent.[34] "Odorama" therefore makes viewers acutely aware of their position as a spectator by demanding their participation. A number flashes on screen, directly addressing the spectator, who scratches the corresponding number on his or her card and then inhales. The olfactory is a particularly intimate sense, as by entering the nose, smells transgress the borders of the body. Aurel Kolnai's phenomenological study of disgust contends that the object of disgust is never merely represented, but encroaches upon the borders of the body, threatening to cross its threshold through the olfactory, tactile, and visual senses in particular.[35] While the visual presentation of a disgusting object is enough to evoke a strong reaction to it, smell is the most intimate sense regarding disgust, as it has the potential to facilitate the incorporation of the disgusting object through particles of scent.[36] Waters' "Odorama" traversed the spectrum of scents from the pleasant (roses, air freshener, pizza) to the abhorrent (flatulence, dirty shoes, skunk). The sense of smell, according to Sigmund Freud, also played a pivotal role in the civilization of humans. Quadrupeds privilege the olfactory senses, so when humans adopted an upright posture, the sense of smell was diminished and sight foregrounded instead. This posture also exposed the genitals, which led to feelings of shame, which in turn led to the onset of the civilization process.[37] While *Polyester* obviously relies most strongly on the viewer's visual and aural faculties, there is a sense in which the incorporation of olfactory stimuli points to the potential for a reversion to an animality that has since been suppressed. In the theatre, such animality bursts open the quiet, civilized contemplation of the film text, as behavioral norms are ruptured by groans of disgust and explosive laughter.

In *Pink Flamingos*, Waters melds comedy with disgust and treats his audience to depravity seldom, if ever, found in more commercial films. The plot follows Divine, who has been forced into hiding under the alias Babs Johnson due to her notoriety as the filthiest person alive. However, her competitors Connie and Raymond Marble (Mink Stole and David Lochary) seek to overthrow her as the filthiest person alive, and the film cycles through escalating acts of filth and revenge between Divine and the Marbles, which are handled with increasing transgression and revulsion. How disgusting objects affect spectators is crucial to understanding how Waters' disgusted laughter operates. In his history and theory of disgust, Winfried Menninghaus argues, via Kant and Mendelssohn, that disgust is the singular emotion that "strains the distinction between 'real' and 'imaginary.'"[38] He emphasizes the proximity of the object in eliciting revulsion, even in works of fiction, and quotes German poet J. A. Schlegel, who stated that it is *"disgust alone"* that "is excluded from those unpleasant sensations whose nature can be altered through imitation."[39] Carolyn Korsmeyer further affirms these sentiments in her aesthetic study on disgust, stating that disgust "achieves a direct and immediate arousal that penetrates the screen of mimesis or artistic rendition. That is, one recoils viscerally whether the object of disgust is aroused by art or by an object in life."[40] In other words, even when a disgusting object is merely represented or described, the reaction of disgust is no less diminished. The immediacy of disgust reduces the mediating function of the screen in disgusting cinema, which Waters uses to his advantage. Waters' incorporation of disgusting subject matter deliberately seeks to elicit a somatic response from his audience, and he facetiously states that, "If someone vomits watching one of my films, it's like getting a standing ovation."[41]

Waters also confronts his audience with unsimulated acts that further disrupt an audience's ability to distinguish a fictional disgusting object from a non-fictional disgusting object. The film culminates in unsimulated coprophagia, as Divine ingests freshly excreted dog faeces to cement her status as the filthiest person alive. Waters conceived of this now-infamous final scene as "a negative publicity stunt" to compensate for the film's tight budget.[42] Like the carnival barker at the freak show, Waters banked on prospective audiences' morbid curiosity about the "filthiest people alive," and the lengths to which they would go to maintain their titles. The single take guarantees that it is unsimulated, and therefore presents it more closely as an unmediated, direct experience. The audience responds more viscerally, more immediately, as it is not a representation of eating excrement; it is a *presentation* of eating excrement. More importantly, the audience laughs with Divine, and retches with Divine, who willingly eats the excrement, laughing and retching as she does so. The simultaneous laugh and retch—or gag—demonstrates the tension between attraction and repulsion that the object of disgust exerts upon those who come into close proximity with it. Waters' effusive cinema depends upon such visceral, bodily responses that have the potential to evoke the "shared experience in showbusiness bedlam" that he enjoyed at Castle's screenings.[43]

The ingestion of dog excrement is a gag, which is to say that it is both a joke about Divine's filthy nature pushed to its extreme, and an inducement for revulsion, even vomiting. Waters co-opts the gimmick as a gag, both in the sense of a joke and a retch, most spectacularly in *Pink Flamingos*. The body's excretions are abject materials that unsettle subjectivity by threatening to disrupt the borders of the body. Corporeal expulsions remind the subject that he or she is not a discrete vessel, but a body that is continually ruptured through ingestion and excretion. The putrefying corpse, according to Julia Kristeva, is "the utmost of abjection," as it reminds the subject of the bodily fluids he or she must continually expel in order to remain alive.[44] The excrement violently expelled from the corpse represents what maintains life, until the body excretes all that it has and succumbs to death, finally collapsing its borders and becoming a corpse itself. These abject materials proliferate in Waters' film, but he does not use them as troubling the subject, but as a source of humor. Although Kristeva states that "laughing is a way of placing or displacing abjection," Waters' laughter is not a coping mechanism for dealing with abjection, but rather is intrinsic to his presentation of disgusting objects as he merges disgust with laughter.[45]

Similarly, Castle uses corpses as props to elicit explosive laughter alongside shock and horror. In *House on Haunted Hill*, one of the guests, Nora, opens her luggage and is horrified to find a decapitated head inside it, doused in blood, grimacing up at her. Another guest, Lance, later finds the severed head in Nora's closet and brings it to the dining room, unceremoniously thumping it down on the table, and demanding to know what a fellow guest knows about it. The shock and horror of being surprised by a decapitated head is assuaged not only by its obvious artifice, but also by the manner in which characters react to it, whether it is comedic hysteria or irreverence. *Pink Flamingos* employs corpses with outrageous campiness in a scene that sees law enforcement arrive to shut down Divine's birthday party. The drunken mob retaliates, swarming from Divine's trailer with axes, guns, and knives, and sets about murdering and dismembering the policemen. Divine cackles with delight as she wrenches a large, bloody bone from a policeman's carcass, and proceeds to tear real, raw meat from it with her teeth. The party descends into a carnivalesque cannibal feast set to raucous Fifties rock and roll, and the carousal is infectious. Horror and laughter merge, creating the contagion of hysterics amongst a rowdy midnight movie audience, as the theatre space itself becomes a carnivalesque site of hedonism and debauchery. Waters uses humor to implore his audience to champion his wildly unconventional characters, stating that in his films he asks his viewers "to root for outsiders," and to "look at people in a different way," using humor to change their opinions.[46] In doing so, Waters works to position his audience *with* his abject characters, to embrace what is disgusting, and to laugh *with* abjection. Humor is crucial to how Waters' use of disgust operates, as the laughter it evokes is reminiscent of the youthful crowd at Castle screenings who engaged in laughter through jumps and scares. Fear, disgust, and laughter all benefit from multiple people sharing a space, as they are contagious reactions that rip through crowds. Laughter especially cannot be contained; it is an uncontrollable excess that bursts from spectators, abetting the riotous atmosphere engendered by Castle's gimmicks and Waters' obscenity.

Waters' abject laughter, his gag, also resonates with the notion of the gimmick as that which both attracts and repels its audience through a series of dualistic, contradictory operations.[47] Sianne Ngai situates the gimmick in relation to capitalist modes of production, and notes that it elicits ambivalent feelings due to its inherent contradictions. These include the gimmick as saving labour/not saving labour, as working too hard/not hard enough, as outdated/futuristic, as a dynamic event/static thing, as unrepeatable/used over and over again.[48] Castle's gimmicks demonstrate how such contradictions work, as the *Macabre* life insurance gimmick, for example, requires both a deficit and a surplus of labour. Castle concocted the gimmick after watching a rough cut of *Macabre* and acknowledging that it didn't "have that bloodcurdling quality that I tried to get."[49] Without the budget or time to reshoot, Castle devised his insurance scheme in lieu of reassembling the cast and crew to create a more frightening production. Instead, he aimed to deceive potential viewers about the film's frightfulness through its paratextual publicity hook. Needless to say, Lloyd's of London initially thought that the idea was preposterous, and Castle had to travel to London to convince them otherwise. The theatres hosting the film subsequently incurred additional labour responsibilities regarding the distribution and administration of the life insurance certificates. The use of gimmicks in a movie theatre also entails both an underinvestment *and* overinvestment of emotional work from spectators. As gimmicks tend to be used in films that do not rely solely on narrative to immerse the audience members in the film through character identification, audience members are less emotionally invested in the characters and the outcome of their fate, and instead anticipate moments of spectacular diversion. The anticipation of spectacle, however, leads to an overinvestment of emotion when the spectacle arrives, which is manifested in bodily reactions such as screams, jumps, gags, and laughter.

Responses to Castle's gimmicks "Emergo" and "Percepto" for *House on Haunted Hill* and *The Tingler* demonstrate this double movement between an excess and a deficit of the spectator's emotional work. Exhibiting disdain for low-budget fare, a *Los Angeles Times* critic called *House on Haunted Hill* the "most monumental and pretentious bore of a film" and said that the "only shocking thing about this film is its utter ineptness," while another critic denigrated *The Tingler* as simply "a gimmick picture and one beneath serious consideration—except, possibly, as a menace to public sanity."[50] Refusing to submit to the lure of the gimmick, these critics overlook how the gimmick compensates for what they perceive as mediocre narrative with spectacle that is driven by an overdetermination of emotional reactions. The reviewers focus on the film text at the expense of the overall cinematic experience. Ngai notes that, "Calling something a gimmick is a distancing judgment, a way to apotropaically ward off, by publicly proclaiming ourselves unconvinced by, or impervious to, the capitalist device's claims and attractions. At the same time the gimmick enables us to indirectly acknowledge this power to enchant, as one to which others, if not ourselves, are susceptible."[51] Ngai notes that the gimmick is often rejected because of its claim to know what we want, an interpellation from which "we recoil, not because the gimmick's claim to knowing us is wrong but because it so often isn't."[52] While the *Los Angeles Times* critic may have claimed to resist the "Percepto" gimmick, it's difficult to imagine anyone sitting completely motionless, stoically refusing the visceral and unconscious reaction to being mildly electrically shocked. Moreover, the derogation of *The Tingler* as a "gimmick picture" fails to consider that it is exactly its purpose as "a menace to public sanity" that appealed so strongly to Castle's demographic, which mostly consisted of children aged eight to fourteen. Waters, who saw these films as a child, calls the gimmick films "childhood bedlam," and recounts how the young crowds got swept up in the moment, screaming and throwing their popcorn at the *House on Haunted Hill* skeleton.[53] Similarly, when the seats buzzed during *The Tingler*, Waters recalls how "the theater would erupt in pandemonium," creating a carnival atmosphere that transcends a reading of the film as an autonomous text.[54] For Castle's young audience, investment in the narrative of the film was irrelevant. Waters claims that no one leaving the theatre after seeing *House on Haunted Hill* commented on whether it was any good or not, but instead focused on the excitement of the experience.[55]

THE CINEMA AS FUNHOUSE: PUBLICITY AND PANDEMONIUM

Castle and Waters follow in the footsteps of the famous carnival entrepreneur P. T. Barnum, whose biographer attributed his "outstanding success as a showman . . . above all to his almost intuitive knowledge of human nature and what the public would pay to see" and his ability to "skillfully [exploit] public opinion through press so as to build interest in his acquisitions to a perfect furor."[56] Like Barnum, Castle and Waters were particularly attuned to their specific demographics, and marketed their films appropriately. Steve Bickel, Castle's friend and personal assistant, affirms that Castle knew exactly who his audience was, and that "he knew he could scare them."[57] Although Castle marketed his films on promises of fear, he was also aware that a "tongue-in-cheek approach" helped to cement his reputation among his youthful audience, who wanted to laugh *and* be frightened.[58] One review of *House on Haunted Hill* lauded Castle's deployment of humor as providing "a release for laughter so it does not explode in the suspense sequences," indicating how Castle used comedic moments to heighten the enjoyment in being frightened.[59] Castle knew that his films appealed to children and teenagers who were looking for some excitement, thrills, and alone time, outside of their parents' homes. Thomas Doherty points out that most Hollywood moguls in the 1950s were reluctant to accept that their major demographic had shifted to the emerging teenage market, despite the evidence presented to them by both exhibitors and the consultants they had hired to do such market research.[60] William Castle, however, had his finger on the pulse, stating in the *New York Times* that, "Over 80 per cent of the movie audience is teen-agers," and, moreover, that he discovered from "talks at high schools all over the country" that "the main thing they are looking for in movies is fun, a good time."[61] Quite aptly, Stuart Samuels traces a lineage between the raucous matinees for adolescents in the 1940s and 50s to the midnight movies of the 1970s, where the "usually young audience smoked joints, drank six-packs, participated, talked back to the screen, yelled insults at characters who couldn't hear them."[62] Castle's and Waters' respective audiences were particularly well-attuned to embracing a pandemonic cinematic experience through loss of inhibitions, either through youthfulness or intoxication. The cinematic experience for Castle's and Waters' crowds speaks to their conception of the theatre as a space for socializing as well as watching movies. Given the address of their films and their B-movie quality, as well as their audience demographics, this socialization was naturally unruly and boisterous.

Castle and Waters directed their promotional campaigns specifically toward their intended audiences, and were directly involved in the publicity, creating a cult of personality around themselves as showmen. The promotional campaign for *The Tingler* saw Castle make appearances around the country with a "live trailer," where he would insert himself into the crowd, then stand up and converse with the William Castle in the trailer on screen.[63] Waters has also cultivated his personality for promoting his films, stating that his fame "happened with my participation from the very beginning because I'm a carny, and publicity is free advertising."[64] Waters and his cast promoted *Pink Flamingos*' Baltimore premiere themselves by handing out press releases and flyering local bars, street corners, and bulletin boards with posters that called the film "an exercise in poor taste."[65] For its New York premiere, Waters insisted that his distributors, New Line Cinema, secure a spot at the Elgin Theatre, which had inaugurated the midnight movie tradition with Alejandro Jodorowsky's *El Topo* (1970). Former Elgin Theatre owners Chuck Zlatkin and Steve Gould recall Waters arriving with his entire cast and crew for screenings of *Pink Flamingos*, and Divine throwing mackerel into the crowd and spilling poppers on the floor, creating chaotic carnage in the theatre space.[66] *Pink Flamingos*' success as a midnight movie with regular screenings was mostly due to word of mouth, a form of advertising crucial to films that lacked a publicity budget. This method of promotion also added to the appeal of the film, as it allowed attendees to feel as though they were "discovering" a film, a feeling that would be negated had they found out through a widespread and expensive advertising campaign.[67] Word-of-mouth advertising is important to the social function of the cinema, as discourse and gossip expand the film text beyond the theatre space.

The official New Line trailer capitalized on this publicity method and eschewed revealing any plot details or scenes from *Pink Flamingos*, focusing instead on the reactions of audience members to tease a future audience. Audience members were interviewed as they left the theatre, and the polarized responses oscillate from one viewer who states that it's "marvellous" to another who calls it "the most disgusting thing I've ever seen in my life." The allusions to outrage and offense are designed to pique the curiosity of those already inclined toward the subversive, if not the outright perverse. The fact that the film generated genuine repulsion—one gentleman declares, "I enjoy dirty things as much as everyone else but this isn't even dirty, it's just disgusting"—is a rallying cry for those seeking pleasure in the grossest extremes of entertainment.[68] By not showing any of the scenes from the movie, it also implores future viewers to imagine what the film could possibly contain to elicit such a spectrum of opinions that were, albeit, mostly unified by the reaction of disgust. For David Sanjek, the exploitation trailer "served as the visual equivalent of the barker's ballyhoo," treading "a fine line between obfuscation and outright deceit."[69] While New Line's trailer for *Pink Flamingos* certainly obfuscates details about the film, few would argue that the film deceives its audience in its promise of obscene disgust. *Pink Flamingos* delivered the disgust and debauchery it promised with aplomb, landing Waters one of his many monikers, "the P. T. Barnum of scatology."[70]

This version of cinema that foregrounds the theatrical experience rather than an autonomous film text encompasses more than just visiting the theatre, and includes the building of anticipation through exploitation-style promotional campaigns. While typically exploitation filmmakers, like the carnival barker, "were more interested in deceiving than arousing or disgusting an audience," the exploitation filmgoer was, as Sanjek notes, "more often than not a willing and conscious participant in their own deception."[71] If Waters banked on potential viewers seeking the grotesque, Castle had similar hopes for his viewer's predilection for fear, and promoted his independent horror films on the promise of fright. *Macabre*'s trailer foregrounds the possibility that a viewer might actually die from fright, and continually insinuates that the viewer might not make it out of the theatre alive. Clearly, Castle did not expect anyone to actually die during the screening, but these ludicrous warnings appealed to his young audience who were willing to believe, or least suspend their disbelief, long enough to hand over their ticket money. Contemporary reviews often disparaged Castle's gimmick films. The *Globe and Mail*'s critic Ronald Johnson admitted that he had been lured to *Macabre* due to "the cleverness of its advertising," but that the film "didn't frighten us out of our wits; it barely wakened us from our early morning torpor," and that the only risk involved was one "of complete boredom."[72] Such reviews, however, concentrate on the film text, failing to take into consideration that the anticipation generated by the promotional campaign is an intrinsic part of the cinematic experience for directors like Castle and Waters.

Building upon anticipation, Castle and Waters both employ tactics of direct address, which, like Gunning's concept of the cinema of attraction, enables films to "explicitly acknowledge their spectator, seeming to reach outwards and confront."[73] *Pink Flamingos* breaks down the barrier between the screen and viewer by introducing the film through the disembodied voice of Mr. Jay. This voiceover that "speaks without mediation to the audience" hails the spectators directly through the collective term "moviegoers," an interpellation which simultaneously draws attention to their position as spectators and involves them in the action of the film.[74] The inspiration for the voiceover was a local wig emporium owner who had a thick Baltimore accent and who, not by coincidence, Waters considers "a showman" due to his "legendary" promotional campaigns.[75] Castle also uses a voiceover at the beginning of *Macabre* to implore viewers to look after one another, and to notify the management if their neighbor becomes overwhelmed with fright. The viewers must therefore actively participate by paying attention not only to the film, but also to their fellow viewers. The voiceover then instructs the audience members to set their watches to the time shown on a clock on the screen, linking them directly to the diegetic time. For his film *Mr. Sardonicus* (1961), Castle as himself introduces the gimmick of an audience poll to determine the fate of the film's titular villain. Near the end of the film, Castle appears on screen again to ask the audience to use their poll cards, which displayed a thumbs up or a thumbs down, to decide whether to punish Mr. Sardonicus for his cruel deeds or not. Waters later mimics such extra-diegetic instructive sequences in *Polyester*, which opens with a scene in a laboratory. In this extra-diegetic scene, the "Prominent Ear, Nose and Throat Specialist" Dr. Arnold Quackenshaw explains how to use the scratch and sniff "Odorama" cards. The inclusion of such extra-diegetic sequences points to the privileging of the cinematic experience in the theatre as opposed to contemplative viewing at home. Such sequences still exist on DVD versions, despite home viewers not having access to the physical material of the gimmick, nor being able to participate in the communal decision-making.

Waters admires Castle most as a purveyor of the cinema as a social institution that engenders experiences that could not be replicated at home. These experiences, moreover, conjure the carnival or funhouse, and encourage active participation from moviegoers, who were more than willing to oblige. Tellingly, Waters extols Castle as a showman as opposed to director, and lauds showmanship more generally, in his ode to him. He even declares that he wishes he *were* William Castle, a wish that he fulfilled in Ryan Murphy's miniseries *Feud* (2017). The television series follows the infamous feud between Bette Davis (Susan Sarandon) and Joan Crawford (Jessica Lange), and in the sixth episode, Waters appears—with his signature pencil moustache—as William Castle at a premiere of *Strait-Jacket* (1964). Waters holds court as Castle, introducing the film and dispensing axes to the excited crowd, portraying Castle's masterful manipulation of his crowd via the cultivation of his showman personality. As Waters' performance in *Feud* displays, Castle worked his audience up through extensive and immersive promotional campaigns that generated an anticipation that exploded in the theatre space. Waters followed suit, playing to the hedonistic midnight movie crowd with debauched disgust and camp humor. As a young fan, Waters relished the theatrical experience, and emulated the creation of an anarchic cinema in his own practice. He attempted to reach *House on Haunted Hill*'s dizzying heights of cinematic frenzy with the infamous final scene of *Pink Flamingos*. However, to his mind, not even *Pink Flamingos* could outdo the carnivalesque cinema experience as achieved by Castle.[76] This cinematic experience is one that is predicated on the understanding of the cinema as a space of encounter between audience members, and between the audience and the screen. Waters uses Castle to determine a productive model for a history of cinema that foregrounds the cinema as a social institution, and as a communal environment for the unleashing of effusive emotions that extends beyond the confines of the theatre itself. Waters ends his ode to Castle by calling upon him to stop people from "getting bored with the theatergoing experience." Waters pertinently asks, "William Castle, where are you when we really need you?"[77] This question remains relevant, as Waters and Castle both put pressure on a cinema that no longer aims for carnival and mayhem. The Castle-Waters mode of cinema does not simply call for spectacle, but for a radical integration of the spectacular into a cinematic experience that is predicated on outrageous publicity, nail-biting anticipation, extraordinary theatrical gimmicks, audience delirium, shouts, screams, gags, laughs, and retches: a cinema of pandemonium.

NOTES

1. John Waters, *Crackpot: The Obsessions of John Waters* (New York: Scribner, 2003), p. 13.
2. He was mistaken about Eisenstein, however, who believed that "mathematically calculated experiential or emotional shocks proved the most successful tools for jolting theatre audiences into more ideologically receptive states. Often these affective categories were conflated; for instance, during Eisenstein's production of *Can You Hear Me, Moscow?*, a series of small fireworks, or 'squibs,' were let off under the seats in the auditorium during a climactic moment" (Catherine Clepper, "'Death by Fright': Risk, Consent, and Evidentiary Objects in William Castle's Rigged Houses," *Film History* 28.3 [2016]: 59).
3. Waters, *Crackpot*, p. 15.

4. Ibid. p. 14.
5. Jonathan Gray borrows the term "paratextual" from literary scholar Gerard Genette, and uses it to refer to "the variety of materials that surround" a film text, and that contribute to the meaning and understanding of a text. See Jonathan Gray, *Show Sold Separately: Promos, Spoilers, and Other Media Paratexts* (New York: New York University Press, 2010), p. 6.
6. Murray Leeder, "Collective Screams: William Castle and the Gimmick Film," *Journal of Popular Culture* 44.4 (August 2011): 775.
7. William Castle, *Step Right Up! I'm Gonna Scare the Pants Off America: Memoirs of a B-Movie Mogul* (Middletown, DE: William Castle Productions, 2010), p. 13.
8. Mary Murphy, "Hawking Horror Films the P. T. Barnum Way," *Los Angeles Times*, November 6, 1973, p. 8.
9. Castle, *Step Right Up!*, p. 20.
10. Julian Tuthill, "Not for Children," *Billboard* 51.31 (August 5, 1939): 15.
11. Castle, *Step Right Up!*, pp. 22–6.
12. "Girl Snubber of Der Fuehrer Hails America," *New York Herald Tribune*, March 17, 1940, p. E2; Ellen Schwanneke, "Now I Belong to This Country," *Philadelphia Inquirer*, January 13, 1945, p. 3.
13. Murphy, "Hawking Horror Films," p. 8.
14. David Sanjek, "The Doll and the Whip: Pathos and Ballyhoo in William Castle's *Homicidal*," *Quarterly Review of Film and Video* 20.4 (January 2003): 254.
15. John Waters, *Shock Value: A Tasteful Book About Bad Taste* (Philadelphia and London: Running Press, 2005), p. 30.
16. *Divine Trash*, dir. Steve Yeager (U.S.A.: Divine Trash, 1998).
17. Tom Gunning, "An Aesthetics of Astonishment: Early Film and the (In)Credulous Spectator," in Leo Braudy and Marshall Cohen (eds.), *Film Theory and Criticism* (New York/Oxford: Oxford University Press, 2009), p. 741.
18. Ibid. p. 743.
19. Ibid. p. 744.
20. Charlie Keil, "Integrated Attractions: Style and Spectatorship in Transitional Cinema," in Wanda Strauven (ed.), *The Cinema of Attractions Reloaded* (Amsterdam: Amsterdam University Press, 2006), p. 199.
21. Leeder, "Collective Screams," p. 779.
22. Waters, *Shock Value*, p. 12.
23. Tom Gunning, "The Cinema of Attraction: Early Film, Its Spectator and the Avant Garde," *Wide Angle* 8.3–4 (1986): 66.
24. Waters, *Crackpot*, p. 15.
25. Peter Bürger, *Theory of the Avant-Garde*, trans. Michael Shaw (Minneapolis: University of Minnesota Press, 2007), p. 22.
26. Kevin Heffernan, *Ghouls, Gimmicks, and Gold: Horror Films and the American Movie Business, 1953–1968* (Durham, NC: Duke University Press, 2004), p. 98.
27. Noël Carroll, *The Philosophy of Horror, or Paradoxes of the Heart* (New York/London: Routledge, 1990), pp. 16–18.
28. Heffernan, *Ghouls*, p. 104.
29. R. H. Gardner, "'Polyester': Best of John Waters," *Baltimore Sun*, May 19, 1981; Lor, "Polyester," *Variety* 302.12 (April 22, 1981): 22.
30. John Engstrom, "The 'Sleaze King' gains respectability," *Boston Globe*, June 16, 1981.
31. Thomas Doherty, *Teenagers and Teenpics: The Juvenilization of American Movies in the 1950s* (Boston: Unwin Hyman, 1988), p. 28.

32. Jack Pitman, "Todd's Odor Epic No 'Critics Pic,'" *Variety* 217.8 (January 20, 1960): 18.
33. "Now You'll Smell—," *Variety* 217.8 (January 20, 1960): 4.
34. "Prime Smell-O-Vision To 'Scent' Up 25–40 U.S. Houses and 40 Abroad," *Variety* 215.13 (August 26, 1959): 5.
35. Aurel Kolnai, *On Disgust*, eds. Barry Smith and Carolyn Korsmeyer (Chicago and La Salle, Illinois: Open Court, 2004), p. 48.
36. Ibid. p. 50.
37. Sigmund Freud, *Civilization and Its Discontents*, trans. James Strachey (New York: W. W. Norton, 1962), p. 46.
38. Winfried Menninghaus, *Disgust: Theory and History of a Strong Sensation*, trans. Howard Eiland and Joel Golb (New York: State University of New York Press, 2003), p. 9.
39. J. A. Schlegel, quoted in Menninghaus, *Disgust*, p. 35.
40. Carolyn Korsmeyer, *Savoring Disgust: The Foul and the Fair in Aesthetics* (New York: Oxford University Press, 2011), p. 39.
41. Waters, *Shock Value*, p. 2.
42. Ibid. p. 15.
43. John Waters qtd. in *Spine Tingler! The William Castle Story*, dir. Jeffrey Schwarz (U.S.A.: Automat Pictures, 2007).
44. Julia Kristeva, *The Powers of Horror: An Essay on Abjection*, trans. Leon S. Roudiez (New York: Columbia University Press, 1982), p. 4.
45. Ibid. p. 8.
46. John Waters qtd. in Jamie Painter Young, "Demented at Heart," in James Egan (ed.), *John Waters: Interviews* (Jackson: University of Mississippi Press, 2011), p. 143.
47. Sianne Ngai, "Theory of the Gimmick," *Critical Inquiry* 43.2 (Winter 2017): 474.
48. Ibid. p. 493.
49. Castle, *Step Right Up!*, p. 153.
50. Charles Stinson, "'Haunted Hill' Opens on Many Area Screens," *Los Angeles Times*, May 14, 1959, p. B8; Philip K. Scheuer, "'Tingler' Gimmick Picture," *Los Angeles Times*, October 29, 1959, p. C8.
51. Ngai, "Theory of the Gimmick," p. 472.
52. Ngai, "Theory of the Gimmick," p. 475.
53. *Spine Tingler!*; *John Waters—This Filthy World*, dir. Jeff Garlin (U.S.A.: Cinemavault, 2007).
54. Waters, *Crackpot*, p. 16.
55. *Spine Tingler!*
56. A. H. Saxon, *P. T. Barnum: The Legend and The Man* (New York: Columbia University Press, 1988), p. 74.
57. Steve Bickel in *Spine Tingler!*
58. William Castle, in K. K., "His Film Gimmicks Reap High Grosses," *Globe and Mail*, July 8, 1960, p. 9.
59. Powe, "Film Review: House on Haunted Hill," *Variety* 21.1 (December 3, 1958): 6.
60. Doherty, *Teenagers and Teenpics*, pp. 62–6.
61. "Gimmicks Pay Off in Box-Office War," *New York Times*, October 26, 1959, p. 36.
62. Stuart Samuels, *Midnight Movies* (New York: Collier Books, 1983), p. 12.
63. Ibid. p. 36.
64. Waters in Dennis Cooper, "John Waters," *Interviews*, p. 180.
65. Waters, *Shock Value*, pp. 19–20.
66. Ben Davis, "Children of the Sixties: An Interview with the Owners of the Elgin," *Film Quarterly* 53.4 (Summer 2000): 6–7.

67. Lawrence Cohn, "Pictures: 10 Years of U.S. Offbeat 'Midnight Movies' Phenom," *Variety* 301.1 (November 5, 1980): 36.
68. Ibid.
69. David Sanjek, "The Doll and the Whip: Pathos and Ballyhoo in William Castle's *Homicidal*," *Quarterly Review of Film and Video* 20.4 (2003): 252.
70. Joe Brown, "Baltimore's Master of Bad Taste: Home-Town Tribute to Filmmaker John Waters and His Divine Comedies," *Washington Post*, February 6, 1985, p. C7.
71. Sanjek, "The Doll and the Whip," pp. 253–4.
72. Ronald Johnson, "Moving with the Movies," *Globe and Mail*, April 30, 1958, p. 11.
73. Gunning, "An Aesthetics of Astonishment," p. 745.
74. Mary Ann Doane, "The Voice in the Cinema: The Articulation of Body and Space," *Yale French Studies* 60 (January 1980): 42.
75. Waters, *Shock Value*, p. 19.
76. *John Waters—This Filthy World*.
77. Waters, *Crackpot*, p. 23.

Index

13 Frightened Girls (1963), 7–8, 171–2, 174, 182–7, 190, 193, 195, 197, 198, 199,
13 Ghosts (1960), 6, 7, 13, 24, 62, 67, 86–7, 94n3, 96n19, 115–36, 171, 172–7, 179, 182, 183, 184, 186–7, 195, 199, 201, 222, 238

Addams, Charles, 157
The Addams Family (1964–6), 179
Adorno, Theodor, 57
Aldrich, Robert, 154, 155, 165
Alexander, Van, 195, 233
Altman, Robert, 195
The Alfred Hitchcock Hour (1962–5), 122
Alfred Hitchcock Presents (1955–62), 122
The Americano (1955), 43, 44, 45–6, 47, 48, 51–2
Arkoff, Sam, 68, 69, 71
Arless, Jean *see* Marshall, Joan
Astin, John, 1, 15n1
Attila (1954), 63
auteur theory, 2–3, 64, 67–70, 167, 173, 193–203
Avatar (2009), 11, 94
The Avengers (1961–9), 68, 185

Babb, Kroger, 57, 237
Backus, Jim, 196
Bakhtin, Mikhail, 58, 65–6, 69
Barker, Clive, 143
Barnum, P. T., 65, 77, 247, 249
Bataille, Georges, 137, 142,
Batman (1966–8), 68

The Battle of Rogue River (1954), 46
Behind the Great Wall (1959), 242
Ben-Hur (1959), 42–3, 61
Black Christmas (1974), 234
Blackbeard (1944), 31
Blackmail (1929), 160
The Blair Witch Project (1999), 130
Bloch, Robert 16n26, 154, 190, 191, 195, 196, 227
Bug (1975), 9
The Black Cat (1934), 156
Blacula (1972), 11
Bonnie and Clyde (1968), 70, 172
Born to Kill (1947), 26
Brottman, Mikita, 41, 87
Bryant, Edwin, 195
Bubba Ho-Tep (2002), 12
A Bucket of Blood (1959), 134n48
Burns, Bob, 91
The Busy Body (1967), 8, 195, 196, 198
Bwana Devil (1952), 80

Caesar, Sid, 196
Cahiers du cinéma, 2
Cameron, James, 22
Cannibal Girls (1973), 11
Caprice (1967), 185
Carrie (1976), 129
Casablanca (1942), 182
Cassavetes, John, 197
Castle, Terry, 10, 93
   Fearmaker: Family Matters (2011), 10

Castle, William
 Step Right Up! I'm Gonna Scare the Pants off America (1976) 4, 5, 8, 15, 64, 77, 96n29, 190
The Cat and the Canary (1927), 156–7
Cecil B. Demented (2000), 241
The Chance of a Lifetime (1943), 5
Chaney, Lon, 143
Chaplin, Charlie, 197
The Children's Hour (1961), 232
Chion, Michel, 23–4
Christie, Agatha, 12
Clepper, Catherine, 11, 41, 111, 119–20, 127, 191, 214n15
Clouzot, Henri-Georges, 77, 87, 101, 104, 154, 155,
Cohn, Harry, 100, 196
The Conquest of Cochise (1953), 48, 50–1
Cook, Pam, 44–5
Coppola, Francis Ford, 3, 93, 194
Corman, Roger, 9, 88, 144, 149n40, 157–8, 178, 194
Corrigan, Timothy, 3, 144, 149n40, 157–8, 177, 194
Cracked.com, 10–11
Crawford, Joan, 8, 16n26, 92, 140, 163, 165, 170n25, 193, 196–7, 208, 228, 251
Crime Doctor (radio series), 140
The Curse of Frankenstein (1957), 63

Dali, Salvador, 93
Danger Man (1960–2, 1964–6), 184–5
Dante, Joe, 10, 94
Dark Castle Pictures, 10, 93
Dark Shadows (1966–71), 179
Dark Waters (1944), 31
Daughters of Bilitis, 219, 220
Day of the Locust (1975), 3
de Toth, André, 194
Dead Alive (1992), 130
death by fright, 112–13
Dexter (2006), 31
Dexter, Von, 195
Les Diaboliques (1955), 31, 63, 77, 82, 101, 104, 154,
Dillon, Robert, 195
A Dog in Flanders (1960), 133n35
Double Indemnity (1944), 21, 28 35, 39n5
Dr. Jekyll and Sister Hyde (1971), 11
Dr. No (1962), 183
Duel in the Sun (1946), 63, 74n24
Durrant, Theo
 The Marble Forest (1951) 101

Earthquake (1974) 93
Eisenstein, Sergei, 64, 237, 251n2
El Topo (1970), 248
Evans, Robert, 8–9
Experiment Perilous (1944), 31
Eyes Wide Shut (1999), 203
Eyes Without a Face (1960), 115, 147

Female Trouble (1974), 240
Ferlinghetti, Lawrence, 221
Feud (2017), 10, 251
Fields, W. C., 197
Fort Ti (1953), 48, 50, 52n3, 80
Foucault, Michel, 220, 232
Fowkes, Katherine A., 176, 179
Frenzy (1972), 170n26
Freud, Sigmund, 141, 204
Fuller, Samuel, 194

Gaslight (1944), 21, 28, 31
Gein, Ed, 226–7, 233
Ghost Story/Circle of Fear (1972–3), 1–3
Ginsberg, Allen, 221
The Glass Bottom Boat (1966), 185
Godard, Jean-Luc, 64, 80, 237
Godzilla: King of the Monsters (1956), 63
Goebbels, Joseph, 239
The Graduate (1967), 70, 71, 172
The Gun That Won the West (1955), 48
Gunning, Tom, 59–60, 76–8, 81, 93, 239–40, 250

Halloween (series), 147
Hammer Film Productions, 63, 158, 169n14, 192
The Haunted Palace (1963), 169n14
Heffernan, Kevin, 65–6, 71, 73n20, 80–1, 154, 162, 163, 241–2
Hermann, Bernard, 233
Herschfield, Ludwig, 4–5
High Wind in Jamaica (1965), 180
Hitchcock, Alfred, 2, 5, 6, 9, 13, 26, 31, 69, 79, 95n19, 122–5, 131, 154–6, 158–63, 165, 169n20, 170,n23, 173, 193, 194, 195, 197, 198, 199, 202, 219, 227, 228, 229, 234
Hitler, Adolf, 4, 239
Hitler's Children (1943), 62
Homicidal (1961), 6, 7, 9, 11, 42–3, 67, 74n44, 83, 95n19, 115, 122, 127, 128, 131, 136n67, 154, 155, 160–1, 167, 169n21, 188n26, 189–90, 193, 195, 197, 198, 202, 208, 210, 214n19, 219, 220, 222, 223–8, 229, 233

Hopper, Edward, 26
Horkheimer, Max, 57
Horror of Dracula (1958; also *Dracula*), 63, 169n14
House of Usher (1960), 149n40, 157,
House of Wax (1953), 79, 80–1, 194
House on Haunted Hill (1959), 6, 7, 10, 12, 15n15, 58, 66, 78, 82–9, 92, 96n30, 111, 115–16, 126, 127, 138, 139, 149n40, 153, 155, 156, 157, 172, 190, 192, 195, 196, 198, 199–200, 201, 204, 210, 212, 238, 241, 245, 246–7, 251,
House on Haunted Hill (1999), 10, 82, 93
Hush, Hush, Sweet Charlotte (1964), 165
The Hypnotic Eye (1960), 9

I Saw What You Did (1965), 8, 155, 163, 166, 169n20, 190, 196, 198, 202, 208, 219, 222, 230–3, 234
I Was a Teenage Werewolf (1957), 178
The Incredibly Strange Creatures Who Stopped Living and Became Mixed-Up Zombies!!? (1964), 9, 79

James, Henry 175
Jason and the Argonauts (1963), 86
Jaws (1975), 9, 93
Jesse James vs. the Daltons (1954), 47–8, 50, 51, 52n3, 80
Jorgensen, Christine, 226

Kafka, Franz, 8
Karloff, Boris, 63, 101
Katzman, Sam, 62
Keil, Charlie, 240
King, Stephen, 16n31, 105
Kinsey, Alfred, 220
A Kiss Before Dying (1956), 26
Kubrick, Stanley, 203

Lacan, Jacques, 21–4, 25, 30, 36, 39
The Lady from Shanghai (1947), 3, 82
Lady in a Cage (1964), 165
The Land is Mine (1943), 62–3
Landis, John, 10
Lansdale, Joe R., 11–12
  "Belly Laugh, or, The Joker's Trick or Treat" (1990), 12–13
Laura (1944), 21, 28
The Law vs. Billy the Kid (1954), 44, 46–7
Leeder, Murray, 52n4, 66–7, 100, 129, 132n7, 140, 190–1, 238
Let's Kill Uncle (1966), 8, 171, 172, 174, 180–2, 186–7, 197, 198, 199, 208

Levine, Joseph E., 57, 63–5, 68, 69–70, 71, 74n37
Lewis, Jerry, 197
The Little Shop of Horrors (1960), 134n48
Lloyd, Harold, 197
Lorre, Peter, 63, 101
Lubitsch, Ernst, 194
Lucas, Blake, 44–5
Lucas, George, 3, 93
Lugosi, Béla, 3, 239
Lynch, David, 24

Macabre (1958), 6, 8, 9, 10, 13, 57, 58, 61, 63–4, 65–6, 82, 83, 88, 89, 91, 92, 96n37, 99–114, 115, 128, 129, 153, 154, 162–4, 173, 189, 195, 196, 198, 200, 202, 212, 237, 240, 241, 246, 249–50
Macumba Love (1960), 134n35
The Mad Martindales (1942), 5
Mädchen in Uniform (1934), 5
Maddin, Guy, 8, 78
The Man from UNCLE (1964–8), 68
The Man Who Laughs (1928), 159
Marceau, Marcel, 8, 78
Marks, Samuel, 4
Marnie (1964), 160
Marshall, Joan, 160–1, 225–6
Marx Brothers, 197
The Masque of the Red Death (1964), 169n14
Masterson of Kansas (1954), 43, 46
Matinee (1993), 10, 94
Mattachine Society, 219, 220, 235n6
Medved, Michael and Harry
  The Golden Turkey Awards (1980), 11, 16n41, 79
Méliès, Georges, 77, 78, 81–2, 84, 86–7
Men of Annapolis (1957), 6
Mr. Sardonicus (1961), 6, 7, 12, 13, 57, 67, 74n44, 82, 115, 127, 128, 131, 137–49, 155, 158, 159–60, 162, 165, 190, 192, 195, 197, 198, 250,
Mizzy, Vic, 195
Mom and Dad (1945), 237
The Monkees (1966–8), 68
Mulholland Dr. (2001), 24, 31
The Munsters (1964–6), 179
The Mystery of the Wax Museum (1933), 80

The Nanny (1965), 11
A Nightmare on Elm Street (1984), 234
Night of the Living Dead (1968), 8
The Night Walker (1964), 8, 13, 93, 154, 155, 163, 164–5, 170n25, 189–215,
North, Alex, 14n28

Not for Children (play), 4–5
The Old Dark House (1963), 15n25, 155, 156–7, 190, 192, 195, 196, 198

Peeping Tom (1960), 115, 130, 132n2
Persona (1966), 91
Pink Flamingos (1972) 240, 243–5, 248–51
The Pit and the Pendulum (1961), 169n14
Poe, Edgar Allan, 143, 144, 157, 158, 174
Polanski, Roman, 8–9, 70, 146, 166
Polyester (1981), 242, 243, 250,
Poston, Tom, 196
The Premature Burial (1962), 169n14
Price, Vincent, 6, 81, 82–4, 87, 88–9, 90–2, 96n30, 116, 149n40, 156, 157, 172, 196–7, 208, 241, 243
The Prisoner (1967–8), 184
Project X (1968), 8, 198
Psycho (1960), 13, 78, 79, 115, 116, 122–5, 129, 130–1, 132n2, 133n16, 154, 156, 159, 160, 162–3, 165–6, 167–8, 170n26, 190, 193, 195, 219, 224, 225, 227, 231, 232, 233, 234

Raimi, Sam, 10
Rashomon (1950), 9
The Raven (1963), 169n14
Rear Window (1954), 165, 170n23
Rebecca (1940), 21, 28
Rebel Without a Cause (1955), 178
The Return of Rusty (1946), 6
The Robe (1953), 79
Robertson, Étienne-Gaspard, 86
The Rocky Horror Picture Show (1975), 94
Rogue One: A Star Wars Story (2016), 72
Rollercoaster (1977), 93
Rope (1948), 79, 158, 170n24
Rosemary's Baby (1968), 3, 8–9, 70–1, 93, 94, 146, 166, 190, 196, 198
Rosenbaum, Jonathan, 5
Rothafel, Samuel, 60, 62, 71–2
Russell, Ray, 195
  "Sagittarius" (1962), 158
  "Sardonicus" (1960), 137, 139

The Saint (1962–9), 185
Sarris, Andrew, 2, 193–4, 196–7
Scent of Mystery (1960), 242
Schwanneke, Ellen, 4–5, 239
Schwarz, Jeffrey, 10, 94
Scorsese, Martin, 3
SCTV (1976–84), 12
The Screaming Skull (1958), 9
Secret Beyond the Door (1947), 27, 31

Shadow of a Doubt (1943), 26
Shampoo (1975), 3
Shanks (1974), 8, 16n28, 78, 197, 198
Sims, Chris, 10–11
Skeleton Dance (1929), 86
Sleep, My Love (1948), 28
Sontag, Susan, 68
Sorry, Wrong Number (1948), 164
Spellbound (1945), 93
Spielberg, Steven, 3, 22, 93–4
Spine Tingler! The William Castle Story (2007), 7, 10, 94, 127, 130n13, 131n30
The Spiral Staircase (1946), 154
The Spirit is Willing (1967), 8, 15n1, 171–80, 187, 190, 195, 196, 198, 199, 202,
The Spy Who Came in from the Cold (1965), 184–5
Stage Fright (1950), 229–30
Stanwyck, Barbara, 164, 170n25, 189, 190, 192, 193, 203, 204, 208, 211, 212–13
Starr, Ben, 195
Steckler, Ray Dennis, 9, 79, 81
Stine, Harold E., 195
Strait-Jacket (1964), 7, 8, 11, 16n26, 92, 140, 154, 155, 163–5, 169n16, 160n25, 179, 193, 195, 196, 198, 200, 202, 208, 210, 212, 219, 228–30, 233, 251
Susina Associates, 6, 99, 101, 195
Suspicion (1941), 27

Tales of Terror (1962), 169n14
Tall Story (1960), 133n35
Taylor, Robert, 164, 189, 190, 192, 193, 203, 204, 208, 211, 213
The Ten Commandments (1956), 61
The Phantom of the Opera (1925), 143
Thirteen Ghosts (2001) (also *Thir13een Ghosts*), 10, 93, 115
This Is Spinal Tap (1984), 130
The Tingler (1959), 6, 7, 10, 11, 12, 16n31, 24, 42, 52n3, 58, 62, 66, 67, 76, 78, 79–80, 82, 87–92, 94, 94n3, 97n43, 111, 115–16, 118–20, 126, 127, 138, 139, 140, 149n40, 153, 154, 155, 156–7, 162, 163, 165, 167, 172, 189, 195–9, 201–2, 210, 222, 238, 239, 241–2, 246, 247, 248
Tol'able David (1921), 90
The Tomb of Ligeia (1964), 169n14
Topper (1948), 179
Torn Curtain (1966), 170n26
Tourneur, Jacques, 194
Towner, Wesley, 5
The Trip (1968), 88
The Trouble With Harry (1955), 170n24

Turner, Terry, 57, 62–3, 72, 73n21
The Two Mrs. Carrolls (1947), 31

Undercurrent (1946), 28
Uranium Boom (1956), 5

The Vanishing Lady (1896), 86
Vertigo (1958), 229
Victim (1960), 232
Visit to a Small Planet (1960), 133n35

Waters, John, 10, 13, 58, 64, 67, 72, 80, 84–5, 94, 95n19, 112, 127, 201, 233, 237–54
Weekend (1967), 80
Weinstein, Harvey, 57
Welles, Orson, 3, 4, 5, 6, 21, 23, 39, 82, 239
West, Mae, 197
Wharton, Edith, 175
Whatever Happened to Baby Jane? (1962), 8, 165

What's Up, Tiger Lily? (1966), 91
When a Stranger Calls (1979), 234
When Strangers Marry (1944), 6, 12, 21–40, 82, 138
The Whistler (1944), 6, 82
White, Robb, 6, 87, 100, 101, 104, 118, 126, 127, 154, 162, 195
The Wild One (1953), 177
Witness to Murder (1954), 164
The Wizard of Oz (1939), 132n4, 157
Wolf, Edmund, 5
Wood, Edward D., Jr., 81, 196
Wood, Robin, 132n2, 198–203, 204, 207, 210, 213
The Worm Eaters (1977), 237

Yes, Mr. Brown (1933), 4

Zemeckis, Robert, 10, 93
Zotz! (1962), 7–8, 127, 195, 196, 197–8, 199

EU representative:
Easy Access System Europe
Mustamäe tee 50, 10621 Tallinn, Estonia
Gpsr.requests@easproject.com

www.ingramcontent.com/pod-product-compliance
Lightning Source LLC
Chambersburg PA
CBHW061709300426
44115CB00014B/2618